CEYLON UNDER BRITISH RULE
1795-1932

CEYLON

UNDER

BRITISH RULE

1795-1932

WITH AN ACCOUNT OF THE EAST INDIA COMPANY'S EMBASSIES TO KANDY 1762-1795

LENNOX A. MILLS

FRANK CASS & CO. LTD.

1964

First published by the Oxford University Press (1933) by whose permission this present edition is now published.

This edition published by Frank Cass & Co. Ltd., 10, Woburn Walk, London, W.C.1.

First Edition   1933
New Impression 1964

Printed and bound by
CHARLES BIRCHALL & SONS, LTD.
LIVERPOOL AND LONDON

PREFACE

NO comprehensive account of the British régime in Ceylon has appeared since the publication of Sir Emerson Tennent's work over sixty years ago. A few valuable articles and books have been written; but these dealt either with the Portuguese and Dutch or with the early British periods. This book is an attempt to trace the development of the colony particularly during the first ninety years of its history. To a considerable extent the chapters dealing with the conquest and the first decade of British rule summarize and in some points supplement the accounts of previous writers. The greater part of the book is almost entirely based upon my own investigations. With the suppression of the Kandyan revolt of 1818 Ceylon ceased to have a history in the old-fashioned sense of the term, apart from the episode of the revolt of 1848. Instead there was a record which was in part administrative and in part economic —the development of the Civil Service, the advancement of Ceylonese prosperity, the conflicts between a benevolent despotism and the European colonists, and the vicissitudes of coffee and cinnamon.

The decade of the 'eighties approximately marked the beginning of the transition to twentieth-century Ceylon, even though the change did not become well-defined until the 'nineties. In agriculture the dependence on the single staple coffee was replaced by a more diversified cultivation. The development of the nation-building services in the 'nineties contrasted with the older and simpler conception of the responsibilities of Government. The Ceylonese movement for constitutional reform began at the same period. Owing to exigencies of space the detailed study closes with the beginning of the change; but in the final chapter the salient features of the modern period are examined. For this part of the book the writer was under the disadvantage that his residence in Minnesota prevented him from consulting all the sources of information at present available.

It is a pleasure to acknowledge my especial obligations to Professor Coupland for his interest and invaluable assistance.

I regret exceedingly that the recent death of my friend, Sir Charles Lucas, K.C.B., has deprived me of his final criticisms. His life-long interest in Ceylon led him to entertain expectations of the book which I hope may prove in some degree justified. I am indebted to Mr. Evans Lewin, the Librarian of the Royal Empire Society, for his help and advice, and particularly for placing at my disposal part of the material on which the map accompanying this book is based. My thanks are also due to Mr. F. Walter, the Librarian of the University of Minnesota, and to Miss A. J. Mayes of Wendover, Bucks., for their assistance in collecting part of the material for the final chapter.

L. A. M.

UNIVERSITY OF MINNESOTA,
1932.

CONTENTS

I

BRITISH RELATIONS WITH CEYLON

1762–1796

'I GOT to Bed just at sunrising, never more fatigued or disgusted with any jaunt in my Life.' An unusual sentence this, in an official report to the Government of Madras, but in truth John Pybus had been sorely tried.[1] Sent as ambassador to Kandy, he had been summoned for his interview with the King at 11.30 p.m., the usual hour for court receptions. It was a night of steamy heat with a pouring rain; but as Kandyan etiquette required, the ambassador and his escort walked 'hand in hand through a very dirty Road' to the palace. Then followed a long wait, hatless and shoeless, in a 'very dirty' courtyard, until finally Pybus was admitted to the hall of audience, rain-soaked and perspiring, and 'pretty well bemired'.

Pybus's mentors now informed him that he must observe the etiquette of the Dutch ambassadors to Kandy, and after indignant expostulations he was compelled to agree. As the ambassador advanced towards the throne he knelt four times, the courtiers prostrating themselves; while on reaching the foot of the dais he again knelt and presented his credentials from the Government of Madras. The conversation with the King continued until nearly morning, nor is this surprising when one considers the manner in which it was conducted. The King spoke to one of his ministers, who prostrated himself and repeated the remark to another official. He in turn prostrated himself and repeated it to an Indian, who prostrated himself and repeated it to Pybus's Indian servant, who repeated it to Pybus. By the same devious channel the reply eventually filtered back to the royal ears. Tired, hungry, and mortified, Pybus at length obtained leave to withdraw. He was informed that he must observe the same etiquette on leaving as on entering the royal presence; but at this point exasperated human nature rebelled. Every time the courtiers prostrated themselves 'I sat down'.

[1] Ceylon Records 1: Oct. 1762. John Pybus entered the Madras Civil Service as a Writer in 1742, became a Member of the Madras Council, and retired in 1768 (Rao, *Ceylon Antiquary and Literary Register*, IV. iv. 206).

The immediate cause of the embassy had been a request from the King of Kandy to the Madras Government for aid against the Dutch. The Dutch held the coastal plains of Ceylon, but like their predecessors, the Portuguese, they had failed to conquer the mountains of the interior, the ancient kingdom of Kandy. The Kandyans were bitterly hostile, and in 1762 were involved in one of their frequent wars with the Dutch. The motives which had induced the Madras Government to send Pybus were partly strategic and partly economic. As a result of Clive's conquests the centre of British power in India had shifted from the western to the eastern coast, and naval actions were generally fought in the Bay of Bengal.[1] The only dock-yards, however, were at Bombay, and there was no harbour on the Bay of Bengal which seemed capable of conversion into a naval base. This involved two serious disadvantages, of which the first was that ships damaged in action in the Bay of Bengal were compelled to make the 'extremely circuitous, tedious and difficult' voyage to Bombay for repairs. Moreover, during the period of the North-Eastern monsoon, from October to March, the fleet had to withdraw to the west coast 'to avoid the violent and dangerous hurricanes which generally happen'. In other words, for several months of the year the heart of the British Empire in India was entirely at the mercy of any enemy who might chance to have a squadron in the Bay of Bengal. The events of 1758 proved that the menace was far from theoretical. After a naval action with the French the British fleet sailed to the dockyard at Bombay, and was absent from October until April 30, 1759. Meanwhile a French squadron appeared in the Bay of Bengal, and co-operated with the land forces under Lally in the siege of Madras. The North-Eastern monsoon prevented the return of the British fleet, and Madras escaped capture only because of the arrival of six of the East India Company's ships in February. The moral was clear: a naval base must be obtained somewhere in the Bay of Bengal. The most suitable was the magnificent harbour of Trincomalee, but this formed part of the Dutch territories in Ceylon, and was for the moment unobtainable. The King of Kandy, however, still held part of the sea-coast of Ceylon, and it was possible that a

[1] Mills, *British Malaya, 1824–1867*, 18–21.

harbour might be found within his possessions. The Madras Government, therefore, welcomed the opportunity to send Pybus to his court, and particularly instructed him to ascertain whether there were such a harbour, and whether the King would 'give us an entire Grant for ever'.[1]

The second motive for Pybus's embassy was economic. The English East India Company had never forgotten nor forgiven their ousting from the spice trade by the Dutch in the seventeenth century. At that time the English had been too weak to resist; but in the year 1762 the wheel had turned almost full circle. The English Company was rapidly becoming a great power in India, while the Dutch were slowly foundering in the seas of bankruptcy. Their monopoly of the spice trade was breaking down, since they no longer had the strength to enforce it.[2] The Directors in London decided that the time had come to reverse in some measure the defeat of a hundred years before. Of all the Dutch monopolies none was more jealously guarded than that of cinnamon. Until the nineteenth century Ceylon was the sole source of supply, the bark being collected partly from the Dutch provinces and partly from Kandyan territory. It is, therefore, not surprising that Pybus was 'most particularly to enquire' whether the King of Kandy would grant the Company a share in his cinnamon trade.[3]

Pybus's mission was a complete failure, since although the King of Kandy was willing to grant the Company a harbour and the monopoly of the cinnamon trade, he demanded armed assistance against the Dutch. The Madras Government refused to make a defensive alliance, because 'it is not our intention by any means at present to enter into absolute Engagements with the king, or to quarrel with the Dutch'.[4] The Company, therefore, refused to ratify the draft treaty which Pybus had made with the King of Kandy. Lamentable to relate, that much-enduring envoy obtained his useless treaty only at the price of a second interview with the King, at half-past two of a rainy morning.[5]

Twenty years elapsed before the East India Company was

[1] C.R. 1: Apr. 6, 1762.   [2] Mills, *British Malaya*, 15–17.
[3] C.R. 1: Apr. 6, 1762.   [4] C.R. 1: Apr. 6, 1762.
[5] C.R. 1: Oct. 1762.

again free to turn its attention to Ceylon. The settlement of
Bengal and the desperate struggles with the Mahrattas and
Mysore had left no leisure for matters of secondary importance.
In the closing years of the War of American Independence,
however, Holland joined the coalition against Great Britain;
and Lord Macartney, the Governor of Madras, determined to
attempt the conquest of Ceylon. Trincomalee was captured in
1782, but was recaptured by the French fleet under Suffrein on
August 30 after a siege of five days.[1]

The abortive attack on Ceylon led to a second embassy to
Kandy. Lord Macartney wished for the co-operation of the
Kandyan army against the Dutch, and he was also anxious to
obtain supplies for the garrison at Trincomalee.[2] His Second
Secretary, Hugh Boyd, therefore accompanied the fleet which
captured Trincomalee, and from there went on to the town of
Kandy, the King's capital. He proposed an offensive and defen-
sive alliance against the Dutch, but his overtures were rejected
owing to the King's anger at the Company's rejection of
Pybus's treaty in 1762. The King refused to negotiate with the
East India Company, and declared that he would make an
alliance only with an ambassador directly accredited by King
George himself. On the way home to Madras Boyd's ship was
captured by Suffrein's fleet.[3]

Boyd had a keen sense of humour which irradiated even the
pages of his official report.[4] He described the manifold dis-
comforts of his journey with a gay light-heartedness which even
his incessant and severe attacks of malaria could not quench.
The jungle paths—there were neither roads nor bridges—were
very rough and overgrown, and the embassy frequently lacked
food. He concluded the account of one trying day with the
remark that he and Ensign Chericke, who commanded his
escort of sepoys, 'adjourn to . . . the discussion of our bowl [of]
curry which we can hardly make hot enough to encounter the
night cold and extreme dampness of the Dews. It penetrates
the tripple covering of my Tent, and not being Used to sleep in

---

[1] *C.A. and L.R.* v. iv. 181–7.
[2] C.R. 1: Oct. 12, 1781.
[3] Pieris, *Ceylon and the Hollanders, 1658–1796*, 140–1; Campbell, ed.,
Miscellaneous Works of Hugh Boyd, ii. 271 and 287; C.R. 1: Nov. 1, 1783.
[4] C.R. 1: Nov. 1, 1783.

a Cold Bath and more than half invalid as I have already been
for some time, I feel its effect very unpleasantly.'

On his reception at court Boyd had to comply with practically
the same rules of etiquette as Pybus. Weak as he was from
malaria he found the tedious ceremonial 'almost intolerably
fatiguing'; but his unfailing sense of the ridiculous never
deserted him. As he struggled to kneel down he noted with
inward joy that the courtiers 'fell to the performance of theirs
[i.e. prostrations], which were in the most perfect degree of
humiliation: they almost literally licked the dust, prostrating
themselves with their faces close to the Stone Floor, and throwing out their Legs and Arms as in the Attitude of Swimming.
Then rising to their Knees by a sudden Spring from the Breast,
like what is called the Salmon Leap by Tumblers, they repeated
in a very loud Voice a certain form of Words of the most extravagant meaning that can be conceived: "that the Head of the
King of Kings might reach beyond the Sun", that he might live
"a hundred thousand Years, etc."' They advanced towards the
throne after 'the aforesaid Concert had been repeated half a
Dozen times'. When one of the ministers had occasion to go to
the end of the hall, 'I saw him, a Venerable grey-headed Old
Man, come trotting down one of the Ailes like a Dog on all
fours!'

Trincomalee was restored to Holland by France in 1783, and
for twelve years more the Dutch East India Company remained
in undisturbed possession of Ceylon. In 1795 Holland joined
France in the war against Great Britain, and once again a fleet
sailed from Madras for the conquest of the island. An embassy
was sent to Kandy to secure the King's assistance in the expul-
sion of the Dutch. The Madras Government wished to obtain
supplies for the army, but they also desired the co-operation of
a Kandyan force in the capture of Colombo, and the monopoly
of the Kandyan cinnamon trade.[1] The British envoy was
Robert Andrews, a member of the Madras Civil Service.[2] The
King was unwilling to agree to a treaty unless the British would

---

[1] C.R. 1: Andrews's Diary of his Embassy to Kandy, 1795.

[2] Rao, *C.A. and L.R.* IV. 206-7. Robert Andrews entered the Madras
Civil Service in 1778, and rose to be Collector of Trinchinopoli. He was
Resident of Ceylon from 1796 to 1798.

pledge themselves never to restore Ceylon to the Dutch. Andrews refused, since at that time it seemed probable that the island might be restored to Holland; but finally the King gave way, and signed the draft of a preliminary treaty on October 12, 1795. Andrews, accompanied by Kandyan ambassadors, returned to Madras to secure the ratification of the Indian Government; and meanwhile the King co-operated with the British troops in Ceylon.[1]

The terms of the treaty were exceedingly favourable to Kandy, establishing a mutual defensive alliance, and pledging the Company to protect the King against all his enemies. The Company reserved to itself the whole sea-coast, while Kandyan trade, especially in cinnamon, would be carried on with the Company in preference to any other power. The King agreed to cede 'a favourable situation to which the Dutch can have no right or title' to build forts and trading posts. In return he received the privilege of employing ten ships for his private trade, which should be free from duty and customs examination.[2] This concession had always been refused by the Dutch, since to give the King the right of private trade would have destroyed the cinnamon monopoly.

The Indian Government signed the treaty on February 12, 1796, but added the proviso that it must be subject to ratification or rejection within two years by the Directors. The promise to protect the King against all his enemies might have been interpreted as a perpetual engagement to defend him against the Dutch, should they be restored to Ceylon. The Indian Government felt that it could not incur this obligation without sanction from London.[3] The King refused to sign the revised treaty, since he insisted upon an unconditional promise of protection, and the grant of a seaport, a demand to which the Company refused to agree.[4] The treaty finally lapsed through the failure of the King to ratify it.[5]

[1] C.R. 1: Andrews's Diary.
[2] C.R. 25: Nov. 19, 1798; Aitchison, *Treaties*, x. 274–5.
[3] Aitchison, *Treaties*, x. 275–8; C.R. 1: Jan. 1, 1796; C.R. 25: Nov. 19, 1798; C.R. 54: Douglass MS. ii, § 47. The volume contains contemporary copies made by a clerk in the Colonial Office of several manuscripts on Ceylon belonging to Sylvester Douglass, later Lord Glenbervie.
[4] C.R. 1: Andrews's Diary.
[5] C.R. 2: Nov. 10, 1798; C.R. 25: Nov. 9, 1798.

In 1798 the Directors informed North, the Governor of Ceylon, that the Governor-General of India would decide whether another attempt should be made to persuade the King to ratify Andrews's treaty.[1] North very strongly urged that no attempt should be made, and Dundas, the President of the Board of Control, approved of his advice.[2] North pointed out that when the treaty was negotiated in 1795 the Company was very seriously misinformed as to the real situation in Ceylon, owing to the shroud of mystery in which the Dutch had carefully enveloped its affairs. At that time the Company believed that the cinnamon was entirely collected from Kandyan territory, and that the King still possessed part of the sea-coast. It was therefore necessary to conciliate him to obtain the cinnamon trade and to secure a seaport to which the Dutch could not lay claim. Since the date of Andrews's embassy it had been learned that the greater part of the cinnamon was collected in the former Dutch territories, and also that the whole of the sea-coast had been ceded to the Dutch Company by the treaty of peace with Kandy in 1766.[3] In other words, Kandy had nothing of value to offer; while the clause of Andrews's treaty allowing the King to trade freely with ten ships meant the destruction of the British cinnamon monopoly. By allowing the treaty to lapse the King had thrown away a unique opportunity; and it was not for the British to repair his short-sightedness at the cost of their own interests.

[1] C.R. 54: Douglass MS. ii, § 50.
[2] C.R. 54: Douglass MS. ii, § 55; C.R. 25: Nov. 19 and 26, 1798.
[3] This was the war in which Kandy was engaged at the date of Pybus's embassy. The Dutch suffered several heavy defeats, but were finally victorious in 1766. The treaty which took from Kandy the parts of the sea-coast which it had hitherto possessed, is given in C.R. 25: Nov. 19, 1798. Kandy was thus cut off from communication with the outer world (Codrington, *Ceylon*, 141–3).

II

THE CONQUEST OF CEYLON
1795–1796

THE century and a half of Dutch rule in Ceylon was fast drawing to a close in weakness and decay. The Dutch East India Company was bankrupt, and its power was only a shadow of what it had been. Since about 1739 the annual expenditure of Ceylon had exceeded the revenue, and the maintenance of the island had been a drain upon the Company's resources. The officials were underpaid and were allowed to make up the deficiency by private trading, with the result that private took precedence over public interests, and maladministration was widespread. During the preceding generation two able and honest governors, Falck and Van der Graaf, had attempted to introduce reforms, but without much success. The Dutch officials sent to Ceylon were not, speaking euphemistically, of the most desirable kind: 'Ceylon was treated as a convenient spot where blockheads, libertines, and bankrupts, who had influence with the Directorate, could easily be dumped.'[1] 'Dry rot had set in among the Hollanders. That retribution which so surely awaits the commercial race which had no ideal beyond the exploitation of the country of another for its own aggrandisement, had fallen upon the men. The one aim of the Hollander was the speedy acquisition of wealth. . . . If Captain Robert Percival . . . is to be believed, the Hollander began his day with gin and tobacco, and he ended it with tobacco and gin. In the interval he fed grossly, lounged about, indulged in the essential siesta, and transacted a little business.'[2]

The Dutch had failed to win the attachment of the Sinhalese, and in their day of trial they were unable to rely on the assistance of their subjects. Dutch rule had been free from the atrocious cruelties which marked the Portuguese, but 'it is painfully observable that no disinterested concern was ever manifested, and no measures directed by them for the elevation and happiness of the native population'.[3] The Sinhalese peasant

---

[1] Pieris, *Ceylon and the Hollanders*, 153–4.
[2] Ibid., 166. [3] Tennent, *Ceylon*, ii. 50–9.

'had a fair measure of personal security, and a reasonable likelihood of even-handed justice'. He 'had the certainty that some portion at least of his labour would enure to his own benefit'. His poverty, however, was still very great: nearly all the trade was in the hands of the Dutch burghers, and the Company was a hard task-master. The Dutch attitude towards the Sinhalese was 'that their chief mission in life was to secure dividends for the Company'.[1]

In 1795 the French armies invaded Holland and overthrew the Stadtholder, who fled to England. With the support of the Dutch people the Batavian Republic was established, and Holland joined France in the war against Great Britain. The British Government was determined that Ceylon should not again be used as a French base for attacking India. To prevent the Dutch colonies from joining the Batavian Republic the Stadtholder agreed that British troops should be landed to support the loyalists against the Dutch and French Republicans. On February 7, 1795, he wrote to the Governor of Ceylon, ordering him to admit British troops to the Dutch towns and forts, and to treat them as allies 'who come to prevent the Colony from being invaded by the French'.[2] The dispatch was forwarded to Lord Hobart, the Governor of Madras, and he at once took steps to carry it into effect.

Lord Hobart was naturally sceptical as to the efficacy of the Stadtholder's letter: the ancient enmity of Dutch and English in the East was unlikely to vanish at the word of a fugitive prince. He decided that if the Ceylon Government should adhere to the Batavian Republic the island must be captured, since Trincomalee could not be left as a French naval base. War was imminent with the Mahrattas and Mysore who had been negotiating with France, and it was feared that a French fleet would be sent to support them. A strong force of European and Indian troops was collected at Madras under the command of Colonel James Stuart; and meanwhile Major Agnew was sent to Colombo with dispatches to the Dutch Governor, Van

---

[1] Pieris, *Ceylon*, 130 and 154.

[2] L. J. B. Turner, *C.A. and L.R.* III. iv. 239. The account of the conquest of Ceylon is largely based upon L. J. B. Turner's articles in *C.A. and L.R.* III. iv. 239–56, and VIII. ii. 93–118. Mr. Turner gives a detailed and exhaustive criticism of the documentary and other sources relating to the conquest.

Angelbeek. Lord Hobart informed him that by the Stadt-holder's orders the Dutch colonies were to be placed under British protection. In the event of obedience the Dutch officials and troops would be retained and the laws and customs respected; but the British would take possession of Ceylon in the name of the Stadtholder, and would restore it to him when peace was made. If any resistance were offered the British would take Ceylon by force.[1]

Van Angelbeek and his Council were seriously perplexed: they resolved to be loyal to the Stadtholder, but at the same time they were most unwilling to admit British troops to their fortresses. They strongly distrusted the Indian Government *et dona ferentes*, and felt convinced that once the British were in possession of Ceylon they would annex it. They realized, how-ever, that a refusal of the unwanted help would be followed by an attack which they were ill-prepared to resist. Finally, on July 26, 1795, the Council determined to defend Ceylon against attack, but to attempt to avoid it by accepting 800 British troops as auxiliaries.[2] Accordingly Van Angelbeek, on July 27, requested that 800 British troops be sent to be divided up amongst the Dutch forts. He declared that the Ceylon Govern-ment was loyal to the Stadtholder and to the English alliance, but he entirely dissented from Lord Hobart's view that the Stadtholder's letter of February 7 placed Ceylon under British protection. Angelbeek concluded by saying that he had ordered the Commandant of Trincomalee to reinforce Fort Ostenburg by 300 British troops.[3]

The Stadtholder's letter was extremely vague and entirely failed to make clear whether the British or the Dutch were to control Ceylon. Probably this was intentional: he was aware that there was a Jacobin party in the colony, and he wished British garrisons introduced to prevent their joining the Batavian Republic. Since, however, he was not certain of the attitude of Van Angelbeek and his Council, he could scarcely declare his mind so openly. 'According to the actual wording of the Stadtholder's letter the Governor is correct. There is no mention of British protection, or of delivering up the Settle-

---

[1] Turner, *C.A. and L.R.* III. iv. 240.
[2] Ibid., VIII. ii. 95 and 102-9.   [3] Ibid., III. iv. 241.

ments.' Lord Hobart 'would have been in a much stronger
logical position if he had relied on the broader issue, namely that
as the Dutch Republic was at war with Great Britain, he was
entitled to act against the Dutch colonies, but that in view of the
relations with the Stadtholder he was prepared to do so pacifi-
cally on certain conditions on both sides'.[1]

Hitherto Van Angelbeek and his Council had been loyal to
the Stadtholder, but at the meetings of the Council held on
August 12 and August 15 they decided to acknowledge the
authority of the Batavian Republic, and to refuse to receive
British troops. The reason for their change of policy was that
they had learned that the revolution in Holland had been
effected with the consent of the majority of the Dutch people,
and had not been a 'French usurpation', as apparently they
had previously considered.[2]

Meanwhile, on August 1, 1795, a British fleet arrived off
Trincomalee, convoying the strong force under Colonel Stuart
which had been collected for the conquest of Ceylon. Major
Fornbauer, the Commandant of Trincomalee, was very suspicious of the British intentions, and on various pretexts refused
to accept the reinforcement of 300 troops whom Van Angelbeek
had requested for Fort Ostenburg. After a fortnight of fruitless
negotiations Colonel Stuart threatened that if the forts were not
surrendered he would attack. Van Angelbeek then withdrew
his request for 300 men, and declared that if he were attacked
he would defend himself.[3] While the Colonel was unaware that
Van Angelbeek and his Council had reversed their policy, he
justly construed Fornbauer's threadbare pretexts as resistance
to the surrender of Trincomalee. The British had shown much
forbearance in their negotiations with Van Angelbeek; and
decisive action was necessary in view of the possibility that a
French fleet might soon arrive for the relief of Ceylon. On
August 18 the British troops were landed, and after a brief siege
Trincomalee surrendered on August 26. Colonel Stuart then
advanced along the sea-coast, and by October 6 he had captured all the Dutch forts from Batticaloa to Mannar.[4] After the
fall of Trincomalee Lord Hobart, on September 22, again offered

[1] Ibid., III. iv. 241–2.   [2] Ibid., VIII. ii. 109–11.
[3] Ibid., III. iv. 242–3.   [4] Ibid., III. iv. 243.

Van Angelbeek the same terms as in his letter of July 7, while at the same time making it perfectly clear that 'protection' meant complete control. The offer was refused on October 13 and the war continued.[1]

A curious incident now occurred at Colombo, the transference to British service of the regiment of Swiss mercenaries which had been raised in 1782 by the Comte de Meuron for the Dutch East India Company. The Comte de Meuron returned to Switzerland in 1786, leaving the regiment under the command of his brother Pierre de Meuron. Hugh Cleghorn, a friend of the Comte, in 1795 suggested to Dundas the advisability of transferring the regiment to the British service.[2] On February 17, 1795, Dundas authorized Cleghorn to negotiate with De Meuron;[3] and on March 30 the Comte consented to accompany Cleghorn to India and bring about the transfer.[4] Dundas was highly pleased, since he considered that 'the withdrawing the Regiment de Meuron from the Dutch service was one of the most essential circumstances which contributed to the conquest of Ceylon'.[5]

De Meuron and Cleghorn arrived in India early in September 1795, and the Comte wrote to his brother ordering the regiment to enter the British service. Lord Hobart sent Major Agnew to Colombo to deliver the letter and to inform Governor Van Angelbeek of the transfer.[6] The news was a complete surprise to the Governor, and he tried to prevent Major Agnew from seeing Colonel de Meuron, in order to keep him in ignorance.[7]

---

[1] Turner, *C.A. and L.R.* III. iv. 243–6.

[2] Neil, ed., *The Cleghorn Papers, A Footnote to History*, 2–4; Lewis, *C.A. and L.R.* VIII. ii. 119–24. Hugh Cleghorn (1761–1836), Professor of Civil History at St. Andrews, was an ardent Imperialist, and had met the Comte de Meuron during his long visits to the Continent to observe the events of the French revolution. As a reward for his services in obtaining the regiment he was appointed Crown (i.e. Colonial) Secretary of Ceylon in 1798, but returned to Scotland in 1800 owing to the hostility of Governor North. He received £5,000 for his services from the East India Company.

[3] Colonial Office Records, Series 55, vol. 61: Feb. 17, 1795. The regiment was to receive British rates of pay and was not to be disbanded until its period of service had expired, while the Comte might receive 'a handsome douceur'.

[4] Neil, *Cleghorn Papers*, 15–18 and 59. The Comte received £4,000 to discharge his debts, his pay from the Dutch East India Company being heavily in arrears. He also insisted that he and his brother receive the rank of general in the British army.

[5] C.O. 55. 61: Aug. 16, 1797.

[6] Neil, *Cleghorn Papers*, 162–96.   [7] Ibid., 202–4.

The Colonel, however, had already been notified by means of a
letter which Cleghorn had sent him concealed in a Dutch
cheese.[1] He approved of the transfer and met the Governor's
threat to imprison the regiment by declaring he would attack
the Dutch garrison. Van Angelbeek permitted the regiment to
leave for India on condition that it took no part in the siege of
Colombo.[2] The De Meuron regiment arrived in India in
November, and almost all of its 860 men enlisted in the British
army.[3] After the departure of what Cleghorn declared to be the
most efficient unit in the Dutch army the garrison of Colombo
was reduced to 2,520, of whom 830 were Europeans and the
remainder natives of dubious value.[4] By abandoning Galle Van
Angelbeek increased the strength of the Colombo garrison to
2,770; but opposed to this somewhat unreliable force was an
army of 5,550 under Colonel Stuart.[5]

The Dutch seem to have made active preparations for the
defence of Colombo, and strong defensive positions were prepared near the town. Meanwhile, the British slowly advanced
along the coast, and arrived near Colombo early in February,
the Dutch abandoning with little resistance their outlying
fortifications. The slow advance of the British was due to the
total lack of means of communication: outside Colombo there
was not a mile of made road on the island, and the troops were
forced to march along the sandy shore at the edge of the jungle.
Van Angelbeek has been accused of treachery because he
ordered the abandonment of the strong defences prepared north
of Colombo. The charge seems unjust since the presence of the

[1] Ibid., 219.

[2] Ibid., 203–4; Turner, *C.A. and L.R.* III. iv. 244–6. Turner's account of
the transfer appeared before the publication of Cleghorn's papers, and while
on the whole accurate is necessarily incomplete.

[3] Neil, *Cleghorn Papers*, 206, 215–16, and Preface, p. xi. The De Meuron
regiment served in India, and was finally disbanded in Canada in 1816. C.O.
55. 61: Aug. 10, 1797. Turner (*C.A. and L.R.* III. iv. 244) gives the strength of
the regiment as 500.

[4] Neil, *Cleghorn Papers*, 231 and 237. Colonel de Meuron reported that
many of the principal European officers in Colombo were disaffected and half-
hearted in the defence. Pieris, *Ceylon*, 167; Turner, *C.A. and L.R.* VIII. ii.
116.

[5] Neil, *Cleghorn Papers*, 282. Cleghorn was present at the fall of Colombo
and gave the strength of the Dutch garrison as 880 Europeans and 1,890
natives. Colonel Stuart's army was composed of 2,050 British, 3,500 sepoys,
and 3,600 pioneers and lascars, a total of 9,150.

British fleet exposed the defenders to the risk of being cut off by a landing party. Another reason for the withdrawal was the presence of a Kandyan army north of the Kelani River and the possibility of their outflanking the Dutch.[1] When the British arrived before Colombo Colonel Stuart offered terms, and after several days of negotiations Van Angelbeek accepted on February 15, 1796. Colombo and all the other Dutch dependencies in Ceylon were surrendered, and the troops sent to Madras. The clergy and the judiciary were to remain in office, the judges for twelve months to decide pending suits. Officials, including Governor Van Angelbeek, were allowed to remain in Ceylon as private individuals, and in point of fact some of them were retained in office. Private property was declared inviolable, and all citizens were free to follow their employments.[2]

Governor Van Angelbeek was accused of treachery because of his surrender,[3] but the charge appears to be without foundation.[4] The Governor seems to have done his best to prepare for

[1] Turner, *C.A. and L.R.* III. iv. 247–53, and VIII. ii. 94 and 114. The Kandyan army co-operated with the British in accordance with the terms of Andrews's treaty of 1795.

[2] Turner, *C.A. and L.R.* III. iv. 250–1; Aitchison, *Treaties*, x. 278–85. After the conquest the majority of the Dutch civilians who had capital went to Batavia, while those of mixed blood remained in Ceylon. They were loyal to British rule, and from their knowledge of English and the native languages practically monopolized the minor Government clerical posts. They proved themselves so essential that Governor Ward about 1856 described them as 'the brazen wheels which, hidden from sight, keep the golden hands of government in motion'. A few held fairly important administrative posts in the higher Civil Service, while many had distinguished careers as barristers or judges (Digby, *The Life of Sir Richard Morgan*, 16–26, 34, 47, and 62; F.B., *Memorials of Sir S. Grenier, passim*).

[3] E.g. Tombe, *Voyage aux Indes Orientales*, trans. Colonel Fyers in the *Journal of the Royal Asiatic Society, Ceylon Branch*, 1888, vol. x, pp. 365–414. Tombe obtained his information from the Dutch officers sent to Batavia, and accused Van Angelbeek of intending to surrender from the time De Meuron's regiment withdrew in 1795.

[4] This is the conclusion of L. J. Turner, who has exhaustively considered all the available evidence in *C.A. and L.R.* III. iv. 251–6, and VIII. ii. 93–8 and 116–18. The British strength was overwhelming while the native troops who formed the great majority of the Dutch garrison were unreliable. The Treasury was empty and no help had come from Holland or from France. With a single exception all the staff officers declared that Colombo could only hold out for three days; and they and the Council approved of Van Angelbeek's decision to surrender on February 14. Moreover, the British offered generous terms; while if Colombo were taken by assault the surrender would perforce be unconditional.

resistance, and there is no indication that he considered surrender until about February 10, when the British were already
encamped before the walls of Colombo. The dominating factor
in the situation seems to have been the overwhelming strength
of the attackers, and the hopelessness of the defence owing to
the unreliability of the native troops. Since the British offered
terms far more generous than Van Angelbeek could have ex-
torted, he can scarcely be censured for deciding that his wisest
course was to agree with his adversary quickly.

For some years after the conquest the ultimate fate of the
island was uncertain, and both the Dutch inhabitants and the
British officials had a strong presumption that Ceylon would
be restored to Holland. In the abortive peace negotiations at
Paris in 1796, and again in 1797, Lord Malmesbury, the British
envoy, was instructed to offer the return of Ceylon or the Cape
of Good Hope if in return peace were made and the Stadtholder
restored.[1] France and Holland rejected the British proposals,
and Ceylon became part of the British Empire.

[1] Malmesbury, *Diaries*, iii. 358, 400–9, 470, 557, and iv. 128. Lord Malmesbury's *Diaries* show that Great Britain was by no means anxious to restore
Ceylon, since Trincomalee was necessary to defend India, 'where we have no
other port' (iii. 470). The island was to be given up only if this were essential
to obtain peace.

III

THE MADRAS ADMINISTRATION
1795–1798

AFTER the British conquest in 1796 Ceylon was made a dependency of the Madras Presidency, since it seemed unnecessary to create a separate government when the island might be restored to Holland. Furthermore, Madras troops had conquered Ceylon at a cost of some £12,000, and the cession may have been made so that the East India Company could recover its expenses from the profits of the Dutch monopolies of pearls and cinnamon.[1] While Ceylon was not formally granted to the Company until 1796 Madras had already established its administration in the conquered districts in 1795.[2]

The Madras Government created a dual civil and military control; and since the respective powers were not clearly defined a considerable amount of friction resulted.[3] The Commander-in-Chief in Ceylon was not only in control of the troops but had 'a discretionary authority, as well Civil as Military', the revenue and commercial officials being subject to his orders. In general, however, he seems to have interfered but little with the civil administration.[4] The civil government was carried on by members of the Madras Civil Service under the general control of Robert Andrews, the Resident and Superintendent of Revenue. After his mission to Kandy was completed he returned to Ceylon and took up his duties early in 1796.[5] The number and duties of Andrews's subordinates are difficult to trace, but there were probably four: John Jervis, Senior Assistant at Jaffna; Alexander, Assistant at Colombo and Galle; and Garrow, Assistant at Trincomalee, Batticaloa, and Mullaittivu. John Macdowall,

---

[1] Brit. Mus. Add. MS. No. 13866: Sept. 28, 1798. C.R. 54: Robertson MS., dated 1799. Robertson was Town Major of Colombo in 1798–9. Turner, *C.A. and L.R.* IV. i. 36–40. The revenue from the three pearl fisheries of 1796–8 was £396,000, and Madras seems to have made a substantial profit out of its conquest.

[2] Turner, *C.A. and L.R.* IV. i. 36; C.R. 1: Dec. 2, 1795.

[3] Turner, *C.A. and L.R.* IV. i. 42 and 44.

[4] Ibid., IV. i. 41; C.R. 53: Feb. 27, 1802.

[5] C.R. 53: Feb. 27, 1802. Andrews's salary was 150 pagodas (£60) a month, plus a commission of 1½ per cent. on the net revenue.

Paymaster to the Ceylon Expedition, was also probably an Assistant.[1]

The duties of Andrews and his Assistants were administrative, financial, and judicial, the most important being to supervise the collection of the revenue. Their judicial powers are uncertain, but they tried civil and criminal cases 'not of a very heinous nature' and 'unconnected with the Military'. Justice was probably of a very summary description, and the Assistants seem to have had wide discretionary powers: a toddy drawer, for instance, was given two dozen lashes for 'impertinent behaviour'. Serious offences such as murder and felony could only be tried by courts martial.[2] Owing to the lack of evidence it seems impossible to trace in detail the work of the civil administration; but probably little attention was paid to anything except the collection of the revenue. Each Assistant had a varying number of native subordinates called Aumildars. They seem to have been in charge of subdivisions of the district, their duties being to collect the revenue, and perhaps also to carry on a certain amount of general administrative work under the Assistant's supervision. The Aumildars were natives of the Madras Presidency, and replaced the Mudaliyars, the Sinhalese officials of the Dutch régime. Subordinate to the Aumildars were Peshcars, Cuttwals, Parpattacarars, and other minor officials who amongst other duties assisted in collecting the revenue.[3]

Little more than a year after the Madras administration was established a formidable revolt broke out amongst the Sinhalese. The duration and events are uncertain, but it probably lasted from June 1797 to the end of the year, or perhaps to February 1798. The British troops drove the insurgents into the jungle, but despite successful skirmishes were unable to force them to submit. The Sinhalese followed their usual guerrilla tactics, refusing to be drawn into a pitched battle and making unexpected attacks upon the columns operating against them. The character of the country, large areas of dense jungle broken only by scattered villages, and with no means of communication save narrow and rough native paths, placed regular troops at

---

[1] Turner, *C.A. and L.R.* IV. i. 37–8; Rao, *C.A. and L.R.* IV. iv. 207–8.
[2] Turner, *C.A. and L.R.* IV. i. 38.   [3] Ibid., IV. i. 38–9.

an immense disadvantage. The losses on both sides are said to have been heavy.[1]

Andrews and his Madras subordinates were almost entirely responsible for the outbreak, although Dutch intrigues were a contributory cause. The Dutch played upon the universal detestation of the Madras rule and incited the natives to revolt, holding out hopes of French assistance.[2] Dutch intrigues, however, were only a minor cause: if Andrews and his Assistants had wished to provoke an outbreak they could not have set about it more effectually. Under the Dutch régime the Mudaliyars and the other native officials had been the essential link between the European administration and the Sinhalese. They collected the revenue, carried out the orders of the Dutch civil servants, and kept them informed of what was going on amongst the Sinhalese. The Dutch had appointed the Mudaliyars from amongst the Sinhalese landholders of good family, and had interfered but little with them so long as they performed their duties satisfactorily. One of the first acts of the Madras administration was to abolish the Mudaliyars and other Sinhalese officials, and replace them by the Aumildars and their subordinates, foreigners from Madras who were entirely ignorant of the customs, language, and prejudices of the people. The Mudaliyars were alienated by the loss of their salary and power, and although they were well aware of the preparations for revolt they made no attempt to check it or to warn the Government.[3]

Not content with alienating the most influential class amongst the Sinhalese the Madras officials abolished the immemorial form of taxation and land tenure in Ceylon, and substituted the Madras revenue system. Even on the very dubious assumption that the Madras was superior to the Ceylon revenue system, the Government should have been aware that suddenly to sweep away the age-old customs of a suspicious and conservative people was to court disaster. The Dutch and the Portuguese

---

[1] Turner, *C.A. and L.R.* IV. i. 48; C.R. 54: Robertson MS.

[2] C.R. 54: Robertson MS.; Turner, *C.A. and L.R.* IV. i. 48; Rao, *C.A. and L.R.* IV. iv. 212; C.R. 2: Feb. 16, 1798.

[3] C.R. 2: Feb. 16, 1798. During the Dutch régime the power of the Mudaliyars over the natives outside the towns was very great and uncontrolled (Tennent, *Ceylon*, ii. 56–8).

were wiser than their successors, and retained the greater part of the system of native land tenure. The subject is exceedingly complicated, but speaking generally the system of taxation and land tenure in 1796 was as follows. The King or the European government which had inherited his rights was the owner of all land, and granted it to individuals in return for the performance of services or the payment of a percentage of the crops. In the course of time the forms of tenure had in many cases become confused: lands held by Service Tenure sometimes paid the tax of a tenth of the produce which was frequently levied on Non-Service lands. Sometimes also the cultivators on Service Tenure lands owed their services not to the State but to an overlord to whom the State had granted the land and the services that went with it. The general principle, however, was clear: Service lands were held free from tax so long as the occupiers rendered the services in return for which the lands had been granted them. In many ways a close analogy existed between Sinhalese Service Tenures and feudal land tenure in Europe.

Service Tenure lands were of two kinds: Accommodessan and Divel or Neinde Paraveni lands. Accommodessan lands were usually granted instead of a salary for the performance of official duties: until the beginning of the nineteenth century the Mudaliyars and almost all the native officers of government were paid by the grant of Accommodessans. These lands could not be alienated by will, sale, or mortgage, nor were they in general heritable. Divel or Neinde Paraveni lands were granted for personal service of a more menial kind, e.g. carrying baggage and general coolie labour. The occupiers owed to Government three months' unpaid service a year, unless they served outside their own district when they received rice and a small wage. These lands were hereditary, but could not be alienated nor sold for debt. The Government was thus assured of an adequate supply of labour without cost to itself.

While land was usually held by Service Tenure there were exceptions, of which the most important was Non-Service Tenure. The holder of Non-Service land did not owe services to the Government, but paid a tax in kind which varied from one-tenth to one-half of the produce. A substantial part of the

Ceylon revenue came from the tenth (for Ande paddy lands one-half) levied upon the cultivators of paddy who held Otu Non-Service lands. Gardens were held either under Tanhool or Ratmahera tenure. In the first case they paid one-third of the produce to Government, either in kind or in money commutation, while in the second they paid one-half. Some time before the conquest the Dutch apparently abandoned the collection of the tax, so that the owners of gardens of coco-nut trees had acquired a sort of prescriptive right to hold them tax free.[1]

Very careful investigation and consideration were essential before any changes were made in a system of land tenures the complications of which were the product of centuries; but the Madras administration was untroubled by such reflections.[2] In 1796 Service Tenures were abolished and replaced by a tax of one-half of the estimated value of the produce. A very large number of Sinhalese were rendered hostile by the abolition of a system which they understood and the substitution of a tax from which they had hitherto been exempt.[3] The rough-and-ready manner in which the new tax was assessed further exasperated the Sinhalese.[4] Another important cause of the revolt was the introduction on September 1, 1796, of a tax of one silver fanam (*2d.*) a year on each coco-nut tree. The Government had a legal right to impose the tax, but owing to its abandonment by the Dutch the Sinhalese had apparently forgotten that any such right existed. It was in the highest degree injudicious for a new and foreign government to revive an obsolete right early in its career, and all the more so because of the other revolutionary changes introduced. The universal

[1] Turner, *C.A. and L.R.* iv. iv. 188–91. A very detailed and well-documented account of land tenures in the Maritime Provinces of Ceylon. C.R. 2: Feb. 6 and Mar. 15, 1798; C.R. 54: Robertson MS.

[2] C.R. 54: Robertson MS. Soon after the conquest, 'when we were almost entirely unacquainted' with Sinhalese land tenures and customs, 'instead of endeavouring to acquire information on these subjects . . . and gradually abolishing all defects and abuses . . . the Madras Government annihilated by one Coup de Plume every feudal tenure and privilege that they had been accustomed to venerate and regard . . . and thus disgusted and offended every native inhabitant of the island.'

[3] Turner, *C.A. and L.R.* iv. i. 44, and iv. iv. 191; Tennent, *Ceylon*, ii. 72; C.R. 2: Aug. 16, 1797.

[4] C.R. 2: Sept. 20, 1797.

rate of one fanam was also unjust, for the value of a coco-nut tree varied with its situation, and the tax was sometimes greater than the annual value of the nuts. Furthermore the Government refused to accept payment in kind, the usual practice in Ceylon, and demanded that the amount be paid in silver. Opposition to the tax was universal and almost instantaneous, for the administration had 'hastily' decided upon the levy best calculated to exasperate its subjects. It is uncertain whether the tax was ever actually collected, but an attempt to do so was made.[1]

The Madras revenue system which was introduced was not only unfamiliar to the Sinhalese, but it also had serious defects. Perhaps the feature which most incensed the Sinhalese was the union in the same person of the functions of tax farmer and magistrate, owing to the 'facility of oppression' thus given to the tax farmer.[2] Farming the taxes, i.e. selling the right of collection by public auction to the highest bidder, was a well-known practice in many Oriental countries; but it was a peculiarity of the Madras revenue system that the farms were often bought by members of the Civil Service. It was in the highest degree undesirable that the person who collected the revenue should sit in judgement upon his own acts as tax farmer. Jervis, Andrews's Senior Assistant, was a tax farmer, and the practice was especially common amongst the Aumildars, who probably had a delegated judicial authority. The abuses produced by this dual position were 'a very prominent feature of all the

---

[1] Turner, *C.A. and L.R.* IV. i. 43–4; C.R. 2: Mar. 15, 1798; C.R. 54: Robertson MS. The tax 'bore most severely on the poorest classes of inhabitants' who depended upon their coco-nut trees for the greater part of their means of subsistence. As an illustration of the importance of coco-nut trees in Ceylon Tennent instanced a suit where the subject in dispute was the 2,520th part of ten coco-nut trees (Tennent, *Ceylon*, ii. 127).

[2] C.R. 2: Sept. 20, 1797. 'The old Revenue System of the Carnatic I cannot consider as a model for imitation, as I have long been of opinion that a worse does not exist.' The taxes on produce and arrack and the monopoly of the pearl fishery were farmed. The tax farmer employed his own subordinates in collecting the tax, and had the support of the Government if the taxpayers refused the amount due from them. The system of farming the taxes was admitted by the Government to be open to the very serious objection that it gave the farmer many opportunities to oppress the ignorant peasantry; but it was long retained on grounds of expediency, as 'the only successful system of revenue collection'. (Turner, *C.A. and L.R.* IV. i. 50; C.R. 2: June 10, 1797.

complaints which have at various times been preferred from the Districts'.[1]

The Aumildars and other native officials from Madras had no bond of common interest with the Sinhalese to restrain their rapacity and cruelty, and they used their authority as an engine of extortion. They were accompanied by a swarm of camp followers, friends and relatives, who came from Madras to make what profit they could out of the tax farms with the active participation of the Aumildars. Lord Hobart condemned their cruelty and rapacity in scathing terms. They were 'a set of wretches, whose speculations are plunder, whose interests are permanently foreign to those of the country, and whose rapacious dispositions are perpetually urged forward by the precariousness of their tenure' (the possibility that Ceylon might be restored to Holland). 'I am certain that no mode for destroying a country could have been devised that was more likely to accomplish its end with despatch and aggravation, and which was more completely calculated . . . to create . . . the most rooted abhorrence of and disgust to the British Government. It is no wonder . . . that General Doyle [the Commander-in-Chief in Ceylon] should remark that the revenue can only be collected at the point of the bayonet . . . the system is so radically bad that it can never be sufficiently reprobated.'[2] The same opinion was expressed in 1798 by Governor North, who after investigating the condition of Ceylon wrote of 'the excesses committed by a set of profligate Malabar Servants of Revenue'.[3] De Meuron's Committee, which investigated the Madras administration in 1798, also considered the conduct of the Madras native officials to be a principal cause of the revolt.[4]

The failure of Andrews and his Assistants to control their native subordinates deserved the severest condemnation. 'Whether oppression upon the unfortunate inhabitants has proceeded from his [i.e. Andrews's] indolence or from worse motives, in his situation indolence and guilt are the same.'[5] North at first believed that Andrews at least was honest:

[1] C.R. 2: Aug. 16 and Sept. 20, 1797; Turner, *C.A. and L.R.* IV. i. 45.
[2] C.R. 2: June 10, 1797.
[3] Brit. Mus. Add. MS. No. 13866: Oct. 27, 1798.
[4] C.R. 2: Sept. 20, 1797, and Mar. 15, 1798.
[5] Cleghorn, quoted by Turner in *C.A. and L.R.* IV. i. 46.

'I have known so many instances of their [i.e. his subordinates']
villainy where he was clearly innocent that, except want of
vigilance and perhaps of activity, I do not believe there is
anything which can be imputed to him as blameable.'[1] Subsequently North revised his opinion as the result of the inquiry
which he held into the conduct of the pearl fisheries of 1797
and 1798. The annual pearl fishery was a government monopoly,
the auction of the right to conduct the fishery being at that
period the principal source of revenue. North found that 'gross
and enormous peculation' took place, and estimated that the
Company had been robbed of 'little less than twelve lacs of
pagodas'.[2] The fisheries had been held under the superintendence of Andrews and some of his Assistants, and there seems
reason to suspect that they cheated the Company of large sums
by allowing twice as many boats to be employed as the Company
was paid for, the profits of the fraud being divided with the
native who bought the monopoly of the fishery. While the
evidence 'was quite sufficient to create suspicion' it was not
conclusive enough to justify the prosecution which the Directors
had originally proposed.[3] By their orders Andrews was suspended from the Civil Service until 1808.[4] Macdowall, one of
Andrews's subordinates, was guilty of extraordinary laxity in
his conduct of the pearl fishery of 1799; while Garrow, the
Assistant at Batticaloa, was suspended by Governor North on
charges of violence and of illegal arrests.[5] The evidence against
Andrews and his Assistants is not conclusive, but it is sufficient
to leave them under suspicion. At best they seem to have done
nothing to check their native subordinates, and with control

---

[1] Brit. Mus. Add. MS. No. 13866: Dec. 29, 1798.

[2] Ibid. No. 13867: Dec. 15, 1800.

[3] C.R. 53: Dec. 1799, May 25 and Sept. 26, 1802, and *passim*; Turner,
C.A. and L.R. iv. i. 45 and 47.

[4] C.R. 53: Oct. 30 and Dec. 29, 1801; Turner, *C.A. and L.R.* iv. i. 46;
Rao, *C.A. and L.R.* iv. iv. 206–7 and 215. Andrews was apparently without
employment from 1798 when North abolished his offices in Ceylon, until he
was reappointed to the Madras Civil Service in 1808. From then until his
death at Trinchinopoli in 1821 he held various positions, principally judicial.
Apparently Andrews did not succeed in dispelling the strong suspicions of his
honesty, and his reinstatement was due to the anger of the Madras officials
at the loss of their patronage in Ceylon, and to 'the influence at Headquarters
which Andrews undoubtedly had'.

[5] Turner, *C.A. and L.R.* iv. i. 47.

in such hands it is not surprising that eighteen months of Madras rule were sufficient to provoke a revolt. It is only just to add that not all of Andrews's Assistants were suspect: Gregory and Alexander were 'honesty itself' and were 'justly beloved'.[1]

Even before the revolt broke out Lord Hobart, the Governor of Madras, was seriously perturbed by the reports which reached him from Ceylon. In an official Minute already quoted he condemned utterly the practice of selling the tax farms to natives of Madras, and ordered that it should cease immediately. On June 9, 1797, he appointed a Committee of Investigation composed of General de Meuron as President, Colonel Agnew, the Adjutant-General of the forces in Ceylon, and Andrews himself. The power of the Committee was 'not to affect the authority of the Superintendent'.[2]

Andrews proved a hindrance rather than a help, but his colleagues were men of marked ability, and carried out a most painstaking and exhaustive investigation of the condition of Ceylon. In a masterly report De Meuron and Agnew proved that the revolt was caused by the blunders and oppression of Andrews's administration, and recommended reforms which removed the hostility of the Sinhalese. The Committee advised that the Madras revenue system be abolished, and the ancient Sinhalese system restored as it had existed under the Dutch régime. The coco-nut tree tax was abolished by Lord Hobart on September 16, 1797, in accordance with the Committee's recommendation.[3] Service Tenure lands should be held as formerly by rendering personal services, and the tax of half the produce which the Madras administration had substituted in 1796 should be abolished. 'The more our system approximates to that heretofore in force (always supposing the abuses of its administration corrected) the better it will apply to this island where, from the . . . long established prejudices of the natives, many of those customs and laws which to a stranger may appear impolitic and oppressive, are in reality gratifying

[1] Turner, *C.A. and L.R.* iv. iv. 215; Brit. Mus. Add. MS. No. 13866: Dec. 30, 1798.

[2] C.R. 2: June 10, 1797.

[3] C.R. 2: Sept. 2 and 16, 1797. The tax had already been suspended in accordance with Lord Hobart's Minute of June 10, 1797.

to the people, and necessary to the welfare and security of the state.'[1] The Committee also advised the restoration of Service Tenures because of the difficulty of obtaining sufficient labour for public works under the Madras system, which had substituted voluntary paid labour for compulsory services. 'The natural indolence of the Cingalese renders the interference of authority necessary to obtain labourers . . . for no temptation of reward within the bounds of reason can induce a Cingalese to labour while he can exist in idleness.'[2]

The last vestiges of the Madras revenue system were swept away when the Committee condemned the union of the powers of magistrate and tax farmer in the same official, and also the employment of natives of Madras in Ceylon. They most strongly advised that all the Madras native officials and tax farmers should be sent back to India, and that the Mudaliyars should be reappointed. They should have magisterial power in minor civil and criminal cases including disputes between the natives and the tax farmers; they should be in charge of the police; and they should 'be the channel of communication' between the Government and the Sinhalese for all official orders affecting their district, except those concerned with the revenue.[3] Despite Andrews's opposition De Meuron and Agnew insisted that the Mudaliyars should be independent of Andrews's Revenue Department, since otherwise they would be subjected to overwhelming pressure by native revenue officials to decide disputes in favour of the tax farmers.[4] Lord Hobart concurred in the restoration of the Mudaliyars, and ordered that they should be independent of Andrews's Revenue Department. They were to be appointed by and subject to 'the chief civil authority on the island', in other words to De Meuron himself.[5]

The recommendations of De Meuron and Agnew were approved by the Madras Government on May 16, 1798; and after that date they concerned themselves largely with devising means of carrying out the reforms without dislocation of the

[1] C.R. 2: Aug. 16, 1797, Feb. 6 and Mar. 15, 1798, and *passim*.
[2] C.R. 2: Aug. 16, 1797.
[3] C.R. 2: Aug. 16, 1797, and Mar. 15, 1798.
[4] C.R. 2: Sept. 20, 1797.
[5] C.R. 2: Oct. 10, 1797, and July 3, 1798. Service Tenures and the Mudaliyars were restored on Sept. 1, 1798.

C

Government service.[1] Their work was brought to a close by the arrival on October 12, 1798, of the Honourable Frederick North, who had been appointed Governor of Ceylon by the Crown. He found the island 'in perfect tranquillity', and wrote that 'the masterly labours of the Committee . . . have left me little more to do than to put into execution the very wise and prudent regulations recommended by them'.[2] De Meuron and Agnew had diagnosed the causes of discontent, and the disappearance of the agitation was due to their skill in solving a difficult problem. North found that for many of the most important problems which confronted him the solution had been laid down by De Meuron's Committee, and he had the wisdom in great part to adopt their recommendations. Where he departed from them, as in the matter of Service Tenures, he merely succeeded in proving the foresight of General De Meuron and Colonel Agnew.

[1] C.R. 2: Feb. 16 and May 16, 1798, and *passim*; Brit. Mus. Add. MS. No. 13866: Feb. 9, 1799. In 1799 De Meuron resigned his post as Commander-in-Chief in Ceylon in order to assist in the defence of Switzerland against Napoleon, and died at Neuchâtel in 1812 (Turner, *C.A. and L.R.* iii. iv. 246).

[2] C.R. 2: July 12, 1798; C.R. 52: Oct. 26, 1798.

IV

THE EXPERIMENT OF DUAL CONTROL
1798–1802

THE arrival of the Honourable Frederick North as Governor in 1798 marked the beginning of a new experiment in the history of Ceylon. The Madras régime was abolished, and from 1798 to January 1, 1802, the control of the Government was divided between the Crown and the East India Company. The reason for the change is somewhat obscure, but it was not as Tennent believed due to the rebellion against Andrews's administration.[1] The Cabinet decided to place Ceylon under the Crown in November 1797, before the news of the revolt could have reached England. It seems more probable that the alteration was the result of the failure of the peace negotiations at Lille, and the consequent decision at least to postpone the return of Ceylon to Holland.[2] The Cabinet at first intended that Ceylon should be a Crown Colony entirely independent of the East India Company; but the Directors protested, urging 'the necessity of preserving an united authority in India'. The final decision appears to have been left to Dundas, who decided upon a compromise. The Governor and the members of the Civil Service were to be appointed by the Crown; but subject to the ultimate authority of the President of the Board of Control they were to be under the control of the Governor-General of India and the Directors 'in the same manner as the Governments of Fort St. George and Bombay'. The revenues of Ceylon, and especially the cinnamon monopoly, were to be under the Company's control; and if the island were eventually ceded to Great Britain Dundas informed the Directors that he knew no reason why it should not be placed under their rule, 'upon the footing of their other possessions'. Although a few posts were to be filled by officials appointed by Dundas it was not the intention of the Cabinet to create a separate Ceylon Civil Service: 'for the collection of the revenues and other purposes of government, the Company's Madras or Bombay Servants would be employed', and would be 'entirely subject' to the Governor's orders. The form of the administra-

---

[1] Tennent, *Ceylon*, ii. 73–4.   [2] Turner, *C.A. and L.R.* IV. iii. 123.

tion in Ceylon was to be similar to that of the Madras or Bombay Presidencies, with the exception that there was to be no Council, all legislative and executive power being vested in the Governor.[1] The principal changes made in 1798 were the abolition of the control of Madras over Ceylon, and the appointment of a civil in place of the military Governor who from 1795 to 1798 had held the supreme authority in the island. Henceforth the powers of the general commanding the garrison were confined to military affairs, and even in these he was under the control of the Governor in his capacity as Commander-in-Chief. This established in Ceylon a basic principle of British colonial administration that 'all the powers of Government . . . as well Civil as Military, shall be vested solely in' the Governor.[2]

Governor North had already had some experience of colonial administration as Chief Secretary of Corsica, and in his new post received a salary of £10,000. He was accompanied by nine officials appointed by Dundas, many of them at the suggestion of North.[3] Amongst them was Hugh Cleghorn, whom Dundas appointed Principal or Chief Secretary to Government (the present Colonial Secretary) with a salary of £3,000, as a reward for securing the transfer of the De Meuron regiment. The Principal Secretary was the head of the permanent Civil Service and the Governor's chief adviser. Four of the officials who accompanied North were to be given suitable appointments at salaries of from £250 to £400 a year. The remainder of his party was composed of Jonville, a naturalist, and Barry, Gordon, and Lusignan, 'young gentlemen going out to learn the languages, and to work under Mr. Boyd' (the First Assistant to the Principal Secretary), until they were fitted for promotion to responsible posts. The other positions in Ceylon continued to be held by members of the Madras Civil Service.[4]

---

[1] C.R. 53: Jan. 16, 1798, Memo. Feb. 27, 1802; C.R. 52: May 5, 1798; C.R. 54: Douglass MS.; C.O. 55. 61: Mar. 26, 1798.

[2] C.R. 52: May 5, 1798. Owing to the vagueness of his Instructions from Dundas North found that his military powers conflicted 'in every Point' with those of the Commander-in-Chief in India (C.R. 52: Feb. 26, 1799); and in 1804–5 his authority was defied and the civil power reduced to impotence by General Wemyss, the officer commanding in Ceylon. This situation was rectified by greater definiteness in the Instructions to later Governors.

[3] C.R. 52: Sept. 28, 1798; Brit. Mus. Add. MS. No. 13866: Jan. 16, 1798.

[4] C.R. 53: May 1, 1798, and Feb. 27, 1802.

The principal officials in the central administration from 1798 to 1802 were the Governor and Treasurer *ex officio* (though the actual work seems to have been done by the Vice-Treasurer); the Commander-in-Chief; the Principal and the Deputy Secretaries; the Commercial Resident, or Head of the Cinnamon Department, the most important branch of the revenue; and the Accountant General and Civil Auditor. Andrews's post of Superintendent of Revenue was abolished in 1798 by North as unnecessary.[1] For provincial administration Ceylon was divided into four Districts, each under a Collector, viz. Jaffna, Galle and Matara, Batticaloa and Mullaittivu, and Colombo (established by North in 1799 and abolished the same year). Each Collector was assisted by native officials, the Mudaliyars and their subordinates, whose 'authority is nearly unlimited' in controlling the inhabitants of the Sinhalese Districts. The Mudaliyars of each District were under the control of the Mudaliyar of the Attepattu, who was attached to the head-quarters of the Collector; while all the Mudaliyars were under the orders of the Maha Mudaliyar of the Governor's Gate, who was in constant attendance on North. North reappointed all the Mudaliyars of good character who had held office under the Dutch.[2] They were indispensable, since as late as 1804 the only official who spoke Sinhalese was an English schoolmaster at Colombo.[3] North charged them with using their power illegally to exact from the raiyats forced labour for their personal benefit.[4] The minor clerical posts both in the provincial and the central administration were filled largely by burghers, or those of mixed Dutch and Sinhalese blood.[5]

The problems which confronted North in 1798 were both difficult and pressing, for De Meuron's Committee had not had time to bring their reforms into operation. This complicated duty fell to North, while in addition there were urgent questions for which the Committee had not supplied a solution. In accordance with De Meuron's Report the Directors had in-

---

[1] C.R. 52: Feb. 26, 1799; C.O. 54. 4: Memo. undated.
[2] C.R. 52: Feb. 26 and Oct. 5, 1799; C.R. 54: Robertson MS.; Cordiner, *Ceylon*, i. 99–102; Brit. Mus. Add. MS. No. 13866: Oct. 27, 1798.
[3] Cordiner, *Ceylon*, i. 119–20; C.R. 52: Sept. 28, 1798.
[4] C.R. 52: Feb. 26, 1799.
[5] C.R. 52: Feb. 26, 1799, and Jan. 30, 1800.

structed North that the Dutch judicial and police system should be retained with such reforms as should prove necessary; and investigation showed that very extensive reforms were required. The Directors also ordered that the Dutch revenue system should be restored, but they authorized North to abolish any taxes which were 'ruinous or vexatious' and substitute others.[1] To make alterations proved a very difficult task, and the situation was rendered much more serious by the failure in 1799 of the pearl fisheries, the principal source of income.[2] The Dutch currency of Ceylon rapidly depreciated, and the country was slow in recovering from the effects of the Madras administration. In place of the large revenue surplus produced by the pearl fisheries in 1796–8 North had to contend with a heavy annual deficit.[3] The Civil Service had to be reorganized and made efficient and free from corruption, a task in which North met with scant assistance from many of the Madras officials.

The Governor's faults of character intensified his difficulties and led to serious mistakes. Honest, talented, and versatile, North's charm of manner won him the warm admiration and attachment of many of his staff. A firm belief that almost all geese were swans frequently resulted in too high an opinion of his subordinates, and this sometimes led to his failing to detect maladministration. A man of sudden and violent likes and dislikes, the trusting friendship of to-day became the bitter enmity of to-morrow; and with his tendency to extremes North was at times as unjust in the one as he had been over-indulgent in the other. In short, he was a bad judge of men. Impulsive, unbalanced, and confident of his own superior wisdom, he was inclined without sufficient investigation to turn quickly from one reform to another, hailing each as a panacea. In his policy towards Kandy the Governor's belief in his own talent involved him in the toils of an abler intriguer than himself, and led to

[1] C.R. 52: May 5, 1798.
[2] Turner, *C.A. and L.R.* IV. i. 39. The three fisheries of 1796–8 produced a revenue of £396,000 but exhausted the pearl banks. The fishery of 1799 brought only £30,000, and no fishing was therefore allowed on the principal pearl banks at Arippu until 1804.
[3] Turner, *C.A. and L.R.* IV. iv. 185–8; VI. i. 26; C.O. 54. 6: Feb. 8, 1803; C.O. 54. 7: Sept. 10, 1802.

a disastrous failure. Nevertheless it should be remembered to his credit that many of his administrative reforms won the approval of so unsparing and competent a critic as his successor, Sir Thomas Maitland.

One of the most serious difficulties with which North had to contend on his arrival was the hostility of the Madras civil servants. The officials in the Madras Presidency itself resented the loss of patronage which they had suffered by the abolition of their control; and in 1798 they tried to hamper North and Cleghorn by giving them as little information as possible about affairs in Ceylon.[1] The hostility of Madras probably explains the re-employment in India of the Madras civilians whom North later dismissed for corruption. The Madras civil servants in Ceylon also resented North's appointment, and were not to be conciliated despite all his friendly overtures. Under the leadership of John Macdowall,[2] the Collector of Colombo, they intrigued to bring about his recall, and rendered the first nine months of his government 'ineffective'. North ascribed their conduct to his attempts to root out corruption: many of them feared a reforming Governor since they were aware that their records would not bear investigation.[3] Another reason for their hostility was jealousy that a Governor who was not an Indian civilian had been appointed to a post which they regarded as a preserve of the Madras Service.[4] Probably their resentment was increased when North removed Andrews from Ceylon soon after his arrival. Andrews had made no attempt to reform any of the abuses in his administration, and the Governor decided that the sooner he left Ceylon the better. For this reason, and because his positions were superfluous, North abolished in 1798 the posts of Superintendent of Revenue and Ambassador to Kandy.[5]

At first North seems to have depended greatly upon Cleghorn's advice in his struggle with the 'Madras Click'; but

[1] Brit. Mus. Add. MS. No. 13866: Sept. 28, 1798.
[2] Ibid.: July 27, 1799.
[3] Ibid.: Aug. 21, 1799; C.R. 26: Oct. 5, 1799; C.R. 27: Aug. 26, 1800; C.R. 52: Oct. 5, 1799 and Jan. 30, 1800.
[4] C.R. 52: Jan. 30, 1800.
[5] Brit. Mus. Add. MS. No. 13866: Oct. 27 and Dec. 29, 1798; C.R. 53: Oct. 30, 1801.

within eight months he had become convinced that Cleghorn was the leader of the malcontents. North ascribed his hostility to the successful efforts of Macdowall;[1] but apparently the principal reason was the charge brought by North against Cleghorn of corrupt management of the pearl fishery of 1799. In that year the Government monopoly of the pearl fishery had as formerly been sold by auction to a native, the three Superintendents of the fishery being Cleghorn, Macdowall, and Turnour. Owing to rumours which had reached him North held an inquiry, and accused the three Superintendents of corruption. An investigation was also held at North's request by General Hay Macdowall, the newly appointed Commander-in-Chief in Ceylon. While his conclusions were more charitable than North's he concurred that 'the grossest frauds, abuses and corruption and even thefts were committed', and that the Company had been defrauded of about 32,690 Porto Novo Pagodas (£10,896 13s. 4d.). There was strong reason to suspect the complicity of the Superintendents, but the evidence was not conclusive since the native witnesses who accused them admitted that they themselves were equally guilty. Furthermore the accused were not present at the inquiry, and thus could not cross-examine the witnesses. It therefore remains doubtful whether the Superintendents were guilty of anything save amazing negligence in blindly committing the exercise of their powers to Macdowall's native servant, who was admittedly the chief criminal, but declared he had acted on his superiors' orders.[2] This seems to have been North's final opinion.[3] As a result of the inquiry Cleghorn was suspended from his post as Principal Secretary in December 1799, and returned to Scotland in February 1800.[4] Macdowall had already been dismissed from office in September for his systematic opposition to North, and

[1] Brit. Mus. Add. MS. No. 13866: July 15 and Aug. 1, 1799; C.R. 27: Aug. 26, 1800.

[2] Brit. Mus. Add. MS. No. 13866: Sept. 3, 1799; Brit. Mus. Add. MS. No. 13867, *passim*; C.R. 26: Dec. 12 and 31, 1799, Jan. 8, 1800, and *passim*; C.R. 53: Sept. 3, 1802; C.O. 54. 14: May 12, 1804.

[3] C.R. 52: Jan. 17, 1800. When the three Superintendents were appointed 'I did not suspect that two of them would resign their powers blindly to a third [Macdowall], nor that third to a Dubash' (Macdowall's native servant).

[4] C.R. 52: Jan. 17, 1800. Turnour was temporarily suspended from his post at Mannar. Brit. Mus. Add. MS. No. 13867: Feb. 3, 1800.

had returned to Madras. His Collectorate of Colombo was abolished as superfluous, and the work divided between the Collectors of Galle and Jaffna.[1]

Garrow, the Collector of Batticaloa, another member of the Madras clique, was suspended in September 1799. North had personally investigated complaints of violence brought against him, and had found him guilty of illegal arrests and other 'acts of arbitrary injustice'. Garrow returned to Madras and was soon reappointed to the Company's service there.[2] In this same year of 1799 Nemesis descended upon another member of the Madras clique, Edward Atkinson, an official of sixteen years' service, who was Commissary of Grain and Provisions, and whom North appointed Paymaster-General of the troops in Ceylon. He kept no accounts and there were strong grounds of suspicion that he and the other paymasters defrauded the soldiers of their pay. He also 'informed a Military Board that he considered the deriving pecuniary advantages to himself by sending in a false return as an allowable though not avowed emolument of the office of Commissary'. North permitted Atkinson to resign before he was aware of the extent of his transgressions.[3] By the beginning of 1800 North's troubles with the Madras clique were at an end: the dismissal of the ring-leaders had taught the survivors a wholesome lesson. At last he was able to report that 'I am now obeyed with an alacrity and exactitude which makes the task of government easy and satisfactory to me'.[4]

Malversation, however, was not confined to the Madras officials. Gavin Hamilton, who was specially appointed by North to succeed Atkinson because 'he has my entire confidence', was found after his death in 1803 to have embezzled

---

[1] Brit. Mus. Add. MS. No. 13866: July 31, Aug. 9 and 14, and Sept. 14, 1799; C.R. 52 : Oct. 5, 1799. Macdowall seems to have been unemployed until 1809, when he was again given a post in Madras. He died in 1814 (Rao, *C.A. and L.R.* IV. iv. 208).

[2] Brit. Mus. Add. MS. No. 13866: July 27 and Aug. 1, 1799; C.R. 52: Oct. 5, 1799. Garrow held various important posts, and died in 1838 at Trinchinopoli (Rao, *C.A. and L.R.* IV. iv. 207).

[3] C.R. 52: Jan. 30 and Feb. 18, 1800. North abolished the post of Commissary.

[4] Brit. Mus. Add. MS. No. 13867: Feb. 15, 1800; C.R. 52: Apr. 5 and Aug. 30, 1800.

£19,675 for private trade. The amount was recovered from his estate.[1] Hamilton's successor, Leslie, had a deficit of over £10,000 after sixteen months' service. The amount was refunded, and Leslie escaped with the loss of his office.[2]

Despite the improved relations between North and his subordinates the employment of Madras civil servants in Ceylon was not a success. The Governor was compelled by the Directors' orders to fill most of the vacancies from that Service, but he was soon protesting vigorously.[3] The salaries and prospects of promotion in Ceylon were so inferior to those in Madras that no Madras civilian of ability or ambition would willingly remain on the island; and North felt that he could not in justice to their 'fair hopes on entering your service' refuse to accept their resignations. Furthermore, the native languages and customs of Ceylon were so totally different to those of Madras that service in the one was almost valueless as a preparation for the other. North urged strongly that the only solution was the creation of a Ceylon Civil Service totally distinct from that of India.[4]

His recommendation had no immediate effect, and in 1801 he established the Board of Revenue and Commerce to control the revenue departments, viz. the provincial administration, the Cinnamon Department, and the pearl fishery. Under the revenue system which had existed since 1798 the island had been divided between three Collectors responsible to the Principal Secretary. Owing to the extent of their districts North had apparently divided them into thirteen provinces, and had allowed each Collector to recommend Europeans for appointment as Agents in the provinces which he was rarely able to visit. The Agents were subject to the Collector's orders, received small salaries, and were apparently not eligible for promotion to higher offices. On the whole the system had worked well, but

[1] C.O. 54. 13: Jan. 1, 1804; C.R. 52: Jan. 30, 1800.
[2] C.O. 54. 13: Jan. 1, 1804; C.O. 54. 23: Feb. 28, 1807. It was typical of North's extraordinary laxity that he reinstated Leslie in his position. Leslie was eventually dismissed and sent to England by order of the Colonial Office.
[3] C.R. 52: May 25, 1798.
[4] C.R. 52: Feb. 26, 1799, and Jan. 30, 1800; C.R. 54: Douglass MS. Strongly supports North's contentions, and contains the comment: 'I am very clearly of opinion that' North's contention 'is perfectly just. H. D.' (i.e. Dundas, the President of the Board of Control).

North considered that its weakness lay in the inevitable changes which periodically occurred amongst the Collectors. He believed that the collective and permanent wisdom of a Board would obviate 'the extensive evils which . . . must follow the appointment of a new Collector, till he becomes thoroughly acquainted with the country he is to govern'. North, therefore, abolished the Collectors and replaced them by Agents of Revenue, who were to administer the thirteen provinces under the control of the newly established Board of Revenue and Commerce.[1] He also abolished the post of Commercial Resident, and placed the control of the Cinnamon Department in the hands of the Board. It had been found inconvenient that the superintendence of the collection, preparation, and shipping of cinnamon, the most important item of revenue, should be in charge of a separate official.[2] North appointed the former Collectors to the Board; but in 1803 he altered the membership so that it was composed of the Chief Secretary, the Vice-Treasurer, the Accountant-General, and the Paymaster-General.[3]

During the first years of his administration North carried out important judicial reforms. When he arrived in Ceylon the only courts were the Courts Martial, the Collectors' Courts which had proved so unsatisfactory during Andrews's régime, and a Court of Equity established by De Meuron. This last proved unworkable because the former Dutch judges whom it was proposed to appoint refused to take the oath of allegiance to Great Britain, or to assist the British by deciding cases brought before them. Since the conquest of Ceylon in 1796 there had been a 'suspension of almost all criminal, and of all civil justice whatsoever'.[4] The attitude of the former Dutch judges very

[1] C.O. 54. 3: Oct. 13 and 17, 1800; C.R. 52: Feb. 18, 1801; C.O. 54. 6: Mar. 16, 1802; C.O. 54. 8: Oct. 31, 1802; C.O. 54. 13: Jan. 1, 1804. Colonel Barbut was continued as Collector of Jaffna, under the title of Commissioner Extraordinary, because of the very great success of his administration. The number of Agents of Revenue actually appointed does not seem to have exceeded eight. Each had one or two Assistants.

[2] C.O. 54. 13: Jan. 1, 1804; C.O. 54. 3: Oct. 13, 1800.

[3] C.O. 54. 3: Oct. 13, 1800; C.R. 52: Feb. 18, 1801; C.O. 54. 7: Sept. 10 and 11, 1802; C.O. 54. 9: May 7, 1803. In 1803 the Colonial Office approved North's proposals to replace the Agents of Revenue by six Collectors; but apparently North changed his mind and retained the existing system.

[4] Brit. Mus. Add. MS. No. 13866: June 28, 1798; C.R. 52: Feb. 26, 1799; C.R. 53: undated dispatch of North to Directors, written from Madras.

greatly increased North's difficulties, and prevented him from carrying out in their entirety the Directors' instructions to re-establish the Dutch system of courts and jurisprudence, with such reforms as should prove necessary.[1] The British were ignorant of the Roman Dutch law which had been in force, and North employed Carrington, a Calcutta barrister, to study the Dutch system of jurisprudence and draw up a code of law for Ceylon. This code apparently came into force in the middle of 1799. On September 23, 1799, North established civil and criminal courts which superseded those of Andrews's régime.[2]

North's Appeal and Supreme Courts were abolished by the Charter of Justice of April 18, 1801, and replaced by a Supreme Court of Judicature and a High Court of Appeal, with a Chief Justice and one Puisne Judge appointed by the Colonial Office. North also became dissatisfied with his Civil Courts, and by November 1802 he had replaced them by five Provincial Courts. The Provincial Judges, who were civil servants, had a wide civil and a limited criminal jurisdiction. In 1802 Justices of the Peace were appointed, and the Fiscals' Courts established in 1800 for minor civil and criminal cases received the new name of the Courts of the Justices of the Peace. The Justices were sometimes civil servants, but more often burghers.[3] In the course of time many alterations were made in the judiciary, such as a large increase in the number of Provincial Courts, but no radical change was introduced. In 1801 the Colonial Office appointed an Advocate Fiscal entitled King's Advocate after about 1815, whose duties were similar to those of the present Attorney-General. He was the legal adviser of the Government,

---

[1] C.R. 53: undated, North to Directors; C.R. 52: May 5, 1798.

[2] C.R. 27: June 23, 1800; C.R. 52: *passim*; C.R. 53: undated, North to Directors; C.R. 54: Douglass MS., § 94–122; C.O. 54. 3: Jan. 15, 1801. In 1801 a code of criminal law based on Dutch law was drawn up by James Dunkin, who was later appointed to a Judgeship in Ceylon.

[3] C.O. 54. 5: Mar. 13, 1801; C.O. 54. 6: Mar. 16, 1802; C.O. 55. 61: Draft of Charter of Justice of 1801; C.O. 54. 7: Sept. 10, 1802; Brit. Mus. Add. MS. No. 13867: Sept. 7, 1801; C.O. 54. 114: Nov. 9, 1831; Cordiner, *Ceylon*, i. 71–3; Turner, *C.A. and L.R.* IV. iii. 132. The appointment of civil servants to the Provincial Judgeships was open to the two disadvantages that they had rarely had legal training before their appointment, and that they seldom studied law very assiduously since the Provincial Judgeship was regarded 'as a mere step to some better situation in the revenue line', e.g. a Collectorship (C.O. 54. 51: Jan. 1, 1814).

drafted Government Bills, and acted as public prosecutor and as counsel for the Crown. He was allowed to carry on his private practice at the Bar when this did not interfere with his duty to Government.[1] As the century advanced the custom became established of reserving this important post for the most eminent member of the Ceylon Bar, which was composed almost entirely of burghers.

In striking contrast to the success of North's judicial reforms was the result of his abolition of landholding by Service Tenure, which he had restored in 1798 as De Meuron had advised.[2] The fate of Andrews's experiment and the considered recommendation of De Meuron's Committee were soon forgotten; and in little more than a year after his arrival the Governor determined to abolish a form of land tenure which was consecrated by centuries of usage.[3] The chief reason for North's policy was the conduct of the Mudaliyars and other native officials who made use of their authority to exact from the peasantry far more than the amount of unpaid services legally due for the cultivation of their own estates. North also considered that to 'men of liberal sentiments and enlightened minds' personal service was an 'onerous and disgraceful servitude'. Ignoring the attachment of the Sinhalese to their own customs, North persuaded himself that 'a vast majority of the people waits for' the abolition of Service Tenures 'with impatience'.[4] He confidently expected that the abolition of personal service would lead to a large increase of cultivation, and that the consequent growth of the land revenue would at least greatly decrease the perennial annual deficit. He dismissed as fantastic De Meuron's warning that only compulsion would compel a Sinhalese to work; North was confident that he would have no difficulty in securing an adequate supply of paid labour for public works, and that the new system would cost the Government less than the old.[5]

[1] C.O. 54. 5: Mar. 13, 1801; Dickman, *Ceylon Civil Service Manual*, 1865 ed., 152. In 1883 the title was changed to that of Attorney-General (C.O. 54. 549: Nov. 3, 1883).

[2] C.R. 52: Oct. 26, 1798.

[3] C.R. 52: Feb. 26 and June 10, 1799; C.R. 54: Robertson MS.

[4] C.O. 54. 6: Mar. 16, 1802.

[5] C.R. 52: Feb. 26 and June 10, 1799, and Feb. 18, 1801; C.O. 54. 6: Mar. 16, 1802; C.O. 54. 7: Oct. 4 and Nov. 24, 1802.

North's first attempt to abolish Service Tenures was made by his Proclamation of May 3, 1800. All who held Service land were given the option of retaining it by their old tenure, or of registering their holdings at the District Registry and commuting their personal service to a tax, the amount of which varied from one-tenth to one-quarter of the produce according to the value of the land. Those who renounced the old form of tenure would be free from all service obligations except 'on the particular order' of the Governor, when their labour would be paid for at the current rates.[1] The result of making the abandonment of Service Tenures optional was that few Sinhalese apparently took advantage of the offer.[2] North lamented 'their want of attention to their own advantages' and embarked on a policy of forcible reform. The Proclamation of September 3, 1801, enacted that after May 1, 1802, 'all obligation to Service on Tenure of Lands . . . shall cease . . . and lands held Duty free . . . on account of such Service shall . . . pay to Government' one-tenth to one-quarter of their produce. The Governor reserved the right to exact labour on giving adequate pay; and 'all Accommodessans at present enjoyed by Native Head Men, and all others of what description soever' were resumed by the Government.[3] In place of their Accommodessan lands the Mudaliyars and other native officials received salaries and a percentage of the land tax collected in their districts.[4]

When Lord Hobart, the Secretary of State for the Colonies, heard of North's abolition of Service Tenures he was far from sharing the Governor's satisfaction. 'We must always assume that antient customs are suited to the manners and disposition of the people where they are in use; and . . . indolence being the predominant feature of the Cingalese character . . . I am apprehensive that abolishing the system of the tenures of service may . . . neither produce an increased cultivation of rice or augmentation of revenue.'[5] Lord Hobart's fears were justified

---

[1] C.R. 52: Jan. 30, 1800; Turner, *C.A. and L.R.* IV. iv. 193.
[2] C.R. 52: Aug. 30, 1800.
[3] Turner, *C.A. and L.R.* IV. iv. 193. North's policy of service commutation applied chiefly if not exclusively to paddy lands.
[4] C.R. 52: Feb. 18, 1801; C.O. 54. 7: Sept. 10, 1802.
[5] C.O. 54. 61: May 1, 1802; C.O. 54. 5: Mar. 13, 1801. Dundas had also been opposed to the abolition of Service Tenures.

by the event. General Maitland, North's successor, arrived in 1805 and spent six months carefully examining the condition of Ceylon. In 1806 he strongly condemned the abolition of Service Tenures, and asked the Colonial Office for permission to restore them. The one feature of North's policy which he approved and intended to retain was the substitution of salaries for Accommodessans, since this diminished the influence of the Mudaliyars and other native officials. The headmen wished to retain their salaries; but the peasantry were 'most anxious to revert to their old tenure'. Service Tenures suited the primitive stage of economic development in Ceylon; and North had been premature and hasty in destroying 'by a single dash of the pen' an institution which had been created by the experience of centuries. The Government had actually lost revenue as a result of the abolition of Service Tenures. 'It is impossible to collect the men with all your money, for their (_sic_) being no penalty, there is not an inhabitant on this island that would not sit down and starve out the year under the shade of two or three cocoanut trees, the whole of his property and the whole of his subsistence, rather than increase his income and his comforts by his manual labour.' To obtain the labour required by Government North had been compelled to establish a paid coolie corps, the maintenance of which more than swallowed up the slight increase in the land revenue, since it was more expensive and less satisfactory than the former system. Far from stimulating agriculture 'it is my decided opinion . . . that in matter of fact its operation has led to a very considerable decrease of cultivation'. One reason for this was that the imposition of North's land tax had brought under the 'fangs' of the tax farmer thousands who had formerly been free from his exactions. He used the power inevitably placed in his hands to extort from the ignorant and submissive peasants more than the amount legally due, despite the efforts of Government to prevent it. Moreover, personal services were still illegally exacted by the Mudaliyars and other Sinhalese officials despite their abolition.[1] Maitland with the

[1] C.O. 54. 20: Feb. 28, 1806. Bertolacci (_A View of the Agricultural, Commercial and Financial Interests of Ceylon_, 304–11) strongly condemned the system of tax farming because of the extortions which the farmers practised upon the peasants. About half the land tax was collected by Government officials, the remainder by the tax farmers.

approval of the Colonial Office allowed North's Proclamations of 1800 and 1801 to become a dead letter, so that Service Tenures were rapidly restored.[1]

[1] C.O. 55. 62: June 11, 1807, and Sept. 30, 1810; C.O. 54. 42: Feb. 26, 1812; C.O. 54. 44: Aug. 22, 1812.

V

THE ESTABLISHMENT OF CROWN COLONY GOVERNMENT IN CEYLON
1802–1811

THE experiment of joint control by the Crown and the Company was not a success, and in December 1800 Dundas informed the Directors that he had resolved to make Ceylon a Crown Colony. The attempt to use Madras officials in Ceylon had failed owing to the dissimilarity between the languages and problems of Ceylon and India. An expert knowledge of Sinhalese conditions could only be obtained by the establishment of a separate Ceylon Civil Service, composed of men who would spend the whole of their official careers on the island. Another reason for the severance from India was that on account of Ceylon's perennial deficit the salaries were considerably lower than in India, while with the small number of posts the chances of promotion were far fewer. Experience had proved that no Madras civilians of ability would willingly remain in Ceylon, nor could they reasonably be expected to do so owing to the serious injury to their prospects which this would entail. Dundas was also influenced by North's severe complaints of the cabal of Madras officials against him.[1]

On January 1, 1802, the control of the East India Company was abolished, and Ceylon became a Crown Colony under the Colonial Office. Legislative and executive power continued to be 'vested in the Governor alone, subject to revision and confirmation or rejection at home'.[2] A very important innovation was the establishment of an advisory Council composed of the Governor; the Chief Justice; the officer commanding the troops in Ceylon; the Principal Secretary to Government; and two other officials nominated by the Governor. The Governor was

---

[1] C.O. 55. 61: Dec. 30, 1800, and Feb. 10, 1801; C.R. 53: Memo. on transfer of Ceylon to the Crown, dated Feb. 27, 1802; C.R. 54: Douglass MS., with comments by Dundas.

[2] C.O. 54. 5: Mar. 13, 1801; C.O. 55. 61: North's Commission and Instructions, dated 1801. The Governor held office during the King's pleasure until 1828, when the Colonial Office adopted the East India Company's rule that the post should be held for six years. (C.O. 54. 104: Feb. 20, 1829. *Parl. Pap. H. C.* 537 of 1836, vol. xxxix: May 31, 1828.)

D

expected to consult the Council on all matters of importance, but was not required to follow its advice, although a dissenting member might enter a protest on the Minutes. The Governor had power to suspend or dismiss members.[1]

A separate Ceylon Civil Service was established, and the Madras officials were encouraged to return to India. About twenty civilians appointed by Dundas were sent to Ceylon in 1801 and 1802, and were amalgamated with those who had gone out with North in 1798, and a few survivors of the Madras régime.[2] While Dundas appointed Robert Arbuthnot Chief or Principal Secretary (the present Colonial Secretary) he left North a considerable degree of freedom in arranging the Civil Service. Dundas advised that salaries should be lower than in India, ranging from £300 to £3,000 for the Principal Secretary, but should permit a decent scale of living and the saving of 'a competence'.[3] All vacancies except writerships, the junior rank

[1] Cordiner, *Ceylon*, i. 73. North did not appoint the two members whose nomination rested with him.

[2] C.R. 54: Douglass MS. In 1800 there were from forty to fifty British officials in the Ceylon Civil Service, and fifty minor posts filled by burghers.

[3] C.R. 53: Feb. 27, 1802. Dundas recommended six of his nominees for the higher posts with salaries of £1,000 and upwards, and the remaining thirteen, who were aged between sixteen and twenty, for Junior Clerkships with promotion as deserved. Most of the junior officials had been educated for writerships (the junior rank) in the East India Company, and included the famous (Sir) John D'Oyly.

The present practice that the post of Colonial Secretary 'cannot be considered as one to which the Civil Servants have any right to look forward' (C.O. 54. 6: Mar. 16, 1802) was apparently not yet fully established. Hobart in his reply entirely disagreed with North (C.O. 54. 112: Feb. 8, 1803). In 1831 Governor Barnes asked the Colonial Office whether the post were open to Ceylon officials (C.O. 54. 112: Feb. 27. 1831). P. Anstruther, who was appointed Colonial Secretary in 1833, was a member of the Ceylon Civil Service (C.O. 54. 114: Nov. 22, 1831; C.O. 54. 128: May 4, 1833). Sir Emerson Tennent, who succeeded him in 1846, and Sir Charles MacCarthy, who replaced Tennent in 1851, were not members of the Ceylon Service. W. C. Gibson, who was Colonial Secretary from 1860 to 1869, was a Ceylon civil servant; but he apparently owed his appointment to the express desire of Sir Charles MacCarthy, who had been appointed Governor (C.O. 54. 437: Oct. 31, 1868). On Gibson's retirement the Ceylon civil servants petitioned that in future the Colonial Secretary should be a Ceylon official. The petition was rejected since the Colonial Office considered that the post 'should be filled up from England or by some officer from another colony'; and in 1869 H. T. Irving, Colonial Secretary of Jamaica, was appointed Colonial Secretary of Ceylon. The position was 'the best and perhaps most important appointment in the Colonies, in the gift of the Secretary of State' (C.O. 54. 437: Oct. 31, 1868; C.O. 54. 444: June 26, 1869; C.O. 55. 117: Jan. 20, May 19 and Aug. 7, 1869;

of the service (the present cadetships), were to be filled by promoting at the Governor's discretion the existing civil servants
in Ceylon. The principle of an exclusive Civil Service was established, since 'nothing can be more unjust and heartbreaking to
young men . . . than to labour under the apprehension of having
their services superseded by favour and interest at home'.
Following the rule in the Indian Civil Service promotion should
normally be by seniority, unless the Governor considered that
this claim was outweighed by superior merit. All appointments
by the Governor were provisional until confirmed by the
Cabinet, 'but this is a power which . . . unless in cases of manifest
injustice or abuse, I am satisfied will seldom or never be
exercised'. Appointments to writerships were to be made by
the Secretary of State for the Colonies in accordance with the
Governor's annual statement of vacancies.[1] The appointment
of army officers to fill vacancies in the Civil Service was strictly
forbidden, since it lessened the civil servants' chances of promotion. For a colony with an annual deficit the expedient of
appointing army officers had much to recommend it: they
often made very efficient administrators especially in the more
backward parts of the country, and they were glad to do the
work in return for a small addition to their army pay. If a civil
servant were appointed he would require a much larger salary
which Ceylon could ill afford. The vacancies in question were
usually minor administrative and judicial positions in the provinces such as Assistant Agents of Revenue, and North and his
successors frequently attempted to fill them with army officers.
The Colonial Office firmly adhered to its veto, although an
exception was very occasionally made when the case for it was
overwhelming.[2]

Jan. 27. 1870). Apparently the modern practice was in process of evolution
in 1802 and gradually increased in rigidity.

[1] C.O. 55. 61: May 1, 1802; C.O. 55. 62: May 7, 1803; C.O. 54. 7: Nov. 24,
1802. The Colonial Office vetoed North's attempt to make permanent appointments to junior administrative positions from amongst Europeans resident in
Ceylon.

[2] C.R. 54: Douglass MS., § 145, Dundas's Memo.; C.O. 55. 61: Feb. 8, 1803;
C.O. 54. 22: June 11, 1807. The administration of Kandy for fifteen or twenty
years after its final conquest in 1818 was largely in the hands of army officers
(v. chapter vi, p. 64, n. 1). The Colonial Office frequently forbade the practice,
but successive Governors had a strong argument in the perennial financial
deficit. With the growth of the coffee industry in Kandy the army officers

The three last years of North's governorship from 1802 to 1805 were spent in arranging the salaries and duties of the civil servants, with the result that the Ceylon establishment was in a state of flux. North complained frequently that the Colonial Office interfered unduly in matters of detail, while the Colonial Office retorted that North had a genius for creating pluralities. Many officials held several posts, each with its attendant salary, and the Colonial Office insisted that the number of positions be decreased by consolidating their duties.[1] The principal officials of the central administration were the Governor and Treasurer; the Chief Secretary; the Deputy Secretary; the Vice-Treasurer, who did most of the work of the Treasury; the Accountant-General and Civil Auditor; the Civil and Military Paymaster-General; and the Board of Revenue and Commerce (the Chief Secretary, the Vice-Treasurer, the Accountant-General, and the Paymaster-General). Under the control of the Board were the Superintendent of Cinnamon Plantations and his staff, and the Revenue Department composed of the members of the provincial administration. Ceylon was divided into eight Districts, each under an Agent of Revenue and Commerce with one or two Assistants. In all there were about forty-five members of the Civil Service. Attached to each office was a varying number of clerks, the majority being burghers.[2]

The Land Survey Department, which was established in 1800 in connexion with North's land reforms, was composed of a Surveyor-General and a small staff. The Public Works Department probably originated in 1800, and in 1802 was placed under a Civil Engineer and Architect. On July 10, 1805, the offices of Civil Engineer and Surveyor-General were combined.[3] The Medical Department in its origin was apparently purely military, and was composed of the army surgeons who were

were gradually replaced by civilians; but as late as 1851 the Colonial Office still found it necessary to protest (Skinner, *Ceylon*, 79; C.O. 54. 234: Mar. 1, 1847; C.O. 55. 93: Dec. 21, 1851).

[1] C.O. 54.6: Mar. 16, 1802, and Feb. 8, 1803; C.O. 54. 7: Oct. 4, 7, and Nov. 22, 1802; C.O. 54.8: Oct. 31, 1802; C.O. 54. 11: April 20, 1803; C.O. 54. 13: Jan. 1, 1804; C.O. 54. 22: Sept. 20, 1806; C.O. 55. 61: Feb. 8, 1803; C.O. 55. 62: May 7, 1803.

[2] C.O. 54. 13: Jan. 1, 1804; C.O. 54. 112: Feb. 8, 1803.

[3] C.O. 54. 112: Feb. 8, 1803; Turner, *C.A. and L.R.* IV. iii. 133; C.O. 54. 5: Mar. 13, 1801; C.O. 54. 6: Mar. 16, 1802; C.O. 54. 7: Sept. 10, 1802; C.O. 54. 18: July 10, 1805.

under the control of the Physician-General to the King's Forces in Ceylon.[1] The Civil Medical Department was established by North in 1800 as a part of his successful fight against small-pox. The early history of the Department is obscure, though it is not improbable that the four physicians who composed it were army surgeons, and were under the Physician-General. From 1802 the Civil and Military Medical Departments were both controlled by the head of the Army Medical Department, whose title was Inspector-General of Hospitals.[2]

A system of pensions which was drawn up by North at Dundas's instructions was approved in 1803, and remained in force until 1834.[3] A pensions fund was established under the trusteeship of the Chief Secretary, the President of the Board of Revenue and Commerce, and three other officials appointed by the Governor. The Ceylon civil servants and the Government each made an annual payment to the fund of 10 per cent. of the salaries, while the trustees were empowered to invest the proceeds. The senior civil servants were entitled to a pension after eight years' service in Ceylon, the amount rising from a pension of £400 for a salary of £1,000 to £700 for the Chief Secretary with a salary of £3,000. All other civil servants received a pension of £400 after twelve years' service in Ceylon, increasing to £600 after eighteen years. An official could receive the pension of the highest office he had held before his retirement. A furlough of two years, during which the annual salary was £300, was allowed 'at any time within the twelve'; but absence on furlough did not count towards the pension. The regulations were open to the serious defect that since the senior civil servants could not increase their pensions by remaining longer than eight years in Ceylon they usually retired as soon as they were eligible for pensions. The administration thus lost its most valuable members, and in 1808 Governor Maitland vainly urged that the length of service required to qualify for a pension should be increased. The Colonial Office refused, but

[1] C.R. 52: May 25, 1798.

[2] C.R. 52: Apr. 5 and Aug. 30, 1800, and Feb. 18, 1801; C.O. 54. 6: Mar. 16, 1802; C.O. 54. 9: May 7, 1803. The salary of the Inspector-General was £1200. C.O. 54. 13: Jan. 1, 1804; Turner, *C.A. and L.R.* IV. iii. 133–4; Bertolacci, *Ceylon,* 65.

[3] C.O. 54. 5: Mar. 13, 1801; C.O. 54. 6: Feb. 8, 1803.

in 1811 gave the Governor discretionary authority in the case of senior civil servants only to pay both pension and salary to those whose services he wished to retain for three years longer. This clumsy device inevitably exposed the Governor to charges of partiality and injustice. No pensions were paid to the widows and dependants of officials, although 'the pay of the Ceylon Civil Servants is too small to admit of their making sufficient savings to procure themselves an independence . . . upon retiring'.[1]

A Crown Agent for Ceylon was appointed in 1802, and the office continued to be separate until in 1833 the business affairs of the different Crown Colonies were combined in the office of the two Crown Agents for the Colonies. The appointments were made and the salary fixed by the Colonial Office, though the actual payment was made by the colony concerned. The duties of the Crown Agent were to buy and ship all supplies required by the Ceylon Government, from locomotives to office stationery, to superintend the sale of cinnamon (after the expiration of the East India Company's monopoly), to float Government loans in London and handle the repayment, to pay pensions and the salaries of civilians on furlough, and in general to act as the London business agent of the Government. The burden of work was very greatly increased in the second half of the nineteenth century, since the development of the planting industry in Ceylon necessitated the construction of railways and a large extension of the road system. The prior consent of the Secretary of State and the Treasury was required before the Crown Agents could carry out orders, the Colonial Office as well as the Ceylon Government being kept closely informed of every step taken.[2]

---

[1] C.O. 54. 28: Aug. 17, 1808; C.O. 54. 40: Nov. 5, 1811; C.O. 54. 44: Jan. 23, 1813; Bertolacci, *Ceylon*, 407–26. The Governors protested at the great hardship inflicted on widows and dependants, e.g. C.O. 54. 51: Feb. 5, 1814. In 1822 the Colonial Office sanctioned the establishment of a Pension Fund for the widows of civil servants (C.O. 55. 66: July 17, 1822). The pensions were limited to members of the Civil Service and did not include the clerical staff and other minor officials, although the pensions were urgently required because the smallness of the salaries prevented much from being saved. In 1822 and 1823 the Governor established a Pension Fund for superannuated clerks or their widows; but the Colonial Office insisted on its abolition in 1828 because of the revenue deficit (C.O. 54. 105: Aug. 25, 1829; C.O. 55. 72: Apr. 20, 1830).

[2] The correspondence with the Crown Agents is filed in the volumes indexed

The relative powers of the Governor and the officer commanding the troops in Ceylon were not clearly defined owing probably to an oversight in the drafting of North's Commission. No ill effects occurred from 1798 to 1804 during the command of General Hay Macdowall, since there was the closest and most friendly co-operation between him and North. With the advent in 1804 of his successor General Wemyss dissension rapidly developed until the Government became 'totally paralysed' and reduced to a condition bordering on chaos. Obstinate and overbearing, and with a volcanic temper, General Wemyss completely disorganized the finances, and in the end achieved the recall of the Governor and of himself. Taking advantage of the Kandyan war which was then in progress and of the undefined nature of North's powers of control over the troops, he refused to discuss his demands in detail, and he hopelessly embarrassed the finances by extravagant expenditure on the army. North complained that he was 'reduced to the office of cashier to the Treasury', since his lack of detailed information and his fear of endangering the success of the war against Kandy made him reluctant to refuse Wemyss's requirements, which were advanced on the plea of 'absolute military necessity'. Again and again North complained of 'the impossibility of carrying on the government without more controul than I have over the army'. General Maitland, who succeeded North as Governor in 1805, strongly condemned Wemyss's expenditure as 'extravagant' and often utterly unnecessary, while he also considered that the army had 'grown far too independent'. He immediately reduced the military to a proper subordination to the civil authority, and drastically cut down the army budget.[1]

in the series C.O. 54 as 'Public Offices and Miscellaneous'. C.O. 54. 5: Mar. 13, 1801; C.O. 54. 109: May 27, 1830; C.O. 54. 115: Mar. 8, 1831; C.O. 54. 119: Jan. 19, 1832; C.O. 54. 130: Oct. 18, 1833; C.O. 55. 75: May 30, 1833; C.O. 54. 515: Oct. 7, 1878; C.O. 54. 521: Sept. 6, 1879: Apr. 23, 1880; Parl. Pap. H. C. 623 of 1845, vol. xxxi, 2–3; *Colonial Office List*, 1927, xxi–xxii; Lucas, *Oxford Survey of the British Empire*, vi. 40–8; Bruce, *Broad Stone of Empire*, ii. 212–24. As an example of the miscellaneous duties of the Crown Agents, in 1872 the Governor asked the Colonial Office to instruct the Crown Agents to dispatch 'a good Plumber . . . there is not one Plumber in the Island' (C.O. 54. 478: Oct. 1, 1872).

[1] C.O. 54. 14: May 31, 1804; C.O. 54. 16: *passim*; C.O. 54. 17: Apr. 13, 1805; C.O. 54. 18: Oct. 19, 1805, and *passim*. Between Aug. 1803 and 1805 the army was increased from 3,700 to over 6,000, in addition to 2,500 expensive

In addition to antagonizing the Governor Wemyss contrived to embroil himself with the Supreme Court, and that so comprehensively that official society became divided into two factions, the military and anti-military, which were not on speaking terms. North essayed the thankless role of peacemaker with the natural result that he 'had the misfortune of seldom satisfying either of the parties'. The first serious quarrel arose in September 1804, over a plot of ground in the Fort of Colombo which North had given to General Macdowall for the exclusive use of the troops as a parade ground. The Supreme Court held its sittings in the Fort near the parade ground, and used it as a convenient spot for administering floggings. The military objected, and in September 1804 Colonel Baillie, the Commandant of Colombo, forbade the use of the ground to any save the troops. The Supreme Court demanded that Baillie withdraw the order since the Charter of Justice of 1801 commanded all officers, civil and military, to aid and assist the Court in the execution of its powers. Baillie refused, and the Court bound him over to keep the peace. North intervened, and while smoothing the ruffled feelings of the Court upheld the action of the military.

The quarrel left both Wemyss and the judges on very ill terms; and on September 24, 1804, at 10 a.m., Wemyss without any warning locked the gates of the Fort on the ground that Kandyan spies were trying to gain access to it. North ordered the gates opened, whereupon General Wemyss declared that as his authority in Colombo had been annihilated he would withdraw to some place where it was still unimpaired. 'Your Excellency will therefore consider yourself responsible for the safety of the Fort of Colombo, so violently seized from my authority.' Meanwhile the Supreme Court was far from idle. Mr. Justice Lushington had found himself locked out of the Fort on the day the gates were closed; and in the middle of the campaign against Kandy General Wemyss was haled into court on a charge of contempt and bound over to keep the peace.

Both Wemyss and the judges seem to have lost all sense of

camp followers to carry baggage. Maitland reported that the newly raised native battalions were unnecessary, ruinously expensive, and often useless. In three months after his arrival he had already decreased the annual military expenditure by about £166,000.

proportion, and incident followed incident until the official
world was rocking on its foundations. 'The merest triviality is
supposed by the General to involve the fate of Empire, and by
the Chief Justice to attack the foundations of the Social Order.'
Witness the Fuel Controversy, when the Chief Justice insisted
on debating in several meetings of the Council whether General
Wemyss's perquisites included the collection of free firewood,
and pronounced that 'an order to cut firewood issued by the
General . . . might have led to riot and bloodshed'. The General
retorted that the Chief Justice had acted from 'the most in-
delicate motives'. By this time the judges had become seriously
alarmed, and declared that the constitution and indeed the
whole social order were in danger of overthrow. They had
irrefutable evidence, for their former friends amongst the army
officers refused to speak to them: 'a voice was heard a few
nights ago in the street near Mr. Justice Lushington's house
d——g the Supreme Court and the Judges'; and the Brigade
Chaplain at Colombo had preached a sermon on St. Paul's trial
before Felix. The judges had no doubt that Felix was a
synonym for the Supreme Court, with the result that they
'induced the officers to read the Bible that they may convince
themselves of the supposed similarity between their General and
St. Paul, with which no one had hitherto been struck'. The
climax came one evening in June 1805. The General met Sir
Edmund Carrington, the Chief Justice, and his wife; and while
politely addressing Lady Carrington he pointedly cut the Chief
Justice. In an interminable dispatch North broke the news to
the Colonial Office, and declared that his action proved General
Wemyss unworthy of his office.[1]

The Secretary of State had already come to this conclusion,
and had appointed General Sir Thomas Maitland officer commanding the troops in Ceylon as well as Governor and Commander-in-Chief, Wemyss being removed from the colony.
North's recall was in all probability hastened by his quarrels
with the General, although his failing health no doubt contributed to the decision. Even before Wemyss's arrival North had
frequently begged for the appointment of a successor, since

---

[1] C.O. 54. 14: Oct. 5, 1804; C.O. 54. 16: Jan. 5, 1805; C.O. 54. 17: June 21,
1805 and *passim*.

under the effects of the climate his health was growing steadily worse.[1] On July 18, 1805, General Maitland arrived at Colombo and assumed office. The union of the positions of Governor and Commander-in-Chief with that of the immediate command of the troops was very unusual; but the Colonial Office probably considered that drastic measures were necessitated by the seemingly hopeless condition of Ceylon's finances and by the incessant quarrels between North and Wemyss.[2]

The new Governor was a most striking contrast to his charming, talented, and somewhat ineffective predecessor. He had an infinite capacity for hard work, and soon acquired an encyclopaedic grasp not only of the main outlines but of the details of the situation in Ceylon. It was entirely typical of the man that his first six months on the island were spent in visiting almost every district and thoroughly familiarizing himself with each aspect of its particular problems. Then, and only then, did he introduce reforms; and in the process he displayed an uncomfortable knowledge of even the most trifling peccadilloes which must have appalled inefficient subordinates. Maitland had proved in the West Indies that he was a very shrewd and able financier and administrator who never made a mistake, and in five years he revolutionized the condition of Ceylon. He paid off a mountain of debt, he stopped large leakages of expenditure, and he balanced revenue and expenses. Nor was this accomplished by cheese-paring economy: he increased salaries and effected his reductions by vigilance, hard work, and by installing a rigorous control of expenditure. The Civil Service was transformed: Maitland found it corrupt and negligent and left it purged from corruption and as efficient as a Service could be that was recruited from boys of fifteen.

While Maitland's subordinates respected and feared him one doubts if any save a very few intimates liked the masterful autocrat. He did not regard even the Colonial Office as sacred:

[1] C.O. 54. 17: Feb. 21 and Apr. 13, 1805; C.O. 54. 14: Mar. 3 and Sept. 25, 1804.

[2] C.O. 54. 18: July 19, 1805; C.O. 54. 22: Sept. 23, 1806; C.O. 54. 35: Oct. 10, 1809. 'As Governor Maitland I have a right to order the troops on this island to be employed on any service I think fit: but I have nothing to do in that capacity with the discipline or detail of the army. As Lieutenant-General Maitland on the other hand, I have everything to do with the discipline of the army, but cannot move a man without the orders of the Governor.'

when he knew that it was wrong he never hesitated to announce that he proposed to disobey orders. On several occasions the Colonial Office ventured to oppose him, but he invariably proved to be right. Maitland was harsh, violent tempered, and overbearing, a man who would not brook disobedience and who worked his subordinates almost as unsparingly as he did himself. To enforce his own standards of honesty and efficiency he found it necessary to remove several of the civil servants; yet paradoxically he felt a genuine concern for their welfare. He had the somewhat rare gift of being able to see both sides of a question, and while he waged a relentless war on abuses he saw clearly that the shortcomings of his subordinates were in many cases beyond their control. The realization of this did not make the Governor deviate a finger's breadth from his goal; but when he inflicted punishment he refrained wherever it was possible from ruining the offender's career. General Maitland was no bully, for even his harshest actions sprang from an extraordinarily lofty sense of duty. 'The honour of His Majesty's service' was a phrase which appeared constantly in his dispatches; and the ideal which he unflinchingly strove after was a service whose honour must be most jealously guarded. Lonely and disliked, the Governor found all the compensation he desired in the immense improvements he brought about in the administration of Ceylon.

Maitland strongly condemned in many respects North's organization of the Civil Service, and especially the laxity of his control. Salaries were too low, and instead of trying to raise them North had rewarded deserving or favoured officers by creating minor posts with insufficient or nominal duties. He had also tacitly allowed the civil servants to engage in private trade, either on their own account or as the agents of Lautour and Company, the Madras firm which had the monopoly of Ceylon commerce and of supplying the Government with most of its requirements. Expenditure was almost uncontrolled owing to the extravagant, confused, and wasteful manner in which the Treasury was conducted. The departments of Government showed a total disregard for economy since a subordinate official could easily commit the administration to heavy expenditure; while several instances had occurred of the misappropriation of revenue by members of the Civil Service. Though Maitland was convinced of 'North's intentions being most honorable and his principles being most pure and patriotic', yet 'the facility of his disposition was such that almost the sight was totally lost of everything like the interests of the King under his government. In some instances a total inactivity prevailed, in others the most pernicious violation of every principle that ought to actuate the servants of the Crown.' Owing to the 'perfectly farcical' laxity of his control 'the system has been administered with so little regard to the maintenance of its own Regulations and with a lenity so extremely bordering upon feebleness as to render it in many points totally inefficient'.[1]   In the District of Jaffna especially Maitland found corruption and abuse of power due in some instances to the civil servants themselves, and in others to the Mudaliyars whom they had neglected to control. The Governor decided that while the Mudaliyars should be maintained 'in a great share of power and influence', their sweeping authority was the most serious evil in the Ceylon administration. 'It approximates so much to a perfect Imperium in Imperio that in t.uth the real government of the island is more that of the Modeliars than of the British Government.'[2]

Maitland saw clearly that North was not wholly to blame: the highest standards of efficiency could not be expected from a Service many of whose members entered at fifteen and retired at twenty-eight. The junior civil servants had a 'good education, fair character and considerable assiduity'; but since their 'principles were not fixed', it was only natural that many proved unsatisfactory when they were sent as Agents of Revenue or Assistants to outlying districts. Without companionship, ignorant of the languages,[3] and insufficiently mature for such heavy responsibility, they tended either to worry over their work if they were conscientious or to neglect it if they were not. Quite a few died of fever since they were too young and unseasoned for so malarial a country; and the majority of the survivors retired about the age of twenty-eight as soon as they

[1] C.O. 54. 18: Oct. 19, 1805; C.O. 54. 21: Feb. 28, 1806; C.O. 54. 22: Feb. 28, 1806; Brit. Mus. Add. MS. No. 13867: Apr. 19, 1800.

[2] C.O. 54. 18: Oct. 19, 1805; C.O. 54. 21: Feb. 28, 1806.

[3] C.O. 54. 33: Mar. 8, 1809. D'Oyly and Tolfrey were the only two officials who could speak Sinhalese.

had completed their twelve years in Ceylon and were eligible for pensions. For the first half of his service the young official was almost useless, and for the remainder he 'thinks of nothing but when his time will be up and just at the period of life when his services are most valuable . . . he is enticed to quit the service'. Owing to low salaries very little could be saved, and 'it may be fairly stated the real, sole and true object of their services is the pension fund'. The average civil servant regarded his career in Ceylon 'as a kind of disgusting but necessary prelude to his deciding what line of life he will adopt'.[1]

As soon as he had mastered the problem Maitland began the work of reform. In 1805 he forbade civil servants to engage in trade, although to encourage agriculture they were allowed to own and cultivate land.[2] He increased inadequate salaries and at the same time effected substantial economies by abolishing the unnecessary posts North had created, and consolidating their duties with other positions. Corruption and abuses were relentlessly rooted out, and in 1806 Maitland was able to report that the civil servants were doing their work satisfactorily, 'and were beginning to think that there was such a thing as the interests of the Crown to be considered'.[3] Perhaps the most important reform which Maitland introduced was the system of very strict control over the expenditure, every official being compelled to submit estimates to the Governor before even the smallest amount could be spent, so that 'not a shilling is advanced or paid without my previous authority'. The Governor was Treasurer *ex officio*, but while North seems to have left the bulk of the work to the Vice-Treasurer Maitland found time to do it himself, and exercised very strict control over the finance departments.[4]

---

[1] C.O. 54. 21: Feb. 28, 1806; C.O. 54. 28: Aug. 17, 1808; Bertolacci (*Ceylon*, 431-3) supported Maitland's criticism.

[2] Bertolacci, *Ceylon*, 73; C.O. 54. 18: Oct. 19, 1805. To prove his charges Maitland was compelled to inform the Colonial Office of those officials who were engaged in trade, but it was typical that he did so unofficially to avoid injuring their careers. In 1813 the rule was extended to include Sitting Magistrates (usually burghers) and all the minor employees of Government, unless special exemption were granted by the Governor (C.O. 54. 47: Ceylon Government Gazette, May 12, 1813, Regulation 4 of 1813).

[3] C.O. 54. 21: Feb. 28, 1806.

[4] C.O. 54. 18: Oct. 19, 1805; C.O. 54. 20: Jan. 31, 1806; C.O. 54. 21: Feb. 28, 1806; C.O. 54. 22: *passim*; C.O. 54. 27: Civil Service Establishment, 1808;

The fate of George Lusignan, Agent of Revenue at Jaffna, was typical of Maitland's relentless determination to uphold efficiency and 'the honour of His Majesty's service'; while at the same time it shows his solicitude for the prospects of his subordinates. Lusignan was a talented and precocious youth who in 1798, at the age of thirteen, had come out to Ceylon as North's protégé. He was rapidly promoted and in 1804 became Agent of Revenue at Jaffna, 'by far the most responsible and valuable situation in the island' since the District comprised nearly a third of British Ceylon.[1] His head turned by North's favour, and ignorant of Tamil, Lusignan allowed his principal Mudaliyar practically to control the District. When Maitland investigated he found 'peculation, fraud and iniquity . . . cruelly oppressive to the natives'. Lusignan also followed the general custom and engaged in private trade, using the same native official as his agent; and being equally indifferent to his own interests and to the Government's, he allowed the Mudaliyar to rob them both impartially. Maitland removed Lusignan from his post, and recovered from him the amounts of which the Government had been defrauded; but at the same time he persuaded the Colonial Office not to ruin his career by dismissing him from the Service. The boy was not flagrantly dishonest, but merely a young fool whose head had been turned by North's favour, the example of the other civil servants, and the temptations to which he had been subjected. Lusignan was appointed to the inferior post of Provincial Judge of Trincomalee, and in time developed into a creditable civil servant.[2]

Maitland completed his reorganization of the Civil Service

C.O. 54. 40: July 16, 1811. Expenditures of less than £75 were sanctioned by the Governor, amounts between £75 and £200 by the Governor and Council, and amounts of over £200 by the Colonial Office (C.O. 54. 122: Dec. 24, 1831; C.O. 54. 118: Oct. 1, 1832). Whenever circumstances compelled the Governor to incur an expenditure of over £200 without the previous sanction of the Colonial Office a full explanation had to be made (C.O. 55. 72: Aug. 3, 1831).

[1] Brit. Mus. Add. MS. No. 13866: Jan. 16, 1798; C.O. 54. 13: Jan. 1, 1804.

[2] C.O. 54. 18: Nov. 10 and Dec. 25, 1805; C.O. 54. 21: Feb. 28, 1806; C.O. 54. 49: Nov. 30, 1813. Governor Brownrigg urged that Lusignan, now Collector of Trincomalee, be restored to favour since he had repaid most of his debt to the Government, and because of the 'faithful zealous and able services and honorable conduct by which Mr. Lusignan has already atoned for errors, which were never attributed to any worse cause than youth and inexperience'. Lusignan became Deputy Secretary to Government with a salary of £2,000 in 1817, and died in 1825 (C.O. 54. 66: Nov. 8, 1817; C.O. 54. 92: Feb. 9, 1826).

in 1808 by dividing it into three classes according to the importance of the positions. Until 1834 no substantial change was made in his classification and scale of salaries, or in the regulations which he drew up for the conduct of the administration.

CLASS I

Chief Secretary to Government . .	annual salary £3,000
Commissioner of Revenue . . .	,, £3,000
Civil Auditor General . . .	,, £2,000
Vice-Treasurer and Accountant-General	,, £2,000
Civil and Military Paymaster-General .	,, £2,000
Comptroller-General of Customs (created 1813)	,, £1,600

CLASS II

Twenty-two positions with salaries of £1,800 to £600, viz.:

11 Collectors at Colombo, Jaffna, Trincomalee, Galle, Matara, Chilaw, Mannar, Kalutara, Batticaloa, Wanni, and Mahagampattu (created 1813);

4 Provincial Judges at Colombo, Jaffna, Matara, and Galle; Superintendent of Cinnamon; Deputy Secretary to Government; First and Second Assistants to the Chief Secretary; Customs Master and the Garrison Store Keeper at Colombo; and Commissioner of Stamps (added 1813).

CLASS III

Ten positions with salaries of £550 or less, viz.:

Postmaster-General (added 1813);

8 Assistants; one each to the Commissioner of Revenue, the Treasurer, the Paymaster-General, the Civil Auditor-General, the Superintendent of Cinnamon, and to the Collectors of Colombo (stationed at Negombo), Jaffna, and Trincomalee; Customs Master at Jaffna.

In addition several Writers were employed at £300 a year as Assistants, principally in the Chief Secretary's office, until they had acquired sufficient experience to be appointed to vacancies in Class III. The Colonial Office refused to agree to Maitland's recommendation that the age at which Writers were eligible for appointment should be raised. No civil servant could be promoted to Class II until after three years' service, or to Class I until after seven years' service in Ceylon. By unwritten custom promotion was almost invariably by seniority despite the regulation that superior merit should also be considered.[1]

Maitland's most important change in the central administration was the abolition of the Board of Revenue and Commerce and the substitution of a Commissioner of Revenue, who was a member of the Council and had complete control over the collection of revenue, though none over its expenditure. The Governor believed that the joint responsibility of a Board could only 'do a good deal of harm', while a single Commissioner could be held responsible for every action of his department. The Commissioner was also required to make periodical tours of the districts to control 'all the different petty abuses that might occur', to see that the natives were well governed, and to report any inefficiency on the part of the district officers. The Vice-Treasurer and Accountant-General was 'the universal receiver' of revenue, and had 'the arrangement of all accounts of the island, both civil and military'. The Civil and Military Paymaster-General controlled 'the whole expenditure of the island, in all its branches'; but could make no payment however small without a warrant signed by the Governor. The Civil Auditor-General had 'the general examination of all civil accounts'.[2] The Chief Secretary to Government remained 'the organ of Government upon all occasions', although during Maitland's omnipresent régime the office was 'almost a sinecure'. The Chief Secretary received all dispatches from the civil servants except those which were concerned only with matters of revenue, and issued all regulations and orders of Government.

[1] C.O. 54. 28: Aug. 17, 1808; C.O. 54. 47: July 10, 1813; C.O. 54. 222: Oct. 5, 1842: C.O. Memo. on history of Ceylon Civil Service. By 1833 the number of positions had increased to 42, viz. six in Class I, twenty-five in Class II, owing chiefly to the creation of additional Collectorships and Provincial Judgeships, and eleven in Class III. Maitland's classification and regulations were brought into force in 1808 although they were not formally sanctioned by the Colonial Office until 1810. In 1813 Governor Brownrigg added the four positions noted in the text. Until 1813 the post of Comptroller of Customs was held by the Auditor-General, that of Distributor of Stamps by the First and that of Postmaster-General by the Second Assistant to the Chief Secretary. The judges of the Supreme Court, the Inspector-General of Hospitals, and the Civil Engineer and Surveyor-General were not members of the Civil Service, and were therefore not included in the list. The office clerks and other minor employees, the majority of whom were burghers, were omitted for the same reason.

[2] C.O. 54. 22: Feb. 28, 1806: and June 11, 1807; C.O. 54. 28: Aug. 17, 1808.

After 1798 all official acts of the Governor were signed by the Chief Secretary before they were published or executed; while his office was also the repository for all documents from every branch of the Service.[1]

In the provincial administration the Agents of Revenue and Commerce were abolished and replaced by ten Collectors under the complete control of the Commissioner of Revenue, who could suspend them subject to the Governor's approval. The Collectors supervised the assessment and collection of the revenue, tried minor civil and criminal cases, and administered their districts. The regulations which Maitland drew up for their guidance illustrated most strikingly his grasp of the principles of colonial administration. The Collector must 'make himself acquainted with the various districts in his province and the various headmen . . . by making frequent circuits through the whole of his province. It is by adopting this measure alone that any Collector can get a thorough knowledge either of the real character of the Headmen under him, or of the actual situation of the country.' The Collector must make a complete tour of his whole district every year, and must give 'an habitual and systematic attention' to all representations and complaints of the people. He must have a 'practically unlimited' knowledge of every aspect of his district—its agriculture, trade, industry, social customs and the manner in which every department of Government 'in practice works'. The annual report to the Colonial Secretary must not be a brief summary of statistics, but must give very full information upon all subjects affecting the district, so as to serve as a guide to the Government in initiating reforms. Close watch must be kept on the native officials to prevent their oppressing the people as their predecessors had done. 'The sole object of Government is and always ought to be considered to be to ensure the prosperity of the island solely through the medium of generally increasing the prosperity and happiness of the natives.'[2]

[1] C.R. 52: May 5, 1798; C.O. 54. 28: Aug. 17, 1808.
[2] C.O. 54. 25: Feb. 28, 1807; C.O. 54. 28: Aug. 17, 1808. As an example of Maitland's detailed knowledge of abuses, he ordered that to prevent the exploitation of the peasantry the tax farms should so far as possible be rented to the villagers and not to the tax farmers. Dickman (*Ceylon Civil Service Manual*, 1883 ed., 291-2) stated that the Collector's 'great guide . . . is the

E

To diminish the influence of the native officials Maitland required the Collectors to watch them closely; while he also appointed burghers and 'such persons of decent character as we can find in the island' to act as Sitting Magistrates in the interior and try minor cases. The Provincial Courts were too few and distant to deal with the native officials' oppression in the country districts. Maitland also reaffirmed North's regulation that all native headmen of the rank of Mohandiram and upwards were to be appointed only by the Governor, the inferior officials being appointed solely by the Commissioner of Revenue on the recommendations of the Collectors.[1]

The necessity of a knowledge of the native languages had been recognized by Dundas in 1801;[2] but hitherto no attempt had been made to compel the civil servants to learn them, and in 1809 only two officials could speak Sinhalese. Maitland therefore passed a regulation that a civil servant who was certified by examination to have mastered Sinhalese should be eligible for promotion to Class II of the Service in two instead of three years, and to Class I in six instead of seven years. As an additional incentive the post of Head Translator to Government was to be held by the most competent linguist irrespective of his rank in the Service. The annual salary was £512 in addition to the pay attached to his existing position.[3] No changes of importance were made during the last two years of General Maitland's régime. The reforms which he had established succeeded in their object, and there were no further complaints of the inefficiency or corruption of the civil servants. In 1810 the General's health which had been seriously affected by the climate suddenly gave way, and he was compelled to return to England in March 1811.[4]

Instructions to Collectors of August 25, 1808'. While obsolete in some details 'in their spirit they are not by any means so'.

[1] C.O. 54. 28: Aug. 17, 1808.   [2] C.O. 54. 5: Mar. 13, 1801.

[3] C.O. 54. 28: Aug. 17, 1808; C.O. 54. 33: Mar. 8, 1809; C.O. 54. 47: July 10, 1813.

[4] C.O. 54. 38: June 5 and Dec. 15, 1810; C.O. 54. 40: July 16, 1811.

VI

THE CIVIL SERVICE
1812–1885

1. *The Old Civil Service, 1812–1833*

DURING the quarter of a century which followed Maitland's reforms few changes of any importance were made in the Civil Service with the exception of the increase in personnel necessitated by the conquest of Kandy. The Colonial Office continually urged the consolidation of offices and the decrease of salaries to lessen the perennial deficit in revenue, while the Governors maintained, and on the whole successfully, that no substantial alterations could be made without serious loss of efficiency.[1] The most important changes in the provincial administration were the reduction of the ten Collectors to eight by abolishing the Collectorship of the Wanni, combining Matara and Mahagampattu in the newly established Collectorship of Tangalla in 1821, and amalgamating the Collectorships of Kalutara and Colombo in 1822.[2] The cost of the central administration was reduced in 1822 by consolidating various offices without any increase of salary. The position of Comptroller General of Customs was abolished, and the work transferred to the Commissioner of Revenue. The duties of the Accountant-General were transferred from the Vice-Treasurer to the Auditor-General, while the Commissionership of Stamps (which had been amalgamated with the office of Comptroller in 1816) was taken over by the Vice-Treasurer.[3]

[1] C.O. 54. 44: Aug. 21, 1812, Jan. 23, 1813; C.O. 54. 47: Apr. 30, 1813; C.O. 54. 51: Apr. 26, 1814; *Ceylon Almanac, 1815*, 40–86, Civil Service Establishment 1815; C.O. 54. 59: Feb. 9, 1816; C.O. 54, 65: Feb. 28, Mar. 13, and May 30, 1817; C.O. 54. 70: Feb. 20, 1818; C.O. 54, 71: July 24, 1818; C.O. 54. 76: Jan. 28, 1820; C.O. 54. 77: Nov. 1, 1820; C.O. 54. 82: Nov. 4, 1822; C.O. 54. 84: C. S. Estab. 1824; C.O. 54. 97: Apr. 8 and 28, 1827; C.O. 54. 101: Aug. 5, Sept. 9, and Dec. 19, 1828; C.O. 54. 104: C. S. Estab. 1829; C.O. 54. 112: C. S. Estab. 1831; C.O. 54. 117: C. S. Estab. 1832; C.O. 54. 128: C. S. Estab. 1833.

[2] C.O. 54. 73: Mar. 2, 1819; C.O. 54. 79: Mar. 12, 1821; C.O. 54. 82: June 1, 1822.

[3] C.O. 54. 59: Feb. 9, 1816; C.O. 54. 79: Feb. 10, Mar. 12 and 14, 1821; C.O. 54. 80: Dec. 26, 1821; C.O. 54. 82: Feb. 7 and Oct. 21, Nov. 4 and 5, 1822; C.O. 54. 101: Dec. 6, 1828. Governor Barnes proposed that the Ceylon Civil

In the same year the Governor, General Barnes, introduced an important reform which gradually remedied a serious weakness in the administration. Governor Maitland had tried to induce the civil servants to study the native languages by a system of rewards, but the results had not been very satisfactory.[1] In 1822 the regulation was made that in future no civil servants would be promoted to a higher rank than that of Assistant until they had 'attained a tolerable proficiency in' Sinhalese or Tamil. While Sinhalese was spoken in the greater part of Ceylon Tamil was the language of Jaffna and the northern districts. Civil servants were allowed to choose which language they wished to study, and were required to pass an examination in reading, writing, and speaking the vernacular. In 1832 the Secretary of State required the civil servants to learn both Sinhalese and Tamil. The regulations seem to have been strictly enforced with very excellent results.[2]

The conquest of Kandy in 1815 entailed an expansion of the Civil Service to administer the kingdom. The circumstances were somewhat peculiar, since British success was due in large measure to the assistance of the great nobles, who deserted to the British because of their King's tyranny. When the British forces invaded Kandy in January 1815 Governor Brownrigg published a proclamation that the only enemy was the King, and that the British would preserve the ancient laws and customs, and continue the chiefs in their ranks and dignities.[3]

Service be abolished and all the positions filled by the army officers in Ceylon with about half the existing salary. He pointed out that eight of the twelve officials in the Kandyan Provinces were military men, and that the arrangement worked well. By his plan the annual salaries of the Civil Service would be reduced from £76,827 to £30,582. The Colonial Office received this suggestion with a notable lack of enthusiasm.

[1] C.O. 54. 65: Feb. 6, 1817; C.O. 54. 74: July 8, 1819; C.O. 54. 76: Jan. 6, 1820. In 1819 the post of Chief Translator to Government was abolished, and instead two annual rewards of £300 and £150 were offered to officials who passed an examination in Sinhalese or Tamil.

[2] C.O. 54. 80: Sept. 21, 1821; C.O. 55. 66: Apr. 12, 1822; C.O. 54. 82: Oct. 21 and 22, 1822; C.O. 54. 84: Mar. 3, 1823; C.O. 54. 86: Jan. 20, 1824; C.O. 54. 88: Feb. 4, 1825; C.O. 54. 92: Feb. 9, 1826; C.O. 55. 74: May 4, 1832. Prior to 1832 very few civil servants had studied Tamil, as they feared that this would interfere with chances of promotion, since the great majority of the more lucrative posts were in the Sinhalese districts. It had therefore often been necessary to appoint an official who knew only Sinhalese to a Tamil district.

[3] C.O. 54. 55: Jan. 16, 1815.

The proclamation was studiously vague as to the form of government which would be established, but justice as well as wisdom forbade the British to treat the kingdom purely as a conquered country. At the same time it was well known that the rule of the Kandyan nobles over the raiyats was very oppressive, and that they could not be given unfettered power to misgovern their people.[1]

The form of administration in Kandy was based upon the Agreement of March 2, 1815, which was made with the Kandyan nobles after the capture of the King.[2] The King and all his family were 'for ever excluded from the throne', and Kandy was annexed to the British Crown, 'saving to the Adigars, Dessaves . . . and all other chief and subordinate native Headmen, lawfully appointed by authority of the British Government, the rights, privileges and powers of their respective offices, and to all classes of the people the safety of their persons and property, with their civil rights and immunities, according to the laws, institutions and customs established and in force amongst them'. Torture was abolished and the death penalty could be inflicted only after the Governor had approved the sentence, but 'subject to these conditions the administration of civil and criminal justice and police' over Kandyans was to be 'according to established forms and by the ordinary authorities, saving always the inherent right of Government to redress grievances and reform abuses'. In other words, the great nobles were restored to the government of their provinces from which the King had deposed them, but at the same time the British were determined to enforce impartial justice to all classes, and prevent the chiefs from abusing their power by oppressing the raiyats in accordance with time-honoured custom.[3]

A provisional administration was set up in 1815, since the Colonial Office had not yet decided on its final form. Governor Brownrigg determined that the government of Kandy should as far as possible be kept distinct from that of the Maritime

[1] For a fuller account *v.* chap. ix.
[2] C.O. 54. 55: Mar. 9, 1815. Campbell, *Ceylon*, i. 381–2: Brownrigg's Proclamation of May 31, 1816.
[3] C.O. 54. 61: Nov. 5, 1816; Marshall, *Ceylon*, 175. The revolt of 1817–18 was caused in large measure by the resentment of the nobles at the curtailment of their power which the British policy inevitably brought about.

Provinces. The Resident, John D'Oyly, was directly responsible to the Governor, and was made a member of the Council. An Agent for the Kandyan Provinces was appointed at Colombo to assist the Governor in supervising the new administration. D'Oyly had two Assistants, one at Kandy and the other at Badulla, while soon afterwards Captain Smith was appointed Agent at Ruwanwella. The Kandyan provinces were administered by the Kandyan nobles whom Brownrigg had appointed as Dissawas or provincial governors under the supervision of D'Oyly and his Assistants.[1] The Governor soon realized that the number of British officials in Kandy must be increased, since the existing staff was too small to prevent the oppression of the raiyats by the nobles. Furthermore, much of D'Oyly's time was required for the report on Kandyan law which he was preparing for the Colonial Office as a guide for the establishment of a permanent form of administration.[2] In 1816 Brownrigg appointed a Board of three Commissioners to control the central administration of Kandy and relieve D'Oyly of part of his burden. D'Oyly as Resident was President of the Board, having 'the superintending authority, with a controuling voice in all measures whatever'. The Second or Judicial Commissioner was the Deputy Resident with special charge of judicial affairs, while the Third or Revenue Commissioner was the Government Agent, whose especial duty was to collect the revenue, manage Government lands, and exact the services owed to Government by the Kandyans in return for their lands. The other members of the new administration were the Magistrate at Kandy, who was also Secretary to the Board, and four Agents at Badulla, Ruwanwella, Kurunegalla, and Ratnapura. The government of the provinces remained in the hands of the Dissawas, but with the increased number of civil servants in Kandy their

---

[1] C.O. 54. 55: Mar. 9 and 15, 1815; C.O. 54. 59: Feb. 9, 1816; C.O. 54. 60: June 5, 1816. John D'Oyly (1774–1824) graduated from Cambridge in 1796, and came to Ceylon as a Writer in 1801. He soon mastered the Sinhalese language and from 1805 to 1816 was Chief Translator to Government. A man of great tact and ability, he was largely responsible for the ease of the British conquest of Kandy, and was created a baronet in 1821 (*Royal Asiatic Society, Ceylon Branch*, vol. xxv, No. 69, pp. xi–xii).

[2] C.O. 54. 56: July 20, 1815; C.O. 54. 60: June 5 and Sept. 14, 1816; C.O. 54. 61: Nov. 5, 1816; C.O. 54. 66: July 8, 1817. D'Oyly's report on Kandyan laws was not completed till 1821 (C.O. 54. 80: May 10, 1821).

powers of oppression were more limited than they had been.[1]

The suppression of the Kandyan revolt in 1818 brought about very important changes in the form of government which lasted until 1833. The rising had shown the dangerous influence of the Kandyan nobles over the raiyats, who had followed their chiefs partly from hereditary loyalty and partly from fear of their power. The Governor determined to destroy the authority of the chiefs, and in so doing he was no longer hampered by the Agreement of 1815, since most of the signatories had joined the revolt.[2] A radical departure from the existing system of 'leaving the general executive government and a great portion of the judicial, to the native chiefs, is absolutely necessary to ensure our maintaining authority in these provinces'. There must be 'a more intimate connection between the British Government and the people' by increasing the number of Agents of Government and giving them more extensive powers.[3] The key-note of the new system was the transfer of authority from the native chiefs to the civil servants, since otherwise the nobles would have used their power over the raiyats to stir up another revolt.[4]

The central administration of Kandy remained in the hands of the Board of Commissioners, who as formerly were directly responsible to the Governor. The officer commanding the Kandyan garrisons was made a member of the Board in 1818, to ensure 'the most intimate and close concert' between the civil and military authorities.[5] On Sir John D'Oyly's death from fever in 1824 the post of Resident was left vacant, and the Board was reduced to three.[6] In the provincial administration very great changes were introduced, all designed to diminish the power of the Kandyan chiefs. Kandy was divided into eleven districts, each under an Agent of Government who had

[1] C.O. 54. 60: June 5, 1816; C.O. 54. 61: Nov. 5, 1816; C.O. 54. 65: May 30, 1817; C.O. 54. 66: passim; Davy, Ceylon, 325–6.

[2] C.O. 54. 71: Oct. 31, 1818.   [3] C.O. 54. 70: Feb. 19, 1818.

[4] C.O. 54. 73: Nov. 21, 1818: Brownrigg's Instructions to the Board of Commissioners. 'It is nearly superfluous to observe the necessity of watching with a jealous eye the conduct of the chiefs . . . and to check . . . any rising discontents which intrigue may excite among the ignorant multitude. The remark relative to chiefs is fully applicable to the great body of the Budhist priesthood.' C.O. 54. 74: Aug. 2, 1819.

[5] C.O. 54. 73: Nov. 17, 1818.   [6] C.O. 54. 86: June 10, 1824.

powers similar to those of the Collector in the Maritime Provinces, and was subject to the control of the Board of Commissioners.[1] Dissawas were appointed in some of the provinces; but they, together with the Ratemahatmeyas and other subordinate native officials of each district, were stripped of much of the power they had had prior to the rebellion, and were under the strict control of the Agents of Government. Henceforth native officials received salaries and held their lands tax free, but they had lost their former right to demand fees and levy arbitrary fines upon the raiyats. They were also with a few trifling exceptions deprived of their former right to exact unpaid forced labour or Rajakaria from the people.[2] After 1818 forced labour could only be demanded by the Agent of Government, the workmen being paid except for the construction and repair of roads and bridges.[3] The Dissawas were appointed and dismissed by the Governor alone, the other native officials by the Resident of Kandy. An Agent of Government had power to fine, imprison, or suspend from office any native official except the Dissawas, while the Dissawas were deprived of their former power to punish subordinate native officials.[4] The jurisdiction of the native officials was limited to petty civil and criminal

[1] In 1818 six of the nine, and in 1831 eight of the eleven, Agents of Government were officers commanding garrisons in Kandy (C.O. 54. 73: Nov. 17, 1818; C.O. 54. 101: Dec. 6, 1828; C.O. 54. 122: Dec. 24, 1831). The reasons for this radical departure from the rule that government appointments must be held by civil servants were: (1) the salary paid the army officers was much lower than to civil servants, an important consideration in the embarrassed state of Ceylon's finances (C.O. 54. 82: Oct. 21, 1822); and (2) the frequent revolts in Kandy made the work of administration more suited to a military officer than a civilian. The North-West Frontier Province of India or the Sudan have similar administrations and for the same reason. The Agents of Government at Saffragam and the Seven Korales, who were civil servants, received a salary of £1,000 each: the army officers who were Agents received on an average £135 apiece (C.O. 54. 128: C. S. Estab. 1833).

[2] For some time the Kandyan nobles continued to levy fines and exact unpaid forced labour, the ignorance and conservatism of the people enabling them to evade the orders of Government.

[3] C.O. 54. 73: Jan. 8, 1819. Much of the land in Kandy as in the Maritime Provinces was held by Service Tenure. In return for this partial abolition of tenure by service a tax was imposed of one-tenth of the produce of paddy lands, save in the case of lands belonging to the Crown, the Buddhist temples, and the native officials. The tax was collected by the native officials under the supervision of the Agents of Government. Forced labour was the means by which Governor Barnes was able to build his Kandyan roads.

[4] C.O. 54. 70: Apr. 12, 1818.

cases, under the strict supervision of the Agents of Government. All other civil and criminal cases except treason and murder were tried by the Agent of Government, who was assisted in important cases by the Dissawa and two other native officials. Their principal duty was to declare the Kandyan law, but the Agent was not required to follow their advice. The Court of the Judicial Commissioner was both a court of first instance with civil and criminal jurisdiction, and also the Kandyan court of appeal, to which were referred all important civil and criminal cases tried by the Agents. From this court the final appeal lay to the Governor, to whom all serious cases, and especially sentences of death, were referred. To a larger extent than the Collectors the Kandyan Agents of Government united in themselves revenue, judicial, and administrative powers.[1]

2. The Reforms of 1833 and the Decline of the Civil Service

The year 1833 is a landmark in the history of the Ceylon Government, for it saw the introduction of sweeping and on the whole unwise reforms. The Colonial Office and the Treasury were determined if possible to balance revenue and expenditure, and they empowered the Commissioners of the Eastern Inquiry to conduct a searching investigation in Ceylon and to propose reforms.[2] Unfortunately two of the three Commissioners who came to Ceylon were dominated by their colleague, Colonel Sir William Colebrooke, and the report was on the whole the expression of his views.[3] He had more than a tinge of the doctrinaire idealist, and was guided by his own notions of abstract justice rather than by actual conditions. While his report contained several excellent suggestions the drastic and ill-considered changes which he advocated played havoc with the efficiency of the Civil Service. The Colonial Office adopted the majority of his recommendations, with the result that for

[1] C.O. 54. 73: Nov. 21, 1818, and Jan. 8, 1819; C.O. 54. 79: Feb. 10, 1821; C.O. 54. 82: Oct. 21 and Nov. 4, 1822; C.O. 54. 101: Dec. 6, 1828.

[2] C.O. 54. 121: Draft of Colonial Office's Instructions to Colebrooke, 1829.

[3] C.O. 54. 121: Apr. 23, 1829; May 23, 1831; Jan. 28, 1832. Colonel Colebrooke entered the artillery in 1803, and from 1805 to 1820 served in India, Ceylon, and Java. From 1822 onwards he was one of the Commissioners of the Eastern Inquiry. He arrived in Ceylon in Apr. 1829 and returned to England in Feb. 1831.

fifteen years the history of the Civil Service was the recital of successive attempts to repair the damage which he had wrought.[1]

Colonel Colebrooke in 1832 submitted a report which strongly condemned the Ceylon Government as costly and 'unfavourable to the improvement of the country'.[2] Omitting the recommendations which were rejected by the Colonial Office, he advised:

(1) The abolition of pensions and a few of the existing positions, and a sweeping reduction in salaries.

(2) The exclusive Civil Service should be abolished, and Ceylon officials should no longer have the sole right to all vacancies. 'The public service should be freely open to all classes of persons according to their qualifications', while 'the unrestricted admission of natives of all classes to the judicial civil offices open to Europeans when they may possess or acquire the necessary qualifications' was most desirable.

(3) A Legislative Council should be established containing European and native unofficial members as well as official.

---

[1] C.O. 54. 118: Oct. 13, 1832. Although Sir Robert Wilmot-Horton, who was appointed Governor to carry out the reforms, was a man of strongly Liberal views, after a few months in Ceylon he was criticizing Colebrooke almost as forcibly as his Conservative predecessor, General Barnes. Horton wrote that he had discussed Colebrooke's report with missionaries and traders as well as civil servants, and that 'I hear but of one view of reprobation' for 'the crude and unpractical views of Colonel Colebrooke'.

After a few years' experience of Colebrooke's reforms the Colonial Office officials were converted to the same view, e.g. Sir James Stephen's memorandum on Horton's dispatch of July 1, 1836: 'I think it is almost demonstrable that the Ceylon retrenchments were made by unskilful as well as unsparing hands, and that they are more distinguished by parsimony than economy' (C.O. 54. 140). In 1842 another memorandum noted that 'almost every project emanating from him was visionary and obscure' (C.O. 54. 222: Oct. 5, 1842).

[2] C.O. 54. 122: Dec. 24, 1831; C.O. 54. 118: Oct. 13, 1832. Colebrooke made recommendations which if adopted would have undermined the whole system of Crown Colony Government, by destroying the greater part of the Governor's power to control his Colony. He advised that the Governor's control of the executive should be largely nullified by transferring the control of the colonial civil servants to the Government departments in London. The Executive Council and not the Governor should practically control the revenue and expenditure; while a Legislative Council should be established from which the Governor should be excluded. Since the members were to take an oath of secrecy he was apparently to be kept in ignorance of its debates. If he rejected a Bill passed by the Council it should be referred to the Secretary of State for his decision. Finally, the Governor's discretionary power should so far as possible be decreased. The report contained many vague generalities, so that it is sometimes impossible to divine exactly what Colebrooke recommended, while he was quite often inaccurate in his references to Ceylon.

(4) The Government monopoly of the cultivation and sale of cinnamon should be abolished, and the industry thrown open to private enterprise.

(5) Land tenure by personal service and Rajakaria, or the right of Government to exact forced labour from those holding land by Service Tenure, should be abolished both in the Kandyan and the Maritime Provinces, and be replaced by an increase of the land tax.[1]

Despite the strong protests of the Governor, Sir Robert Wilmot-Horton, the Secretary of State for the Colonies accepted most of Colebrooke's recommendations, and at the end of 1833 the reforms came into operation.[2] The position of Commissioner of Revenue was abolished and the work transferred to the Chief Secretary.[3] The post of Paymaster-General was also abolished, and the work transferred to the Treasurer, who retained his duties as Commissioner of Stamps. The salaries of the Treasurer and of the Accountant and Auditor-General were each reduced from £2,000 to £1,500, and that of the Collector of Customs from

[1] C.O. 54. 122: Dec. 24, 1831, and May 28, 1832; C.O. 54. 121: May 22, 1832; C.O. 54. 118: Oct. 23, 1832. Governor Barnes on the whole strongly condemned Colebrooke's Report. Since the Sinhalese had originally been given their land in return for personal service, he could see nothing unjust in exacting it. The Sinhalese would not work voluntarily for pay, nor could the Government afford to hire labourers for the immense amount of road construction which was essential to develop the island. The abolition of the Government monopoly of cinnamon, one of the most important sources of revenue, was a strange way to reduce the annual deficit. To admit the natives to the Civil Service was 'ludicrous' in view of their lack of Western education. Justly indignant at the charge that his Government had retarded the development of Ceylon, Barnes wrote that if only he could obtain the revenue he 'could prepare such an appalling list [of essential public works] as, from the amount of expense, would startle the most zealous advocate for improvement' (C.O. 54. 112: Sept. 10, 1830, and Jan. 12, 1831).

[2] C.O. 55. 73: May 29, 1834; C.O. 55. 74: *passim*; C.O. 55. 75: July 29, 1833; C.O. 55. 77: May 6, 1835; C.O. 54. 127: *passim*; C.O. 54. 128: *passim*; C.O. 54. 130: *passim*; C.O. 54. 131: Proclamation of Oct. 1, 1833; C.O. 54. 135: May 1, 1834; C.O. 54. 140: Feb. 10, 1835.

[3] C.O. 55. 85: Nov. 30, 1844. About 1843 the control of the collection of revenue was transferred to the Auditor-General. The reforms fell most heavily upon Robert Boyd, the only survivor of the senior civil servants sent out in 1801, who had a very fine record of thirty-four years of uninterrupted service in Ceylon. By the abolition of his post of Commissioner of Revenue he fell from a salary of £3,000 to £300 as an unemployed civil servant. It proved impossible to give him one of the higher appointments, and in 1836 he was retired on an annual pension of £1,000 (C.O. 54. 128: Aug. 30, 1833; C.O. 54. 129: C.O. Memo.; C.O. 54. 136: Oct. 4, 1834; C.O. 54. 147: July 13 and Aug. 2, 1836).

£1,574 to £1,000. The provincial government was entirely re-modelled, for the former districts were done away with, and the separate administration of Kandy was abolished. The whole of Ceylon was divided into five provinces, each under a Government Agent with a varying number of Assistant Agents. In an attempt to weaken the national feeling of the Kandyans parts of the former kingdom were included in the new provinces, the arrangement being as follows:

> Northern Province—composed of the former Districts of Jaffna, Mannar, and the Wanni, and the Kandyan Province of Nuwarakalawiya.
>
> Southern Province—the Districts of Galle, Tangalla, Matara, and Hambantota, and the Kandyan Provinces of Saffragam, Lower Uva, and Welasse.
>
> Eastern Province—the Districts of Trincomalee and Batticaloa, and the Kandyan Provinces of Tamankaduwa and Bintenne.
>
> Western Province—the Districts of Colombo, Chilaw, and Puttalam, and the Kandyan Provinces of the Seven Korales, Three Korales, Four Korales, and Lower Bulatgamme.
>
> Central Province—the central districts of the Kandyan kingdom.

The duties of the Government Agents and their Assistants were the same as those of the former Collectors, while the Mudaliyars and other native officials had the same powers as formerly.[1]

The District Judges received the new title of Provincial Judges, but otherwise no change was made save that the Colonial Office wrote that barristers and not civil servants would be appointed to fill future vacancies. The existing practice was condemned since the District Judges had no legal training before appointment, and because the system of promotion by seniority entailed frequent changes of office from the revenue (administrative) to the judicial department.[2] The regulation,

---

[1] C.O. 54. 128: May 20, 1833; C.O. 54. 130: Nov. 22, 1833. The number of native officials was reduced and the Kandyan native officials lost their right to exemption from the land tax while in office, but were recompensed by additional salaries.

[2] C.O. 55. 73: May 29, 1834; C.O. 54. 222: Oct. 5, 1842: C.O. Memo. Vacancies due to retirement or furlough entailed the promotion of all officials whose

however, remained a dead letter for twenty years. The Cinnamon Department was abolished as a natural consequence of
the abandonment of the Government monopoly of cinnamon,
while the Department of the Civil Engineer and Surveyor-
General was reorganized and placed in charge of all public
works in Ceylon.[1]

The number of positions in the Civil Service—thirty-eight in
1831[2]—was not greatly altered, and with the exception of
Robert Boyd, the ex-Commissioner of Revenue, all the civil
servants were given posts.[3] In the provincial administration,
for example, the substitution of five for some seventeen provinces
necessitated the appointment of a large additional number of
Assistant Agents, and most of the former Collectors retained
their former districts under this new title. Salaries were reduced
from £43,976 to £24,985, the average decrease being 33 per cent.,
though in some of the minor posts it amounted to 60 per cent.
The heaviest loss fell upon those who could least afford it, since
in a country where the cost of living was expensive the Treasurer
with a salary of £2,000 was less affected by a reduction to £1,500
than, for example, the Assistant Agent of the Seven Korales
whose salary fell from £1,000 to £400.[4] Horton protested
strongly at the reductions, which fell 'with the most ruinous
severity' upon the junior civil servants; and he vainly warned
the Colonial Office that insufficient pay would inevitably lead
to inefficient work.[5] The events of the next few years proved
conclusively the short-sighted parsimony of the Treasury and

posts were inferior in seniority to the vacancy. As a result civil servants were
frequently moved from one district to another, or from administrative to
judicial work and vice versa.

[1] C.O. 54. 127: *passim*; C.O. 54. 128: May 2, 1833; Skinner, *Ceylon*, 169.
Hitherto the Civil Engineer had been responsible for only part of the public
works, the remainder (including public buildings, roads, and bridges) being in
charge of the Quartermaster-General and the Royal Engineers.

[2] C.O. 54. 122: Dec. 24, 1831.

[3] C.O. 54. 130: Nov. 22, 1833. The civil servants were given the alternative
of retiring upon the pensions due to them, or of remaining in the Service at the
reduced salary for their posts, plus half the difference between the new and
the old salary. Thus the District Judge of Jaffna, whose salary was reduced
from £1,500 to £1,000, would receive £1,250. When the old civil servants as
they were called retired, the new appointees would receive only the reduced
salary. Boyd, who had no alternative, was the only civil servant who retired.

[4] C.O. 54. 128: Aug. 29, 1833.

[5] C.O. 54. 114: Dec. 14, 1831; C.O. 54. 130: Nov. 22, 1833.

the Colonial Office, and within a few years the Secretary of State was trying to undo the harm wrought by his predecessor.

The decline of the Service was not attributable solely to the decrease of salaries: two other causes were equally effective. The first was the abolition of pensions, and the second the slowness of promotion. The old civil servants as they were called received the pensions due to them on retirement, but the Secretary of State announced that no pension would be granted to any official appointed after the date of the reforms, unless as a special reward for exceptional services.[1] Maitland and other Governors had pointed out that the pension was the principal attraction to the Service, since salaries were too low to permit of much being saved. Inevitably therefore the civil servants appointed after 1833 were of inferior ability to their predecessors, and were also less interested in their work. The slowness of promotion reinforced the effect of abolishing pensions and reducing salaries. In so small a Service promotion was necessarily slower than, for example, in the Indian Civil Service, where the large number of positions entailed a correspondingly large number of retirements. The abolition of the Paymastership and the Commissionership of Revenue removed two of the few prizes of the Service and weakened the incentive for exertion. The unwritten law of the Ceylon Service that promotion was by strict seniority still further discouraged zeal. Theoretically the Governor was expected to consider the relative efficiency of the candidates, but despite occasional condemnations promotion by seniority was the almost invariable rule.[2]

[1] C.O. 55. 73: May 29, 1834; C.O. 55. 74: Nov. 28, 1832, and Mar. 23, 1833.
[2] C.O. 54. 86: Jan. 20, 1824; C.O. 54. 114: Nov. 9, 1831; C.O. 55. 74: Sept. 14, 1832; C.O. 54. 222: Oct. 5, 1842: C.O. Memo. About 1831 Anstruther, the Chief Secretary, condemned 'the ruinous system of making promotion dependent on mere seniority' (C.O. 54. 114). In 1832 Governor Horton reported that the result of promotion by seniority was 'the constant change of situation which takes place. The retirement or even departure to England of a single civil servant frequently causes the removal of a very considerable number, and all members of the service consider their remaining long in any situation so precarious, that they are induced to look forward anxiously to a change instead of devoting their whole attention to the duties of their office; and in almost every instance no sooner has a public officer made himself master of the duties of his situation than he is removed to another of which he knows comparatively little' (C.O. 54. 117: Jan. 31, 1832). Sir Emerson Tennent, who was Chief or Colonial Secretary from 1846 to 1850, condemned 'the pernicious system of

The result of these causes was that after 1833 an Assistant
Agent had the prospect of long service in subordinate posts on
an inadequate salary of a few hundred pounds. His principal
incentive to efficiency was the possibility of attaining one of
a very few well-paid positions—which carried no pension. The
same situation had of course existed since the establishment of
the Ceylon Service, but the changes introduced in 1833 intensified the conditions which discouraged zeal and efficiency.

The reforms also discontinued the appointment of Writers,
with the result that newly appointed civil servants entered upon
their duties at once, without the necessary period of preparatory
training to acquaint them with conditions in Ceylon. Dundas's
regulation of 1801 that vacancies would be filled by promotion
from amongst the existing members of the Ceylon Service was
abolished. 'Offices which may hereafter become vacant in the
Colony will be either filled up by candidates already on the
spot, or by persons appointed to them direct from home.'[1]
Colebrooke and the Secretary of State for the Colonies were
determined 'to break through the principle of an exclusive
civil service',[2] since they believed that it excluded the natives
of Ceylon from their fair share of appointments. Henceforth
the Service was to be open to all competent English-speaking
natives or British colonists in Ceylon. The Governor was to
recommend to the Secretary of State suitable candidates for
appointment. Unfortunately the Secretary of State's instructions followed closely the wording of Colebrooke's report, and
were therefore so vague as to what constituted competency that
the Governors were in great perplexity how to apply them.
Scarcely any appointments were made as a result of this

promotion by mere seniority. Exertion was felt to be ineffectual . . . by the
consciousness that no services however zealous were sufficient to achieve distinction when opposed to the claims of ante-dated incompetence' (Tennent,
Ceylon, ii. 174).
    [1] C.O. 55. 73: May 29, 1834. The former allowance of £300 for civil servants
temporarily unemployed was abolished. Horton vainly urged that the appointment of Writers be continued. Anticipating Macaulay he also advised that the
minimum age for appointment should be raised to eighteen or twenty, and that
an 'indispensable preliminary' was 'an adequate examination' which should
show that the candidate had a liberal education and a general knowledge of the
principles of English law (C.O. 54. 114: Nov. 9, 1831). Lord Goderich dismissed
the plea for examination as 'impracticable' (C.O. 55. 74: May 4, 1832).
    [2] C.O. 55. 74: May 4, 1832.

regulation.[1] The discouragement to zealous service can be imagined, when to low salaries, no pensions and slow promotion was added the possibility that a vacancy might be filled by a stranger from England or Ceylon.

One of the few beneficial changes was the alteration of Ceylon's constitution. Prior to 1833 the Governor had had complete executive and legislative power, assisted by an advisory Council of officials. This body now became the Executive Council, and was composed of the Governor, the officer commanding the troops in Ceylon, the Chief Secretary, the Queen's Advocate (the present Attorney-General), the Treasurer, and the Government Agent of the Central Province. The Governor was required to consult the Executive Council on all matters except when they were trivial or too urgent to admit of delay. In this latter case he must inform the Council as soon as possible of his measures and the reasons for them. The Governor was given discretionary power to act in opposition to the Council's advice; but he was required immediately to send a full report of the case to the Colonial Office.[2] An important change was introduced by the establishment of a Legislative Council composed of nine official and six unofficial members.[3] The unofficial members were nominated by the Governor from the principal natives and European colonists in Ceylon. The control of the executive remained in the hands of the Governor, but the assent of the Legislative Council was required for legislation. The Governor had power to veto any Ordinance, and all Ordinances to which he assented were subject to the final decision of the Crown, which had full power to sanction, disallow, or alter them.[4] The Governor's control of legislation was not substantially affected by the establishment of the Council owing to the official majority and his power of veto. The appointment of the unofficial members gave the natives and colonists official spokesmen for discussing grievances or making

[1] C.O. 55. 74: May 4 and Sept. 14, 1832, and Mar. 23, 1833; C.O. 54. 222: Oct. 5, 1842: C.O. Memo.

[2] Parl. Pap. H. C. 698 of 1833, vol. xxvi. 1–9; C.O. 55. 74: Sept. 14, 1832. In 1841 the Auditor-General replaced the Government Agent of the Central Province.

[3] V. chap. vii for fuller accounts of the Executive and Legislative Councils.

[4] C.O. 55. 74: Sept. 14, 1832; Parl. Pap. H. C. 698 of 1833, vol. xxvi. 3–7.

known their wishes. They could criticize freely all actions of the administration, and were to some extent a check upon the power of the Governor.

From the point of view of the natives the most important reform was the abolition of Rajakaria, or the Government right to exact forced labour from the holders of Service Tenure lands. North's abolition of Service Tenures in the Maritime Provinces in 1801 had been premature, and Maitland had allowed his laws to become a dead letter. Forced labour was paid at rates fixed by the Government, and continued to be exacted for the building of public works, the collection of cinnamon, &c. In 1809 the construction and repair of roads and bridges was declared an unpaid labour for the raiyats through whose districts the roads ran. Rajakaria in Kandy was exacted for similar purposes, and was paid save for road construction. While Rajakaria could only be demanded by the civil servants, the work of calling out the raiyats was done by the native officials in both Kandy and the Maritime Provinces. They abused their power by taking bribes for exemption and by illegally exacting labour for their own estates.[1] In 1801 the raiyats had clung to Service Tenure, but in 1832 they wished for its abolition. This was the result of the economic progress which had been brought about by thirty years of British rule. The raiyats also complained strongly of the exactions of the native officials for which Rajakaria furnished the pretext.[2] Colebrooke, Governor Horton, and many Ceylon civil servants advocated the abolition of Rajakaria for this reason, and because the native officials would lose much of their power over the raiyats when deprived of the right to impress them for service.[3] At the same time Horton strongly urged that Rajakaria should be temporarily retained until coolies had been recruited for the urgent work of completing the Kandyan roads begun by Governor Barnes. In contradiction to Colebrooke the Governor wrote that it was excessively difficult to hire labour in Ceylon.[4] The Secretary of State for the Colonies refused to sanction any delay, and

[1] C.O. 54. 73: Nov. 21, 1818; C.O. 54. 122: Dec. 24, 1831; C.O. 54. 145: Mar. 16, 1832; Tennent, *Ceylon*, i. 427 and 428; ii. 93.
[2] C.O. 54. 114: Nov. 10 and Dec. 14, 1831; Skinner, *Ceylon*, 168.
[3] C.O. 54. 114: Jan. 12, 1831; C.O. 54. 122: Dec. 24, 1831.
[4] C.O. 54. 118: *passim.*

F

peremptorily abolished Rajakaria by the Order in Council of April 12, 1832. The reform affected only the Government's right to Rajakaria since it expressly reserved the right of the Buddhist temples and the Kandyan nobles to exact forced labour from their tenants.[1] These last relics of Service Tenures were increasingly resented by the raiyats, and were extinguished by Ordinance Number 4 of 1870 which empowered all tenants to commute their services into an annual money rent fixed by the Government.[2]

The first breach in the reforms was made in 1837, less than four years after their adoption. Sir Robert Horton had been unflagging in his efforts to convince the Colonial Office that the reduction of salaries had been too drastic, and he was at length partially successful in spite of the opposition of the Treasury. The Governor contended that the scale of salaries was too low 'to induce young men of education and respectability to embark in the service'. He begged also that the reduced pensions which could be obtained by the old civil servants should be increased, to persuade them to remain in Ceylon after they had completed their twelve years of service.[3] Lord Glenelg, the Secretary of State for the Colonies, granted substantial increases of salary to the junior civil servants, viz. the Assistant Government Agents and minor District Judges whose salaries varied from £300 to £850. He made practically no change in the salaries of senior officials who received over

[1] C.O. 55. 72: May 3, 1832, and Mar. 14, 1833; C.O. 54. 121: Mar. 16, 1832. The Order in Council was drafted by the Commissioners of the Eastern Inquiry. Horton continued to regret the summary abolition of Rajakaria owing to the difficulty experienced in recruiting enough labour for road construction. In 1834–5 he and the Secretary of State concurred in the wish that the abolition had been accompanied by an Ordinance giving the raiyats the alternative of paying a tax for road construction, or of working on the roads a few days a year. This anticipation of Torrington's Road Tax of 1848 was rejected from fear of the discontent it would occasion among the people, who would look upon the measure as a revival of Rajakaria (C.O. 54. 135: Aug. 30, 1834; C.O. 55. 75: Mar. 19, 1835).

[2] C.O. 54. 446: Sept. 18, 1869; C.O. 54. 448: Nov. 30, 1869; C.O. 54. 454: Mar. 5 and 22, 1870; C.O. 55. 117: May 13, 1870; Digby, *Life of Sir Richard Morgan*, ii. 77–84.

[3] C.O. 54. 148: Glenelg's Memo. to the Treasury on Horton's dispatch of July 1, 1836. Before 1833 a civil servant might reasonably expect to attain an average pension of £550, but owing to the reduced salaries after that date the pension was only £400, being a percentage of the salary.

£1,000. A moderate increase of pension was given to the old civil servants, but Glenelg refused to establish pensions for officials appointed after 1833.[1]

In 1839 Governor Stewart Mackenzie condemned the regulations of 1833 that no more Writers would be appointed, and that civil servants would only be sent out to Ceylon to fill an actual vacancy. The Governor protested that it was absurd to appoint as Assistant Agent or District Judge a young man who had just arrived from England, and who was as totally ignorant of law and methods of colonial administration as he was of the native languages and customs. On his own initiative the Governor ordered that all newly arrived officials must spend six to nine months as Assistant to a Government Agent, and that they would be appointed to a vacancy only after the Government Agent had reported favourably on their competence.[2]

3. *Lord Stanley's Reforms*

The measures adopted in 1837 and 1839 were totally inadequate: while they repaired in some minor particulars the harm done in 1833, they did not touch the roots of the evil. Under the combined effect of low salaries, poor prospects of promotion, and the abolition of pensions, the Service continued rapidly to deteriorate. The event which finally brought about reform was a series of pessimistic dispatches in 1841 from the new Governor, Sir Colin Campbell. He reported 'that the Civil Service was yearly deteriorating in point of ability, and . . . that it was hardly possible to make satisfactory arrangements to fill the places of the few able men, whose applications for leave of absence' he found it impossible to refuse. Lord Stanley, the Secretary of State for the Colonies, asked for further information, with the result that he learned that 'seven of the chief officers of Government are in positions for which they are unsuited'. The reason for these peculiar appointments was that promotion was governed by seniority and not by ability.[3] By

---

[1] C.O. 54. 222: Oct. 5, 1842: C.O. Memo.; C.O. 55. 79: *passim*.
[2] C.O. 54. 169: Jan. 18, 1839.
[3] C.O. 55. 83: Oct. 7, 1842. e.g. Campbell reported that Turnour, a good Auditor, was a poor Treasurer; Wright, a good Treasurer, was an indifferent Auditor; Wodehouse, an excellent Government Agent, was not a success as

Stanley's orders Campbell rearranged the higher appointments so as to place the best man in the position most suited for him. Stanley condemned strongly the constant transfers which were the result of promotion by seniority. He insisted that Campbell 'put an immediate and peremptory stop' to 'the continual shifting of all the public servants on the temporary absence' on leave 'of any of their colleagues . . . at the present moment a large proportion of the offices . . . are filled by gentlemen who nominally occupy other situations'.[1]

The Governor's dispatches had reported that few officials had a satisfactory knowledge of the native languages. Governor Barnes's regulation of 1822 had fallen into such complete disuse since 1833 that many civil servants were unaware that no one could be appointed to a higher post than that of Assistant until he had passed an examination in the vernacular. Of the twenty-three civil servants appointed since 1833 two had passed the examination, while only two more had sufficient knowledge to run the risk of taking it.[2] Very few of the junior civil servants had 'any competent knowledge of native languages', while many of the most valuable senior officials were in no better case.[3] Lord Stanley ordered that Barnes's regulation of 1822 be strictly enforced. This, however, applied only to junior officials, so to stimulate their seniors Stanley directed that ignorance of the languages should be a disqualification for promotion.[4] The enforcement of Lord Stanley's regulations produced a gradual improvement, but in 1848 the civil servants' knowledge of the vernaculars was still far from satisfactory.[5] To a considerable extent their ignorance caused the serious mismanagement of the Kandyan revolt of 1848.

Lord Stanley had also been disquieted by the large number of

District Judge of Kandy; while Buller, Government Agent of the Western Province, was unequal to his post.

[1] C.O. 55. 83: Aug. 1, 1843. To fill a vacancy among the higher offices often entailed moving ten or fifteen civil servants from their posts to the ones next above them in seniority. Apparently Stanley's orders failed permanently to remedy this situation. ([C. 1825] of 1877, vol. lix, May 7, 1877; Ridgeway, *Administration of Ceylon*, 130.)

[2] C.O. 54. 196: Apr. 30, 1842.

[3] C.O. 55. 83: Feb. 21, 1843, and Feb. 23, 1844; C.O. 54. 216: Feb. 15, 1845.

[4] C.O. 55. 83: July 18, 1842; C.O. 55. 85: May 23 and 24, 1845.

[5] C.O. 54. 223: Jan. 26, 1846; C.O. 55. 87: Apr. 9, 1846, and May 22, 1847; C.O. 54. 259: July 30, 1849; C.O. 55. 93: Oct. 1, 1851.

civil servants who had engaged in coffee-growing.[1] While the
rules of the Service forbade them to take part in trade, they
were expressly permitted to own estates and sell the produce.[2]
Coffee-growing in Ceylon became very profitable during the
later 'thirties, and the civil servants joined in the mania for
plantations which seized upon all classes of Europeans in Ceylon.
The Governor, Stewart Mackenzie, many of the judges and
Government Agents, the Treasurer, the Auditor-General, the
Colonial Secretary—in fact every official who could obtain the
capital, became the owner of a plantation, convinced that in
a few years he would make his fortune. The Governors encouraged the civil servants in their enterprise, for at that time
they were almost the only Europeans in Ceylon who had capital
to invest, and the one hope of making revenue balance expenditure was to develop the new industry. Furthermore the Governors realized that since salaries had been 'reduced to a bare
subsistence' a coffee plantation was 'the only prospect a public
servant can ever have of realizing independence'. Unfortunately
as the result of the reforms many of the civil servants had
become indifferent to their work, so that in some cases they
paid more attention to their coffee plantations than to the
service of the Government.[3]

Lord Stanley took prompt measures to deal with the situation.
In 1844 he ordered that 'no civil servant will hereafter be permitted to engage in any agricultural or commercial pursuit for
the sake of profit, and that all who may have done so must
within a reasonable time dispose of their property or retire from
the public service'.[4] Governor Campbell pointed out that this
stringent and unexpected regulation would work great hardship, and in 1846 the Secretary of State modified his instructions. No civil servant might in future acquire any land in
Ceylon save a house and grounds, nor might he sell the produce.
All estates must be sold which had been bought since the
publication of Lord Stanley's prohibition on February 1, 1845.
A civil servant might, however, retain estates bought prior to

[1] C.O. 55. 83: Oct. 7, 1842.   [2] C.O. 55. 77: Nov. 30, 1836.
[3] C.O. 54. 276: Tennent's list of civil servants who owned coffee estates in
1841. C.O. 54. 202: Jan. 24, 1843; C.O. 55. 85: Nov. 30, 1844; C.O. 54. 216:
Feb. 12, 1845.
[4] C.O. 55. 85: Nov. 30 and Dec. 4, 1844, May 23 and 24, 1845.

this date, provided that he did not himself cultivate them or superintend the cultivation, and that in the Governor's opinion 'the possession of land shall in no degree interfere with the due and impartial performance of his public duties'. The alternative was retirement from the Service; while 'in all questions of promotion a preference should be given, *ceteris paribus*, to an officer who does not hold land, over one who does'.[1] The Secretary of State's orders were carried out, the civil servants apparently regarding the decision as wise and lenient.[2]

Lord Stanley's correspondence with the Governor had convinced him that the Ceylon Service was suffering from far more serious defects than land-holding or an ignorance of native languages. It was evident that on the whole the civil servants 'are far from being so zealous and efficient as they ought to be . . . while I fear that none of the alterations which you have recommended are likely to produce a remedy'. He therefore asked for a comprehensive report on the Service, especially from Anstruther and Dyke, its two ablest members.[3] As the result of their disclosures Lord Stanley in 1844 wrote to Sir Colin Campbell that 'the Government are resolved no longer to tolerate the inefficiency which for several years past has disgraced the civil servants at Ceylon' 'I find a most unhappy unanimity as to the low state of public feeling which has of late years crept in among the Junior members of the Civil Service—their want of energy and proper pride, and their indifference to improvement. They are represented as listless in the discharge of their functions—contented with the bare performance of those duties which can be exacted from them—and wanting in the zeal without which their services cannot be advantageous.'[4]

[1] C.O. 55. 87: Aug. 24, 1846. The prohibition against owning plantations did not extend to minor native officials (C.O. 54. 554: Aug. 7, 1884).

[2] C.O. 54. 226: Oct. 13, 1846.

[3] C.O. 55. 83: Feb. 15, 1844. Anstruther, the ablest member of the Service, had come to Ceylon about 1822. He had unbounded influence over the Sinhalese, and had been Colonial Secretary since 1833. Dyke, who had formerly been a midshipman, entered the Ceylon Service about 1822. He was Government Agent of the Northern Province for thirty-eight years, and died in 1867. He refused promotion and devoted his great ability with remarkable success to the task of increasing the prosperity of his province (C.O. 54. 101: Dec. 6, 1828; C.O. 54. 321: Apr. 9, 1856; C.O. 55. 115: Dec. 4, 1867).

[4] C.O. 55. 85: Nov. 30, 1844. The reforms of 1845 were based largely on the

A principal cause, and one which antedated the reforms of 1833, was 'the paralysing effect of a constant attention to seniority in promotions—the consequent absence of any hope of advancement by reason of superior merit'. Equally important were the changes for which Colebrooke was responsible—the small salaries, the abolition of pensions, and the abandonment of the principle that all promotions should be made from within the ranks of the Civil Service.

The remedy was to abolish the greater part of the reforms of 1833 and 'to revert in a considerable measure to the system existing previously to 1832 under which those of your officers who are most distinguished for their ability and zeal were brought up'. Pensions must be restored and salaries increased in all cases where they were insufficient. The principle of an exclusive Civil Service must be re-established, all vacancies being filled by the promotion of Ceylon civil servants, and not by men brought in from outside. At the same time Lord Stanley made an important reservation which had not existed in the Service of pre-reform days: promotion by strict seniority was not restored. 'No individual whatever his length of service should be entitled to promotion unless he should be not only competent, but the most competent person whom the Civil Service might offer . . . and in the event of there being no competent officer on the spot, or of public circumstances requiring such a measure, the Secretary of State should appoint to any of the superior offices direct from home.'[1] A knowledge of the language of the district in which the vacancy occurred was also required.[2] The restoration of an exclusive Civil Service entailed the weakness that in filling vacancies the Governor's field of choice was limited to a small number of candidates. Experience had proved that it was sometimes difficult to find efficient officers. Stanley therefore directed that the number of candidates should be increased by including in the Civil

confidential reports of Dyke and Anstruther. The great majority of the Ceylon dispatches between 1841 and 1845 deal with the defects of the Service and the proposed remedies. They are contained in C.O. 54. 189, 190, 196–8, 202–4, 216–18, and 222.

[1] C.O. 54. 518: Mar. 24 and May 8, 1879. The rule was sometimes drastically applied: e.g. in 1879 on grounds of superior ability Saunders was appointed Government Agent of the Western Province over the heads of ten civil servants.

[2] C.O. 54. 222: Feb. 14, 1845.

Service the minor judicial and executive positions which had formerly been excluded.[1] To fill the periodical vacancies in the junior positions caused by promotions the Secretary of State reverted in a modified form to the practice of appointing Writers. Lord Stanley had left very little of the reforms of 1833 except the establishment of the Legislative Council and the abolition of Rajakaria.

The example of the Indian Army and Civil Service strongly influenced Lord Stanley, especially as regards promotion, the establishment of pensions, and the qualifications of Writers. William Cabell in 1840 drew up a very detailed report in which he pointed out that the Ceylon rule of promotion by seniority had been copied from the practice of the Indian Civil Service.[2] In India as in Ceylon the custom discouraged zeal since 'a civilian is almost sure of splendid provision however inefficient he may prove, because he is nearly without a competitor at some time or other for a lucrative appointment'. In the East India Company's Army promotion by seniority was the rule for ordinary posts, but appointments to the staff or the Political Department were made on grounds of merit. These were the prizes of the Service, and officers spared no exertion to qualify themselves, since they could not obtain them 'as a matter of course, or nearly so'. Cabell advised that the Ceylon Service should follow the army rule, filling the ordinary posts by seniority, but making promotion to the important offices dependent on merit. Liberal pensions should be established, as Indian experience showed that otherwise it was impossible to make a tropical Civil Service efficient. The amount of the pension should increase in proportion to the length of service, since the result of this in India had been that officials usually remained in the Service after they were eligible for the minimum pensions. Candidates for Ceylon Writerships should be between sixteen and twenty-two, and before appointment should pass an examination similar to that required for entrance into Hailey-

---

[1] C.O. 55. 85: Nov. 30, 1844. The majority of these minor positions were District Judgeships, held chiefly by burghers. There were also a few posts as Assistant Agent, held principally by army officers, and the two important positions of Civil Engineer and Surveyor-General, and Commissioner of Roads (the official in charge of road construction).

[2] C.O. 54. 222: Dec. 8, 1840.

bury, the training college for Writers in the Indian Civil Service.

The new classification of the enlarged Civil Service came into force in 1845, and arranged the positions in the following manner.[1]

SENIOR BRANCH

	Salary.
Colonial Secretary	£2,000
Auditor-General . . . . ⎫	
Treasurer . . . . . ⎬ . . each £1,500	
Government Agent Western Province ⎭	
,, ,, Northern Province	
,, ,, Central Province	£1,400
,, ,, Southern Province ⎫	
,, ,, Eastern Province ⎬ . . each £1,200	
District Judge Colombo . . ⎭	
,, ,, Jaffna . . .	
Principal Assistant to the Colonial Secretary ⎫	
District Judge Galle . . . . ⎬ . each £1,000	
,, ,, Kandy . . . . ⎭	
,, ,, Trincomalee . . .	
Second Assistant to Colonial Secretary . £800 increasing to £1,000	
Commissioner of the Court of Requests and Police ⎫	
Magistrate Kandy . . . . . ⎬ each £800	
Civil Engineer and Surveyor-General . . ⎭	
Commissioner of Roads.	

[1] C.O. 54. 222: July 3, 1845. The District of Ratnapura was sometimes called Sabaragamuwa, and Anuradhapura, Nuwarakalawiya. A few new positions were created, e.g. the Second and Third Assistants to the Colonial Secretary, and the Service also included many long-established posts which hitherto had not formed part of it. There was a substantial increase of salaries, especially in the Junior Branch. The combination of the duties of Assistant Agent and District Judge was continued owing to the necessity for economy imposed by the small annual revenue of Ceylon (C.O. 54. 216: Feb. 15, 1845). So far as possible, however, they were separated, and candidates for legal appointments were required to pass an examination in law (C.O. 55. 85: May 23, 1845). The list does not include the Government Agent of the North-Western Province, which was created in 1845 with its head-quarters at Puttalam (C.O. 54. 265: Dec. 13, 1849). Despite the enlargement of the Civil Service the small number of positions frequently resulted in a virtual 'stagna-tion of promotion', e.g. in 1877–81 there were only four vacancies amongst the senior posts. The situation was made more serious since there was no age limit for retirement. To alleviate the situation the Colonial Office in 1882 empowered the Governor to require any civil servant to retire at fifty-five, when he became eligible for a pension (C.O. 54. 535: Dec. 19, 1881, and Mar. 14, 1882).

JUNIOR BRANCH

Salary.

Class I. 2 Assistant Agents (Kurunegala and Matara) . . . . . | each £700
4 Assistant Agents and District } rising to £850
Judges (Mannar, Anuradhapura, | by £30 yearly.
Batticaloa, and Badulla . . |

Class II. Postmaster-General . . .
5 District Judges (Matale, Negombo, Kurunegala, Kalutara, and Matara) . . . . . } each £550
Fiscal for the Western Province . rising by £25
4 Assistant Agents and District yearly to £650
Judges (Ratnapura, Chilaw, Hambantota, and Kegalla) . .

Class III. 5 Assistant Agents, one at headquarters of each province (Colombo, Galle, Jaffna, Kandy, and } each £400
rising to £500
by £25 yearly.
Trincomalee) . . . .

Class IV. Third Assistant to the Colonial Secretary. . £300
rising to £375

Class V. Secretary to the Central School Commission . £200
Commissioner of the Loan Board . . . £200
The Assistants to the Engineer and } salaries ranging
Surveyor-General and to the Commissioner of Roads . . . } from £200 to £500

Writers did not rank as members of the Service until they had passed their examination in the native languages.

A system of pensions was established in 1845 for all civil servants appointed since 1832, the old civil servants receiving their pensions in accordance with the former regulations.[1] The

[1] C.O. 54. 216: Feb. 12 and 15, 1845; C.O. 55. 85: May 23, 1845; C.O. 54. 222: July 3 and 11, 1845. The pension for fifteen to twenty years' service was $\frac{4}{12}$ of the annual salary, while there was an increase of $\frac{1}{12}$ for each additional five years' service or fraction thereof. The maximum pension was $\frac{8}{12}$ of the annual salary, attained after thirty-five years' service. The pension was computed on the salary received at retirement, 'provided he shall have been in the receipt of same or in the same Branch and Class for at least three years: otherwise the pension shall be calculated upon the average amount of salary received' in the three years preceding retirement. No pension was granted to any official who resigned before the age of fifty-five, unless the head of his department and two physicians certified that he was physically incapable of his work. No pension could be granted without the sanction of the Imperial

new rules were greatly superior to the old ones: henceforth the amount of the pension depended on the length and value of an official's service, no special privileges being attached to the higher offices. No pension was granted to a civil servant who retired before the age of fifty-five unless his resignation was necessitated by ill health. The object of the regulations was to induce civil servants to remain in the Service after they were eligible for pensions, and to exert every effort to merit promotion since by so doing they increased the amount they would receive. Under the former system the strong tendency had been for officials to retire as soon as they had completed the minimum period of twelve years' service.

Lord Stanley also reverted to the practice of appointing Writers to fill the periodical vacancies in the junior ranks. The regulations differed in important respects from those which had

Government; and no civil servant had 'an absolute right . . . to any pension . . . Her Majesty's Government will retain their power to dismiss any civil servant from the Service without compensation'. The pension rates formed a maximum, and might be diminished or (for very exceptional merit) increased according to the value of the individual's services. No pension would be granted in cases of 'obvious negligence, irregularity or misconduct'. The same scale of pensions applied both to European and to native civil servants. Five per cent. was deducted from the annual salary of each official as a contribution towards his pension. In 1853 the Colonial Office ordered that Writers should 'date the commencement of their Civil Service . . . and of their claim to Pension' from the period at which they passed their preliminary examination in the native languages (C.O. 54. 362: Aug. 16, 1861).

In 1861 the rates of pensions for civil servants and for minor Government officials were altered. The pension for ten to eleven years' service was $\frac{15}{60}$ of the annual salary, while there was an increase of $\frac{1}{60}$ for each additional year's service. The maximum pension was $\frac{40}{60}$ of the annual salary, attained after thirty-five years' service. The remainder of the pensions regulations were almost identical with those of 1845 (C.O. 54. 362: Aug. 16, 1861).

In 1885 after eleven years' consideration the Colonial Office sanctioned the grant of pensions to the widows and orphans of civil servants, the officials contributing a percentage of their salaries to the fund. This much needed reform had been urged by successive Governors for two generations, since they received 'constantly appeals for relief from utter destitution' (C.O. 54. 494: Oct. 7, 1874; C.O. 54. 497: Aug. 4, 1875; C.O. 54. 498: Oct. 26, 1875: and Mar. 23, 1876; C.O. 54. 535: Dec. 9, 1881; C.O. 54. 549: Oct. 23, 1883; C.O. 54. 552: passim; C.O. 54. 555: Feb. 10 and Mar. 26, 1885; C.O. 54. 561: Sept. 9, 1885).

Gregory, Autobiography, 344–5. In 1847 a scale of pensions was established for the minor employees of Government who received a yearly salary of £25 or more. The regulations as to rates of pension, length of service, &c., were similar to those of the Civil Service. At the same time inadequate salaries were increased. The staff of clerks had been too large, underpaid, and inefficient (C.O. 55. 85: May 29, 1844, Jan. 25 and Sept. 18, 1845; C.O. 54. 222: passim; C.O. 55. 87: May 19, 1847).

prevailed prior to 1832, and showed a distinct improvement. At the commencement of each year the Governor informed the Secretary of State of the number of Writers required to fill the probable vacancies; while at the same time he had the right to recommend for appointment any of the natives or colonists. The Secretary of State nominated the Writers from his own and the Governor's candidates. Before the Writers were formally appointed they were required to pass the examination for entrance into Haileybury College taken by candidates for Writerships in the Indian Civil Service. Candidates must be between seventeen and twenty-one; while the character of the examination ensured their having received the usual public school education.[1] Upon their arrival in Ceylon Writers were attached to one of the Government offices upon a salary of £200 a year to learn their duties. No Writer could be appointed to a position in the Service until he had passed a preliminary examination in Tamil or Sinhalese, eighteen months being allowed to study the language. Failure to pass the examination entailed the loss of the Writership.[2]

In striking contrast to the doctrinaire innovations of 1833 Lord Stanley's reforms were not dominated by preconceived theories. His regulations were based on a careful study of the existing situation, and were well designed to repair the damage caused by his predecessor. Nearly ten years passed before his object was attained, for the Service had become seriously demoralized by inefficiency and indifference. The blunders

---

[1] C.O. 54. 222: June 11 and 28, 1845, and *passim*: Col. Office Printed Circular of 1845 on appointment of Writers. The subjects of the entrance examination to Haileybury included Greek, Latin, Mathematics, Euclid, English History, and Geography. The Colonial Office was at first inclined to send Ceylon Writers who had passed their examination to Haileybury, but the idea was abandoned as impracticable.

[2] C.O. 54. 216: Feb. 15, 1845; C.O. 54. 222: Feb. 14, 1845; C.O. 54. 223: Jan. 16, 1846; C.O. 55. 87: Mar. 26, 1846. By the regulations of Aug. 15, 1853, two examinations were instituted. In the first which qualified the Writer 'for holding a first appointment in the Public Service', the candidate was required 'to speak with fluency the colloquial language, to read and explain . . . printed books', and to read and write typical official documents. The second examination, which was held one year after the first, must be passed before a civil servant was eligible for promotion. The requirements were 'the reading of the classical books, a knowledge of Grammar, and translating from English authors' and Government Ordinances into Sinhalese or Tamil (*Ceylon Almanac*, 1859, pp. 114–15: Governor's Minutes of May 27, 1852, and Aug. 15, 1853).

made in suppressing the Kandyan revolt of 1848 were a commentary on the necessity for reform and the difficulty of achieving it.[1]

4. *The Civil Service, 1846–1885*

Lord Stanley had raised the cost of the Civil Service by £40,000 through the introduction of pensions and the increase of salaries, but no alarm was felt, since in 1844 and 1845 the revenue exceeded the expenditure owing to the rapid growth of coffee cultivation.[2] In 1846, however, there was a deficit of £100,000, and the abolition of most of the customs duties in 1847, together with the temporary collapse of the coffee industry, still further diminished the revenue. To relieve 'the immediate and pressing embarrassments of the colony' the Colonial Office ordered drastic reductions in the cost of the Civil Service. The Governor, Lord Torrington, in consultation with his Legislative Council, was to submit proposals for 'a total and organic change'.[3] Lord Torrington appointed a committee of three of the senior civil servants to propose economies, and in December 1849 they presented a painstaking and detailed report. Few alterations were made in Stanley's reforms: the posts of Surveyor-General and Commissioner of Roads were combined, a few minor positions were suppressed, and salaries were somewhat reduced.[4] The unofficial members of the Legislative Council were dissatisfied, and advocated drastic reductions in

---

[1] *V.* chap. x.

[2] C.O. 54. 224: Apr. 14, 1846; C.O. 54. 251: Oct. 16, 1848.

[3] C.O. 55. 90: Apr. 22, 1847; C.O. 55. 89: July 17, 1848.

[4] C.O. 54. 265: Dec. 14, 1849. Printed as Parl. Pap. H. C. 568 of 1852. The sixty-six posts in the Civil Service were reduced to sixty-three. One of the principal criticisms of the committee was that the Service suffered from over-centralization and unnecessary red tape. The insistence, for example, that even the smallest extra expenditure required the previous consent of the Governor, conveyed through the Colonial Secretary, meant that the latter was so overwhelmed with trivialities that important affairs suffered. 'I had a correspondence extending to thirteen despatches in regard to a pewter ink-stand for a police office'. Since 'every instrument has to be prepared in triplicate and sometimes in quadruplicate', it compelled every Government department to maintain a large and increasing staff of 'trumpery' clerks to cope with the floods of correspondence (Tennent, *Ceylon*, ii. 172–3; C.O. 54. 228: Oct. 22, 1846). In 1883 the complaint was again made that the time of the higher officials was too much occupied by minor details; but apparently the Colonial Office was not convinced that the situation was serious (C.O. 54. 547: May 16, 1883).

the Service, but these proposals were not approved by the Colonial Office, nor eventually by the Legislative Council itself. For seven years the expense and inefficiency of the Civil Service were a perennial subject of debate, and only in 1855 did the Legislative Council finally agree on its report. The result of its deliberations was a document which differed in no essential particulars from the report of 1849: salaries were moderately reduced and a few minor positions abolished. The Colonial Office sanctioned a part of the proposed minor alterations.[1] The changing attitude of the unofficial members of the Council reflected the vicissitudes of the coffee planters: during the period of collapse they demanded sweeping economies, but with the return of prosperity no more complaints were heard about the cost of the administration.[2]

The rapid growth of the coffee industry was reflected in the Ceylon revenue: the deficit which until about the middle of the 'fifties had been almost an expected item in the annual budget was at last converted into a surplus which steadily increased. Prior to this date the Treasury had usually opposed increases of salary for the civil servants, although there seems to have been general agreement that they were barely adequate in view of the high cost of living in the colony. In 1858 the salaries were increased, the general result being approximately to restore the maximum fixed by Lord Stanley in 1845.[3]

---

[1] C.O. 54. 251: Oct. 3, 1848; C.O. 54. 272: Jan. 15 and Mar. 11, 1850; C.O. 55. 93: Jan. 20, 1851; C.O. 54. 317: Oct. 25–30, 1855. In 1852 the Imperial Government transferred the control of the Ceylon Customs Department from the Board of Trade to the Ceylon Government, and incorporated the Customs officials in the Ceylon Civil Service. Hitherto the more important Customs officials had been appointed and controlled by the Board of Trade, although they had apparently been selected from the Ceylon Service (C.O. 55. 93: Dec. 28, 1852).

[2] C.O. 54. 317: Oct. 25–30, 1855; C.O. 54. 344: June 7, 1859.

[3] C.O. 54. 344: June 7, 1859; C.O. 54. 415: Oct. 12, 1866; *Ceylon Almanac, 1859*, 60–80; Tennent, *Ceylon*, ii. 174; *Speeches and Minutes of Ward*, 215–27. Stanley's principle of an initial minimum salary with annual increments was abolished, and a fixed amount substituted. For the junior positions the new salary was on the whole slightly less than the 1845 maximum, and for senior posts, the same or somewhat larger. The Colonial Secretary continued to receive £2,000, and the Treasurer and Auditor-General each £1,500. The six Government Agents received from £1,200 to £1,500, a moderate increase in certain cases. The eighteen Assistant Government Agents received from £450 to £800, on the whole slightly less than Stanley's maximum. The sixteen District Judges received from £1,200 (at Colombo and Kandy) to £400. Writers con-

During the years which had elapsed since Stanley's reforms the Civil Service had on the whole recovered its efficiency, and there was no repetition of the condemnations which were so frequent in the 'forties. In one important respect, however, conditions remained unsatisfactory; a disappointingly high percentage of officials were ignorant of the native languages. This was not unnatural in the case of the senior civil servants who had been appointed long before the date of Lord Stanley's rule that ignorance of the vernacular was an impediment to promotion. The Colonial Office directed that the rule should not be rigidly enforced against them since they 'from their age may fairly be regarded as unfit to acquire proficiency in native languages'.[1]

No such excuse could be put forward for Writers appointed after 1845; yet the Governors and the Colonial Office found frequent cause to complain of their lack of knowledge. The evidence is somewhat scanty, but the constant injunctions to enforce the regulations requiring civil servants to pass examinations in native languages leave a strong suspicion that the rule was enforced only spasmodically.[2] In 1858 Governor Ward explained and defended the 'general laxity' on the grounds of 'the smallness of the salaries, . . . the slowness of promotion, the

tinued to receive £200, increased to £300 in 1873 (C.O. 54. 484: Jan. 9, 1873). Salaries in the Customs Department were from £350 to £1,200 for the Collector of Customs at Colombo. The Queen's Advocate, who was a barrister and not a member of the Civil Service, received £1,500. Twenty Police Magistrates received from £600 to £350. The Surveyor-General and the Civil Engineer and Commissioner of Roads each received £1,200, while the Director of the Botanic Gardens at Peradeniya received £450. The Education Department had a small staff of Inspectors and Masters whose salaries varied from £750 to £150. The salaries were in many cases lower than before the reforms of 1833, especially for the senior civil servants. The salaries of office clerks were increased in 1864 by about 16 per cent., a tardy relief since they had on the whole been underpaid.

In 1866 the civil servants petitioned Parliament for an increase in salary of 25 per cent. owing to the heavy rise in the cost of living since 1859. The Governor supported the petition, but it was rejected by the Colonial Office in 1868 (C.O. 55. 115: Mar. 17, 1868). In 1877 the salaries of civil servants were increased by 20 per cent. owing to the rise in living expenses combined with the depreciation of the rupee, in which salaries were paid after 1872 (C.O. 54. 501: Mar. 15, 1876, and Nov. 9, 1877; C.O. 54. 502: Aug. 9, 1876; C.O. 54. 512: Feb. 28, 1878).

[1] C.O. 55. 93: Apr. 8, 1852.
[2] C.O. 54. 259: July 30, 1849; C.O. 55. 93: *passim*; C.O. 55. 95: June 14, 1855; C.O. 55. 100: Sept. 8 and Dec. 18, 1858.

little care that has been taken to keep the number of Writers complete, or to make a strict examination in the native languages an absolute condition of promotion, and I may add the very large number of natives who have acquired a proficiency in the English tongue . . . the fact of having passed an examination in his earlier years . . . is no proof among the senior civil servants that they can speak Cinghalese now, the number of those who can . . . not exceeding four or five'.[1] Writers found it 'very difficult' to pass the preliminary examination within the prescribed eighteen months after their arrival, since they 'are generally employed in public business the whole or a great part of the day, and are often before they have passed their examination appointed to act as Police Magistrates'. No civil servant had as yet succeeded in passing the second and much more difficult language examination, which a regulation of 1853 established as a qualification for promotion. 'Since they are busy all day . . . the necessary study . . . has been found to be utterly incompatible with' Government duties.[2] To remedy the situation Governor MacCarthy in 1863 revised the examination rules and decreased the amount of Government work assigned to Writers.[3] The new regulations were apparently successful,

[1] C.O. 54. 337: Oct. 25, 1858.
[2] C.O. 54. 37I: Oct. 16, 1862. While successive Governors deplored the practice of appointing Writers to acting appointments as Magistrates or Assistant Government Agents before passing their first language examination, they declared it to be unavoidable. Vacancies in the Service frequently occurred; and since positions could not be left unfilled the only alternative to using the Writers was temporarily to appoint men who were not in the Civil Service. This last expedient evoked very strong objections from the Colonial Office, but it was not infrequently resorted to for junior positions owing to the lack of civil servants (C.O. 54. 322: May 22, 1856; C.O. 54. 424: Feb. 27, 1867; C.O. 54. 428: Oct. 4, 1867; C.O. 54. 436: Sept. 12, 1868; C.O. 55. 115: Aug. 21, 1867; Nov. 8, 1868).
In 1881 of the ninety-two positions in the Service non-civil servants temporarily held six, of which five were Police Magistracies (C.O. 54. 531: Feb. 12, 1881).
[3] C.O. 54. 371: Oct. 16, 1862; C.O. 54. 375: Mar. 13 and Apr. 25, 1863; C.O. 55. 106: Dec. 24, 1862, and Apr. 25, 1863. MacCarthy's regulations provided that for eighteen months after his arrival in Ceylon a Writer received an allowance of £3 a month for a teacher in native languages, while the amount of official work required of him was reduced to two hours daily. If he passed the examination in eighteen months his period of study would count as part of his active service for pension and rank in the Service. If he failed his period of service would date from the time he passed the examination; while failure to pass in three years entailed the loss of the Writership. The examination in

for very little more was heard of the civil servants' ignorance of the native languages.

For some years there was a curious inconsistency in the method of appointing Writers. Lord Stanley directed in 1845 that the Secretary of State should nominate them from his own and the Governor's candidates; and in 1852 the Secretary of State provided that half should be chosen from each group.[1] From about 1845 to 1856 the Secretary of State's nominees were required to pass the Haileybury entrance examination before they were appointed to Writerships. After 1856 the Colonial Office substituted a competitive examination held by the Civil Service Commissioners. Neither examination was a test of specialized knowledge of colonial administration; but while the Haileybury examination was based upon public school training, its successor was designed to obtain as Writers university graduates who had received a liberal education. No examination was required of the candidates nominated by the Governor.[2] Governor Ward successfully opposed the establishment of a competitive examination for his nominees, since he believed that personal selection obtained more suitable men.[3]

the native language was both oral and written, and required the ability to read, write, and speak it. Writers were also required to pass examinations in précis writing, the Government system of accounts, the elements of Ceylon law, and in 'general attainments'. This last included English composition, arithmetic, geometry, and the classics. The second language examination (for promotion from Class III to Class II of the Junior Branch of the Civil Service) must be passed within six years after arrival in Ceylon. An official was required to pass in both Tamil and Sinhalese, and not in one language only as hitherto. He was also required to pass an examination in Ceylon law. In 1875 the rules were slightly modified: henceforth the examination required 'a thorough proficiency in the . . . modern colloquial' and not in the 'archaic' classical language (C.O. 54. 498: Dec. 17, 1875).

[1] C.O. 55. 93: Apr. 8 and Oct. 25, 1852. The Governor was given the right of virtually appointing so that 'a door should be always open for . . . both British and natives who may be resident in the Colony'. The number of Writers in 1852 varied from four to six, while by 1865 it had risen to twelve (C.O. 55. 110: Aug. 12, 1865).

[2] C.O. 55. 98: passim; C.O. 54. 321: Feb. 10, 1856; C.O. 54. 322: May 22, 1856; C.O. 54. 349: passim. In 1859 the Secretary of State's nominees passed a preliminary and a final competitive examination before the Civil Service Commissioners. The age limit was eighteen to twenty-five, and the principal subjects were Greek, Latin, mathematics, modern history, constitutional law, international law, political economy, English composition, précis writing, and book-keeping.

[3] C.O. 55. 103: Feb. 9, 1860; C.O. 54. 353: June 23, 1860; C.O. 55. 106:

G

Ward's successor, Sir Charles MacCarthy, was dissatisfied with the calibre of the Governor's candidates, and in 1863 he required them to pass a non-competitive examination in Ceylon on their 'general attainments'.[1] The standard of MacCarthy's examination was lower than that of the Civil Service Commissioners, since otherwise the Governor's nominees would have been unable to compete successfully owing to the inferiority of Ceylon's educational facilities. Experience proved that the Secretary of State's Writers were 'as a body far superior to the Governor's nominees'.[2] In 1870 the Colonial Office ordered them to pass the same competitive examination as was required of candidates nominated by the Secretary of State. The examination was held simultaneously every year in England and in Ceylon.[3] The entrance requirements for the Ceylon were closely modelled upon those for the Indian Civil Service.[4] In 1880 the examination for Writerships ceased to be held in Ceylon, all candidates being required to compete in London. At the same time the system of competition limited by the nomination of the Secretary of State was abolished and replaced by open competi-

Nov. 18, 1862. Ward considered that if a competitive examination were established the great majority of the successful candidates would be natives, since they were intellectually more precocious than Europeans of the same age. In later years they failed to retain their superiority; and also they were generally inferior to Europeans in impartiality, honesty, and willingness to accept responsibility. Moreover, the native races of Ceylon preferred European officials since they 'universally dislike and distrust each other'. Appointment by nomination enabled the Governor to select those natives who could be advantageously employed. Ward himself nominated Europeans, natives, and burghers.   [1] C.O. 54. 371: Oct. 16, 1862; C.O. 54. 375: Mar. 13, 1863.

[2] C.O. 54. 435: June 26, 1868; C.O. 54. 445: July 6, 1869.

[3] C.O. 55. 117: Dec. 8, 1868: Sept. 10 and Nov. 30, 1869; C.O. 54. 445: July 6, 1869; C.O. 54. 447: Oct. 2, 1869. The virtual effect of the reform was to compel all candidates to obtain their education in England. The same examination qualified for the Civil Services of Ceylon, the Straits Settlements, and Hong Kong, collectively known as the Eastern Cadetships. Owing to the small number of the annual vacancies (two to eight on the average) it proved difficult to attract the best candidates to a competition which offered so few prizes. After 1896, therefore, the same examination qualified for the Home and Indian Civil Services and the Eastern Cadetships (Lowell, *Colonial Civil Service*, 30–1, 65–71).

[4] C.O. 55. 117: *passim*; C.O. 55. 120: *passim*; C.O. 54. 445: July 22, 1869. Following the model of the Indian Civil Service successful candidates were to be 'trained to business habits' by work at the Colonial Office, and were also to study law and native languages before being sent to Ceylon. The training in England was soon abolished, and successful candidates were sent out to Ceylon at once.

tion. Both systems produced much the same type of civil servants.[1]

The appointment to District Judgeships of civil servants who had not received a legal training had been criticized as early as the days of Governor Maitland. The system had worked fairly well, but with the growth of the coffee industry complaints from the colonists and burghers became more frequent.[2] In 1856 the Colonial Office ordered that the District Judgeship of Colombo must be held by a member of the Ceylon Bar, since the development of the coffee trade had made it the most important court of original jurisdiction on the island. While it was preferable that the other District Judgeships should be held by barristers the Governor was allowed to use his own discretion.[3] The majority of the judicial positions continued to be filled by civil servants, but a tendency developed to appoint barristers to the important District Judgeship of Kandy. In 1872 the Colonial Office ordered that owing to the increase of the coffee industry the District Judgeships of Kandy and Colombo must always be held by barristers and not by civil servants. This established the rule that the same course must be adopted with the other District Judgeships as their importance increased.[4]

An analysis which was made in 1868 of the personnel of the Civil Service showed that it was composed of 1,084 appointments, of which 894 were held by natives and burghers and 190 by Europeans.[5] Of the positions 282 were classed as higher appointments with salaries of £200 and upwards, while 802 formed the lower Service, with salaries of £50 to £300. The lower

---

[1] C.O. 54. 528: Oct. 15 and Dec. 9, 1880. The object of the change was to compel all candidates to obtain their education in England, owing to the inferiority of educational facilities in Ceylon. Natives of Ceylon continued to be eligible; but in practice the percentage who competed successfully was about as small as in the earlier period when appointment was by nomination. In 1878 the age for candidates was fixed at twenty-one to twenty-four (C.O. 54. 514: July 20, 1878).

[2] C.O. 54. 238: Sept. 13, 1847; C.O. 54. 309: Sept. 26, 1854; C.O. 55. 98: May 14, 1856; Digby, Morgan, i. 184–6; Sirr, Ceylon and the Cingalese, ii. 239–40.

[3] C.O. 55. 98: May 14 and Aug. 16, 1856. Governor Ward appointed as District Judge of Colombo Sir Richard Morgan, a burgher, who later became the Queen's Advocate.

[4] C.O. 54. 402: June 13, 1865; C.O. 54. 444: June 26, 1869; C.O. 54. 477: Aug. 29, 1872; C.O. 54. 478: Sept. 2, 17, and 30, 1872.

[5] C.O. 55. 115: Mar. 17, 1868; C.O. 54. 434: May 23, 1868.

Service was entirely staffed by burghers or natives, and included the Mudaliyars and other native officials, the office clerks, constables, &c. Of the 28*7* higher appointments natives and burghers held 92, but the majority of them in this division of the Service as well as about half the Europeans had minor technical positions such as that of Assistant Surveyor, Master Attendant (i.e. Harbour Master), &c.[1] In the 'Civil Service Proper', that is the administrative and judicial service to which entrance could be obtained only through a Writership, the salaries ranged from £200 for a Writer to £2,000 for the Colonial Secretary. Of the 84 positions 10 were held by natives and burghers, and 74 by Europeans.[2] The technical branch of the Service comprised the Departments of the Surveyor-General, the Director of Public Works, the Principal Civil Medical Officer, and the Director of the Royal Botanic Gardens at Peradeniya (the Department of Tropical Agriculture). The scientific departments on which most emphasis was laid were the first two, which were concerned with the survey of land and the improvement of means of communication. The Medical Service may perhaps be described as fairly adequate to the needs of the Colony.[3]

In 1873 the number of provinces was increased to seven by the creation of the North Central Province, composed of the Kandyan Districts of Nuwarakalawiya, Tamankaduwa, and

[1] In the judiciary burgher members of the Ceylon Bar frequently held high office, e.g. the District Judgeships of Colombo and Kandy (salary £1,200). In 1881 there were 208 Mudaliyars and other principal native headmen. Admission to all positions in the lower Civil Service was by competitive examination, except for Mudaliyars and other native headmen, who continued to be appointed by the Governor (C.O. 54. 531: Feb. 8, 1881).

[2] Thirty-two of the Europeans were the sons of colonists or of civil servants, and had been nominated as Writers by the Governors. In 1881 the Civil Service Proper was composed of 84 Europeans and 7 natives (C.O. 54. 531: Feb. 8, 1881).

[3] In 1867 the title of Civil Engineer and Commissioner of Roads was changed to that of Director of Public Works (salary £1,500). On the completion of the Government railway from Colombo to Kandy in 1867 a Railway Department was created under the Chief Resident and Locomotive Engineer whose salary was £1,000 (C.O. 54. 463). The Surveyor-General and the Principal Medical Officer received salaries of £1,200. The next twenty years saw a large increase in the staff of the medical and the other scientific departments, together with the first tentative steps in the creation of the Departments of Forestry and of Irrigation, e.g. C.O. 54. 518: Mar. 22, 1879. In 1868, however, the principal task of the Ceylon Government was the maintenance of law and order, together with the improvement of means of communication.

Demala Pattu. The former Assistant Government Agent at Anuradhapura was replaced by a Government Agent and an Assistant Government Agent. The new Province had formerly been famous for its fertility, but owing to the decay of the tanks and other irrigation works it had long since become an almost uninhabited wilderness. To restore its prosperity Governor Gregory carried on a vigorous policy of repairing the tanks, and made it a separate province. Although the inhabitants were Kandyans they had hitherto been incorporated in the Tamil Northern and Eastern Provinces. It was 'morally impossible' for the Government Agents of these large provinces to deal adequately with the Kandyan districts, since they were rarely acquainted with the Kandyan language and customs, and were, moreover, fully occupied with the needs of the Tamil districts.[1] The Government Agent of the Northern Province, for example, was largely concerned with the affairs of the Tamil District of Jaffna. He and his two Assistants at Mannar and Mullaittivu had little time to spare for the outlying districts, even after the area under their control had been reduced by the formation of the North Central Province. For this reason the District of Vavuniya Vilankulam was established in 1874 in the Northern Province, and was placed under a third Assistant Agent. The District was on the border of the North Central Province, and one of the most important duties of the Assistant was to carry out the Governor's plans for the restoration of the irrigation works.[2] During the eleven years which elapsed between 1874 and 1885 few alterations were made in the Civil Service, apart from the creation of a small number of minor positions which became necessary owing to the growth in planting and population.[3]

---

[1] C.O. 54. 486: May 12 and June 24, 1873; C.O. 54. 487: July 7 and Aug. 25, 1873; C.O. 54. 488: Oct. 10, 1873; C.O. 54. 492: Jan. 31, 1874.

[2] C.O. 54. 474: Dec. 24, 1874; C.O. 54. 547: Nov. 6, 1882.

[3] e.g. C.O. 54. 474: Dec. 24, 1874. Two additional Assistant Agents were appointed at Kalutara and Negombo in the Western Province. Between 1846 and 1874 the population had increased from 554,000 to 776,000, but no change had been made in the number of civil servants, viz. the Government Agent at Colombo, and three Assistant Government Agents at Colombo, Ratnapura, and Kegalla. In 1886 the District of Badulla became the Province of Uva, and in 1889 the Districts of Kegalla and Sabaragamuwa became the Province of Sabaragamuwa.

A valuable memorandum on the Civil Service was written in 1882 by Mr. Dickson, who had been thirty-seven years in the Ceylon Service and was the Government Agent of the Central Province.[1] The average length of service in Ceylon was as follows:[2]

Class I	. . . . .	27 years
Class II	. . . . .	20 ,,
Class III	. . . . .	13 ,,
Class IV	. . . . .	9 ,,
Class V	. . . . .	5 ,,
Sixteen Writers .	. . .	3 ,, (varying from 5 years to 2 months).

The central administration was composed as formerly of the Colonial Secretary and his two Assistants, the Auditor-General and his Assistant, and the Treasurer. The Colonial Secretary was not chosen from the Ceylon Civil Service, but was appointed by the Secretary of State for the Colonies from the staff of the Colonial Office or from a Crown Colony. The head of the Ceylon Civil Service, he supervised and controlled the administration and was responsible for its efficient operation. He was also the Governor's principal adviser, and in this capacity his influence was increased by the practice of appointing a new Governor every six years. Although the Governor could overrule the Colonial Secretary, he would hesitate to do so owing to the much greater local experience of his adviser. The Colonial Secretary was 'in truth the organ of Government upon all occasions. . . . To this Office all applications or references from any officer of Government connected with his situation are to be made, and from it all the Regulations and Orders of Govern-

---

[1] C.O. 54. 547: Nov. 6, 1882, and May 16, 1883.
[2] C.O. 54. 478: Sept. 2, 1872, Col. Office Memo., and Nov. 15, 1872, draft dispatch; C.O. 54. 484: Jan. 7 and Feb. 20, 1873; C.O. 54. 486: May 12, 1873. In 1873 the former division of the Civil Service into the Senior Branch and the Junior Branch (subdivided into Classes I to IV) was abolished. The Senior Branch was renamed Class I, and the Junior Branch became Classes II to V. The Treasurer had been in the Ceylon Service 47 years; the Government Agents from 21 to 37 years; the Assistant Government Agents from 8 to 21 years; and the Assistant Auditor-General (a burgher) 37 years (C.O. 54. 547: Nov. 6 1882).

ment will, in the first instance, be issued.' It was 'the office in which all the traditions of Government are carried on. . . . The conduct of it [i.e. the Government] mainly depends upon the vigilance and system that prevail in the office of the Colonial Secretary.'[1]

The Treasurer was concerned with the collection and expenditure of the revenue. He received the accounts of the Assistant and the Government Agents for all the revenue collected in their districts, and had charge of all public money paid into the Treasury. No money could be paid out from the Treasury without the signed warrant of the Treasurer. As Commissioner of Stamps he had the general superintendence of the receipt and issue of all revenue stamps, and as Deputy Paymaster-General of the troops, he controlled the Army Pay Department.[2]

The duties of the Auditor and Accountant-General and Controller of Revenue extended far beyond the audit of the accounts of Ceylon. As Auditor he had the power to advise the Governor to abolish any position which he considered superfluous, while he also viewed with a critical and wary eye any increase of the annual expenditure. As Controller of Revenue he had 'both the control of the Revenue and of the whole accounts of the Colony in every Department'. He must, for example, be fully acquainted with the system of revenue collection in each province, must see that the revenue was 'regularly collected', and must endeavour to secure 'uniformity of system'. The Auditor represented 'the controlling . . . function of Government. In point of fact the Auditor is a check not only upon the Colonial Secretary, but likewise upon the Governor himself', in the matter of controlling the expenditure and preventing its increase.[3]

For provincial administration Ceylon was divided into seven

---

[1] C.O. 54. 28: Aug. 17, 1808; C.O. 54. 547: Nov. 6, 1882; Dickman, *Ceylon Civil Service Manual*, 1865 ed., 38–9. All dispatches except those from the Colonial Office were addressed to the Colonial Secretary. He submitted to the Governor a summary and when necessary an explanatory memorandum, together with a draft reply which was usually accepted. The Colonial Secretary was also responsible for the preparation of the annual budget which was submitted to the Legislative Council, and of the Blue Book, or annual report to the Colonial Office on the affairs of the colony.

[2] C.O. 54. 547: Nov. 6, 1882; Dickman, *C.C.S. Manual*, 1865 ed., 39–40.

[3] Ibid., 40–4.

provinces under the Government Agents of the Western, Central, Northern, Southern, Eastern, North-Western, and North Central Provinces. The provinces were subdivided into a varying number of districts, the total number being twenty-one, of which fourteen were administered by Assistant Government Agents.[1] Each Government Agent had sole charge of the principal district of his province, the seven districts thus controlled having a population of 1,540,000 as opposed to 1,219,678 in the remaining districts. The Government Agents were responsible to the Colonial Secretary, and exercised general supervision and control over their Assistant Government Agents. In addition to the Assistant Government Agents in charge of districts a junior civil servant with on the average nine years' service was attached to the head-quarters of each province with the rank of Assistant Government Agent. The principal duties of Government and Assistant Government Agents were to foster the prosperity of their districts, maintain law and order, and collect the revenue. While they controlled the village headmen, who had petty police powers, they had no authority over the police who were under the control of the Inspector-General of Police at Colombo. The ability of the Government Agents to repress lawlessness was apparently impaired since the divided control led to 'uncertainty as to the authority having jurisdiction in the matter'. Like the Indian District Officers the Government Agents were concerned with almost every phase of the Government's activities. The restoration and maintenance of irrigation works, the improvement of means of communication, the condition of the planting industry, the state of native agriculture—these were only a few of their manifold duties. In accordance with Maitland's regulations of 1808 each Assistant Government Agent was required to visit every part

---

[1] C.O. 54. 547: Nov. 6, 1882. The Government Agents, each of whom was assisted by an Assistant Government Agent, directly administered the Districts of Colombo, Kandy, Jaffna, Galle, Batticaloa, Kurunegala, and the North Central Province. This last comprised the Districts of Nuwarakalawiya and Tamankaduwa, the administrative centre being at Anuradhapura. The fourteen Districts under Assistant Government Agents were: *Western Province*: Kalutara, Negombo, Kegalla, Sabaragamuwa (or Ratnapura); *Southern Province*: Hambantota, Matara; *Eastern Province*: Trincomalee; *Northern Province*: Mullaittivu, Mannar, Vavuniya Vilankulam; *North-Western Province*: Puttalam; *Central Province*: Matale, Nuwara Eliya, and Badulla.

of his district at least once a year, about one hundred days being occupied by this duty. The Government Agent similarly made at least one annual tour of his whole province, and was consequently absent from his head-quarters for more than half the year.[1]

The judicial and executive powers were separated in all except 'four of the most outlying districts', Anuradhapura, Trincomalee, Vavuniya Vilankulam, and Mannar, where the Assistant Agents were also District Judges. The majority of the twelve District Judgeships and of the fifteen Police Magistracies continued to be held by civil servants in the ordinary course of promotion, with the exception of the District Judgeships of Colombo and Kandy, which since 1872 had been reserved for members of the Ceylon Bar. The District Judges were independent of the administrative service, and were under the control of the Supreme Court at Colombo.

Each Government and Assistant Government Agent had a large staff of native subordinates who formed an essential link between the civil servants and the people. The same grades existed as in the early days of British rule, with varying powers and duties from Maha Mudaliyars to village headmen. In 1881 the native officials numbered 208, with 34 presidents of Gansabhawas (minor native courts). The powers of the native officials were wide and important despite the curtailments of the preceding eighty years. The suspicion which had marked the attitude of Government during the first half of the century had by the 'seventies been replaced by a frank appreciation of their value as trusted and indispensable auxiliaries. The native officials were 'men of independent means, gentlemen by birth and manners . . . there is a career open as native Chiefs, the advantages of which are to be found not so much in salary as in power, in influence and in the respect of their countrymen. . . . [They are] gentlemen of high character . . . upon [whom] depends

---

[1] Public health, irrigation, and communications were under the control of the Medical and Public Works Departments which were independent of the Government Agents. Nevertheless the Agents were in close and constant touch with these matters, and their opinions carried great weight, since it was they who had the most intimate knowledge of their own provinces. On the whole the regulations in force in 1882 were merely a modernized version of Maitland's regulations of 1808 (Dickman, *C.C.S. Manual*, 1883 ed., 291–2).

the administration of the Government among the native population everywhere except in the great towns. They have a wide jurisdiction by positive enactments. They have yet a wider one by custom.' In the Kandyan provinces especially the inherited contempt for a man of low caste made it 'absolutely essential . . . that the Headman . . . be a pure Sinhalese of good family. A Burgher or a Jaffna Tamil' with a European education 'would be utterly unable to fulfil his duties'. The native officials 'exercise a power which may perhaps at rare intervals have been abused, but which is in the main used for the good of the people; and the maintenance of this power has done much to reconcile the people to British rule'.[1]

[1] C.O. 54. 531: Feb. 8, 1881.

VII

THE GOVERNOR OF CEYLON

THE office of Governor was established in 1798, when Ceylon was placed under the dual control of the Crown and the East India Company. The Governor was appointed by the Crown, but obeyed all orders received from the Directors or the Governor-General of India so long as these were consistent with the Cabinet's instructions. The Governor's dispatches were addressed either to the Court of Directors or to Dundas, the President of the Board of Control, these last being sent in the first instance to the Directors. The civil servants, of whom the majority were drawn from Madras, were 'entirely subject' to the Governor's orders. No Council was appointed, all legislative and executive power being vested in the Governor.[1]

In 1802 the authority of the East India Company was abolished, and Ceylon became a Crown Colony under the control of the Colonial Office. The new Instructions which were issued to Governor North in 1801 were similar to those of 1798 apart from the omission of all articles concerning the Company. Until 1828 the Governor held office during the royal pleasure, but after that date the term was limited to six years.[2] A Council

---

[1] C.O. 55. 61: Mar. 26, 1798: Dundas's Instructions to North; C.R. 52: May 5, 1798. For a fuller account v. chap. iv. The Governor had discretionary power in emergencies to act without awaiting the sanction of the East India Company. He was required to report all such occurrences at once to the Company.

[2] C.O. 54. 104: Feb. 20, 1829; *Parl. Pap. H.C.* 537 of 1836, vol. xxxix, May 31, 1828. On the death or absence of the Governor, the officer commanding the troops held a dormant commission as Lieutenant-Governor, e.g. C.O. 54. 40: July 16, 1811. After 1840 the post was usually held by the Colonial Secretary, although the officer commanding was occasionally appointed. Dormant commissions as Lieutenant-Governor were issued to successive Colonial Secretaries, viz. to P. Anstruther in 1840 (C.O. 381. 26: Dec. 7, 1840); to Sir J. E. Tennent in 1845 and 1849 (C.O. 381. 27: Aug. 8, 1845, and Mar. 20, 1849); and to Sir C. J. MacCarthy in 1851 (C.O. 381. 27: Jan. 2, 1851). In 1864–5 General O'Brien, the officer commanding, was Acting-Governor owing to the death of Governor MacCarthy (C.O. 54. 388–400: *passim*). In 1867 General Hodgson held office as Lieutenant-Governor during the Governor's absence, in accordance with the Secretary of State's ruling of the same year (C.O. 55. 115: Sept. 24, 1867). In 1872 H. T. Irving, the Colonial Secretary, was given a dormant commission as Lieutenant-Governor (C.O. 381. 28:

was established composed of the Governor, the Chief Justice, the officer commanding the Ceylon garrison, the Principal Secretary to Government, and two other officials appointed by the Governor. The Council was purely advisory, for while the Governor was expected to consult it on all matters of importance, he was not required to follow its advice. Legislative and executive power 'must remain, as it now is, vested in the Governor alone, subject to revision and confirmation at home'.[1]

The Governor had complete control over the civil servants, and could suspend them for misconduct pending the final decision of the Colonial Office. Appointments to the higher Civil Service were made by the Secretary of State; and while the Governor had power to promote civil servants his action was provisional until confirmed by the Colonial Office. With rare exceptions the Governor's promotions were ratified.[2] The supremacy of the civil over the military power was established by appointing the Governor Commander-in-Chief of the Ceylon forces.[3] The action of the executive was kept within legal

---

Jan. 9, 1872); and he held office in that capacity during the Governor's absence in 1872 and 1873, although the officer commanding the troops was then in Ceylon (C.O. 54. 485: Mar. 18, 1873). In 1873 the Colonial Office declined to appoint the officer commanding Lieutenant-Governor *ex officio*, since 'there are advantages in making the temporary administration a personal and not an *ex officio* appointment' (C.O. 54. 485: Mar. 12, 1873, C.O. Memos. and Draft Dispatch).

[1] C.O. 54. 5: Mar. 13, 1801; C.O. 55. 61: 1801: North's Instructions and Commission. Dissentient members of the Council could enter their reasons in the Minutes. The Governor had power to suspend or dismiss members pending the final decision of the Colonial Office. Insertions in pencil show that with some alterations the same Instructions were issued in 1813 to Sir Thomas Maitland as Governor of Malta.

[2] C.O. 55. 61: 1801: North's Instructions.

[3] *V*. chap. v, p. 50, n. 2; Mills, *Colonial Constitutions*, 367–8. The Governor's control over the military is limited to broad questions of policy, e.g. he gives general instructions 'for such military service as the safety and welfare of the Colony may appear to him to require'. He may not interfere in technical military matters, e.g. the maintenance of discipline. For all military details the officer commanding is solely responsible, although he must report his proceedings to the Governor, and must conform in every respect to the Governor's general instructions. 'The Governor is the single and supreme authority.... He is ... entitled to the obedience, aid and assistance of all military and civil officers; but although bearing the title of captain general or commander-in-chief and although he may be a military officer ... he is not, except on special appointment from His Majesty, invested with the command of His Majesty's regular forces in the Colony. He is therefore not entitled to ... take the immediate direction of any military operations, or except in cases of urgent necessity to

bounds by the Supreme Court, the judges of which were independent of the Ceylon Government, since they held office during good behaviour, and were appointed and dismissed by the Imperial Government. The Governor was answerable to them as well as to the English courts for breaches of the law. In the case of misconduct by the judges the Governor could make representations to the Colonial Office.[1]

While the power of the Governor was supreme in Ceylon he was subject to the complete control of the Colonial Office. In practice the Colonial Office usually confined its intervention to questions of general policy, leaving the details to be arranged by the Governor, who necessarily possessed a much fuller knowledge of local conditions. He must obey all instructions of the Secretary of State for the Colonies, and in matters of importance he must, if possible, postpone action until he had obtained the prior consent of the Colonial Office. He was forbidden to declare war except to repel invasion 'or in the event of unavoidable emergencies'. If an emergency arose the Governor had discretionary authority to take immediate action or even to disobey his instructions. The Colonial Office must be at once informed, and the measures taken were provisional until confirmed. Indirectly the Treasury exercised strong control, since its approval was required for all matters of finance. This control was greatly strengthened in the first half of the century by the very frequent occurrence of an annual deficit which was met by the Treasury. In consequence desirable and even necessary expenditure was often vetoed or at least postponed for fear of increasing the deficit. The Governor must issue signed warrants for the expenditure of all revenue, and must send annually a detailed account of revenue and expenditure to the Treasury.[2]

communicate officially with subordinate military officers' (Colonial Office, *Regulations for His Majesty's Colonial Service*, p. 6).

[1] Keith, *Constitution, Administration and Laws of the Empire*, 28–9. The normal procedure is to refer the Governor's charges for investigation to the Privy Council. The Governor had power to remit fines of less than £10 and to pardon minor offenders. In the case of heavier fines or of convictions for murder or treason the sentence could be suspended pending the decision of the Imperial Government (C.O. 55. 61: 1801: North's Commission and Instructions).

[2] C.O. 55. 61: 1801: North's Instructions; C.O. 54. 5: Mar. 13, 1801. V. chaps. v and vi for examples of the control exercised by the Colonial Office and the Treasury.

The Governor must also transmit to the Colonial Office 'upon all occasions . . . a particular account of all your proceedings and of the condition of affairs within your Government'. The Instructions which were issued to each Governor remained substantially unaltered from 1801 until 1831.[1] The Instructions to Governor Horton in that year were more detailed, but in other respects showed little change.[2] The Council could meet only when summoned by the Governor, and could discuss only such matters as he laid before it. Any member could enter in the Minutes his reasons for dissenting from the Governor, or for believing that any question should be considered or any Ordinance enacted.[3] While the Governor should usually refer all questions to the Council and accept their decision, he was empowered to overrule their opinion. In an emergency he could act without consulting the Council, but in such an event he should lay the question before them as soon as possible. All Ordinances were to be introduced by the Governor and enacted 'with the advice and consent of the said Council'. The Governor was forbidden to assent to legislation on a variety of subjects, of which the most important were Ordinances affecting the constitution of the Council, imposing any tax or duty on the trade or shipping of the United Kingdom, laws to which the royal assent had once been refused, unless express permission had first been obtained, and laws which diminished the revenue or prerogative of the Crown, or which altered the number or salary of Government officials, 'without Our special leave or consent therein first received'. No Ordinance could be enforced until it had received the royal assent, unless the delay would cause 'serious injury or inconvenience'; while unless the decision of the Crown was announced within two years from the date of enactment the Ordinance became null and void. The Crown reserved full power to confirm, reject, or amend all Ordinances. Horton's Instructions of 1831 gave

[1] C.O. 55. 62: Jan. 16, 1805: Maitland's Commission and Instructions; C.O. 55. 62: Nov. 4, 1820: Paget's Commission and Instructions. Accounts of revenue and expenditure were to be transmitted to England annually instead of semi-annually. Insertions in pencil show that the same Instructions were issued to Paget's successor, Sir E. Barnes.

[2] C.O. 55. 72: Instructions to Horton.

[3] The Governor must immediately send the Colonial Office full information regarding any disagreement.

fuller information as to the procedure required before the Governor could suspend from office any civil servant. The accused must be informed in writing of the charges against him and be called upon to make a written defence, while both documents must be sent to the Colonial Office immediately.[1]

The Supplementary Instructions to Governor Horton in 1833 established what has been called the classical form of Crown Colony Government.[2] During the period from 1802 to 1833 the Governor had exercised his legislative and executive powers with the advice of a Council composed entirely of officials. After 1833 the Council, renamed the Executive Council, continued to advise him on all questions connected with the executive government of the island, but its legislative powers were transferred to a Legislative Council which contained a minority of unofficial members. The Instructions of 1833 made no other changes of importance, although they defined the Governor's powers in somewhat greater detail than formerly.

No change was made in the Governor's powers of control over the civil servants. Any appointment to office made by him was provisional until the decision of the Crown was announced. The Governor had power to suspend any civil servant from the performance of his duties; but only the Colonial Office could dismiss him from the Service. Before any official was suspended the Governor must inform him in writing of the charges against him, must call upon him to make a written defence, and must lay the case before the Executive Council.[3] All the evidence must then be sent to the Colonial Office for final decision. In the very few instances where the

---

[1] 'For the further discouragement of Vice and encouragement of Virtue and Good Living', the Governor was forbidden to appoint to Government service any 'whose ill fame and conversation may occasion scandal'.

[2] *Parl. Pap. H.C.* 698 of 1833, vol. xxvi: Mar. 19 and 20, 1833.

[3] C.O. 381. 27: Mar. 8, 1855. The Instructions to Governor Ward, which were repeated in all subsequent Instructions, required that the full evidence must be submitted to the Executive Council, and their opinions entered in the Minutes. While suspension was the normal procedure, the Governor might interdict an officer from the performance of his duties pending the final decision of the Crown. This could be done 'if in any case the interests of Our Service shall appear to you to demand that a person shall cease to exercise the powers and functions of his office instantly, or before there shall be time to take the proceedings herein before directed'.

Governor suspended a civil servant; the Colonial Office appears carefully to have reviewed the evidence.

The Colonial Office Regulations supplemented the information given in the Instructions as to the Governor's power of appointment and dismissal. Appointments to the minor Government posts were very largely in the hands of the Governor. When the initial annual salary was £100 or less the Governor had full power of appointment. When the initial annual salary was between £100 and £300 the Governor made a provisional appointment and recommended his candidate to the Colonial Office, which usually accepted his choice. When the initial annual salary exceeded £300, in other words in the higher Civil Service, the Governor might either recommend a candidate or make a provisional appointment, at the same time apprising the appointee that the position was temporary until the Colonial Office had made its decision. The Colonial Office had the right to make a different appointment, although in practice it usually confirmed the Governor's selection. Practically all the appointments in the first two classes were clerical and other minor positions, while positions with a salary of over £300 were in the administrative and judicial Civil Service. The Governor had full power to dismiss the minor officials whose salary was less than £100 without the confirmation of the Colonial Office. The only requirement was that the accused be informed of the charges and given a hearing before the Governor and the head of his department. Officials whose appointment had been made or confirmed by the Colonial Office could be suspended by the Governor and the Executive Council, pending the final decision of the Colonial Office.[1]

The Executive (formerly the sole) Council was composed of the Governor, the officer commanding the troops, the Colonial or Principal Secretary, the Queen's Advocate, the Treasurer, and the Government Agent of the Central Province, all of whom were members of the Legislative Council.[2] The Executive

---

[1] Colonial Office, *Regulations for H.M. Col. Service*, 11–12. pp. 8–20 give a brief summary of the Governor's Instructions. Dickman, *Ceylon Civil Service Manual*, 1883 ed., 187–90.

[2] C.O. 381.26: Jan. 9, 1840. In 1840 the Auditor-General replaced the Government Agent of the Central Province. In 1841 the Colonial Office directed that when the officer commanding the troops was Acting Governor

Council was to meet when summoned by the Governor 'to consult with and advise you upon any question connected with the Executive Government of Our said Island which may by you be proposed for their consideration'. As hitherto the Governor was required to consult them on all matters, save when these were too trivial or too urgent to admit of delay. In the latter case the Governor must inform the Council of his action and of the reasons for it.[1] The Governor had power in all cases to reject the advice of the Council, but he must then send a full report of the circumstances to the Colonial Office. Three members formed a quorum, and the Minutes were to be sent to the Colonial Office bi-yearly. The Council was purely an advisory body, which gave its opinion on such questions only as the Governor laid before it.

The Legislative Council was composed of nine official and six unofficial members nominated by the Governor from amongst the principal natives and European colonists of Ceylon. The appointments of unofficial members were subject to confirmation by the Secretary of State, while they held office during the King's pleasure, which in practice meant until they resigned.[2]

his place in the Legislative and Executive Councils should be taken by the next senior officer of the garrison (C.O. 381. 26: Jan. 15, 1841). In 1883 the title of Queen's Advocate was changed to that of Attorney-General (C.O. 54. 549: Nov. 3, 1883).

[1] C.O. 55. 81: May 31, 1841. 'There will be some instances of confidential correspondence with Her Majesty's Government which will not safely admit of their intervention.' Governor Robinson's Instructions in 1865 directed that the Governor need not consult the Executive Council on questions 'of such a nature that in your judgment Our Service would sustain material prejudice by consulting the said Council thereon' (C.O. 381. 28: Mar. 4, 1865).

[2] The native members were required to speak English, while colonists must have lived at least two years in Ceylon. Governor Horton nominated three burgher and native members in 1835, but he did not appoint the three European members until 1837 owing to the difficulty of finding suitable candidates. Owing to the delay the colonists accused Horton of despotism, and when appointed refused to serve. The native members already appointed would take precedence over them; while they also demanded that the number of official and unofficial members be made equal. This is the first instance of the demand for popular control of the Legislative Council. The colonists in 1834 declared that the acts of the Legislative Council were illegal since its membership was incomplete, but the Colonial Office refused to agree. The Colonial Office supported the Governor, and in 1837 the European members gave up their opposition and took their seats in the Council. C.O. 54. 131: Nov. 23, 1833; Mar. 8 and Aug. 1834; C.O. 54. 135: Apr. 17 and Sept. 5, 1834; C.O. 54. 140: Feb. 24 and June 26, 1835; C.O. 54. 141: Jan. 14 and July 15, 1835;

H

The official members were the officer commanding the troops, the Colonial Secretary, the Chief Justice,[1] the Auditor-General, the Treasurer, the Government Agents of the Western and Central Provinces, the Surveyor-General, and the Collector of Customs at Colombo. The President of the Council, who had both an original and a casting vote, was the Governor or in his absence the senior official present. Seven members constituted a quorum, and questions were decided by the vote of the majority.

Ordinances were passed by the Governor 'with the advice and consent of the said Legislative Council', the Executive Council being deprived of its legislative power. All Ordinances and subjects for debate must be introduced by the Governor, although any member could enter in the Minutes his reasons for wishing to propose any Bill or debate any question. 'A full and exact copy of the Minutes' was sent to the Colonial Office semi-annually. The Governor had power to veto all legislation; while he was also forbidden to propose or assent to Bills on a variety of subjects, of which the more important were Ordinances: (1) affecting the constitution of the Legislative Council— the Council was thus debarred from increasing its own power; (2) making grants of money, land, &c., to the Governor or to any member of the Council; (3) 'whereby any increase or diminution might be made in the number, allowance or salary of any Public officers . . . without Our special leave or command therein first received'; (4) imposing any new rate or duty which would in any way lessen the Crown's revenue or prerogative;[2] (5) reintroducing Ordinances 'to which Our assent has once been refused without express leave for that purpose first obtained from Us'; (6) hindering any form of religious worship

C.O. 54. 146: Jan. 8, 9, and 18, 1836; C.O. 54. 147: Feb. 10 and 11, and Mar. 17, 1836; C.O. 54. 154: Feb. 11 and July 24, 1837; *Colombo Observer*, Feb. 14, 1834.

[1] C.O. 55. 79: May 18, 1838. In 1838 the Chief Justice was replaced by the Queen's Advocate, so that the Ceylon practice was brought into conformity with the one which prevailed in most of the Crown Colonies.

[2] C.O. 381. 28: Mar. 4, 1865. The Instructions to Governor Robinson substituted the following clause: 'Any Ordinance of an extraordinary nature and importance, whereby Our prerogative or the rights and property of Our Subjects not residing in Our said Island, or the trade and shipping of Our United Kingdom and its Dependencies may be prejudiced.'

conducted 'in a peaceable and orderly manner';[1] (7) 'by which persons not being of European birth or descent might be subjected or made liable to any disabilities or restrictions to which persons of European birth or descent would not be also subjected'. In addition to these definite restrictions the Governors always adhered to the principle that no important or novel legislation should be introduced without the previous consent of the Secretary of State. The Crown reserved full power to confirm, amend, or reject all Ordinances, which were suspended pending its decision with the exception of the annual supply ordinances. An Ordinance might, however, be provisionally enforced when the delay 'would be productive of serious injury or inconvenience'. Any Ordinance was 'deemed to be disallowed' if the Crown's decision were not announced within three years from the date of enactment.[2] Although the unofficial minority of the Council could speak and vote freely, legislation remained under the control of the Governor and ultimately of the Colonial Office. The function of the Legislative Council was advisory: it enabled the Governor to gauge popular feeling.

Few changes were made in the Governor's Instructions after 1833, with the exception of those which have been already noted.[3] In 1847 the Colonial Office directed that all Ordinances should be provisionally enforced from the date of promulgation by the Governor, instead of remaining in abeyance pending the final decision of the Crown.[4] An important change was made in 1860 which abolished the Governor's control of subjects for debate in the Legislative Council. Henceforth any member

[1] C.O. 55. 61: 1801. North's and all the subsequent Instructions granted complete religious freedom to all, 'provided they can be contented with a quiet and peaceable enjoyment of the same without giving offence or scandal to Government'.

[2] To enable opponents to present their case every proposed Ordinance must be published in the Government Gazette 'for at least three weeks next before the enactment thereof'. 'Due notice' of all private Bills must be given to all those affected, while 'a full and impartial examination' must 'take place of the grounds upon which the same may be proposed or resisted'.

[3] The Governors' Commissions and Instructions from 1833 to 1872 are given in: C.O. 381. 26: Apr. 20, 1837; May 18 and July 2, 1838 (Mackenzie); Jan. 15, 1841 (Campbell); C.O. 381. 27: Mar. 27, 1847; Mar. 13, 1848 (Torrington); Sept. 24, 1850 (Anderson); Mar. 8, 1855 (Ward); Aug. 28, 1860 (MacCarthy); C.O. 381. 28: Mar. 4, 1865 (Robinson); Jan. 8, 1872 (Gregory).

[4] C.O. 381. 27: June 28, 1847.

could propose any Bill or question for debate which was not concerned with finance. No Ordinance or resolution could be passed and no question debated the object of which was 'to dispose of or charge any part of Our revenue', unless the Governor himself introduced the proposal or authorized it.[1]

The official majority in the Legislative Council was one of the most important means by which the Governor could control legislation. In theory he could require their support on measures which he considered essential, but in practice his control over their votes was not altogether absolute and varied at different periods. The question was first raised by Governor Sir R. Wilmot-Horton in 1837. He wrote that all Bills were drafted by the Governor, the Colonial Secretary, and the Queen's Advocate, and were then discussed by the Executive before they were submitted to the Legislative Council. Any member was free to oppose the measure and enter his protest in the Minutes. The question that perplexed the Governor was how far the same unfettered liberty could be allowed to the official majority when the Bill was debated by the Legislative Council. 'Very considerable difference of opinion' on this point prevailed in the Executive Council, but Horton had 'never felt any serious *practical* inconvenience from that independence on the part of the Executive members of the Legislative Council which has been assumed and acted upon by them as their undoubted right'.[2] The Colonial Office considered that it was impossible to lay down a universal rule: much would depend on the circumstances of the particular case. 'Generally speaking', all nine official members should be permitted to speak and vote freely in the Legislative Council. On rare occasions, 'involving the main principles upon which the administration of the Colony is conducted . . . it may be expedient that the Governor should have it in his power to require the resignation, or even to proceed to the suspension of any public officer who may be unwilling . . . to support him. . . . But this . . . is a very extreme case, and . . . the utmost reserve will be necessary in resorting to the exercise of such a power.'[3]

[1] C.O. 381. 27: Aug. 28, 1860.   [2] C.O. 54. 153: Jan. 23, 1837.
[3] C.O. 54. 153: June 27, 1837: C.O. Draft Dispatch and Memo. dictated by J. S. (Sir James Stephen?). Marginal notes show that the draft dispatch

The question again rose in 1841, and the Secretary of State laid down the rule that in non-essentials 'the utmost freedom of debate' might be allowed the official members of the Legislative Council. However, 'when the question in debate is one in which the character or the general policy of the local government may be at stake, or when it is one which the Governor himself regards as affecting the reputation or the successful conduct of his Government', the Legislative Councillors who were also members of the Executive Council must support the Governor's measure at least 'by a silent acquiescence or by neutrality'. A member who refused even this tacit support must 'withdraw from the Legislature by resigning the office in respect of which he is a member of it':[1] in other words, he must resign from the Civil Service. In 1848 the Secretary of State directed that while official members of the Legislative Council must vote for all measures which the Governor considered 'necessary', they were 'entitled as well as the unofficial to express their opinion upon all subjects with the utmost freedom. . . . If they should altogether disapprove of them it would in my opinion be their duty to enable him to pass them upon his own responsibility, recording by a Minute, if they should deem it requisite, the objections which they might entertain.'[2]

This decision failed to settle the question, for Sir William Anderson, who was Governor from 1850 to 1855, frequently complained that he was 'powerless and yet responsible'. Owing to the revenue deficit he stringently curtailed the expenditure upon roads, and his measures of economy were frequently opposed by the unofficial members of the Legislative Council. Many official members refused to support the policy 'previously determined in the Executive' Council. 'In theory they are bound to support the Government, but . . . they can always offer . . . the tacit resistance of not voting, and the Governor must then often be in a minority, and the measures of Government be lost.'[3] The difficulty was solved by Anderson's

was never sent to Ceylon, since 'there is always some risk and rarely much advantage in handling questions, . . . with so little practical bearing'.

[1] C.O. 55. 81: May 31, 1841.
[2] C.O. 54. 247: Mar. 8, 1848; C.O. 55. 89: May 18, 1848.
[3] C.O. 54. 314: Jan. 13, 1855: the Memorandum of H. M. (Herman Merivale?)

successor, Sir Henry Ward. He came to an understanding with the five officials who were members of both Councils 'that after a measure has been fully discussed amongst themselves, as is always the case', they must all vote for it in the Legislative Council. Considerably greater latitude was allowed to the four remaining official members: the Governor did not consider that he had 'any other claim to their support than that which the merits of the measure proposed may give me. This system works most satisfactorily.'[1]

The liberty accorded by Ward to the four officials who were not members of the Executive Council was subsequently curtailed. In 1875 the Governor reported that 'at present the understanding is that unless an intimation be given the official members shall on all occasions vote with the Government'.[2] In this year the Colombo Chamber of Commerce petitioned the Secretary of State that 'the official members may be permitted on *all* occasions to vote in accordance with their private opinions'.[3] The Secretary of State rejected the petition, since 'the essence of the present system is to leave the sole responsibility for all action both in legislative and administrative matters in the hands of the Governor, subject to the control of the Secretary of State'. 'The demand is for an alteration of what really is the essence of a Crown Colony—namely that the votes of the Official Members must be considered as at the disposal of the Governor. . . . The Unofficial minority does all that is required, or can be permitted, by resisting and calling attention to anything which the public may deem objectionable in the Government Policy.'[4] In spite of this decision the Governor informed the Colonial Office in 1884 that even with 'the sternest

supported the Governor: 'The unofficials, with very little aid from the official ranks, can always overpower the Governor, who cannot make a "cabinet question" of every discussion on the estimates.' The majority of the unofficial members represent the small European mercantile community, 'and their object seems invariably to be "economy", except in those items of expenditure which tell for their own immediate purposes'. C.O. 54. 344: June 7, 1859.

[1] C.O. 54. 344: June 7, 1859.   [2] C.O. 54. 497: June 19, 1875.

[3] C.O. 54. 497: May 13, 1875. The petition apparently referred only to the four officials who were not members of the Executive Council: the Chamber of Commerce seems to have conceded that the five who were members of both Councils could not 'stultify themselves by opposing measures they had themselves prepared' (C.O. 54. 497: June 19, 1875).

[4] C.O. 54. 497: Aug. 24, 1875: C.O. Draft Dispatch and Memos.

use of official obligations' he could not entirely count on the votes of the two Government Agents in the Legislative Council. They 'have been accustomed to exercise a certain independence of judgment in their votes, and are not regarded as being bound by the same strict obligations as their colleagues who are also members of the Executive Council'.[1] In 1910 the rule was that while officials who were members of both Councils must support Government measures or resign from the Civil Service, the other official members 'have a larger liberty, but may be called on to support the government or to resign their seats as members of Council, but not necessarily their departmental office'.[2]

The European colonists and the burghers were far from content with the minor role assigned to the unofficial members of the Legislative Council, and they periodically made vain attempts to limit the Governor's power. The natives of Ceylon appear to have taken little or no part in the movement. The agitation was spasmodic, usually coinciding with periods when the coffee industry was in difficulties, or when the Governor's expenditure upon means of communication was less than the merchants and planters demanded. The serious decline of the coffee industry between 1848 and 1853 resulted in numerous demands for reform. A petition to the House of Commons complained that the taxes were excessive, the civil servants overpaid and inefficient, the roads in need of repair, and the unofficial members of the Legislative Council rendered powerless by the official majority. The petitioners begged that the number of the unofficial members be increased, and that they be empowered to originate Bills and subjects for debate. Other petitions demanded that the Crown Colony form of government be abolished and replaced by responsible government.[3] The fundamental cause of the agitation appears to have been economic: owing to the heavy deficits the Government had limited

[1] C.O. 54. 552: Mar. 30, 1884.
[2] Bruce, *Broad Stone of Empire*, i. 231.
[3] C.O. 54. 251: Oct. 3, 1848; C.O. 55. 89: May 18, 1848; C.O. 55. 93: July 4, 1851; C.O. 55. 98: Feb. 23, 1856. Doctor Elliott, the editor of the *Colombo Observer*, was one of the leaders of the agitation, and sent several petitions to the Secretary of State asking for the establishment of responsible government. He demanded that natives be given the franchise, maintaining that their total ignorance of parliamentary government was no impediment, e.g. C.O. 54. 251: Oct. 16, 1848; C.O. 54. 314: Jan. 13, 1855. -

its expenditure upon the maintenance and construction of roads in the coffee districts. The European merchants and planters were profoundly dissatisfied, and demanded a popular majority in the Legislative Council in order to control the budget and increase the appropriations.[1] The revival of the coffee industry about 1853 was reflected in a large and increasing revenue surplus, and the Government was enabled rapidly to develop the system of roads. 'The change was magical', and no more was heard of the attacks on the form of government.[2]

In 1855 the Governor, Sir Henry Ward, introduced a modified form of election for the three European unofficial members of the Legislative Council. 'Finding that there were two bodies with a sort of permanent organization—the Chamber of Commerce in Colombo, and the Planters' Association—which might perform the functions of a constituency, I have constantly delegated to them the right of selecting their own member', subject to what was in practice the nominal confirmation of the Colonial Office. The three unofficial members who represented the Sinhalese, Tamils, and burghers continued to be nominated by the Governor.[3]

Demands for popular control of the Legislative Council were again made by the colonists and burghers in 1859, but they were strongly opposed by the Governor and the Colonial Office. Sir Henry Ward wrote that 'in a Colony the population of which consists of seven or eight thousand European settlers, a small though intelligent class of Burghers, and two million of Cinghalese, Tamils and Moormen, wholly unaccustomed to the working of a constitutional system, you cannot introduce the principle of Representative and Responsible Government as it is applied in Canada . . . the Crown for many years must hold the balance between European and native interests, if it wish to see order maintained and legislation impartially conducted'. Furthermore the burghers, who outnumbered the Europeans, possessed 'neither the respect nor the affection of the natives . . . if you

---

[1] C.O. 54. 317: Oct. 25–30, 1855.   [2] C.O. 54. 344: June 7, 1859.
[3] C.O. 54. 344: June 7, 1859; C.O. 54. 318: Nov. 15, 1855. In 1889 two additional unofficial members were added, one to represent the Moormen, and one the Kandyan Sinhalese. The Colonial Office also directed that henceforth unofficial members were to hold office only for three years, but were eligible for reappointment (*Governors' Addresses to the Legislative Council*, iii. 327).

value the peace of Ceylon you must never give these gentlemen a preponderance in the Legislative Council. That is their present object.'[1] As a result of the agitation the Governor, with the somewhat reluctant assent of the Colonial Office, gave unofficial members the right to introduce Bills.[2]

The constitutional issue was revived in 1864 in connexion with the question of Ceylon's military expenditure. During the first half of the century the expenditure had very frequently exceeded the revenue, the deficit being met by the Imperial Treasury. After about 1853 the prosperity of the coffee industry transformed the financial situation, and by 1864 the annual surplus of revenue had increased to £100,000. The colony was able to pay the whole expense of its civil administration, and gradually to increase its annual contribution towards the cost of its defence. By 1864 the annual cost of the Ceylon garrison was about £200,000, of which the island paid £100,000.[3] For many years the amount of the annual military contribution had been a standing cause of contention, the colonists protesting that it was excessive, and the Imperial Government complaining that it was insufficient.[4] In 1861 Parliament held an inquiry and passed a resolution that the cost of a colonial garrison should, whenever possible, be borne by the colony, unless the troops were maintained there for Imperial and not for local needs. Ceylon was referred to 'more particularly' as quite able to bear the cost of its defence.[5]

As a result of this resolution the Secretary of State in 1864 instructed the Governor that Ceylon must henceforth pay for

[1] C.O. 54. 344: June 7, 1859; C.O. 54. 361: July 30 and Oct. 20, 1861. Ferguson, *Pioneers of the Planting Enterprise in Ceylon*, 75 and 79. The revival of the agitation was largely the work of Wall and Lorenz, respectively the representatives of the Planters' Association and of the burghers. The collapse of the Government plans for building a railway from Colombo to Kandy was also responsible for reviving the constitutional question.

[2] C.O. 55. 103: Jan. 4, 1860. The Governor was censured by the Colonial Office for taking so important a step without first obtaining permission.

[3] C.O. 55. 110: Sept. 26, 1864. In 1864 the garrison numbered about 1,000 European and 1,500 Indian and Malay troops.

[4] From 1838 Ceylon was required to pay annually £24,000 to the Imperial Treasury as a contribution towards the cost of its defence. C.O. 54. 172: Sept. 2, 1839; *Parl. Pap. H.C.* 414 of 1851, vol. xxxv; C.O. 54. 265: Dec. 13, 1849; C.O. 55. 93: Jan. 20 and July 4, 1851; C.O. 54. 281: Feb. 2, 1852; C.O. 55. 98: Feb. 23, 1856; C.O. 54. 367: Feb. 13, 1862.

[5] C.O. 55. 110: Sept. 26, 1864.

the whole of its military expenditure. He agreed with the colonists that the amount could be reduced, and to this end he proposed to appoint a Commission of Inquiry composed partly of officials and partly of Europeans in Ceylon. The amount of the annual military expenditure would be determined by Parliament in accordance with the Commission's report, and would be charged upon the revenues of Ceylon by a permanent Ordinance of the Legislative Council. The Commission's report, however, would not be available for several years, and in the meanwhile the Treasury could not be expected to pay £100,000 annually when Ceylon had a yearly surplus of the same amount. The Legislative Council was therefore to pass a provisional Ordinance by which the annual military contribution of Ceylon would be increased from £100,000 to £135,000 pending the final settlement. Until that date the remainder of the military expenditure would continue to be borne by the Treasury. When the permanent Ordinance was passed 'the existing practice of making payments out of the Ceylon revenue by simple direction of the Secretary of State will be discontinued . . . and Legislative enactment in future required for all expenditure whatever'.[1] In 1848 the Secretary of State, Earl Grey, had laid down the abstract principle that the budget ought to be controlled by the Legislative Council, but he had not conferred this right upon it as the colonists and burghers asserted.[2]

The Secretary of State had chosen a most unpropitious time for his proposals, because both Europeans and burghers were incensed at the policy of economy in road construction which had been followed since 1861. The Governor, Sir Charles Mac-

[1] C.O. 55. 110: Sept. 26, 1864.

[2] C.O. 55. 110: Sept. 26, 1864. Until 1838 the budget was not submitted to the Legislative Council, but after that date the Council was empowered to criticize and partially to revise it (C.O. 55. 79: Sept. 16, 1838). The fixed civil and military expenditure received its validity solely from the orders of the Secretary of State, only the annual contingent expenditure requiring the sanction of the Council. Earl Grey instructed the Governor that the control of the budget would be given to the Legislative Council, but only *after* the passage of 'an Ordinance permanently charging upon the revenue of the Colony the fixed expenses' both civil and military (C.O. 55. 89: July 17, 1848). In 1858–9 a permanent Ordinance was passed by the Council for the annual payment of the civil expenditure, but the military expenditure was not similarly provided for. In ordering the passage of a permanent military Ordinance in 1864, the Secretary of State was fulfilling the conditions laid down by Grey as a necessary preliminary to surrendering the control of the budget.

Carthy, had curtailed the expenditure in order to finance the construction of the railway from Colombo to Kandy. He was charged with failing to build new roads in the coffee districts, and with allowing existing roads to fall into disrepair. The annual surplus of £100,000 was the result of his 'generally parsimonious policy', and should be devoted to road construction or to reducing taxation. A large part of the garrison was maintained for Imperial and not for local needs, and therefore should continue to be paid for by the Treasury. The colonists grudged the expenditure upon the troops, since it decreased the funds available for means of communication. They declared that they were willing to pay their fair share of the military expenses, but they insisted that the Legislative Council alone should determine the amount. As to the Secretary of State's offer to place the budget under the Council's control in return for the permanent Ordinance, this 'acknowledged right' had been granted by Earl Grey in 1848, and systematically violated ever since.[1]

The colonists' discontent reached a climax unprecedented in the decorous proceedings of the Legislative Council: owing to

[1] C.O. 54. 367: Feb. 13, 1862; C.O. 54. 377: July 4, 1863; C.O. 54. 378: *passim*; C.O. 54. 388: Apr. 5, 1864; C.O. 54. 392: Aug. 30, 1864; C.O. 54. 394: Nov. 30, 1864; C.O. 55. 110: Sept. 26, 1864; Feb. 27 and Mar. 27, 1865; Digby, *Morgan*, i. 263–83; Mellor, *The Case of Ceylon, passim*. The Acting Governor, General O'Brien, reported in 1864 that on a recent tour of Ceylon he had found the roads in a 'sad state'. Between 1860 and 1863 MacCarthy accumulated a surplus revenue of £525,505, of which £106,198 came from sums voted but not expended upon public works (C.O. 54. 394: Nov. 30, 1864). The Secretary of State considered that General O'Brien's strictures referred only to particular roads and not to the whole island. MacCarthy had spent over £500,000 on public works from 1860 to 1863, a slightly larger amount than that of his predecessor, Ward, who had been universally praised by the colonists for his liberality in road construction (C.O. 55. 110: Mar. 27, 1865). Admittedly MacCarthy had practised strict economy at the orders of the Colonial Office, to accumulate a surplus which would meet all possible expenses for the construction of the Colombo–Kandy railway. It appears impossible to decide how true the charges were that the roads had fallen into serious disrepair. The official policy was to pay off the whole cost of building the railway in about twelve years, while the colonists wished the repayment to be extended over a much longer period, 'so that it might be shared by those who are to succeed them' (C.O. 54. 392: Aug. 30, 1864). One is inclined to suspect that the administration carried retrenchment too far, so that the colonists had ground for complaint. It would also seem that the colonists were unreasonable: they insisted on the railway and at the same time objected to any economies which accompanied it.

the absence of several official members the unofficials found themselves in a majority and passed a vote of censure on the Government.[1] This 'snap division' had no effect upon the outcome, and the Ordinance embodying the Secretary of State's instructions was passed by the official majority of the Council.[2] On November 15, 1864, the six unofficial members resigned in protest against these 'unconstitutional', 'unworthy, and humiliating' proceedings. On the advice of the Executive Council the Governor refused to accept the resignations.[3] The Colonial Office was informed by its legal advisers that the resignations did not affect the validity of the Ordinance, since they were not accepted by the Governor. To remove all doubts, however, an Order in Council was passed on March 9, 1865, that the absence of some of the members did not affect the validity of any Ordinance passed by a Legislative Council.[4]

Great indignation was aroused amongst colonists and burghers, and in 1865 they formed the Ceylon League to obtain an unofficial majority in the Legislative Council, and thus gain popular control of the budget. For several years the League carried on a vigorous agitation in Ceylon and England, but the Colonial Office refused to give way. In 1868-9 the League 'as good as collapsed altogether' owing to the rapid development of the coffee plantations. The increase in prosperity was due in considerable measure to Governor Robinson's large expenditure upon roads.[5]

Meanwhile the Commission of Inquiry into Ceylon's military expenditure was appointed in 1865,[6] and it unanimously reported that the annual cost of the garrison could be reduced from £200,000 to about £160,000. The Colonial Office approved

---

[1] C.O. 54. 392: Aug. 30, 1864. [2] C.O. 54. 400: Jan. 9, 1865.
[3] C.O. 54. 394: Nov. 30, 1864.
[4] C.O. 55. 110: Mar. 27, 1865; C.O. 381. 28: Mar. 9, 1865: Order in Council, applying to Ceylon, Mauritius, Malta, Trinidad, and St. Lucia.
[5] C.O. 54. 432: Feb. 12, 1868; C.O. 54. 433: Mar. 21 and Apr. 4 and 5, 1868; C.O. 54. 434: Apr. 20, 1868; *Parl. Pap. H.C.* 39 of 1867, vol. xlviii; Digby, *Morgan*, i. 322-3; ii. 39-49; Ferguson, *Pioneers of the Planting Enterprise*, i. 82-3.
[6] C.O. 54. 402: June 28, 1865. The Commission was composed of three Ceylon civil servants, three military officers, and three colonists (Colonel Byrde, a leading coffee planter; Wise, the President of the Colombo Chamber of Commerce; and Smith, the Ceylon representative of the important Ceylon Company).

the report, and directed that Ceylon should pay £150,000 in 1867, and £160,000 thereafter. At the end of seven years the Imperial Government would reconsider the amount of the colony's military expenditure. In 1867 a permanent Ordinance was passed to this effect by the Legislative Council, and the Colonial Office surrendered its control of the budget.[1]

This concession did not seriously affect the Governor's control of the Legislative Council. Subject always to the ultimate authority of the Colonial Office, the final decision in legislation and administration lay with him, although his policy was frequently based upon the advice given by the Executive or Legislative Councils. 'In a Crown Colony such as Ceylon . . . the powers of the Governor constitute a paternal despotism, modified only by the distant authority of the Queen. The functions of his councils are consultative, but the adoption or rejection of their recommendations rests exclusively with himself.'[2] Responsibility was never divorced from power, and the Colonial Office held him solely accountable for every act of his Government. 'So long as a Colony remains a Crown Colony the Governor is really the only person responsible. If things go well, however ably supported he may be by his Executive he gets the credit of success; if things go ill, however badly supported he may be, he gets the discredit of failure.'[3] While the situation in Ceylon itself remained essentially unchanged throughout the century, the Governor's relations with the Colonial Office underwent important modifications owing to the development of steamships and ocean cables. During the earlier decades of British rule about twelve months often elapsed before a reply was received to a dispatch: and it was therefore necessary to entrust the Governor with a considerable measure of

[1] C.O. 55. 110: Sept. 19, 1865; C.O. 55. 112: Aug. 27 and Nov. 3, 1866; C.O. 55. 115: Apr. 4 and Nov. 26, 1867; C.O. 55. 117: Mar. 1 and 31, 1869; C.O. 54. 406: Dec. 13, 1865; C.O. 54. 417: Dec. 13, 1866; C.O. 54. 425: May 28, 1867. In 1874 Ceylon's military expenditure was lessened by disbanding the Ceylon Rifles, a Malay corps raised at the beginning of the century (C.O. 54. 485: Apr. 16, 1873; C.O. 54. 487: Sept. 3, 1873; C.O. 54. 494: Sept. 12, 1874). The Ceylon Government urged strongly that even the reduced garrison was excessive, and in 1884 the annual military expenditure was decreased to Rs. 600,000 (C.O. 54. 552: Feb. 4 and 15, and Mar. 30, 1884; C.O. 54. 553 and 554: *passim*).

[2] Tennent, *Ceylon*, ii. 167.

[3] C.O. 54. 497: June 19, 1875.

discretionary power in carrying out the policies laid down by the Secretary of State. Rapidity and ease of communication greatly increased the Colonial Office's power of control, and led to more interference in matters of detail. On the whole the 'stronger and more continuous control' tended to diminish the Governor's independence and self-reliance. The control, however, was 'more intelligent', and was based upon 'better and more sympathetic knowledge of local conditions'. This was due to modern means of communication which gave the Colonial Office a knowledge that was 'far fuller, more accurate, and more up-to-date than was available in old days'.[1]

The legal supremacy of the Governor involved a certain risk to the interests of Ceylon, since at the beginning of his term of office his knowledge of conditions was necessarily limited. The danger was increased by the practice of appointing a new Governor every six years. With a few exceptions, however, he had had previous experience in the administration of other colonies, while the control of the Colonial Office tended strongly to make for continuity of policy. Furthermore, the Governor could always obtain advice from his Executive and Legislative Councils, which had a full knowledge of Ceylon's problems. Despite his legal supremacy, in practice he was guided to a considerable extent by the advice of his Councils.

The colonists were more powerful than the unofficial minority in the Legislative Council would indicate. The complete freedom of the press enabled them to make known their wishes or to criticize the administration—a weapon which never suffered from disuse. Any inhabitant of Ceylon could freely petition the Secretary of State, while questions in Parliament were a check upon the Governor. Since the trade and plantations of Ceylon were to a large extent controlled by financial interests in Great Britain, the colonists could count upon powerful support at home in their contests with the colonial administration. Moreover, while the Colonial Office would naturally tend to support the Governor, constant friction between him and the unofficial members of Council might create a suspicion of tactlessness and lack of discretion which would militate against his chances of

---

[1] Lucas, *Oxford Survey of the British Empire*, vi. 22–6; Bruce, *Broad Stone of Empire*, i. 181–91, and 221–3; Ireland, *Far Eastern Tropics*, 36.

promotion. To be successful the Governor had to gain the co-
operation of the natives and the colonists.[1]

Under the conditions of the nineteenth century the Crown
Colony form of government was inevitable. 'The principal bar
to the establishment of representative governments in Colonies
is their being inhabited by a population of which a large
proportion is not of European race, and has not made such
progress in civilization as to be capable of exercising with
advantage the privileges of self-government. Of such colonies
Ceylon affords the best example. The great majority of its
inhabitants are Asiatics . . . having the character and habits of
mind which have from the earliest times prevented popular
governments from taking root and flourishing among the nations
of the East. Amidst a large population of this description there
are settled, for the most part as temporary residents engaged
in commerce or agriculture, a mere handful of Europeans. . . . In
such a Colony the establishment of representative institutions
would be in the highest degree inexpedient. If they were established in such a form as to confer power upon the great body
of the people . . . the experiment would be attended with great
danger, or rather with the certainty of failure. If on the other
hand the system of representation were so contrived as to ex-
clude the bulk of the native population from real power, in
order to vest it in the hands of the European minority, an
exceedingly narrow oligarchy would be created—a form of
government which experience certainly does not show to be
favourable to the welfare of the governed. . . . It can hardly be
supposed that narrow views of class interests would not exercise
greater influence in the legislation of the colony than a comprehensive consideration of the general good. To anticipate [this
result] . . . implies no unfavourable opinion of the character
and intelligence of the European inhabitants of Ceylon, but
only a belief that they would act as men placed in such a
situation have generally been found to do.'[2] The only alternative

---

[1] Bruce, *Broad Stone of Empire*, i. 224; Grey, *Colonial Policy of Lord John
Russell's Administration*, i. 29. All petitions to the Secretary of State must
be sent to the Governor, who was required to forward them to the Colonial
Office. This rule enabled the Governor to accompany the complaint by his
own explanations.

[2] Grey, *Colonial Policy*, i. 26–8; Bruce, *Broad Stone of Empire*, i. 232–3.

was to give the Governor control of the legislature and the executive, while at the same time the presence of the unofficial members in the Legislative Council enabled him to learn the needs of the merchants, the planters, and the native races. The economic interests of the Europeans and the natives were frequently opposed, but while the former vigorously put forward their demands, the latter relied upon the Government to protect them. The official majority in the Legislative Council were really the guardians of the native interests, trying to hold the balance even between the legitimate development of Ceylon's resources and the preservation of native rights.

VIII

ASPECTS OF NATIVE POLICY
1798–1889

THE record of British policy in Ceylon is not free from
blemishes, but on the whole it is one of which the Empire
has no occasion to be ashamed. Throughout the nineteenth century the British Government conscientiously tried to
improve the condition of the people, and to hold the balance
even between the conflicting interests of the planters, the native
aristocracy and priesthood, and the raiyats. A century before
the League of Nations enunciated the principle of the trusteeship of backward peoples the Ceylon Government had acted
in its spirit without ostentation, and without definition.

One of the most difficult problems was to prevent the oppression of the raiyats by the native officials, without at the same
time destroying their power and prestige. Especially in Kandy,
where the feudal respect for birth was exceptionally strong, the
officials were drawn very largely from the aristocracy, so that
their administrative was strengthened by their hereditary
power and influence. Immemorial custom sanctioned the
illegal exaction of taxes and unpaid labour from the raiyats,
and in the earlier part of the century they were too ignorant
and timid to carry their grievances to the courts or the Government Agent. The Ceylon Government realized that to prevent
these exactions it must curtail the power of the native officials.
At the same time they must be left sufficient authority and
prestige to preserve their loyal co-operation and the raiyats'
respect and obedience. Inevitably they possessed an influence
over their countrymen and a knowledge of their actions and
wishes which could not be equalled by the British civil servant,
alien in race and religion and destined after a few years of service
to be moved to another district.

At the beginning of the nineteenth century Governor North
found that the Mudaliyars and minor officials, while nominally
under the control of the Government Agent, had 'nearly unlimited' authority over the natives. They used their position
illegally to exact unpaid forced labour for the cultivation of

I

their own estates.[1] Governor Maitland confirmed the charge
in 1806 ;[2] and he agreed with North that their power must be
diminished, both in the interests of the raiyats, whom they
oppressed, and of the British Government, which they systematically defrauded and deceived.[3] The peasantry were too timid
and too ignorant of their rights to complain, while the civil
servants were too imperfectly acquainted with the country
and the languages to detect their practices. The Mudaliyars
realized the strength of their position, and used it to establish
'a species of *imperium in imperio* which could only be tolerated
as long as we are kept in the dark with regard to the nature of
their conduct'. They were 'a paralysing medium between
Government and the people', concealing from the British
official whatever it was undesirable he should know. The only
remedy was to diminish the power of the native headmen, and
bring the civil servants into more intimate touch with the
people.[4]

Maitland offered rewards for proficiency in Sinhalese, since
a knowledge of the vernacular would destroy the Mudaliyars'
position as the sole channel of communication between the
administration and the people. He increased the number of
Magistrates, to curb the power of the headmen in remote districts
far removed from the control of the Provincial Courts. The
Collectors were ordered to watch their headmen closely, carefully investigate all complaints, and make frequent circuits of
their districts to gain the confidence of the people and learn
their needs. Maitland's regulations were continued by his
successors, and the diminution of the power of native officials
became a settled policy of the Ceylon Government. Success
was gradually achieved as the civil servants increased in numbers and in knowledge of the languages and the people. The
weapons used were close supervision of native subordinates,
the prompt punishment of offenders, and the readiness of the
courts to redress the wrongs of any who appealed to them.[5]

[1] *V*. chap. iv, notes 8–10.   [2] C.O. 54. 20: Feb. 28, 1806.
[3] C.O. 54. 31: Jan. 25, 1809.
[4] C.O. 54. 31: 1809, undated dispatch of Maitland. C.O. 54. 122: Jan. 31,
1832. Colebrooke's Report described the oppression of the raiyats by the native
officials and the tax farmers when collecting the revenue.
[5] Skinner, *Ceylon*, 223–8. 'The pernicious and oppressive influence exercised

A very important cause of the change was the growing refusal of the raiyats to submit to injustice as they came to realize that the Government would uphold their rights against all infringement.[1]

The form of administration established in Kandy after the revolt of 1818 was avowedly designed to weaken the native officials by abolishing the greater part of their power and influence, and by bringing them under the strict control of the Agents of Government. The Government acted partly from the desire to free the Kandyan raiyats from heavy exactions and also under the belief that the Kandyan nobles were a menace to the security of British rule. The power of the Kandyan was greater than that of the other native nobles owing to the very strong feudal loyalty of their raiyats. As a result of the series of Kandyan revolts, particularly that of 1818, the Kandyan nobles were as late as 1848 looked upon with suspicion as secretly hostile to British rule.[2] Justifiable in its inception, the policy was carried to undesirable lengths. Many British officials failed to realize that by the 'forties the raiyats were no longer in bondage to their chiefs, and were 'very little disposed to submit tamely to exactions of any kind'. The power and prestige of the native officials were unnecessarily weakened, and their influence declined. The Kandyan revolt of 1848 was partly due to this mistaken policy, owing to the increasing lawlessness which resulted from the refusal of the raiyats to give heed to the restraining counsels of their chiefs. The Government had also alienated the Kandyan nobles, and they did little to assist it when the crisis came.[3]

by the headmen and petty officials has been to a great extent done away with, at least so far as it is practicable for the law or the influence of the Executive to detect it' (C.O. 54. 228: Oct. 22, 1846). References are difficult to cite since the dispatches seldom give more than at most a passing reference to the gradual weakening of the power of the native officials, or to the desirability of still further curbing it.   [1] Skinner, *Ceylon*, 229.

[2] Skinner, *Ceylon*, 223–4, 229–30. The suspicion with which the Kandyan nobles were regarded was shown by the trials for treason in 1835 and by the promptness with which the responsibility for the revolt of 1848 was ascribed to them. From the same motive the Government during the 'thirties appointed few Dissawas, who corresponded to the Mudaliyars in Maritime Ceylon, and temporarily substituted for them a larger number of inferior chiefs (C.O. 55. 79: Dec. 17, 1839; C.O. 55. 83: Dec. 22, 1843; C.O. 55. 85: June 7, 1844; C.O. 54. 210: Mar. 19, 1844).

[3] Skinner, *Ceylon*, 223–30.

While the evidence is very scanty, it would seem that after 1848 the Ceylon Government alternated between two policies towards the native officials. At times it followed what might be called the traditional view, that 'the Kandyan chiefs acted tyrannically, that conceding power to them was giving them illegitimate influence, and that it was unjust to the lowly born Kandyan that he should be prejudiced by reason of birth'. Sir Charles Layard, the Government Agent of the Western Province and the principal advocate of this policy, appointed as Mudaliyars in some districts men who though able were of low birth. 'They were undoubted failures. The proud Kandyans despised them, and evaded and unwillingly obeyed their orders.' The alternative policy was that as far as possible the native officials in Kandy should be men of aristocratic descent as well as of ability. 'There was no doubt that matters went on far more smoothly and efficiently when the native officers were selected from families of ancient lineage rather than from men who, though of excellent character and of experience, had risen from the ranks.'[1]

Governor Sir William Gregory in the 'seventies successfully followed the second policy in the Kandyan districts.[2] His successor, Sir James Longden, imitated him and regarded the native officials as trusted and indispensable auxiliaries of the Government Agents. They were 'gentlemen of high character and good descent . . . upon [whom] depends the administration of the government among the native population everywhere except in the great towns. They have a wide jurisdiction by positive enactments. They have yet a wider one by custom.' They 'exercise a power which may perhaps at rare intervals have been abused but which is in the main used for the good of the people; and the maintenance of this power has done much to reconcile the people to British rule'.[3]

The relation of the British Government with the Buddhist Church in Kandy was a recurrent problem which was not

[1] Gregory, *Autobiography*, 287–8.
[2] Gregory, *Autobiography*, 288 and 364. The Governor's policy was 'to give them confidence and encouragement, to reward even ostentatiously good conduct, fidelity, and strength, but to be down on offenders with relentless severity'.
[3] C.O. 54. 531: Feb. 8, 1881; C.O. 54. 533: June 15, 1881.

finally settled until 1889. Buddhism was the religion of the great majority of the people, and Buddhist temples and monasteries existed in all parts of Ceylon. The Church had received such large gifts of land from the kings or from individuals that by the nineteenth century 'in every district of the island the priests are in the enjoyment of the most fertile lands'. Owing, however, to three centuries of Portuguese and Dutch hostility, the wealth and power of the Buddhist priesthood were much greater in Kandy than in Maritime Ceylon. The king himself was the spiritual and temporal head of the Church, while Buddhism was the State religion. The Church's lands in Kandy were free from taxation, and the priests received from their tenants a large revenue which took the form of a percentage of the crops or of compulsory labour.[1] By the Convention of March 2, 1815, 'the religion of Budhoo . . . is declared inviolable, and its rights, ministers, and places of worship are to be maintained and protected'.[2] 'In the practical working out of the Convention the British Sovereign succeeded to all the rights and obligations of the Kandyan King in respect of the Buddhist Church.' The custody of the Sacred Tooth of Buddha, 'the appointment and dismissal of priests, and the control of other domestic matters of the Buddhist Church were vested in the Governor', as the representative of his Sovereign.[3] The priesthood were hostile to British control, and took a prominent part in organizing the revolt of 1818. The British Government was therefore free to modify the vague and sweeping Convention of 1815. The Proclamation of November 21, 1818, which established the new form of administration in Kandy, merely stated that the priests and 'all the ceremonies and processions of the Budhoo religion shall receive the respect which in former times was shown them'; but the British would also protect 'the peaceable exercise of all other religions and the erection of places of worship'. Confirming the immemorial right of the

---

[1] Tennent, *Ceylon*, i. 363–6; C.O. 54. 122: Dec. 24, 1831. Amongst the compulsory services were providing food or transport for the priests, repairing the temples, taking part in religious ceremonies, &c.

[2] Aitchison, *Treaties*, x. 290.

[3] G. W. Woodhouse, *C.A. and L.R.* iii. iii. 175–6. The Governor selected and appointed the priests, though he usually adopted the recommendations of the priesthood (C.O. 54. 122: Dec. 24, 1831).

Buddhist Church, the Government 'exempted all lands, which now are the property of temples, from all taxation whatever'.[1]

Owing to the exemption of Church lands from taxation and from the Crown's right to Rajakaria, many Kandyans made fraudulent transfers of their lands to the temples. The Government therefore issued Proclamations in 1819 and 1822 forbidding grants of land to the temples without its sanction; while it also tried to investigate the genuineness of grants already made, and to register lands which had belonged to the Church before November 1818. The attempts failed owing to the evasions of the Kandyans and the insufficient staff of the Survey Department; and in 1846 Tennent reported that 'the evil continues to the present hour in all its original magnitude'. He estimated that one-third of the paddy lands in Kandy, besides much waste land, belonged ostensibly to the temples.[2] Nothing was done until 1856, when Governor Ward investigated the Church's title to its estates, and compiled a register giving the area and location. Bona-fide temple lands continued to be free from taxation, but fraudulent grants were deprived of their immunity.[3] The abolition of Rajakaria in 1832 applied only to tenants on Government lands, and did not affect the right of the chiefs and priests to the compulsory services of their Kandyan tenants.[4] Service tenures were increasingly resented by the tenants, and were entirely abolished in 1870 by an Ordinance which empowered all tenants to commute their services into an annual money rent fixed by the Government.[5]

A new phase of the Buddhist question developed in the 'forties, owing to the hostility of the Ceylon missionaries and their powerful adherents in Great Britain to the British Government's connexion with 'idolatry'. They objected especially to

[1] Aitchison, *Treaties*, x. 296–7 (also given in C.O. 54. 73: Nov. 21, 1818); C.O. 54. 112: Dec. 24, 1831.

[2] C.O. 54. 122: Dec. 24, 1831; C.O. 54. 228: Oct. 22, 1846.

[3] C.O. 55. 98: Apr. 20, 1857; C.O. 54. 348: Mar. 31, 1859; C.O. 54. 346: Nov. 12, 1859. Many fraudulent grants escaped detection since it was often impossible to disprove the Church's claim of immemorial possession owing to the lack of registers showing the area of temple lands in the past.

[4] C.O. 55. 72: Apr. 12 and May 3, 1832.

[5] C.O. 54. 122: Dec. 24, 1831; C.O. 55. 85: July 24, 1844; C.O. 55. 87: Apr. 13, 1847; C.O. 54. 446: Sept. 18, 1869; C.O. 54. 448: Nov. 30, 1869; C.O. 54. 454: Mar. 5 and 22, 1870; C.O. 55. 117: May 13, 1870; Digby, *Morgan*, ii. 77–84.

the appointment of priests by the Governor, and demanded a complete severance of relations between Church and State. Carried away by religious scruples, Governor Mackenzie in 1840 refused to sign the warrants appointing priests to the chief temples, because to do so was 'a direct encouragement to' Buddhism. The result was that while the priests themselves filled the vacancies as they occurred, the appointments were technically illegal since they were not confirmed by the British Government. The temple tenants refused to pay their rents or their labour services; and in one instance a Dissawa seized a temple and ejected the incumbent. The courts refused redress since the priest had not been legally appointed by the Government; and the Church found itself powerless to enforce its just claims.[1] This was the situation when, in 1844, Lord Stanley, the Secretary of State for the Colonies, was won over by the missionaries and instructed the Governor to sever all connexion with Buddhism.[2] He approved of the refusal to sign the priests' warrants of appointment, and condemned the annual Government grant of £300 made for 'Devil Dances and other idolatrous festivals'. Buddha's Tooth must be made over entirely to the custody of the priests, and the British sentry withdrawn from the temple, since his presence must tend to increase 'Idolatrous Veneration' for the relic. The Ceylon Government's reason for guarding the temple was to make certain that the Tooth was not stolen, since the Kandyans believed that the possessor was the rightful ruler of Kandy. The relic had been stolen by the rebels in 1818, and had greatly stimulated their resistance.[3]

Lord Stanley's orders caused 'much alarm and dissatisfaction' amongst the priests and a 'large section' of the Kandyans; while Governor Campbell and many of his advisers were opposed to a complete severance of relations. They enacted an Ordinance which was rejected by Lord Grey, who was now Secretary

[1] C.O. 54. 258: May 10, 1849.

[2] *Parl. Pap. H. C.* 106 of 1850, vol. xii, p. 269; Anon., *History of Connection of British Government and Buddhism*, 28–32. A Reverend Mr. Peggs, who had apparently never been to Ceylon, took an active part in the agitation. Governor Torrington in 1849 described his letters to Lord Stanley as misleading and exaggerated (C.O. 54. 258: May 10, 1849).

[3] C.O. 55. 85: July 24, 1844. On the outbreak of the Kandyan revolt in 1848 the Government again took possession of the Tooth, but restored it to the priests in 1853 (C.O. 54. 250: Aug. 14, 1848; C.O. 54. 300: June 10, 1853).

of State, on the ground that it failed completely to sever the Government's connexion with Buddhism.[1] In 1847 Governor Torrington resigned Buddha's Tooth to the custody of the priests, discontinued the annual allowance of £300 made towards the cost of the temple rites, and informed the priesthood that the Government's decision to sever all connexion with Buddhism was irrevocable. Since Lord Grey refused to permit the appointment of priests by the Governor, it was essential to substitute some arrangement which would give the Church a legal status in the courts and thus enable it to protect its rights from infringement.[2] Torrington found the problem insoluble, and in 1849 he drafted an Ordinance which was vetoed by the Secretary of State. Grey also refused his request that he be permitted to appoint the priests as formerly.[3] In 1851 Governor Anderson asked for permission to sign the warrants appointing the chief priests, since the courts refused to entertain suits brought by priests whose appointments were technically invalid.[4] As a temporary measure Lord Grey reluctantly agreed, since he could see no other way to preserve the Church from spoliation.[5] The Anglican Bishop of Colombo supported the Governor, and they were both bitterly attacked by many of the clergy in Ceylon and their supporters, including Doctor Elliott.[6]

A solution of the problem was at last found by the Secretary of State in December 1852. Henceforth each of the Kandyan chief priests was to be elected by the priests of his temple. The Government was to take no part in the election beyond granting to each appointee a certificate 'which while avoiding altogether the form of an appointment . . . should simply profess to be a certificate or recognition by Government of the title of the party elected'. The Buddhist Church would thus have a legal status in any suits brought to enforce its rights.[7] In 1853

---

[1] C.O. 54. 223: Jan. 7, Feb. 7, and June 25, 1846; C.O. 54. 227: Nov. 7, 1846; C.O. 55. 87: Apr. 13, 1847; *Parl. Pap. H. C.* 106 of 1850, vol. xii. 247–69.

[2] C.O. 54. 249: July 9, 1848; C.O. 55. 89: July 19, 1848; C.O. 55. 91: Mar. 23 and Apr. 23, 1849.

[3] C.O. 54. 257: Jan. 13, 1849; C.O. 54. 258: May 10, 1849.

[4] C.O. 54. 281: Aug. 14, 1851; C.O. 54. 288: Jan. 13, 1852.

[5] C.O. 55. 93: Dec. 21, 1851: Jan. 10 and Dec. 4, 1852.

[6] C.O. 54. 282: Nov. 4, 1851; C.O. 54. 288: Jan. 10 and 13, 1852; C.O. 54. 293, *passim*.   [7] C.O. 54. 290: Aug. 6, 1852; C.O. 55. 93: Dec. 4, 1852.

Anderson reported that he had carried out his instructions, and that the Buddhist priests declared that they were satisfied with the arrangement.[1]

For twenty years the Buddhist Question ceased to perplex the Ceylon Government, but in 1876 the Governor discovered that there had been 'scandalous misappropriation of temple revenues, widespread corruption, and systematic fraud' by the clerical and lay trustees who administered the Church's endowments. Since the priests had proved unable to protect their property of 376,000 acres, the Governor proposed to transfer the management to three Commissioners appointed by himself; but the Secretary of State rejected this solution as involving too drastic an interference with Buddhist affairs.[2] Amendments to the Penal Code intended to give the Church effective power to prosecute dishonest trustees failed to achieve their purpose.[3] 'Great and scandalous abuses' continued until the passage of the Buddhist Temporalities Ordinance of 1889, which gave the Church efficient machinery for exercising control over the management of its property. The Ordinance established in each district a committee of Buddhist laymen elected by the Buddhist priests and laity of the district. The trustees were henceforth all Buddhist laymen, and were, in the majority of cases, elected by the committee of the district where the temple was situated. A provincial committee of five members was elected by the temple trustees and district committees of each province. Each trustee administered the endowments of his temple under the supervision of the district and ultimately of

[1] C.O. 54. 298: Mar. 24, 1853; C.O. 54. 300: June 10, 1853; C.O. 55. 95: Aug. 18, 1853. These dispatches, together with Pakington's instructions of Dec. 4, 1852, are printed in *Parl. Pap. H. C.* 410, 927, and 985 of 1852–3, vol. lxv. C.O. 54. 310: Nov. 24, 1854; C.O. 55. 98: Dec. 19, 1855; C.O. 54. 321: Feb. 5, 1856; C.O. 55. 98: Apr. 8, 1856. The severance from Buddhism 'did no more than delegate certain prerogatives which the British Sovereign succeeded to from the Kandyan King into other hands, to be resumed whenever it was found necessary to do so. The King in fact is still . . . the head of the Buddhist Church. The final decision in all matters not purely domestic or doctrinal lies with him. The appointment of a priest is nothing; his dismissal is everything, and the King has not renounced his right of dismissal' (Woodhouse, *C.A. and L.R.* III. iii. 176).

[2] C.O. 54. 507: May 7, 1877; *Papers Relating to Buddhist Temporalities*, passim.

[3] C.O. 54. 527: Aug. 7, 1880; C.O. 54. 533: June 15, 1881; C.O. 54. 547: June 28, 1883.

the provincial committee, which were empowered to dismiss
and to prosecute him for dishonesty. The trustee's accounts
were audited half-yearly by an independent auditor appointed
by the District Court.[1]

One of the principal benefits of British rule to the native
population has been the restoration of irrigation works. While
irrigation was much less necessary in the mountain area, it was
essential in the plains owing to the long and frequent droughts
caused by failure of the monsoons. The ancient kings of Ceylon
had regarded the construction of irrigation works as one of
their principal duties, and by the use of Rajakaria they were
able to build on a stupendous scale. Owing to centuries of war
and neglect the greater part of these works had fallen into
decay by the middle of the nineteenth century, and large and
fertile areas like the districts around Anuradhapura had become
practically uninhabited. Ceylon had formerly grown sufficient
rice to feed its population; but by the beginning of the nineteenth century it was largely dependent on imported Indian
rice. This dependence increased with the influx of Tamil coolies
to work on the coffee plantations, since their principal food was
rice.[2]

From the beginning of British rule the Government recognized that the restoration of irrigation works would be of immense benefit to the native cultivators. The question was
discussed at various times, but nothing was done until 1856
since with a recurrent deficit the expense was too great.[3] Soon
after his arrival as Governor, Sir Henry Ward made a tour of
the greater part of Ceylon, and decided that the two most
urgent needs were roads and the repair of irrigation works. The
Governor was particularly impressed with the work which was
being done in the District of Uva by Mr. J. Bailey, the Assistant

---

[1] C.O. 57. 106: Oct. 31, 1888; C.O. 56. 12: Buddhist Temporalities Ordinance
of 1889; Woodhouse, *C.A. and L.R.* III. iii. 177.

[2] Tennent, *Ceylon*, i. 423–5 and 432–4; Skinner, *Ceylon*, 162–5; E. Elliott,
Journal of the Royal Asiatic Society, Ceylon Branch, 1885, vol. ix, pt. ii, No. 31,
pp. 160–71; C.O. 54. 492: Jan. 8, 1874.

[3] C.O. 54. 5: Mar. 13, 1801; C.O. 54. 20: Feb. 28, 1806; C.O. 54. 25: Feb. 28,
1807; C.O. 54. 43: June 12, 1812; C.O. 54. 126: *passim*; C.O. 54. 127: Feb. 5,
1833; C.O. 54. 228: Apr. 13, 1847; C.O. 54. 252: Nov. 13, 1848; C.O. 55. 91:
Jan. 24, 1849; C.O. 54. 314: Jan. 13, 1855; Bertolacci, *Ceylon*, 131–2 and 200;
Skinner, *Ceylon*, 167.

Government Agent, and with the report which he submitted.[1]
While the report dealt with the District of Uva, much of the
description was equally applicable to many other parts of
Ceylon. 'Irrigation in the flat parts of this District was carried
on chiefly by means of tanks . . . canals, and water courses.
The large canals have for centuries been out of use, and are
only traceable by the remnants of their vast embankments, but
some six or seven tolerably large ones yet irrigate a considerable
extent of land; but they are in a most dilapidated condition,
and hastily and imperfectly patched up; seldom or never cleared,
they are rendered sufficiently waterproof for each year's cultivation only with great and constant toil. I know of but one stone
dam in the whole District, and that is in . . . bad order. . . .
A masonry sluice is a thing unknown, and each cultivator cuts
a hole in the bank wherever it suits him when he wants water
for his field. . . . We find the whole of the low country dotted
with tanks' from 'vast sheets of water to little ponds . . . we
find every village with its one or more tanks, almost all now
ruined and useless.' Owing to the frequent and 'long protracted
droughts . . . the destruction of the tanks therefore has almost
depopulated the country', and the raiyats have become 'sickly
. . apathetic' and poor farmers, too listless even to repair their
own village reservoirs.[2]

While many irrigation works had been dilapidated for centuries the British Government had completed the evil by its
abolition of Rajakaria and its failure to maintain the Gansabhawas. As in many primitive agricultural communities the village
had possessed an organ of self-government in the Gansabhawa,
a council composed of representatives of the raiyats which
regulated the affairs of the village and enforced its ancient
customary law. A very important part of this law was the
binding customs which regulated every detail of agriculture,
and in particular assigned to each cultivator his share in the
use and preservation of the irrigation works. The Gansabhawa
punished dishonest or lazy raiyats for such matters as taking
more than their share of the water or neglecting to do their

[1] C.O. 54. 316: July 11, 1855; C.O. 54. 318: Nov. 15, 1855; C.O. 54. 321:
Jan. 28 and Apr. 9, 1856; C.O. 54. 322: June 9 and July 24, 1856; C.O. 54. 323:
Aug. 15, 1856; C.O. 55. 98: *passim*.
[2] C.O. 54. 323: Dec. 19, 1855.

part in keeping the works in repair.[1] The Gansabhawa, however, could not maintain its authority without the support of the Government; while the use of Rajakaria by the State was the only means which could compel the different villages to assist one another in keeping the irrigation works in repair. Under the Dutch and the early British régimes Rajakaria was employed for this purpose; but its abolition destroyed the means by which the co-operation of the raiyats had been enforced. Deprived of the coercive support of the administration, the villages proved unable to combine, each quarrelling with its neighbour in a struggle for water. Even in the village itself the Gansabhawa was unable to enforce the customary law, since the British 'tacitly permitted the national customs' and the authority of the Gansabhawa to fall into disuse. The industrious cultivator who tried to maintain the irrigation works might lose his entire crop because of the laziness or dishonesty of his neighbours, because the Government did not, and the Gansabhawa could not, compel co-operation. 'A single idle or litigious man could neutralize the efforts of a whole village.' The only remedy was 'the lottery of litigation' in the District Court, an expensive and slow proceeding at best, and one moreover in which the judge often gave a wrong decision from ignorance of the minute and complicated details of rice cultivation. Gradually many irrigation works which had already fallen into serious decay became useless, and cultivated fields relapsed into jungle.[2]

Governor Ward in 1856 enacted an Irrigation Ordinance which was based to a considerable extent upon Mr. Bailey's report.[3] The Ordinance gave the Government no power to appoint a Gansabhawa and revive the ancient customs regulating the maintenance and use of irrigation works, unless the

---

[1] Tennent, Ceylon, ii. 461. In some districts of the Eastern Province a lazy raiyat was whipped by the village overseer, and was also compelled to give him part of his own share of the harvest 'as payment for his trouble in whipping him'.

[2] C.O. 54. 323: Dec. 19, 1855, and Sept. 27, 1856; C.O. 54. 328: Feb. 27, 1857; A. O. Brodie, J.R.A.S.C.B., 1856–8, vol. iii, pt. i, No. 9, pp. 141–4.

[3] C.O. 54. 323: Dec. 19, 1855. Originally enacted for five years, the Ordinance was renewed in 1861 (C.O. 54. 361: July 2, 1861; C.O. 54. 367: Jan. 9, 1862); and in 1868 it was re-enacted for an indefinite period (C.O. 54. 432: Jan. 12 and 14, 1868).

majority of the rice landowners of a district voluntarily requested it. The Government Agent together with a committee elected by the cultivators then drew up a code of the ancient customs, which became legally binding when approved by the Governor and Executive Council. A Gansabhawa of three to thirteen members was appointed from amongst the landowners of the village by the Government Agent, who acted as President. The Gansabhawa had power to punish all breaches of the ancient customs, and might inflict a fine up to £2. Its proceedings were summary and informal, no lawyers being allowed to appear, and no appeal being permitted.[1] The Irrigation Ordinance was one of the most important achievements of Ward's governorship. It was brought into operation in many districts by the votes of the raiyats; and Ward reported that 'there is nothing that the people have received with so much satisfaction'.[2]

Governor Ward spent over £78,000 in restoring irrigation works, particularly the Irakkamam and Amparai Tanks in the Eastern, and the Urubokka and Kirama works in the Southern Province. These provinces received special attention since they had been seriously neglected; but the Governor also did much for Uva, where Bailey's achievements were 'really marvellous'. Under the stimulus of road-building and the restoration of irrigation works the rice crop increased, abandoned fields were reclaimed from the jungle, and the population rapidly grew in numbers and in prosperity.[3] The repair of only the most important works was supervised by trained engineers owing to the small number of the staff. The majority were restored by the voluntary unpaid labour of the local raiyats, under the supervision of the Assistant Government Agents, and the native headmen, the Government contributing part of the cost.[4]

[1] C.O. 54. 323: Oct. 23, 1856. The Assistant Government Agents had the same powers in their districts as the Government Agents.

[2] C.O. 54. 334: Mar. 20, 1858.

[3] C.O. 54. 328: Feb. 27, 1857; C.O. 54. 329: July 22, 1857; C.O. 54. 333: Jan. 30. 1858; C.O. 54. 334: Mar. 20, 1858; C.O. 54. 335: July 21, 1858; C.O. 55. 100: Apr. 2, Sept. 22, and Oct. 23, 1858; C.O. 54. 345: July 22 and 23, 1859; C.O. 54. 353: June 25, 1860; C.O. 54. 478: Sept. 25, 1872; Gregory, *Autobiography*, 297–8. Ward's irrigation policy increased the yield of the tax of a tenth on rice from £36,000 in 1854 to £81,000 in 1859 (C.O. 55. 112: Nov. 10, 1866).

[4] C.O. 54. 328: Feb. 27, 1857; C.O. 54. 334: Mar. 20, 1858. Sir Hercules Robinson appointed Lieut. Woodward, R.E., Irrigation Assistant in the Public

Governor Sir Hercules Robinson in the 'sixties rivalled Ward in the vigour with which he restored irrigation works in every part of Ceylon.[1]

Governor Sir William Gregory was especially interested in the Wanni, a part of the Northern Province which included Mannar, Nuwarakalawiya, and Mullaittivu. 'This magnificent district . . . was once the granary of the island; it is now utterly neglected.' With 1,700 tanks, some of immense size but almost all in ruins, it had a population of only 60,000 'miserable, half-starved, and dejected looking wretches . . . dying out by disease and starvation'. The province was far too large to be administered by a single Government Agent. Practically nothing had been done for this isolated region, the few roads built by earlier Governors having fallen into almost total disrepair.[2] In 1873 Gregory incorporated Nuwarakalawiya in the new North Central Province, and in 1874 he created the new District of Vavuniya Vilankulam in the Northern Province. Roads were built connecting the area with Trincomalee, Jaffna, Puttalam, and Kandy, with the result that the cultivators were able to bring their crops to market. Hitherto the raiyats had been too apathetic to adopt Ward's Irrigation Ordinance, but their reluctance was overcome by Dickson, the Government Agent of the North Central Province. Several hundred of the village tanks—small reservoirs irrigating about 50 acres apiece—were restored, the Government providing the masonry sluice on condition that the villagers themselves completed the work.[3] The repair of the village tanks was not sufficient since they were dependent on local rainfall, and in times of drought the supply would fail. Centuries before they had been connected by canals with storage reservoirs such as the Kalawewa Tank, which had

Works Department, but the post was soon afterwards abolished. In 1900 Governor Sir West Ridgeway created a separate Irrigation Department (Keane, *Report on Irrigation in Ceylon*, 7–8).

[1] C.O. 54. 438: Dec. 15 and 24, 1868; C.O. 54. 444: June 12, 1869; C.O. 54. 448: Nov. 30, 1869; C.O. 54. 457: Sept. 16, 1870; C.O. 54. 467: Sept. 14, 1871; C.O. 55. 115: Mar. 17 and Oct. 26, 1868; Keane, *Irrigation*, 5.

[2] C.O. 54. 478: Sept. 25, 1872; Gregory, *Autobiography*, 305–10; Skinner, *Ceylon*, 162–5.

[3] C.O. 54. 478: Oct. 15, 1872; C.O. 54. 484: Jan. 7 and 31, 1873; C.O. 54. 493: June 10, 1874; C.O. 54. 494: Sept. 8, 1874; C.O. 54. 501: Mar. 28, 1876; C.O. 54. 503: Sept. 18, 1876; Gregory, *Autobiography*, 310–11, 386–7; Ievers, *Manual of the North Central Province*, 73–6 and 132–61.

a bund 60 to 80 feet high, a circumference of 35 miles, and a catchment area of 120 square miles. The water had been brought to Anuradhapura by the Giant's Canal, 60 miles in length, and distributed to the village tanks by a system of lesser canals and storage reservoirs. Between 1873 and 1877 Gregory repaired a large part of the Giant's Canal. Governor Gordon began the repair of the Kalawewa Tank in 1884 and completed it in 1887.[1] As a result of Gregory's policy the rice crop increased fivefold: 'there is ample food for every one, and now they are exporting large quantities. . . . This child of mine—this North Central Province . . . is a splendid success.'[2] In addition to his work in the Wanni Gregory restored irrigation works in every province of Ceylon. In the Eastern Province he repaired the Kantalai Tank, irrigating 23,000 acres of rice land. The expense of building the tank would have been £1,000,000: to restore it perfectly cost £7,597. The repair of the Tissamaharama Tank, begun in 1871 by Sir Hercules Robinson, was completed in 1877 at a cost of £12,950, and brought under cultivation 'a vast tract of land . . . which from a flourishing and populous condition had relapsed into solitude and sterility'.[3]

The destruction of the coffee plantations compelled Sir James Longden, Governor from 1877 to 1882, to abandon the expensive restoration of the large reservoirs owing to the decline of the revenue. He was forced to content himself with 'the humbler but not less essential task of repairing the Village Tanks'.[4] Sir Arthur Gordon, the next Governor, arrived when the revenue was recovering as the planting industry regained its prosperity. He expended large amounts upon the repair of village tanks, and also of the storage reservoirs, such as the Kalawewa Tank.[5]

During the generation which had elapsed since the date of

[1] C.O. 54. 501: Mar. 28, 1876; C.O. 54. 554: Oct. 10, 1884; Ievers, *N.C. Province*, 162–7; Gregory, *Autobiography*, 311–12.
[2] C.O. 54. 553: Apr. 26, 1884; Gregory, *Autobiography*, 362–4, 387, and 393.
[3] C.O. 54. 477: July 1 and Aug. 14, 1872; C.O. 54. 488: Oct. 13, 1873; C.O. 54. 493: Aug. 11, 1874; C.O. 54. 507: Mar. 15, May 18 and 24, 1877; C.O. 54. 508: June 5 and 28, 1877; Gregory, *Autobiography*, 327–8.
[4] C.O. 54. 512: Feb. 10, 1878; C.O. 54. 522: Nov. 20, 1879; C.O. 54. 527: Aug. 10, 1880; C.O. 54. 529: Dec. 6, 1880; C.O. 54. 531: Jan. 8 and Feb. 23, 1881; C.O. 54. 535: Dec. 28, 1881; C.O. 54. 540: July 20, 1882.
[5] C.O. 54. 552: Feb. 18, 1884; C.O. 54. 554: *passim*; C.O. 54. 555: Nov. 11, 1884; C.O. 54. 557: Feb. 24, 1885.

Ward's Irrigation Ordinance, what might almost be described as a revolution had taken place in rice cultivation. The raiyats had a far more abundant supply of water than they had known for centuries. Large areas had been reclaimed from the jungle and the well-being of the people had grown to a remarkable degree. Their prosperity was still further increased by the abolition on January 1, 1893, of the immemorial tax of a tenth on rice, which in the earlier years of British rule had been one of the principal sources of the revenue.[1]

The excellent results which had followed Sir Henry Ward's revival of the Gansabhawa in 1856 for irrigation purposes led to a very important extension of its powers in 1871. By this, the crowning act of Sir Hercules Robinson's governorship, the Gansabhawa was empowered to control all matters of purely local concern. The reason for the reform was the 'extraordinarily large number' of petty criminal cases in the minor courts, and 'the very large proportion which are dismissed without trial'. In 1869 charges were laid in the courts of the Magistrates and Justices of the Peace against 168,426 persons, or about one-thirteenth of the total population. Of these 112,301 were dismissed without trial, while only one-tenth of the accused were convicted. Including those summoned as witnesses approximately 1,000,000, or one-third of the population, appeared in the minor courts in 1869. 'Nearly the whole population are habitually in the Courts . . . where nearly every case is supported by false evidence, and perjury is unblushingly committed. The villages and smaller towns are infested by Petition Drawers and Proctors [i.e. lawyers] who foment litigation and devour the substance of the people.' The courts were congested by a flood of frivolous charges, the raiyats incurred heavy expenses in court and lawyers' fees, and their farms suffered by their long absences. The number of assaults and murders largely increased, since men who could not afford the expense of a suit took the law into their own hands.[2]

To increase the number of courts would merely have augmented the evil by increasing the facilities for litigation, since

[1] Keane, *Irrigation*, 7–8.
[2] C.O. 54. 474: Feb, 4, 1872; Digby, *Morgan*, ii. 99–102. 'One individual for a trifling suit may . . . withdraw from their village and necessary occupations ⅓ of its population as witnesses.' (Skinner, *Ceylon*, 233–5.)

two principal causes of the situation were the existence of the courts combined with the Sinhalese passion for lawsuits. Owing to the 'inordinate' love of litigation charges were laid 'on the most slender pretexts, to gratify spite or often merely to enjoy the excitement of having a case in court'.[1] The fundamental cause of the evil was the decay of the Gansabhawas, which followed the establishment of British law courts throughout Ceylon. Formerly, all breaches of custom and all disputes had been decided summarily by a village council which knew the whole circumstances and could not be deceived by perjured evidence. The British courts did not interfere directly with the Gansabhawas; but as their judgements alone were legally binding the raiyats gradually turned to them, since the Gansabhawas had no power to enforce 'the traditional law of the villagers'. The love of litigation was no longer held in check by a summary tribunal which was well aware of all the facts, and the raiyats exploited to the full the latent possibilities of English legal procedure.[2] The revival of the Gansabhawa for irrigation purposes was insufficient to cope with the evil, since 'the great majority of petty criminal complaints . . . originate I believe in disputes about property or land'.[3]

The Gansabhawa Ordinance No. 26 of 1871 gave the Government Agents no authority to extend the scope of Ward's Gansabhawas except at the request of the raiyats. The raiyats were empowered to frame rules for the regulation of 'purely village affairs', such as agriculture, fisheries, village schools, and paths, &c. The ancient customs thus revived were enforced by the Gansabhawa, composed of five members chosen by lot from the substantial landowners of the village, and a President. The Mudaliyar was appointed by the Governor as the President of all the Gansabhawas of his district with power to overrule the other members. The Gansabhawa tried all offences or complaints arising from breaches of the ancient customs; while it also had jurisdiction in petty civil and criminal cases, and could inflict fines up to £2. Its proceedings were summary, no lawyers being permitted to appear; but all decisions were subject to an

[1] C.O. 54. 467: Oct. 4, 1871; C.O. 54. 474: Feb. 4 and 5, 1872.
[2] C.O. 54. 474: Feb. 4, 1872.
[3] C.O. 54. 467: Oct. 4, 1871.

K

appeal to the Government Agent.[1] The success of the Ordinance was so striking that it was rapidly adopted at the petition of the natives themselves. The number of petty or frivolous cases in the courts showed a marked decrease, and the Gansabhawa became a valuable part of the executive and judicial system of British rule.[2]

[1] C.O. 54. 467: Oct. 4, 1871. The Ordinance considerably increased the power of the Mudaliyars by making them responsible for all minor matters in their districts. The supervision of the Government Agent was a safeguard against abuses (C.O. 54. 474: Feb. 4 and 5, 1872). Mesurier, *Manual of Nuwara Eliya District*, 92–105.

[2] C.O. 54. 478: Sept. 25, 1872; C.O. 54. 480: Dec. 11, 1872; C.O. 54. 484: Jan. 9, 1873; C.O. 54. 528: Sept. 20, 1880; C.O. 54. 529: Dec. 23, 1880; C.O. 54. 542: Dec. 8, 1882; C.O. 54. 558: Mar. 20, 1885.

IX

THE CONQUEST OF KANDY

WHEN the British replaced the Dutch as the rulers of Maritime Ceylon they inherited a problem which had never been solved by their predecessors. The mountain kingdom of Kandy had formerly ruled the whole island, and it was naturally hostile to whatever European power held the coast. It frequently stirred up disaffection in the Maritime Provinces, and waged periodical wars against the Europeans. The situation was intolerable, and in 1815 the problem received its inevitable solution with the British conquest of the kingdom. In 1798 Kandy was weak, and far behind the Maritime Provinces in wealth and civilization. The army was an untrained and ill-armed peasant militia, while the only important article of trade was cinnamon. The King had despotic powers, tempered however by the authority of his nobles who ruled over the provinces as his more or less obedient deputies.[1] So far as possible the Kandyan rulers had prevented intercourse between their subjects and Maritime Ceylon. Reliable information of the politics and topography of the country was most difficult to obtain, and throughout his governorship North was very seriously hampered by his vague and inaccurate idea of Kandyan affairs.

The most powerful of the Kandyan nobles in 1798 was Pilama Talawuwé, the Maha Adigar or chief minister. Able, ambitious, and completely unscrupulous, his design was to overthrow the Malabar dynasty which ruled in Kandy and make himself king. King Raja Sinha died without issue in 1798, and through Pilama's influence a distant relative of the late ruler was chosen as his successor by the ministers. It seems probable that the jealousy of the other nobles prevented Pilama from carrying out his plans, and that he placed a young and inexperienced prince upon the throne until a favourable opportunity should arise for removing him.[2] Apparently Pilama soon realized that he was unable to succeed without assistance, and in 1799 he

[1] Pieris, *Ceylon and the Hollanders*, 156–7; Marshall, *Ceylon*, 31–6.
[2] L. J. Turner, *C.A. and L.R.* iii. iii. 219; Tennent, *Ceylon*, ii. 61 and 75–6; Valentia, *Travels*, i. 233.

tried to enlist Governor North as his ally. The relations between Kandy and the British were friendly at this time, and in February 1799 Pilama was sent on an embassy to Colombo.[1] He had other interviews with North in December 1799 and January 1800, and informed the Governor that he proposed to dethrone or preferably to murder his puppet and make himself king. In return for armed assistance he would place Kandy under British control. North indignantly refused his help, and warned Pilama that he would hold him responsible for the King's life. The obliging Adigar then suggested that as an alternative he would persuade the King to attack the British; in the ensuing invasion of Kandy the change of dynasty could be expeditiously effected. The Governor again refused, and warned Pilama that if war broke out, he and not the King would be held responsible.[2]

Although North realized that the Adigar was 'a man whose profligate and perfidious ambition had announced views which we could not countenance with honour', the whole basis of his Kandyan policy from 1800 to 1803 was his alliance with Talawuwé.[3] The motives which induced North to ally himself with a self-proposed murderer and traitor sprang from the curious complexity of his character. He was ambitious to make the British power paramount in Ceylon by establishing a protectorate over Kandy with a subsidized British garrison at the capital, after the model of the Indian Protected States.[4] A poor judge of character and far from clear-sighted, it rarely crossed his mind that an ambitious minister who would turn traitor to make himself king would never be content merely to exchange a native for a foreign ruler. Talawuwé's secret plan was to use

---

[1] C.O. 54. 1: Feb. 21 and Oct. 5, 1799. The King wished North to cede to him Tamblegam and the seashore under Trincomalee. The Governor refused, since the cession of a port would have destroyed the British monopoly of the Kandyan cinnamon trade.

[2] C.R. 27: July 1, 1800; C.O. 54. 2: Jan. 13, 1800; Brit. Mus. Add. MS. No. 13867: Feb. 7, 1800; Turner, C.A. and L.R. iii. iii. 219–20; Cordiner, Ceylon, ii. 160–1.

[3] C.R. 27: May 19, 1800.

[4] C.O. 54. 2: Jan. 13, 1800. North had communicated his plans to his friend the Marquess Wellesley, the Viceroy of India (Brit. Mus. Add. MS. No. 13867: Dec. 25, 1799): and had received his approval (Brit. Mus. Add. MS. No. 13865: Jan. 23 and Mar. 7, 1800; C.R. 54: Douglass MS. § 60). Dundas also approved (C.O. 54. 5: Mar. 13, 1801).

the British to overthrow the King, and then trust to a favourable opportunity to get rid of them. He was very much superior to North in Oriental diplomacy, and the Governor's blundering machiavellianism ended in disaster. From one point of view North's policy was short-sightedly aggressive, but from another it was chivalrous. With little reliable information as to Kandyan affairs he greatly overestimated Talawuwé's power and chances of success; he did not allow for the jealousy of the other Kandyan nobles, and above all, he had a totally false idea of the young King. The new ruler had ability and determination, and in a few years the puppet of 1798 had become a ferocious and dreaded tyrant. North believed, however, that unless he aided Talawuwé 'the poor Pageant' would be murdered; and his anxiety to preserve the King's life persuaded him that both duty and inclination required him to join in a plot against the power of an independent and friendly ruler.[1]

Eventually North and Talawuwé came to terms: the King was to retain his life and titular sovereignty, and in return the Adigar was to become the real ruler of Kandy under British suzerainty. A British garrison was to be stationed at the town of Kandy, and if possible the King should be persuaded to live in Colombo. Immemorial custom required that an embassy be sent to congratulate the King on his accession to the throne; and North appointed as his ambassador General Macdowall, the Commander-in-Chief in Ceylon. The ambassador received the distinctly unusual escort of 1,164 troops and six six-pounder guns; and he also carried the draft of a treaty which embodied the terms arranged by the Governor and the Adigar. He was secretly instructed to ascertain the relative power of the King and his minister. North stipulated that he would abandon the plan unless the King agreed to the escort and to the treaty: he declined to adopt Talawuwé's advice that the arrangement should if necessary be carried through by force.[2] If the King

---

[1] C.O. 54. 2: Jan. 13, 1800; Brit. Mus. Add. MS. No. 13867: Jan. 19, 1800; C.R. 27: May 19 and July 1, 1800; Valentia, *Travels*, i. 234–48; Marshall, *Ceylon*, 71–83 and 95. North occasionally had doubts of his wisdom in depending on Talawuwé's support, e.g. 'I hope that I have not done wrong, but I am not yet certain whether I have acted like a good politician or a great nincompoop' (Brit. Mus. Add. MS. No. 13867: Mar. 16, 1800).

[2] C.O. 54. 2: Apr. 4, 1800, and *passim*; C.R. 27: June 23, 1800; Brit. Mus.

refused his consent it would be clear that he and not the Adigar was the real master of Kandy, and in that event North refused to enter into 'an unjust conspiracy' against a ruler who was 'in the enjoyment of his authority'.[1]

The King agreed to the size of the escort, and on March 12, 1800, General Macdowall and his force set out under the guidance of Talawuwé. The Adigar led the column over so difficult a route that the artillery had to be abandoned at Ruwanwella, thirty miles from the town of Kandy. Since he wished to have a British garrison at Kandy, his action may probably be ascribed to the growing strength of his enemies at court. After Macdowall's departure North discovered that the King had 'rendered himself in some sort independent of his first Adigar', and he ordered the General to leave the bulk of his force at Ruwanwella. Macdowall at length reached Kandy with only four companies of native troops, but the dispatch of so large an escort probably confirmed the King's suspicion and hostility.[2] Macdowall found that while the Adigar's power was great, it was less than North had believed. The fear that the King's life was in danger was probably not very well founded. It seems probable that he was already beginning to show his ability and, aided by Talawuwé's enemies, to free himself from his tutelage. The King did not wish to have a British garrison in Kandy, and Macdowall returned to Colombo without making a treaty.[3]

After the failure of Macdowall's embassy various attempts were made to frame a treaty; but they failed since North refused to grant the Kandyan demand for a seaport.[4] Meanwhile the

Add. MS. No. 13867: *passim*; Valentia, *Travels*, i. 234–49, 424–5; Tennent, *Ceylon*, ii. 77–9. General Hay Macdowall (1756–1809) joined the army in 1773, and in 1783 was captured when Suffrein regained Trincomalee. He seems to have had North's entire confidence, and commanded the troops in the Kandyan war of 1803. In 1807 he was appointed Commander-in-Chief of the Madras army, and was drowned at sea while on the way to England in 1809. Sydney Smith described him as 'a weak, pompous man ... whom any man of common address might have managed with the greatest ease' (J. P. Lewis, *C.A. and L.R.* VI. i. 1–5).

[1] C.O. 54. 2: Jan. 13, 1800; C.R. 27: July 1, 1800; Cordiner, *Ceylon*, ii. 161–2.

[2] C.O. 54. 2: Apr. 4, 1800; Cordiner, *Ceylon*, ii. 287–92; Percival, *Ceylon*, 377–409; Turner, *C.A. and L.R.* III. iii. 220–1.

[3] Brit. Mus. Add. MS. No. 13867: Apr. 18, 1800; C.R. 27: May 19, June 23, and July 1, 1800; Cordiner, *Ceylon*, ii. 299–319.

[4] C.R. 27: Aug. 4, 1800; C.O. 54. 6: Mar. 16, 1802; Cordiner, *Ceylon*, ii. 162.

Adigar found himself unable to overthrow his master since his power steadily waned as that of the King and his party increased. He therefore attempted to bring about a war between Kandy and the British, since he believed that they would dethrone the King and place himself on the throne. North was aware of the Adigar's machinations, and warned him 'that any aggressive war which he should excite against our possessions would end in his personal ruin'.[1] In April 1802 Talawuwé's servants seized the baggage and areca nuts, valued at £1,000, of a party of native merchants from Puttalam. Despite lengthy negotiations North was unable to obtain compensation for this robbery of British subjects; and in 1803 he declared war. The Adigar had at last achieved his object of provoking a British invasion.[2]

On the declaration of war North offered to 'recognize' the King and his heirs in return for the cession of the Seven Korales as security for the payment of the full costs of the war. The Province was the 'richest' in Kandy, and its possession would ensure the British control of the State. The King must also allow the construction of a road and canal through his territory from Colombo to Trincomalee on pain of being dethroned.[3] At the same time instructions were sent to General Macdowall which shed much light on North's vacillating and tortuous policy. The Seven Korales were to be annexed and the King brought under British control. North could not decide whether to retain the existing ruler or to remove him. If the latter policy should appear preferable he was equally uncertain which of the rival pretenders he should support. Talawuwé was 'the chief instigator of the war' and untrustworthy; and North would never support him except to 'place the King beyond his

[1] C.R. 27: passim; Brit. Mus. Add. MS. No. 13867: Jan. 13, 1801; C.O. 54. 6: Mar. 16, 1802; Cordiner, Ceylon, ii. 162–3; Tennent, Ceylon, ii. 81; Turner, C.A. and L.R. iii. iii. 221; Miss V. Methley, Transactions of Royal Historical Society, Ser. iv, vol. i, pp. 96–8.

[2] C.O. 54. 6: Sept. 4, 1802; Methley, T.R.H.S. iv. i. 98; Cordiner, Ceylon, ii. 164–7; Marshall, Ceylon, 84; Percival, Ceylon, 424–6. Prior to the outbreak of the war North proposed to insist that the King either pay a subsidy which was beyond his means or else cede territory to cover the cost of a force stationed in British territory to protect him (C.O. 54. 7: Oct. 15 and Nov. 21, 1802; C.O. 55. 62: May 7, 1803).

[3] C.O. 54. 10: Feb. 2, 1803; Methley, T.R.H.S. iv. i. 98.

murderous reach'—or unless he should really prove to be very powerful. In that event North would revive his plan of 1800, making him the ruler of Kandy in all but name, 'and in complete subordination to my government'. The third possibility was Prince Muttusamy, a brother-in-law of the late King Raja Sinha who had escaped from Talawuwé's hostility and had been living under British protection since 1798. He had claims to the throne, and his party was 'numerous and powerful'. The British could not in good faith support him unless the King persisted in fighting or fled from the town of Kandy and refused to return. 'In that case Buddha Sawmy [Muttusamy] must be raised to the station from which he has been unjustly excluded.'[1]

North seems to have been absolutely confident of an easy victory, and he entered light-heartedly upon the most disastrous war in the history of British rule in Ceylon. Yet even a slight knowledge of the Portuguese and Dutch wars with Kandy should have warned him that every attempt to conquer the kingdom had failed. The Kandyans were untrained, ill-armed, and not particularly warlike, and on the few occasions when they fought in the open they were easily defeated. Two centuries of warfare, however, had taught them that they had two faithful allies who largely atoned for their own deficiencies. The greater part of the kingdom, both mountains and plains, was covered with dense jungle; and the British were even more ignorant of its geography than they were of Kandyan politics. The roads were merely trails, so narrow that the troops were often compelled to march in single file, and so rough that pioneers had constantly to be employed to make a way for the guns. Rivers were numerous and could be crossed only by fords; but owing to the frequent and heavy floods during the rainy season the streams were often impassable.[2] All stores

---

[1] C.O. 54. 1: Nov. 26, 1798; C.O. 54. 10: Feb. 2 and 7, 1803, and *passim*; C.R. 26: *passim*; Methley, *T.R.H.S.* IV. i. 99. *As early as 1802 North had regarded Muttusamy as a more desirable ruler than Talawuwé or the 'unfortunate' King (C.O. 54. 6: Sept. 4, 1802).

[2] About 1820 Skinner had to put his troops near Nuwara Elia on third rations, since owing to the swollen rivers their supplies took six weeks to cover three days' march (Skinner, *Ceylon*, 21–2, 26–9, and 162).

'There are no roads in Ceylon, and wheeled carriages can only be used in the neighbourhood of the larger European settlements. . . . In travelling foot-paths are sometimes discernible . . . but vegetation is so rapid and general that . . .

had to be carried by porters since it was impossible to use bullock carts; and one important reason for the failure of the campaign was the breakdown of the Commissariat Department.[1] The Kandyan kings had forbidden the construction of roads, since they regarded a broad belt of thick jungle as the surest safeguard of their independence. 'There are . . . few countries in the world where . . . the rude and undisciplined peasant is so nearly on a level with the trained soldier. The broken and rugged nature of the ground, the impassable swamps, the impervious character of the jungle that covers the face of the country, all these baffle the operations of regular troops and reduce a Kandian action to a multitude of single combats.'[2]

Fever was at least as potent an ally as the difficult nature of the country, owing to the numerous swamps and ruined tanks which formed breeding places for the mosquitoes. Ignorance both of the cause and cure of 'jungle fever' immensely aggravated the danger, and the mortality among the British was appalling.[3] The troops appear on the whole to have been in good health on their departure from the coast; but the march through malarial districts showed its effects soon after the arrival in Kandy, and the hospitals filled to overflowing. When the 51st Regiment left Colombo on January 31, 1803, its strength was 625; when it left Kandy on April 11, 1803, it mustered about 400. Within a few days of its return to Colombo 'there was scarcely one of them who did not soon go into the hospital, and in less [than] three months three hundred died'.[4] The ravages of the fever were greatly augmented by stationing detachments 'in the most pestilential places', and the garrisons

it is often with difficulty that a palanquin is pushed forward through the surrounding thickets.' Many of the Kandyan paths were impassable for horses (Cordiner, *Ceylon*, i. 15–16, 167–8; ii. 290–3).

[1] Cordiner, *Ceylon*, ii. 172, 176, 203, and 207; de Bussche, *Ceylon*, 21 and 68–9; Marshall, *Ceylon*, 93; Methley, *T.R.H.S.* iv. i. 104, 110, and 114.

[2] de Butts, *Ceylon*, 170–1; Bertolacci, *Ceylon*, 7.

[3] Cordiner, *Ceylon*, ii. 194; Turner, *C.A. and L.R.* v. ii. 69. The average annual mortality amongst infantry in Great Britain was about 15 per 1,000, while in Ceylon from 1817 to 1836 it was 75 per 1,000. The 19th Regiment, which served in Ceylon from 1796 to 1819, had an annual average mortality of 76 per 1,000 (Marshall, *Ceylon*, 33, 41–4).

The outbreak of fever in 1803 was unprecedented in its violence, the Kandyans themselves suffering severely from it (Methley, *T.R.H.S.* iv, i. 107–8).

[4] Cordiner, *Ceylon*, ii. 168, 193–9.

of some of the British forts were almost wiped out.[1] The exact strength of the British troops in Ceylon in 1803 is uncertain, but was probably between 4,000 and 5,000 of all arms. It has been estimated that in addition to the 661 killed or captured in the Davie massacre in 1803, the number of deaths from January 1 to June 30, 1803, was 1,091.[2]

Kandyan strategy made the fullest use of the unhealthiness and the inaccessibility of the country. On the rare occasions when the Kandyans fought a pitched battle the British easily routed them with trifling loss. They showed, however, a high degree of skill in guerilla tactics, sniping from ambush and withdrawing as soon as the attack became serious. Isolated detachments and convoys were frequently attacked, and in the end the commissariat completely broke down owing to the heavy losses suffered by the coolies bringing up stores. Owing to the inaccessible nature of the country the British were rarely able to inflict serious loss on the enemy. The experience of the army in 1803 was very similar to that of its Dutch predecessors, an easy initial success followed by failure due to fever and to the cutting of the lines of communications.[3]

The invasion of Kandy was carried out by two columns, the combined strength of which was 3,344. The Colombo column 1,900 strong under General Macdowall set out on January 31, 1803; and on February 4 the second division under Colonel Barbut left Trincomalee. The troops were almost unopposed, and on February 20 the two columns arrived at the town of Kandy, which they found deserted, the King having retreated to Hanguranketa.[4] By Colonel Barbut's advice North decided

[1] Forbes, *Ceylon*, i. 41, ii. 53; Marshall, *Ceylon*, 112–13.

[2] Turner, *C.A. and L.R.* v. ii. 60–4; C.O. 54. 11: Aug. 31, 1803; de Bussche (*Ceylon*, 65) stated that the death list of 1,091 was incomplete.

[3] Methley, *C.A. and L.R.* IV. ii. 66–76. The uniform of the British troops was most unsuitable, for it consisted of a red tunic, white trousers and belt, and large brass plates on the shako. The Kandyan, himself invisible, could discover his enemy from a distance of several miles. The brass plates became burning hot in the sun and caused headaches; while the varnished shako sometimes stuck to the head and gave no protection from sunstroke. When it rained, as it frequently did, all the water which collected on the shako ran down the soldier's back, so that the troops were constantly wet through, and fell easy victims to chills and fever (Johnston, *Narrative of an Expedition to Candy*, 109–14).

[4] Cordiner, *Ceylon*, ii. 168–80; Turner, *C.A. and L.R.* III. iii. 222; Methley, *T.R.H.S.* IV. i. 101–4. The dispatches relating to the war are in C.O. 54. 10–18.

about the middle of February to enthrone Muttusamy. On March 14, 1803, Muttusamy ceded the Seven Korales and the cinnamon monopoly, acknowledged the British suzerainty, and agreed to pay for the cost of maintaining a British garrison. The dethroned King was to live in Colombo, receiving a pension from Muttusamy.[1] The haste with which Muttusamy was raised to the throne is the more remarkable when it is remembered that about a fortnight earlier North had written that the British could not in good faith support him unless the King persisted in his resistance.[2] The folly of this hasty decision is no less evident, for it very soon became clear that the vast majority of the Kandyans remained faithful to their King and refused to acknowledge Muttusamy. He had been publicly punished by the late King for fraud, and was therefore legally incapable of ruling.[3] Moreover, the coronation drove Talawuwé to support the King against the British, whereas hitherto he apparently had secretly aided them in hopes of their support.[4]

The ravages of fever now began to show themselves, and with the advent of the rainy season supplies commenced to run short owing to the increased difficulties of transport. On March 13 a detachment sent at Talawuwé's instigation to seize the King at Hanguranketa was ambushed in the mountains by the Adigar, and was forced to retreat with heavy casualties. Talawuwé's object was to weaken the army as a preparation for ejecting it from Kandy, and the losses were so great that he succeeded. General Macdowall realized that the campaign must be suspended until the next dry season; and on April 1 he returned to Colombo with the army. He left in Kandy Colonel Barbut with a garrison of 300 Europeans, 700 Malays, and some Indian artillerymen.[5]

The moment for which Talawuwé had been waiting had arrived: he still hoped to attain the throne through British assistance, and the increasing weakness of the troops combined

[1] C.O. 54. 10: *passim*; Aitchison, *Treaties*, x. 286–8; Cordiner, *Ceylon*, ii. 184, 187–8.
[2] C.O. 54. 10: Feb. 2, 1803.
[3] Cordiner, *Ceylon*, ii. 188; Valentia, *Travels*, i. 252–3.
[4] Turner, *C.A. and L.R.* iii. iii. 222.
[5] Turner, *C.A. and L.R.* iii. iii. 222; Marshall, *Ceylon*, 87–9; Cordiner, *Ceylon*, ii. 185–95.

with the powerlessness of Muttusamy induced North to accept his alliance. On March 28 they signed an agreement by which the King was to be handed over to the British, Muttusamy and his court were to live in Jaffna, and Talawuwé as 'Grand Prince' was to become the ruler of Kandy. The province of the Seven Korales was to be ceded, and all hostilities were to cease. 'It was now thought that the Adigar was sincere, and that he had at length determined to act with good faith.' It is an illuminating commentary on North's credulity that when he met the Adigar on May 1 at Dambadeniya to ratify the treaty, he was only saved from capture through the chance arrival of a British force.[1] Nevertheless the Adigar seems to have wished to help the British as far as he could—at any rate until the King was safely in their hands; but he was powerless to do so. Some slight knowledge at least of his treachery had come to the ears of the King, although the full extent was probably unknown since he retained his head and part of his power. To safeguard himself he reluctantly joined the King's party, who refused to recognize the truce and continued the war.[2]

The garrison at Kandy was now to pay the penalty for North's blind trust in Talawuwé. From the day when General Macdowall and his army left for the coast their safety depended upon the honour and good faith of the Adigar; and the responsibility for the disaster which befell them must be borne in great measure by the Governor.[3] The fever increased rapidly, and before the end of April Colonel Barbut reported that the Europeans were unfit for duty. By June 20 they were dying at the rate of six a day. Supplies also began to run short since many of the food convoys were captured, and by the middle of June almost the sole remaining food was paddy, or unhusked rice, which the troops were too weak to separate from the husk.[4] General Macdowall himself came to Kandy on May 23 to meet Talawuwé, but the Adigar evaded coming, perhaps because the King's suspicions made the interview dangerous for him. On June 11

---

[1] Aitchison, *Treaties*, x. 288–9; C.O. 54. 11; Cordiner, *Ceylon*, ii. 195–201; Valentia, *Travels*, i. 430.
[2] Cordiner, *Ceylon*, ii. 204–5; *C.A. and L.R.* iii. iii. 223–4.
[3] Marshall, *Ceylon*, 90.
[4] Methley, *T.R.H.S.* iv. i. 109–10; Cordiner, *Ceylon*, ii. 206; Marshall, *Ceylon*, 93.

the General, who was extremely ill from fever, returned to Colombo. During his visit the fever increased with startling rapidity: most of the officers were incapacitated and hardly a European was fit for duty. The Malays also suffered severely, and began to desert to the Kandyans. The General left Kandy with the determination that unless reinforcements and provisions were sent the troops must be withdrawn immediately. He did not reach Colombo until June 19, and before measures could be taken the garrison surrendered on June 24.[1] About the middle of June North decided that Kandy must be evacuated; but he then discovered that the transport service had broken down. More than 1,000 coolies were required to carry the invalid Europeans at Kandy; and it was impossible to obtain them since so many had died of fever or been killed in the food convoys ambushed by the Kandyans. The British at Colombo were still trying to recruit coolies when the news arrived of the disaster at Kandy.[2]

One final piece of ill-fortune had befallen the garrison shortly before General Macdowall's arrival: on May 21 Colonel Barbut had died of fever. An experienced officer with some years of service in Ceylon, it is conceivable that he might have saved the garrison. This was not to be expected from his successor, Major Adam Davie. Major Davie had entered the army in 1787, but had never seen active service; and nothing in his experience or, it would seem, his character, fitted him to be the leader of a forlorn hope. Moreover he had a severe attack of fever, and on June 24 he was still convalescing.[3] It seems probable that his physical weakness undermined his morale and his powers of decision. After Macdowall's departure he was 'left to struggle with insurmountable difficulties; his position being an open town, surrounded by wooded hills; a feeble, sickly garrison, part of which was of very doubtful fidelity, without provision, or the means of procuring a supply; cut off from all communications with the maritime provinces; surrounded by a vigilant

---

[1] Cordiner, *Ceylon*, ii. 202–4; Methley, *T.R.H.S.* iv. i. 112–13.

[2] Cordiner, *Ceylon*, ii. 203 and 207.

[3] Cordiner, *Ceylon*, ii. 201. Major Davie, a Scotsman, was recruiting officer in Edinburgh from 1787 to 1793, and served in India from 1794 to 1799. In 1801 he was gazetted Major in Colonel Champagné's newly raised Ceylon Malay Regiment (Methley, *T.R.H.S.* iv. i. 114).

enemy; and as may be presumed, in great doubt whether to consider the adikar a friend or a foe'.[1]

On June 23 Talawuwé warned Davie that an attack would be made the following morning, and on June 24 he himself led the assault with a force which has been estimated at 10,000 Kandyans. To meet the attack Davie had about 35 Europeans, most of them invalids, and about 390 unreliable native troops. The Malays had been reduced from 700 to 250, largely it would seem by wholesale desertion. The attack began about 4 a.m., the British being gradually driven back to the King's palace, where they held out till 2 p.m. The officers then advised Davie to surrender since the position could not be defended much longer.[2] Davie surrendered to the Adigar on the conditions that the garrison together with Muttusamy and his attendants were to evacuate Kandy immediately, and were to have safe conduct to Trincomalee. They were to surrender all stores and powder, retaining their muskets and side arms but no ammunition whatever. Talawuwé promised to care for the 120 Europeans who were in hospital too ill to be moved, and to send them to Trincomalee when they recovered.[3] At 4 p.m. on June 24 the troops marched out in a drenching rainstorm on the road to Trincomalee. Of the 300 Europeans and over 700 natives who had composed the garrison there remained 34 Europeans (14 officers and 20 privates), 250 Malays, and 140 gun lascars. Many of the Europeans were in no condition to make a long march; while the Malays were unreliable, and provisions were scanty. To reach safety Major Davie must 'cross a rapid unfordable river the Mahaweli [Ganga] in the face of a hostile force said to amount to many thousands, and march 142 miles opposed by a vigilant adverse population'.[4] Unless

---

[1] Marshall, *Ceylon*, 95–7. On June 23 the Kandyans captured Fort Girihagama, and completely cut off communications with Colombo (Cordiner, *Ceylon*, ii. 207).

[2] Cordiner, *Ceylon*, ii. 208–9; Marshall, *Ceylon*, 96–8; Methley, *T.R.H.S.* IV. i. 115.

[3] Cordiner, *Ceylon*, ii. 209–10; Methley, *T.R.H.S.* IV. i. 120. Turner (*C.A. and L.R.* III. iii. 224–5) believed that the Adigar probably intended to adhere to the terms of surrender, and that he massacred the garrison only because of the King's imperative orders. It would seem that throughout the campaign he was as friendly to the British as was consistent with his own safety.

[4] Marshall, *Ceylon*, 98, 116–18.

Talawuwé for once was faithful to his word the garrison was lost.

The troops reached Watapuluwa on the Mahaweli Ganga at 7 p.m. on June 24, and passed the night in the open under a heavy rain. The Adigar had promised boats; but on June 25 the Kandyans informed Davie that the King would only supply them if Muttusamy and his attendants were first surrendered. Major Davie was well aware that to give up Muttusamy was to send him to almost certain death; but he handed over the prince in the hope that this would mollify the King. Muttusamy was taken before the King and immediately beheaded.[1] No boats were provided, and on the afternoon of June 25 one of the British soldiers who had been left behind in hospital arrived with the news that the Kandyans had massacred the European invalids in Kandy.[2] On June 26 the British succeeded in passing a rope across the river, but it was cut by the Kandyans before a raft could be built. The Kandyans now began to close in, and about the same time the native troops commenced to desert to the enemy in small parties.[3] The Kandyans promised to supply boats providing the troops first laid down their arms. Major Davie complied, and the way was cleared for the final massacre. The majority of the natives joined the Kandyans; the few who remained faithful were murdered. The 34 Europeans were led away in pairs and murdered, with the exceptions of Major Davie and Captains Rumley and Humphreys who were spared.[4] Of the 300 European troops only one escaped to the coast. Corporal Barnsley of the 19th Regiment was left for dead by the executioners; but after nightfall he contrived to reach a British outpost at Fort Macdowall. Supporting his head in his hands, since the gash of the executioner's sword made it fall forward, he stumbled through the jungle and brought the news of the massacre. Captain Madge had only 39 European and Malay troops at the fort, and he at once

---

[1] Cordiner, *Ceylon*, ii. 210–11; *C.A. and L.R.* v. iv. 211–17.
[2] Methley, *T.R.H.S.* iv. i. 121.
[3] Cordiner, *Ceylon*, ii. 212; Marshall, *Ceylon*, 99. The failure to build rafts earlier, although the troops had been over thirty-six hours on the river bank, was another proof of Major Davie's incompetency.
[4] Cordiner, *Ceylon*, ii. 214 and 217. The two captains died in a Kandyan prison before 1807.

retreated to Trincomalee, abandoning 19 European invalids who were massacred. His detachment was saved from destruction by the arrival of 150 Malay troops from Trincomalee.[1] Major Davie would have met a happier fate if he had died with his companions. Governor Maitland made several efforts to obtain his release; but the King would only liberate him in exchange for a seaport. This demand was of course refused, and he remained a prisoner in Kandy until his death, which probably occurred in 1812.[2]

When the news of the disaster reached Colombo North made Davie his scapegoat, asserting that the massacre was entirely due to his cowardice and incapacity.[3] With this view it is impossible to agree: the Governor himself was ultimately responsible, although General Macdowall bore a share of the blame. The Davie massacre was the natural result of the blunders both political and military which marked the campaign. Given North's blind optimism and blundering policy, his credulous trust in Talawuwé, the breakdown of the transport service, the outbreak of fever, and the decision to leave the garrison in Kandy, only a *deus ex machina* could have saved the troops from destruction. The war of 1761 to 1766 should have taught the Governor that although the Dutch finally starved the Kandyans into surrendering the sea coast, they suffered severe losses and were three times forced to retreat from Kandy. There was even an ominous forerunner of the Davie massacre: 1,800 troops under Marten Rain who were left in the town of Kandy were cut off from communication with the coast, and were almost destroyed by fever and starvation.[4]

[1] Cordiner, *Ceylon*, ii. 214–15; Johnston, *Narrative of an Expedition to Candy*, 135: Barnsley's Narrative.

[2] Methley, *C.A. and L.R.* IV. iv. 181–2; D. P. Hettiarati, *C.A. and L.R.* VIII. ii. 164–5; *Journal of the Royal Asiatic Society, Ceylon Branch*, xxv, No. 69, 1917, Diary of Sir John D'Oyly, *passim*.

[3] The accounts of Cordiner and Valentia echo North's views. Cordiner was biased by his friendship for North, while Valentia, who paid a brief visit to Ceylon in 1803 and 1804, received most of his information from North. Marshall is impartial and on the whole accurate. He used the material available to Cordiner, and also the valuable notes of Simon Sawers, Commissioner of Kandy from 1819 to 1827, who obtained the Kandyan view of the massacre. The latest and most authoritative account is that of Miss Methley (*T.R.H.S.* IV. i). It is based on a careful examination of all the documentary material, and is on the whole very impartial, although there is a slight tendency unduly to exonerate Major Davie.   [4] Pieris, *Ceylon and the Hollanders*, 104–19.

While the ultimate responsibility lies with North and General Macdowall, Major Davie cannot be acquitted of incompetence for his conduct at Watapuluwa on June 24 to 26. In all fairness allowance must be made for an officer with no previous experience of active service, whose morale and powers of thought had probably been weakened by his severe attack of fever. Even if Davie had shown both energy and courage it seems very improbable that he could have extricated his garrison. Colonel Forbes strongly condemned him because he did not cut his way through to Colombo or Batticaloa, since the road across the Mahaweli Ganga to Trincomalee was barred.[1] In 1804 Captain Johnston retreated successfully from Kandy to Trincomalee with about 280 troops, European and native. The circumstances, however, were different; Johnston had food and ammunition, and his men were in good health. Despite these advantages he narrowly escaped destruction, and almost all the European survivors died at Trincomalee from fever and exhaustion.[2] Davie had no powder and little food, many of the Europeans were able to walk only a short distance; and to reach safety he must traverse over 100 miles of mountain and jungle, surrounded by thousands of active enemies. The Kandyans' repeated treachery should have shown Davie that his troops were doomed; but his anxiety to save them led him to snatch at the most unlikely chance of safety. In no other way can one mitigate the severity of one's condemnation for the surrender of Muttusamy and the final order to the troops to lay down their arms. Thirty-four fever-stricken Europeans and 390 unreliable native troops armed with bayonets probably would not have been very formidable antagonists for several thousand Kandyans; but at least they would not have been cut down unresistingly like cattle in a slaughterhouse. Whatever course Davie adopted the destruction of his force was probably inevitable; but unfortunately for his reputation he chose the least commendable.

'Universal consternation' reigned in Colombo when the news

[1] Forbes, *Ceylon*, i. 28–38.

[2] Johnston, *Narrative of an Expedition to Candy*, passim. As against Johnston's success, in 1764 400 troops under Major Frankena tried to cut their way out from Kandy to Colombo, but were annihilated at Sitavaka (Methley, *T.R.H.S.* iv. i. 123–4).

arrived; but a punitive expedition was out of the question for 'the hospitals were crowded with sick and dying'.[1] In August and September the Kandyans invaded British territory, on one occasion advancing to within twenty miles of Colombo, while they also stirred up numerous revolts amongst the Sinhalese. Weakened though the British were by fever, and greatly inferior in numbers, they easily routed the Kandyans with heavy losses.[2] The 66th Regiment, 800 strong, was sent as reinforcements, but owing to the Napoleonic War it was impossible to spare the 3,000 or 4,000 troops for which North asked to conquer Kandy.[3] The Secretary of State instructed North to make peace on the conditions that the Kandyans restored all British captives and evacuated Maritime Ceylon. The political independence of the country would be respected, but it would be held in economic dependence by the British possession of the coast and monopoly of the supply of salt.[4] North unsuccessfully attempted to make peace on these terms; and a desultory border war continued until 1805.[5] The campaign of 1804 was the occasion for a brilliant feat of arms. General Wemyss, who had succeeded General Macdowall in command of the troops, determined to invade Kandy with six columns, each starting from a separate seaport and meeting at the town of Kandy. Orders were issued on September 3, but a few days later the General decided that the six columns should merely ravage the borders of Kandy. On September 8 the new instructions were sent to Captain Johnston, the officer commanding at Batticaloa. Incredible as it may seem they were so vaguely worded that he justifiably construed them as a confirmation of his original orders to march to the town of Kandy.[6] Captain Johnston left Batticaloa on September 20 with about 280 troops, Europeans, Malays, and sepoys, and 550 pioneers and coolies. After heavy fighting he reached the town of Kandy on October 6 and

[1] Cordiner, *Ceylon*, ii. 218 and 221.
[2] Cordiner, *Ceylon*, ii. 221–35.
[3] Brit. Mus. Add. MS. No. 13867: Feb. 9, 1804.
[4] C.O. 55. 62: Mar. 29, 1804.
[5] Brit. Mus. Add. MS. No. 13867: July 29, 1804; C.O. 54. 16: Jan. 11, 1805; C.O. 54. 17: Feb. 21 and June 4, 1805, and *passim*; Tennent, *Ceylon*, ii. 84–6; Valentia, *Travels*, i. 253–4; Cordiner, *Ceylon*, ii. 257–8; Marshall, *Ceylon*, 131–2; Davy, *Ceylon*, 315.
[6] Marshall, *Ceylon*, Appendix V, 254–6.

remained there until October 9, when he retreated towards Trincomalee. The path was so narrow that in many places the troops were compelled to march in Indian file. They also suffered severely from rain, heat, and lack of food, many being so exhausted that they could not carry their muskets. So many of the coolies deserted that the doolies were abandoned, and the wounded either walked or were carried. The Kandyans made incessant attacks from ambush, and for the first three days no halt could be allowed even to attend to the wounded. The sepoys and to some extent the Europeans showed a loss of morale. Only the skill and bravery of the officers, and especially of Captain Johnston, saved the column from destruction. The troops reached Trincomalee on October 20 utterly exhausted, with a loss of at least 34 killed and 37 wounded. Of the European survivors almost all died in hospital from fever or exhaustion.[1]

The arrival in 1805 of General Sir Thomas Maitland as Governor of Ceylon brought about a change in policy towards Kandy. He saw that the Kandyans were far from defeated, and that the Government lacked the financial and military resources to bring them to terms. North's plan of campaign during 1804 and 1805 of devastating the border districts of Kandy was inhumane, and merely sacrificed the lives of the troops by exposing them to the pestilential climate. Maitland would remain strictly on the defensive, and would make peace on the sole conditions that the survivors of the Davie massacre were restored, and that 'we keep everything we had antecedent to the war'. A formal treaty was of little value, since no peace would 'continue one hour longer than we maintain' a garrison

---

[1] Johnston, *Narrative of an Expedition to Candy*, passim; Alexander, *Autobiography*, i. 148–66. Captain Arthur Johnston entered the army in 1794, retired in 1816 with the brevet rank of Lieutenant-Colonel, and died in 1823 or 1824. He was court-martialled for disobedience to orders, but was acquitted owing to the obscure wording of General Wemyss's dispatch of September 8 (Marshall, *Ceylon*, 121–30).

The strength of the column and the number of casualties is not quite certain: Marshall, usually a reliable authority, gave the number of troops as 82 Europeans and 202 natives, of whom 10 Europeans and 24 natives were killed and 6 Europeans and 31 natives wounded (Marshall, *Ceylon*, 123 and 126). Governor North stated that the force was composed of 60 Europeans and 220 natives, and that the number killed was 9 Europeans, 60 natives, and 76 coolies (C.O. 54. 16: Feb. 8, 1805).

strong enough to overawe the Kandyans. Their troops, however, were too contemptible to endanger Maritime Ceylon, so that 'in point of security we are now just as well as if peace was actually signed'.[1] The Governor failed to obtain a formal treaty of peace since the Kandyans insisted on the cession of a seaport. By tacit agreement hostilities ceased from 1805 to 1815, and the British suffered no inconvenience from the state of nominal war.[2]

During the years of peace the King of Kandy gradually made himself the real ruler of the country. Talawuwé was eventually deprived of all his offices, and being detected in a plot to murder the King and cause a revolt, he was beheaded in 1811.[3] The growing power of the King caused increasing hostility on the part of the Kandyan nobles, and there were several revolts which were put down with great cruelty. The British formed the erroneous opinion that the King was universally hated; but in fact he appears to have been popular except with his nobles since he protected the people against their exactions. By 1814 the majority of the nobles had been alienated by the loss of their power, and were prepared to welcome British intervention.[4] The execution of Talawuwé was followed by the appointment as First Adigar of his nephew, Ehelapola, the Dissawa or Governor of Saffragam. In 1814 he revolted but was quickly defeated by his rival, Molligoda, who succeeded him as First Adigar. The revolt was followed by an orgy of executions in Kandy which completed the alienation of the nobles.[5]

After their defeat Ehelapola and many other refugees fled to

[1] C.O. 54. 18: *passim*; C.O. 54. 21: Feb. 28, 1806; C.O. 55. 62: Feb. 21, 1805; June 11, 1807; Sept. 30, 1810; C.O. 54. 43: Mar. 31 and April 13, 1812; Lord, *Maitland*, 89–94.

[2] C.O. 54. 22: May 21 and Sept. 20, 1806; C.O. 54. 25: Feb. 28, 1807; C.O. 54. 26: Dec. 1, 1807; C.O. 54. 28: Mar. 9 and Sept. 1, 1808; C.O. 54. 34: Apr. 27, 1809; C.O. 54. 40: Sept. 11 and 29, 1811; C.O. 54. 42: Feb. 26 and Mar. 29, 1812; C.O. 54. 43: June 12, 1812; C.O. 54. 44: Nov. 3, 1812; C.O. 54. 47: Mar. 15, 1813.

[3] Turner, *C.A. and L.R.* III. iii. 225; C.O. 54. 40: July 16, 1811.

[4] Davy, *Ceylon*, 316–23; Marshall, *Ceylon*, 151, 163, and 170; *J.R.A.S.C.B.* xxv, No. 69, D'Oyly's Diary, *passim*.

[5] C.O. 54. 52: *passim*; Marshall, *Ceylon*, 134–7; Kehelpannala, *Ehelapola*, 1–32; Tennent, *Ceylon*, ii. 87–9. Ehelapola's young children were all beheaded by the King, who compelled their mother to witness the executions and to pound the severed heads with a pestle, or else be publicly raped. She was then drowned in a tank near Kandy (Davy, *Ceylon*, 320–2).

British territory and proffered their aid in overthrowing the King. The Governor, General Brownrigg, refused to move since he had received no instructions from the Secretary of State. Moreover he was not yet certain of strong Kandyan support against the King. The Davie massacre, however, was neither forgotten nor forgiven; and the Governor frankly avowed his 'strong conviction . . . of the expediency of reducing this hostile and annoying power when any good opportunity offers'. He would not attack Kandy unless British territory were invaded, 'important as the entire sovereignty of this island would prove to the British Crown, and naturally ambitious as I am that such an event might take place during the period of my' governorship.[1]

A few months later the King committed the act which was to destroy him. Ten native merchants trading in Kandy were falsely accused of being British spies; and by the King's command they were mutilated, the nose, right ear, and right arm being cut off. The victims were sent back to Colombo with the severed members tied round their necks, nine dying on the road.[2] The Governor rightly regarded this 'wanton, arbitrary, and barbarous piece of cruelty' inflicted on British subjects as ample cause for war. A transport service was built up which came triumphantly through the campaign of 1815. Promises of assistance were received from a large number of the Kandyan nobles, including Molligoda, the King's most trusted minister. The negotiations with the Kandyan chiefs were carried on by John D'Oyly, the Resident of Colombo, ably assisted by Ehelapola. General Brownrigg later declared that the conquest would have been impossible if it had not been for the help received from the Kandyans themselves, and the tact and ability with which D'Oyly had enlisted their support. By the end of the year all preparations for the invasion were completed. The Governor had no fears for the outcome: in 1803 the whole nation

---

[1] C.O. 54. 51: Feb. 10, Mar. 20, and June 28, 1814; C.O. 54. 52: Aug. 16, 1814; C.O. 54. 53: Sept. 5, 1814.

[2] Davy, *Ceylon*, 324. According to Kandyan testimony obtained after the war, the merchants were robbed by Kandyans, who then accused them of being spies in order to cover their own crime. 'It was generally supposed in the Kandyan country that the King had no doubt that the men were spies' (Marshall, *Ceylon*, 142).

was hostile, whereas in 1814 he believed that the King had lost the support of all save his immediate followers.[1]

On January 10, 1815, the Governor issued a proclamation to the Kandyans in which he assured them that the Britsh were the enemies only of the King. They would respect the Buddhist religion and temples, continue the nobles in their ranks and dignities, protect the people from all tyranny, and preserve the ancient laws and customs of the country.[2] The invasion began on January 11, 1815, but apart from a few skirmishes there was no fighting. The campaign seems indeed to have been rather in the nature of a triumphal procession, chief after chief joining the British as they advanced. Molligoda himself surrendered on February 8 after a feigned resistance, and on February 13 the troops occupied the town of Kandy. The King took refuge in the mountains with his few remaining adherents, but he was captured on February 18 by followers of Ehelapola, and handed over to the British. Within less than six weeks the ancient kingdom of Kandy had ceased to exist. The total strength of the British army was 3,744, of whom none were killed in action. In striking contrast to 1803 the health of the troops was excellent and supplies were ample, owing to the careful thoroughness with which General Brownrigg had organized his Transport and Medical Services.[3]

By the Convention of March 2, 1815, Kandy was annexed, King Vickrema Sinha and all his family being 'for ever excluded from the throne'.[4] The new form of government was 'carefully adapted to the wishes of the chiefs and people, with a particular degree of attention to some prejudices the indulgence of which

[1] C.O. 54. 53: Oct. 30, and Dec. 31, 1814; C.O. 54. 55: Mar. 9, 1815; C.O. 54. 60: June 1, 1816; *J.R.A.S.C.B.* xxv, No. 69, D'Oyly's Diary, *passim*; Marshall, *Ceylon*, 144; de Bussche, *Ceylon*, 16, 20–1, and 68–9.

[2] C.O. 54. 55: Jan. 16, 1815.

[3] C.O. 54. 55: Jan. 17 and Feb. 25, 1815; *J.R.A.S.C.B.* xxv, No. 69, D'Oyly's Diary, 183–99; Marshall, *Ceylon*, 143–58; Tolfrey, *A Narrative of Events Which Have Recently Occurred in Ceylon*, passim; Davy, *Ceylon*, 324–5; de Bussche, *Ceylon*, 17–34, 52–5, and 69.

[4] The King and about 94 of his Tamil relations and adherents were banished to Colombo, and in 1816 were removed to Vellore in India. They were given liberal pensions, and while State prisoners, were treated with great consideration. The King died of dropsy at Vellore in 1832; and in 1893 the descendants of the exiles were still living in southern India in receipt of pensions (C.O. 54. 59: Feb. 9, 1816; C.O. 54. 117: Feb. 29, 1832; *C.A. and L.R.* v. iv. 213–17; vi. i. 54–5).

was plainly understood to be a *sine qua non* of their voluntary submission to an European power'. The Kandyans were assured that their new rulers would respect their 'laws, institutions and customs'; while 'the religion of Boodhoo . . . is declared inviolable, and its rights, ministers, and places of worship are to be maintained and protected'. The nobles who had assisted the invasion were restored to the rule of their provinces from which the King had deposed them, and the British Government promised to respect their 'rights, privileges, and powers'. They administered the country in accordance with Kandyan laws and customs, subject to the general supervision and control of British civil servants, who were empowered 'to redress grievances and reform abuses'. While the Convention gave wide power to the nobles, it curbed abuse of their position by placing them under the authority of British officials.[1] A garrison of 1623 was left in Kandy, of which 752 were stationed in the town itself, while the remainder were scattered in detachments through the provinces.[2]

The annexation of Kandy was followed by three years of peace, during which the British tried hard to conciliate the nobles and the Buddhist priests. The country appeared to be peaceful and contented, but an undercurrent of uneasiness ran through General Brownrigg's dispatches: he knew that British rule was unpopular, and was constantly on his guard against possible revolts. In 1816 the Government arrested some of the priests and nobles who had formed a plot to destroy the garrison and expel the British from Kandy.[3] The motives of the conspirators were the same as those which led to the revolt of 1818.[4]

[1] Aitchison, *Treaties*, x, 289–92; C.O. 54. 55: Mar. 9 and 15, and Apr. 1, 1815.

[2] de Bussche, *Ceylon*, 39. [3] C.O. 54. 61: Nov. 5, 1816.

[4] C.O. 54. 56: July 20 and 21, 1815; C.O. 54. 59: Feb. 9, 1816; C.O. 54. 60: June 5, 1816; C.O. 54. 61: Nov. 5, 1816; C.O. 54. 65: Feb. 6 and May 29 1817; C.O. 54. 70: Feb. 19, 1818; Davy, *Ceylon*, 326–7; Marshall, *Ceylon*, 175–80. It is uncertain how far the British Government had effectively diminished the power of the Kandyan nobles. The civil servants were far too few adequately to control them, and they were compelled to use as their subordinates the very men whose abuse of power they were attempting to restrain (C.O. 54. 60: June 5, 1816). The raiyats were strongly attached to their chiefs and to their time-honoured abuses, and refused to co-operate with their new rulers. One is inclined to doubt whether the British were more than moderately successful in curbing the power of the nobles in the first years after the conquest.

'The Priests appear to be the grand movers of these plots, by their influence over the chiefs.' They were dangerous and secret enemies with whom it was difficult to cope. Despite the scrupulous respect paid to Buddhist rites the Church was bitterly offended by 'our manner of treating their priests, who require respect amounting almost to adoration'. The Kandyan nobles were alienated because 'their consequence [was] most sensibly fallen and their powers considerably abridged as well as their emoluments'. An especial grievance was the impartiality of British justice, which disregarded their immemorial right to extort 'undefined and arbitrary dues' from the raiyats. 'Before, no one but the King was above them; now they were inferior to every civilian in our service,—to every officer in our army. Though officially treated with respect, it was only officially: a common soldier passed a proud Kandyan chief with as little attention as he would a fellow of the lowest caste . . . . Ignorant of their distinctions, high caste and low caste were treated alike by most Englishmen who came in contact with them: and undesignedly and unknowingly we often offended and provoked them when we least intended it.' Like all Kandyans the nobles were strongly attached to the institution of monarchy, and deeply resented its disappearance. The distant court of George III was no substitute for the court of a visible monarch where they had enjoyed elaborate ceremonial, unbounded flattery, and the opportunity to display their magnificence. The whole nation 'wanted a King whom they could see, and before whom they could prostrate and obtain summary justice'. They disliked the British as foreign conquerors: 'they made no complaint of oppression or misrule, contenting themselves with expressing a wish that we should leave the country'. The partially successful attempts to protect the raiyats from the oppression of their chiefs failed to win their support. Intensely conservative, they were firmly attached to aristocratic rule, and they preferred its immemorial abuses to the strange reforms of the foreign conqueror. So when the Kandyan nobles revolted in 1818 their people followed them partly from traditional loyalty and partly from fear of their power. One circumstance alone prevented the formation of a formidable conspiracy: the jealousies of the nobles prevented them from accepting one of their number as king. The principal noble, Ehelapola, was apparently ambitious to gain the throne; but he had no general ascendancy over the other chiefs, and rather than submit to him they preferred a temporary acquiescence in British rule.[1]

'The outbreak of the rebellion in the province of Velassy was purely accidental, and the chiefs and people of the other provinces were as much taken by surprise as were the English authorities.'[2] A pretender to the throne named Wilbawa established himself in the jungle, and with the assistance of Buddhist priests incited the province to revolt. Wilson, the Assistant Resident at Badulla, was not aware of the seriousness of the situation, and in October 1817 advanced against Wilbawa with twenty-four Malay soldiers. They were forced to retreat by the rebels, and the survivors returned to Badulla with the news that Wilson had been killed and several Malays captured. Sir John D'Oyly sent Molligoda and a force of troops into the Provinces of Uva and Welassi, and by the end of December the revolt was apparently quelled.[3] 'The outbreak of revolt in Velassy acted like a match thrown into a barrel of gunpowder upon the dissatisfied and disaffected population of the whole country.'[4] Although there was no organized conspiracy for a general rising the universal hostility to the British formed a fairly effective substitute. Many of the principal nobles soon joined the rebels, including Kapitipola, Dissawa of Uva and nephew of Ehelapola, who became the pretender's First Adigar and the leader of the insurrection. By February or March of 1818 the whole of Kandy was in revolt, with the exception of Molligoda's Province of the Four Korales and a few other small provinces. Apart from Molligoda himself, who was heartily loyal, every chief of importance had either joined the revolt or

---

[1] C.O. 54. 56: July 20 and Sept. 26, 1815; Marshall, *Ceylon*, 178–9; Kehelpannala, *Ehelapola*, 33 and 36. After the conquest Ehelapola was given estates and money, but the refusal to appoint him Regent 'embittered him considerably'. He refused to accept any office, and contented himself with the position of the premier Kandyan noble (C.O. 54. 55: Apr. 1, 1815). He affected royal state, and roused the suspicions of General Brownrigg who watched him closely (C.O. 54. 61: Nov. 5, 1816; C.O. 54. 66: Sept. 25, 1817).

[2] Marshall, *Ceylon*, 179.

[3] C.O. 54. 66: Nov. 7, Dec. 15 and 28, 1817; Marshall, *Ceylon*, 180–8.

[4] Marshall, *Ceylon*, 188.

had been arrested.[1] The loyalty of the Four Korales was of great importance to the British, since in that Province lay the mountain passes through which ran the path from Colombo to Kandy.[2] Serious though the situation was in March it grew steadily worse during the next three months: 'not a leader of any consequence had been taken, and not a district subdued or tranquillised'. In May an event occurred which very greatly strengthened the cause of the pretender: a Buddhist priest stole the sacred Tooth of Buddha from its shrine in Kandy and brought it to Kapitipola. The Kandyans believed that whoever possessed the relic was the lawful ruler of the kingdom.[3] The rebels followed the same tactics as in 1803, avoiding pitched battles and ambushing small detachments or convoys. The revolt often flared up again in districts which had apparently been pacified; and on April 12 General Brownrigg reported that if reinforcements had not been sent from India it might have been necessary to evacuate Kandy.[4] The army was divided into a large number of small detachments which were scattered through the revolted provinces, while chains of fortified posts were built. The troops were exhausted by constant and often fruitless marches over unknown and difficult country; they were drenched by torrential rains, and at times suffered seriously from lack of supplies. Owing to the frequent attacks made on convoys the transport service partially broke down. Losses from disease were heavy, particularly from fever and dysentery. The strength of the British army 'hardly amounted to five thousand, and I believe it is not too high to estimate our total loss at about one thousand', of which barely one-tenth was incurred in action.[5] General Brownrigg found that the only way

[1] C.O. 54. 66: Nov. 7, 1817; C.O. 54. 70: *passim*; Davy, *Ceylon*, 328. Molligoda's loyalty was probably caused by his ancient animosity against Ehelapola. Molligoda rendered valuable service and died in 1823 (Marshall, *Ceylon*, 190, 199, and 277).

[2] Forbes, *Ceylon*, i. 50.

[3] C.O. 54. 71: July 24, 1818.

[4] C.O. 54. 66: *passim*; C.O. 54. 70: Apr. 12, 1818, and *passim*; C.O. 54. 71: July 24, 1818; Davy, *Ceylon*, 329; Marshall, *Ceylon*, 207–10.

[5] C.O. 54. 70: Jan. 30 and Apr. 12, 1818; C.O. 54. 71: July 24 and Oct. 9, 1818; Davy, *Ceylon*, 331, 488–94; Marshall, *Notes on Medical Topography*, passim. In 1818 the European troops in Kandy had an average strength of 2,863, of whom 678 died, most of them from disease. The 73rd Regiment, 864 strong in 1818, lost in 1818 and 1819 621 men, of whom 516 died and 105

to counter the Kandyan tactics was 'to burn and lay waste the property of the Headmen'. 'When a district rose in rebellion one or more military posts were established in it; martial law was proclaimed; the dwellings of the resisting inhabitants were burnt; their fruit trees were often cut down, and the country was scoured in every direction by small detachments.'[1] Regrettable as was the necessity of starving the Kandyans into submission, the only alternative was an indefinite continuance of guerilla fighting.

The tide turned about July or August 1818, and by the end of October the rebellion had collapsed. Kapitipola suffered several defeats, Buddha's Tooth was recovered, and all the principal rebel leaders surrendered or were captured. Kapitipola and Madugala were tried by court martial and beheaded.[2] The revolt failed since the rebels lost heart owing to their heavy losses, and because the rivalry of their chiefs prevented them from effectively uniting under a single leader. It was estimated that perhaps 10,000 Kandyans had been killed in action or had died from disease or famine. They had lost most of their cattle and crops, while for two seasons they had been unable to cultivate their land, and had been forced to live in the jungles and mountains.[3] In September 1818 their cause was still further weakened when Madugala discovered that the pretender Wilbawa was a former Buddhist priest and not, as he had declared, a relative of the ex-King. Madugala for a time imprisoned the impostor and his Adigar Kapitipola, and set up a rival claimant to the throne.[4] The recovery of Buddha's Tooth had also a very important effect upon the superstitious Kandyans, who 'declared that now indeed we were masters of Kandy, since the country went with the tooth'.[5]

The pretender Wilbawa escaped and is said to have lived in concealment amongst the Veddahs of Bintenne. In 1830 he was

were invalided home, the majority from disease contracted during the rebellion. In 1820 the regiment had only 38 deaths (Marshall, *Ceylon*, 191, 210–12).

[1] C.O. 54. 66: Nov. 27, 1817; C.O. 54. 70: Feb. 28, 1818; Marshall, *Ceylon*, 190; Davy, *Ceylon*, 330–2, and 431.

[2] C.O. 54. 71: *passim*; C.O. 54. 73: Jan. 8, 1819; Davy, *Ceylon*, 329.

[3] C.O. 54. 65: Nov. 27, 1817; Marshall, *Ceylon*, 192–7, and 331.

[4] C.O. 54. 70: Feb. 19 and Apr. 12, 1818; C.O. 54. 71: Oct. 9, 1818; Marshall, *Ceylon*, 196.

[5] C.O. 54. 73: Jan. 8, 1819; Davy, *Ceylon*, 369.

captured, tried for high treason, and condemned to life imprisonment; but he was given a 'free and unconditional pardon' by the Secretary of State, Lord Goderich.[1] About twenty of the rebel leaders were banished to Mauritius, while others were imprisoned at Colombo. By 1830 they had all been gradually released with the exception of Talawuwé. He was liberated in 1832 but was required to live in Colombo, since his 'influence and talents . . . might even now be in some degree dangerous'.[2] Amongst the prisoners was Ehelapola, who was arrested in March 1818 on suspicion of complicity in the rebellion. He always protested his innocence, and it is impossible to decide whether he was guilty or not. The evidence against him was too vague to justify a trial: but General Brownrigg considered that in the disturbed state of Kandy it would be dangerous to release him owing to his great influence and his suspicious conduct in 1815 to 1817.[3] He was kept in easy confinement at Colombo and later at Mauritius, where he died of dysentery in 1829.[4]

The revolt of 1818 was the most serious attempt of the Kandyans to regain their independence; but for nearly a generation the Government was occasionally troubled by small risings. The procedure became almost stereotyped: the 'rightful King'—an impostor rarely if ever related to the deposed royal family—appeared in a remote district, and gathered a small local following which often included Buddhist priests. An Agent of Government soon learned of his appearance, and a small force of troops sufficed to capture him and disperse his followers. The execution or more frequently the imprisonment of the leaders ended the incident. The great majority of the Kandyans held aloof from the rebels, and indeed assisted in capturing them. The outbreaks showed, however, that Kandy

[1] C.O. 54. 107: Nov. 20, 1830; C.O. 54. 117: Mar. 6 and May 29, 1832; C.O. 54. 121: Nov. 23, 1830, and *passim*; C.O. 55. 72: Sept. 12, 1831.

[2] C.O. 54. 73: Jan. 8 and Feb. 8, 1819; C.O. 54. 74: Apr. 24, 1819; C.O. 54. 77: Feb. 25, 1820; C.O. 54. 80: May 10, 1821; C.O. 54. 88: May 14, 1825; C.O. 54. 117: Mar. 6, 1832; C.O. 54. 118: Sept. 22, 1832.

[3] C.O. 54. 70: Apr. 12, 1818; C.O. 54. 71: July 23, 1818; C.O. 54. 73: Nov. 27, 1818, and Jan. 8, 1819; C.O. 54. 84: July 1, 1823; Kehelpannala, *Ehelapola*, 37–8.

[4] C.O. 54. 88: May 14, 1825; C.O. 54. 104: Jan. 27, 1829; C.O. 54. 105: Oct. 29, 1829; Kehelpannala, *Ehelapola*, 38–43.

was not reconciled to British rule, and led the administration to watch carefully for signs of disaffection. Two petty outbreaks of this nature occurred in 1820, two more in 1823, and others in 1824, 1842, 1848, and 1858.[1]

A curious incident occurred in 1834 which may perhaps have been a plot to overthrow the British Government in Kandy. Mahawalatenna, Dissawa of Saffragam, who had been 'uniformly attached to the Government', and several Buddhist priests gave information of a treasonable conspiracy. Government secret agents also unearthed rather vague evidence of a plot. Some of the principal Buddhist priests and Kandyan nobles were accused, including the Dissawa Dunawilla and the First Adigar Molligoda (a brother of the Molligoda of 1815). Their plan was to poison the Governor and principal officials at a banquet, corrupt the Malay troops, and with their assistance destroy the European garrison and re-establish the independence of Kandy. The Executive Council was at first sceptical, but in July it became converted to the Governor's belief in the reality of the conspiracy, and the suspects were arrested.[2] Further information was subsequently obtained which made it 'morally impossible' to doubt their guilt, and it was decided to bring them to trial.[3] The King's Advocate examined the evidence and concurred in the decision: there was clearly a plot to restore the Kandyan monarchy, while at the same time the evidence was too vague and unsatisfactory to allow 'any certain decision' as to the number and character of the conspirators. 'A public trial is the only satisfactory test of truth.'[4] The prisoners were tried for high treason at Kandy in January 1835, and were all acquitted by the jury 'in direct opposition

---

[1] C.O. 54. 76: Jan. 22, 1820; C.O. 54. 77: *passim*; C.O. 54. 79: Nov. 11, 1820; C.O. 54. 84: *passim*; C.O. 54. 86: Oct. 26, 1824; C.O. 54. 197: May 9, 1842; C.O. 55. 100: Aug. 14 and Sept. 27, 1858; Campbell, *Ceylon*, i. 80–2, and 111–14.

[2] C.O. 54. 135: Sept. 15, 1834, and *passim*. While the guilt of the accused was 'unquestionable', the evidence 'legally available' against them was 'extremely meagre', since they had been arrested before they committed any overt act of rebellion. The Government ordered the arrests as it feared that a longer delay to secure evidence might afford it in the shape of an open revolt.

[3] C.O. 54. 135: Sept. 23, 1834; C.O. 54. 136: Oct. 15, 1834; C.O. 55. 75: Apr. 2, 1835.

[4] C.O. 54, 136: Dec. 24, 1834; C.O. 54. 137: *passim*.

to the summing of the judge'. Despite the acquittal the Government dismissed all the chiefs from their offices, since it was 'so manifest that they were at least cognizant of a treasonable conspiracy'.[1]

To determine the truth is even more impossible now than in 1835. The Government acted in all sincerity, being convinced of the guilt of the accused even if they doubted their ability legally to prove it. It is a truism that moral certainty is not necessarily false because it lacks the support of legal proof. That some plot existed is perhaps confirmed by the evidence of Molligoda himself. He stated that he was aware of a treasonable conspiracy of which he had intended to inform the Government, but that he was prevented by his sudden arrest.[2] The Kandyan nobles and the Buddhist priests admittedly chafed under British rule. The especial grievance of the Church was that when temple tenants refused to perform their services the priests were compelled to take legal action since the Government refused to interfere. The nobles strongly resented the steady diminution of their power and prestige, the abolition of Rajakaria, and the attempt to break up Kandyan national unity by incorporating parts of the country in the Maritime Provinces. The latest measure adopted to weaken the nobles was the announcement that the Government intended to abolish the positions of Adigar and Dissawa. Though shorn of almost all their former power these traditional offices of the old kingdom still commanded much respect amongst the Kandyans; and the nobles clung to them as almost the last relics of their great estate before the days of the British conquest.[3] On the other hand Major Skinner always denied the existence of any plot. He had a unique and unrivalled knowledge of the natives,

[1] C.O. 54. 140: Feb. 9, 1835; C.O. 55. 77: Aug. 13, 1835; Marshall, *Ceylon*, 219–20.

[2] C.O. 54. 135: Sept. 15, 1834; C.O. 54. 140: June 26, 1835. It seems highly probable that the informers' evidence was to some extent at least perjured; and it is not impossible that Molligoda became frightened and hoped to better his case by himself inventing a plot and declaring he had intended to reveal it. To meet perjury by counter-perjury is a device not unknown in Sinhalese courts.

[3] C.O. 54. 122: Dec. 24, 1831; C.O. 54. 137: Printed report of the trial in January 1835, and Memorial of April 1834 of Molligoda and Dunawilla to the King on the grievances of the Kandyan chiefs; C.O. 55. 79: Dec. 17, 1839; C.O. 54. 210: Mar. 19, 1844.

and his opinion is entitled to great weight.[1] Years later, similar testimony was given by Philip Anstruther, the Colonial Secretary, whose knowledge of the natives rivalled that of Major Skinner. 'I do not believe that there was one word of truth in the evidence either for the Crown or for the prisoners on the trials. The trials were sanctioned by myself, and of course I had at the time the opinion that the prisoners were guilty. . . . It is a circumstance that has puzzled me more than anything I ever met with in my life.'[2] The Government itself seems eventually to have modified its opinion, for the chiefs were reinstated in office.[3] According to Major Skinner the effect of the trials 'was seriously to impair the influence and authority of Government in the minds and affections of the people.'[4]

[1] Skinner, *Ceylon*, 189–90, and 217–18. Skinner believed that the informers had either fabricated their evidence to ruin their enemies, or else that they had 'wilfully exaggerated . . . to ingratiate themselves with Government'.
[2] *Parl. Pap. H.C.* 36 of 1851, VIII. i. pp. 750–1.
[3] C.O. 54. 210: Mar. 19, 1844.
[4] Skinner, *Ceylon*, 218.

X

LORD TORRINGTON AND THE KANDYAN REVOLT
1847–1850

VISCOUNT TORRINGTON, Governor of Ceylon from 1847 to 1850, had had no experience in colonial administration. His principal qualifications appear to have been that he was a Lord of the Bedchamber, a Whig peer, and a relation of the Prime Minister, Lord John Russell. For many years, however, Ceylon had had an uneventful history, and Lord Torrington might safely be expected to deal adequately with such matters of routine as road construction and balancing the budget. Moreover, he would be guided by a brilliant Colonial Secretary, Sir Emerson Tennent. Under ordinary conditions the selection would probably have been justified by results; but the situation in Ceylon was already far from normal, and in the next two years it became distinctly worse. To a considerable extent Lord Torrington's failure was due to difficulties which he inherited; but his personal qualities went far to aggravate what must have been a critical period for even the most experienced and tactful of Governors. Lord Torrington seems to have been tactless, arrogant, and hot-tempered, and he soon alienated the Europeans and burghers by the scarcely veiled contempt with which he treated their opposition. It appears equally evident that his opponents were frequently unreasonable in their demands and intemperate in their criticisms. Long before the revolt broke out in 1848 the relations between Torrington and a large part of the European and burgher community had hardened into contemptuous dislike on the one hand and deep hostility on the other.

Soon after his arrival in Ceylon in 1847 the Governor became involved in a dispute which had originated under his predecessor, Governor Campbell. The Verandah Question was in itself a very trifling affair, but Lord Torrington's method of handling it created enemies who turned to good account the blunders which he made in the Kandyan revolt of 1848. The burgher and native inhabitants of Colombo had built verandahs on the fronts of their houses which encroached from six to ten feet on the streets, and which were frequently converted into shops. While the Dutch and British had issued stringent Ordinances forbidding this practice the regulations had rarely been enforced. Although some of the verandahs dated from the eighteenth century the majority had perhaps been built within the preceding thirty years. The growth of the coffee industry had transformed the somnolent seaport of Colombo, and the increased traffic made it imperative to widen the principal streets. Legally the verandahs were usurpations of Crown land; but the occupants denied the Government's right uncompromisingly to enforce its claims in view of their 'long and uninterrupted' possession.[1]

In February 1846 Governor Campbell enacted that all verandahs adjudged by the Government to obstruct the streets should be removed without compensation. When the verandah did not form an obstruction the owner might obtain a legal title by buying the land at a price of from threepence to ninepence a square foot.[2] The Ordinance was exceedingly unpopular amongst the burghers and natives; but very few Europeans took part in the protests which were sent to the Ceylon Government and to the Secretary of State. The principal organizers of the opposition were Doctor Elliott, the editor of the *Colombo Observer*, and Richard Morgan, an able burgher barrister.[3] Doctor Elliott's medical skill had made him very popular and influential in Colombo; and from first to last he opposed Lord Torrington with vehemence and gusto. A warm-hearted and pugnacious Irishman, his hatred of any semblance of oppression and his love of a quarrel both combined to make him the enemy of the Governor.[4] The Secretary of State at first approved the

---

[1] C.O. 54. 224: Mar. 9, 1846; C.O. 54. 225: July 7, 1846; C.O. 54. 236: June 28, 1847.

[2] C.O. 54. 224: Mar. 9, 1846; C.O. 54. 225: July 7, 1846; C.O. 54. 227: Nov. 14, 1846.

[3] C.O. 54. 225: July 7, 1846; C.O. 54. 227: Oct. 26, 1846; C.O. 54. 237: July 7, 1847. Richard Morgan was later appointed Queen's Advocate, and eventually was knighted and became a Judge of the Supreme Court (Digby, *Morgan*, passim).

[4] Christopher Elliott, M.D. (1810–59), came to Colombo in 1834 as Colonial Assistant Surgeon, but in 1835 he resigned and built up a large private practice. He became the owner and editor of the *Colombo Observer* (Ferguson, *Pioneers of the Planting Enterprise*, i. 21–4). Governor Sir Colin Campbell described him as 'a restless and not over scrupulous person' who 'endeavoured

M

Ordinance; but in April 1847 Lord Grey advised Torrington to pay moderate compensation where the verandahs removed had stood for more than twenty or thirty years.[1] He preferred to enforce a rather harsh policy by tactless methods, and the Ordinance was carried into effect during 1848 and 1849. It may be granted that the burghers were not guiltless of exaggeration and misrepresentation, and that Doctor Elliott in the *Observer* filled his columns with bitter abuse of the Governor and the Civil Service. Despite the provocation Torrington was not justified in dismissing the claims of the occupiers as the 'most consummate effrontery', and in treating with brusqueness and discourtesy the deputation of Elliott, Morgan, and others who called upon him to protest at the Ordinance.[2] Torrington's final decision was that compensation would only be granted on the removal of verandahs which had stood for over fifty years. If a verandah which had been built within fifty years were left undisturbed the occupier must pay for the land the price fixed in 1846. Torrington refused to accept oral testimony as to the age of the verandahs and insisted on the production of the title deeds—a difficult matter, since often both the originals and the Government copies had disappeared.[3] The Colonial Office was distinctly critical, feeling that the Governor had been somewhat harsh and arbitrary 'in the sudden exertion of the legal powers of the Crown . . . beyond the limits of natural equity'.[4]

The Verandah Question had affected only the burghers and natives, but about the same time the Governor became involved in a dispute with the Europeans as well. The reason was that perennial source of strife, official control of the Legislative Council; and on this question the Europeans and the educated

to attract attention to his newspaper by a pretty general abuse of the European officers in the Colony'. The circulation of the *Observer* was about 300, 'chiefly amongst the Burghers' (C.O. 54. 234: Apr. 14, 1847).

[1] C.O. 55. 87: Oct. 26, 1846, and Apr. 23, 1847.

[2] C.O. 54. 236: June 28, 1847; C.O. 54. 237: July 10, 1847. The tone of Torrington's dispatches is distinctly less restrained and judicial than that of his predecessor, Governor Campbell.

[3] C.O. 54. 236: June 28, 1847; C.O. 54. 237: July 10, 1847; C.O. 55. 89: Oct. 22, 1847; C.O. 54. 244: Jan. 12, 1848; C.O. 54. 245: Feb. 3, 1848; *Parl. Pap. H.C.* 106 of 1850, vol. xii, 124–9; Digby, *Morgan*, i. 142–7. In 1847 many of the Colombo land surveys were also found inaccurate (C.O. 54. 240: Nov. 12, 1847).

[4] C.O. 54. 245: Feb. 3, 1848: and Colonial Office Memos. of Hawes ('a hard case'), Strachey, and Merivale; C.O. 55. 89: Apr. 13, 1848.

burghers and natives were apparently united. They were influenced partly by democratic theory, holding that self-government or some advance thereto was the inalienable right of
British subjects. The European merchants and planters had
also a more practical motive: they wished to control the Legislative Council in order to increase the expenditure upon roads.
Dislike of the Governor seems to have played its part: one at
least of the petitions for reform hinted at his dictatorial and
discourteous attitude towards unofficial members.[1] The leaders
of the movement were Richard Morgan and Doctor Elliott.
Petitions were sent to the Secretary of State demanding that
the Legislative Council should be placed under the control of
elected unofficial members, and that the official members should
be permitted to speak and vote freely. Morgan and Elliott
went further than most of their followers in advocating the
establishment of responsible government. Even less support
was forthcoming for Elliott's proposal that the franchise should
be rapidly extended to the uneducated native population.[2]
The Governor strongly opposed the petitions as 'unworthy of
attention', and the Colonial Office while condemning his tactless
attitude refused to make any concessions. The demand for
reform persisted for several years, but finally died down with
the return of prosperity to the coffee plantations and the increased expenditure upon roads by Governor Ward.[3]

One of the most important measures of Torrington's administration was his financial reforms. Ever since the British conquest
the Treasury had cherished the hope that the colony would soon
become self-supporting. Sometimes this consummation was
attained through a lucrative pearl fishery or an increased export
of cinnamon; but usually the annual accounts showed a deficit.
The budgets of 1843 to 1845 inclusive produced a total surplus
of £133,000, which was derived from the export tax on coffee
and the large sale of Crown lands for plantations. In 1846 the
Treasury and the Colonial Office decided that financial stability
had been attained, and that the time was ripe for a reform of

[1] C.O. 54. 247: Feb. 11 and 24, 1848.
[2] Digby, *Morgan*, i. 136–40; C.O. 54. 247: Feb. 11 and 24, 1848; C.O. 54.
250: Aug. 15, 1848: C.O. 54. 252: Nov. 14 and 15, 1848; C.O. 55. 91: Feb. 1
and May 15, 1849.
[3] C.O. 55. 89: May 18, 1848; C.O. 54. 247: Mar. 8, 1848: and C.O. Memos.

the system of taxation. Reports were sent home in 1846 by the principal members of the Civil Service, the most valuable being that of the Colonial Secretary, Sir Emerson Tennent.[1] The committee of Colonial Office and Treasury officials who examined the reports adopted almost entirely Tennent's proposals for the reduction of taxation, but they rejected some of his most important recommendations for reducing expenditure. They based their decision upon the belief that the revenue would continue to increase. They recommended the abolition of all export duties and the establishment of a uniform import duty of 5 per cent. on all imports. The committee approved the proposed licence tax on muskets, and advised that a general land tax should be substituted for the tenth on rice lands as soon as a survey of Ceylon had been carried out.[2] On June 18, 1847, Lord Grey instructed Torrington to carry out the committee's report 'so far, and only so far, as' he considered that it was 'just and can be successfully brought into execution'.[3]

The Ceylon Government soon discovered that the treasury could not afford the cost of making an accurate survey and imposing a fair rate of tax on each variety of soil and produce. Moreover, the work presented unexpected difficulties owing to the minute subdivision of land amongst the natives.[4] The Secretary of State had based his recommendations on the assumption that the annual surplus of revenue would continue, and that there was in the Ceylon Treasury an accumulated surplus of £200,000. Owing, however, to the collapse of the

[1] C.O. 54. 150: Aug. 15, 1848; C.O. 54. 224: Apr. 14, 1846; C.O. 54. 227: Nov. 4, 1846; Grey, *Colonial Policy of Lord John Russell's Administration*, ii. 163–5; Tennent, *Ceylon*, ii. 168–72. From 1803 to 1829 the annual deficit varied from £30,000 to £140,000, except for a surplus of £15,323 in 1822. In 1829–36 inclusive the annual surplus varied from £30,000 to £50,000, due chiefly to successful pearl fisheries. In 1837–42 the average annual deficit was £15,937 due to the failure of the pearl fisheries. In 1843–5 inclusive the average annual surplus was £44,430 (C.O. 54. 228: Oct. 22, 1846).

[2] C.O. 54. 228: Apr. 13, 1847; C.O. 55. 90: Apr. 22, 1847. Originally paid in kind, the tenth on rice lands had to a considerable extent been commuted into a tax in money between 1827 and 1842. All other cultivated lands had been declared tax free in 1824.

[3] C.O. 55. 87: June 18, 1847; C.O. 55. 91: Feb. 8, 1849. The most important dispatches and reports on the financial reforms are printed in *Parl. Pap.* [933] of 1848, vol. xlii of 1847–8.

[4] C.O. 54. 247: Mar. 16, 1848. Torrington inquired how he should assess the land tax on a raiyat whose holding was 1/22,000 part of a coco-nut tree.

coffee industry the budget of 1846 had a heavy deficit, which swallowed up half the surplus. The bulk of the remainder was required to cover the £87,400 of paper currency which was in circulation, and further deficits were anticipated. The proposed land tax was abandoned, and the tenth on rice was retained for another half-century.[1] In spite of the declining revenue the proposed customs tariff was adopted with the single exception that the export duty on cinnamon was retained, although reduced from 1s. to 4*d*. a pound. The loss of revenue was £25,644, and to make up the deficit Lord Grey ordered the imposition of additional taxes and a drastic curtailment of every branch of expenditure.[2]

The new taxes aroused strong and in some instances justifiable opposition, but the Governor did not deserve all the censure which was heaped upon him. Some of his taxes had already been proposed by his predecessor, Governor Campbell, and had received the endorsement of the Colonial Office. The whole financial policy 'was strictly in accordance with our views, and had been fully explained to Lord Torrington previously to his departure from this Country'.[3] Owing to his recent arrival in Ceylon he was naturally guided by the advice of his Executive Council, and especially by that of Sir Emerson Tennent. The charge against Lord Torrington would have been more correctly stated if it had been said that he carried through what was in some respects an ill-advised financial policy designed by other men, in a hasty and arbitrary fashion. In 1848 Lord Torrington increased the existing stamp duties, which were 'singularly productive' because of the Sinhalese love of litigation. The natives were incensed by the regulation that all owners of shops, boats, carriages, and bullock carts must pay an annual licence of £1. Two measures which aroused very strong native opposition were the imposition of an annual licence of 2s. 6*d*. on each firearm, and of 1s. on each dog. These taxes were first

[1] C.O. 54. 261: Nov. 15, 1849. The exact amount of the deficit of 1846 is uncertain. It was variously given as £100,000 (C.O. 55. 89: July 17, 1848), £81,801 (C.O. 54. 249: July 4, 1848), and £74,000 (Grey, *Colonial Policy*, ii. 164–72).

[2] C.O. 55. 90: Apr. 22, 1847; C.O. 55. 89: July 17, 1848; Grey, *Colonial Policy*, ii. 164–72.

[3] Grey, *Colonial Policy*, ii. 170–1; C.O. 54. 252: Nov. 14, 1848; C.O. 55. 91: Oct. 24, 1848, and Jan. 16, 1849.

proposed by the Legislative Council in 1841, and were intended
as police measures as much as to increase the revenue. The
villages swarmed with an 'immense quantity' of pariahs, and
outbreaks of rabies had become an 'intolerable nuisance'. The
gun tax was designed to restrict the increasing use of firearms
in crime.[1] Very brief experience showed what preliminary investigation would have revealed, that the gun and dog taxes
were unenforceable. The village pariahs were useful scavengers
and watchdogs, but as they were usually masterless they all ran
the risk of being destroyed for non-payment of the licence.
The annual gun licence was far too heavy, being often equivalent
to 20 or 25 per cent. of the value of the weapon, which was
frequently 'utterly useless'. Moreover, 'firearms may be deemed
in Ceylon an agricultural implement: they are essential to protect the crops from elephants and wild beasts'. The licences
for shops, firearms, and dogs produced little revenue and were
repealed in 1848 after the revolt.[2]

The most important of the new measures, the Road Ordinance
of 1848, was originated by Mr. Philip Wodehouse, Government
Agent of the Western Province. It required every inhabitant
of Ceylon to work six days annually on the repair or construction of the roads, or else to pay a commutation tax of 3s. One-
third of the labour was to be used solely for village roads, the
remainder for the principal highways, and no man could be
employed beyond a radius of twenty miles from his home. The
Ordinance applied to all races and classes with the exception of
Buddhist priests;[3] while the 3s. commutation tax could be
earned by a few days' labour. The Ordinance aroused the
strongest opposition amongst the natives and their European
sympathizers as a revival of Rajakaria. It was an absurd

[1] C.O. 54. 190: Oct. 21, 1841; C.O. 54. 196: Apr. 5, 1842; C.O. 54. 244:
Jan. 10, 1848; C.O. 54. 247: Mar. 7, 1848; C.O. 54. 261: Nov. 15 and Dec. 14,
1849; C.O. 55. 89: Mar. 24 and July 14, 1848; C.O. 55. 91: Oct. 24, 1848;
Sirr, *Ceylon*, ii. 8–9; Tennent, *Ceylon*, ii. 171.

[2] C.O. 54. 249: Sept. 9, 1848: and C.O. Memo.; C.O. 54. 252: Nov. 14, 1848;
C.O. 54. 257: Jan. 12 and Feb. 14, 1849; C.O. 55. 91: Jan. 16, 1849; *Colombo
Observer*, Nov. 7, 1848.

[3] C.O. 54. 251: Sept. 13, 1848; C.O. 54. 252: Nov. 13, 1848. After the suppression of the revolt of 1848 Buddhist priests were exempted from the
provisions of the Road Ordinance. The exemption was dictated by expediency:
during the revolt they had stirred up disaffection by citing the Ordinance as
a proof that the British were oppressing the Buddhist religion.

exaggeration to compare so moderate and carefully regulated
a corvée with the unrestricted and often oppressive exactions of
the former system. The natives, however, were content with
jungle paths, were indifferent to increased prosperity, and
regarded the measure as intended solely for the benefit of the
European coffee planters. It is true that the majority of the
main roads at this period were designed primarily to develop
the plantations. The native standard of living, however, was
considerably improved by the increased prosperity which was
brought to Ceylon by the coffee industry. The allocation of
one-third of the labour to village roads ensured that the natives
would benefit directly as well as indirectly. Native cultivation
was extended to fertile areas which had been abandoned owing
to the impossibility of bringing the crops to market. The
economic development of Ceylon was dependent upon the
prosperity of the plantations, and this in turn could only be
attained by the building of roads. The revenue had always
been inadequate for this purpose, and the amount available
had been still further decreased by the coffee *débâcle* and the
reduction of taxes in 1847–8. The only solution was the Road
Ordinance of 1848, and the measure was sanctioned by the
Colonial Office. The Ordinance was first enforced in 1850, and
the protests of the natives soon subsided when they realized
that it did not involve the restoration of the old form of
Rajakaria.[1] The Ordinance proved of immense value in developing the magnificent network of roads in Ceylon.

At the same time that the new taxes and the Road Ordinance
were promulgated the Government began searching inquiries
for the annual Ceylon Blue Book. For many years the returns
had 'been a fiction, one set being a mere transcript from those
of a previous year'. The raiyats were asked a series of some
thirty questions as to their economic situation. The unusual
attempt to obtain accurate statistics aroused their suspicions,
and agitators persuaded them that the real object of the Government was to obtain information on which to base thirty new
taxes. Other absurd rumours obtained credence, such as that

[1] C.O. 55. 81: May 31, 1841; C.O. 54. 228: Apr. 13, 1847; C.O. 54. 249:
July 4, 1848; C.O. 54. 252: Nov. 14, Dec. 11 and 13, 1848; C.O. 54. 268:
Mar. 8, 1850; Grey, *Colonial Policy*, ii. 171–2; Skinner, *Ceylon*, 168.

'for . . . identification the breasts of the women were to be measured in the same way that the dogs and guns were to be'.[1] The Kandyan rebellion of 1848 followed hard upon these events, and it was ascribed by Torrington's enemies largely to the native hostility to his 'unjust' measures.[2] The Governor himself and his advisers believed that the nobles and priests brought about the revolt in order to restore the kingdom of Kandy, and that they aroused the raiyats by stirring up discontent against the new taxes, the Road Ordinance, and the Blue Book inquiries.[3] The real causes of the revolt went deeper than either Torrington or his enemies realized. The Governor's measures excited strong resentment, but they were the immediate occasion and not the fundamental reason for the outbreak. To explain the revolt as a Kandyan plot on the old familiar lines was far from being the whole truth.

The principal causes of the revolt appear to have been the growing lawlessness of the Kandyans, the inefficiency of the Civil Service, the alienation and declining influence of the Kandyan nobles, and the partial demoralization of the raiyats which resulted from the development of the coffee industry.[4] The rapid growth of the plantations between 1837 and 1848 profoundly unsettled the raiyats. Prior to this time Ceylon, and especially Kandy, had always suffered from a scarcity of currency; but in the short space of eleven years the coffee industry brought into the island an estimated capital of £3,000,000. A very large percentage of this was paid in wages to the labourers on the plantations. While the majority were Tamils, 'the most profligate of the low country Singhalese flocked' into Kandy attracted by the good wages. 'Temptations to and examples of intemperance and vice of every kind were rife'; and the newcomers 'spread far and wide their contaminating influences over a previously sober, orderly, honest race. Robberies and bloodshed' grew common, drunkenness became 'an enormous

---

[1] C.O. 54. 249: July 9, 1848, and *passim*; C.O. 54. 250: Aug. 4, 1848; C.O. 54. 264: *passim*; Tennent, *Ceylon*, ii. 569–70.

[2] C.O. 54. 250: Aug. 15, 1848.

[3] C.O. 54. 264: *passim*; Tennent, *Ceylon*, ii. 570–1.

[4] *Parl. Pap. H. C.* 106 of 1850, vol. xii, 278–98, and 524–33, evidence of Major Skinner, Commissioner of Roads, before the Parliamentary Commission of Inquiry. The report is also given in Skinner, *Ceylon*, 213–33.

evil', and there was a very serious decline in Kandyan morality.[1]
The Kandyans also resented the sale of unoccupied Crown lands
to the coffee planters. Moreover, the plantations brought an
influx of Europeans of whom there 'were not a few whose habits
and conduct tended much to diminish the respect in which the
English character had previously been held by the natives'.[2]

The policy of weakening the power and prestige of the
Kandyan nobles was another potent cause of demoralization
and eventually of the revolt. The Government held the un-
shakable belief that this course was essential to protect the
raiyats from oppression and to prevent a repetition of the revolt
of 1818. 'Without any avowed determination to destroy it [i.e.
the position of the nobles] we have practically discouraged and
undermined it.' By the 'forties the raiyats were well aware of
their rights, and they no longer showed that docile submission
to their chiefs which had marked them twenty years earlier.
Justifiable in its earlier stages the Government's policy was
carried to unwise lengths. The nobles from whom the majority
of the Kandyan native officials were appointed formed the
essential link between the civil servants and the raiyats. Their
authority depended far more upon their prestige and moral
influence than upon their legal powers. By lessening their power
and undermining their influence the Government appreciably
decreased their ability to check the growing demoralization and
lawlessness of the Kandyan raiyats. Furthermore the nobles
were alienated by the British policy, and in 1848 the majority
made little attempt to give the Government information and
assistance. A very striking feature of the revolt was the fog of
ignorance which enveloped the civil servants; and there is no
doubt that the nobles could have considerably diminished it if
they had felt inclined. Their attitude was denounced as treason,
but it seems more accurate to describe it as neutrality. While
it is true that some lesser nobles and priests were implicated
in the rising, the important nobles took no part in it. If they
had originated the plot 'they would not have condescended to

---

[1] Skinner, *Ceylon*, 219–20; C.O. 54. 251: Sept. 15, 1848; Forbes, *Recent
Disturbances in Ceylon*, 16; Anon., *Days of Old*, 1–11.
[2] C.O. 54. 250: Aug. 4, 1848; C.O. 54. 261: Nov. 15, 1848; Skinner, *Ceylon*,
222–3.

select as their leaders a set of low country vagabonds of inferior caste, for whom they entertain the greatest possible repugnance and contempt'.[1]

A very important cause of the revolt was the inefficiency of the Civil Service produced by the changes introduced in 1833. The demoralization was too deep-seated immediately to be eradicated by Lord Stanley's reforms, and the revolt occurred before they had achieved their purpose. The calibre of the officials appointed after 1833 showed a distinct decline owing to the decreased prospects offered by the Service. The civil servants as a whole became marked by a disinclination to perform more than the minimum of official duties. This tendency was strengthened by the permission given them to supplement their salaries by establishing coffee plantations. A very large number availed themselves of the offer, with the result that they neglected the work of Government in order to develop their plantations. Their dual position 'weakened the moral influence and authority which they previously possessed' amongst the Kandyans, who came to regard them as coffee planters.[2] Barnes's regulations requiring study of the native language became a dead letter, and by 1845 few civil servants could speak the vernacular fluently. They were compelled to rely for their information and for the execution of their orders upon the native officials, the very class who had been alienated by the undermining of their authority.[3] Social intercourse with the Kandyans diminished, and the absence of friendly relations brought as its inevitable result the withholding of information.[4] Maitland's regulations that civil servants must tour their districts were neglected, and many seem to have spent most of their time at their headquarters. The civil servants were unaware

[1] Skinner, *Ceylon*, 223–8; C.O. 54. 251: Sept. 15, 1848; C.O. 54. 261: Nov. 15 and Dec. 6, 1849; Forbes, *Recent Disturbances in Ceylon*, 18–26. Major Skinner's opinion that the majority of the nobles while alienated were not implicated in the revolt was shared by the ablest and best informed of the civil servants, viz. P. Anstruther, Colonial Secretary 1833–46, P. Wodehouse, Government Agent of Colombo in 1848, and Sir Anthony Oliphant, the Chief Justice (*Parl. Pap. H.C.*, 106 of 1850, vol. xii, 97–149, 169, 278, and 343–9; *Parl. Pap. H.C.*, 36 of 1851, vol. viii, i. 584–603 and 748–52).

[2] Skinner, *Ceylon*, 222–3.

[3] C.O. 54. 250: Aug. 4, and Oct. 1, 1848 (Lord Grey's Memo.); *Parl. Pap. H.C.* 36 of 1851, vol. viii. i. 590–1 and 749.

[4] Skinner, *Ceylon*, 213 and 223–4.

of the increasing lawlessness especially in the more remote districts, and the revolt came upon them as a complete surprise.[1]

Major Skinner, the Commissioner of Roads, had been in Ceylon for more than a quarter of a century. His fluent knowledge of the vernaculars combined with his friendship with many of the Kandyan nobles and his constant tours of road inspection gave him a knowledge of the country which was far superior to that of the civil servants in charge of the districts. He marked the growing lawlessness and lack of respect for British authority especially in the Seven Korales and Matale. In 1847 he informed Lord Torrington of 'the state of anarchy to which the two rebellious districts were approaching' and warned him of the imminence of revolt. He was 'disregarded if not disbelieved' since he 'was not supposed to be as well informed of the internal state of the country as the presiding local judicial and revenue officials'. Less than twelve months later the revolt broke out in these very districts.[2] If the Government had been less ignorant of the condition of Kandy the rebellion could have been avoided at the eleventh hour. Major Skinner considered that Lord Torrington was unjustly blamed as the cause of the revolt: he arrived in Ceylon only one year before it broke out, and he could not be held responsible for 'the general disorganization which alone led to the outbreak', and 'which had its origin at a date long antecedent to his assuming the Government'.[2]

With the exception of a small riot at Colombo on July 26, 1848, there were no disturbances in the Maritime Provinces. During the earlier part of July the natives and burghers of Colombo protested strongly against the new taxes, and Doctor Elliott assailed them vigorously in the *Observer*. He urged the natives to demand representation on the Legislative Council, instancing the victory achieved for democracy by the French revolution of 1848. Finally a meeting of protest on the outskirts of Colombo was called for July 26. Torrington sanctioned the

---

[1] Skinner, *Ceylon*, 224 and 231–3; C.O. 55. 85: Nov. 30, 1844; C.O. 54. 250: Aug. 4, 1848. In Lord Grey's opinion the revolt disclosed 'what seems to me the principal fault in the system of Government', viz. 'the absence of sufficient communication between the Government and the natives of the more remote districts'. 'Nothing, it is obvious, can so effectually contribute to this important object as a knowledge of the native languages' (C.O. 55. 91: Oct. 24, 1848).

[2] Skinner, *Ceylon*, 213, 222–4.   [3] Skinner, *Ceylon*, 213 and 224–6.

meeting, but gave orders to the police that while he would receive a petition he would not permit a large crowd to enter the town. Many thousands of natives assembled at the meeting and marched towards the Fort of Colombo to present their petition. The Colombo police force of forty-two men attempted to halt the mob, but were driven back after suffering several casualties. Torrington advanced with a strong body of troops which had been held in readiness in case of trouble. Doctor Elliott learned of the riot and hastened to the scene before the arrival of the troops. He persuaded the mob to disperse and allow him to present their petition.[1]

Meanwhile more serious trouble had been developing in Kandy. Early in July, Tennent and Buller, the Government Agent of the Central Province, made tours through part of Kandy and erroneously believed that they had quieted the discontent.[2] On July 6 an excited but unarmed crowd of three thousand entered the town of Kandy to protest against the new measures. Buller tried to address them but apparently lost his head and ordered the police to disperse the meeting. The police were too few to control the crowd, and Buller summoned Colonel Drought and two companies of the 15th Regiment. On their appearance the raiyats quietly dispersed to their villages, and Buller reported to Torrington that he believed the trouble was ended. With unconscious irony the same dispatch chronicled the appearance in the more remote districts of another 'of the many Malabar Pretenders to some relationship with the late King of Kandy'. There was no reason to connect him with the Kandy meeting; but Buller had ordered his arrest as a vagrant.[3]

The scene of action now shifted to the District of Matale. The Police Magistrate in charge, Waring, was in poor health and also cherished the belief that his duty was solely to hear cases, and not to maintain the peace of his district. The pretender and his following were therefore enabled to mature their plans undisturbed, only fourteen miles from the town of

[1] C.O. 54. 250: July 25, Aug. 9 and 15, 1848.
[2] C.O. 54. 249: July 5 and 8, 1848; C.O. 54. 250: Aug. 4, 1848; Millie, *Thirty Years Ago: or Reminiscences of the Early Days of Coffee Planting in Ceylon*, chap. 13.
[3] C.O. 54. 249: July 9 and 12, 1848.

Kandy, the head-quarters of the province. On July 26 Waring wrote to Buller that there was no danger of revolt; on July 27 he reported that there was; and on July 28 he fled for his life just as the rebels entered the town.[1] It is a striking illustration of the Government's lack of information that Buller received no definite information of the pretender until July 25. On that date the Superintendent of Police at Kandy, Loco Banda, reported the assemblage of many armed men near Matale. He was at once sent there with a strong force of police, and on July 27 he warned Buller that the condition of the district was very unsatisfactory, and that the pretender was said to have been crowned at Dambulla. At the same time Buller received confirmatory evidence from Waring's second letter and from two native headmen. On July 28 he set out for Matale to investigate, but returned to Kandy when he encountered Waring in full flight. Meanwhile the rebels sacked the public buildings and the bazaar at Matale, and plundered the bungalows of a few planters. At 10 p.m. on July 28 Captain Lillie and 200 troops marched from Kandy, accompanied by Buller and Selby, the Queen's Advocate. The troops were fired on near Matale, and after a skirmish in which one British soldier was wounded the rebels were routed. Captain Watson and 100 men of the Ceylon Rifles were left as a garrison on July 29.[2] On July 28 the rebels threatened Kurunegala in the Seven Korales, twenty-five miles from Kandy, and plundered the adjacent coffee plantations. The following day thirty-five men of the Ceylon Rifles under Lieutenant Annesley were sent from Kandy. On their arrival they found the rebels plundering the town, and after a brief skirmish expelled them with a loss of sixteen killed. On August 1, 4,000 rebels made two attacks on Kandy, but fled when attacked by the Ceylon Rifles.[3] With these four skirmishes active resistance came to an end owing to the promptitude with which the rising had been crushed. About the beginning of August the true identity of the pretenders was discovered.[4]

[1] C.O. 54. 261: Dec. 13, 1848. After the revolt Waring was retired on pension.
[2] C.O. 54. 250: Aug. 14, 1848: Henderson, *The History of the Rebellion in Ceylon*, 14.
[3] C.O. 54. 250: Aug. 14, 1848; C.O. 54. 264: Aug. 15, 1848.
[4] C.O. 54. 250: Aug. 14, 1848.

There were two kings, one at Matale and one in the Seven Korales, of whom the Matale pretender who claimed descent from Raja Sinha was the more important. He had been concerned in the revolt of 1842, and had escaped punishment from lack of sufficient evidence to convict him. Both were Sinhalese of low caste from the Maritime Provinces, professional robbers; and their chief ministers who bore the high titles of the old Kandyan court were thieves like themselves or else minor Kandyan headmen. Their following was eventually discovered to be small and to be composed partly of robbers, the scum of the Maritime Provinces who had come to the plantations, and partly of the discontented Kandyan raiyats of Matale and the Seven Korales. The real object of both pretenders was probably to amass plunder and then disappear.

The rebellion came as a complete surprise to the Government, and owing to the scarcity of reliable information they failed to realize that the revolt had been put down after August 1. Metaphorically speaking a single shell had suddenly burst about their ears, and they mistook it for a general bombardment. In the shock of the reaction from contented ignorance it was perhaps natural that they should exaggerate the danger. Torrington's inexperience caused him to trust largely to his advisers, and especially, it would seem, to Tennent, to General Smelt, the officer commanding in Ceylon, and to Sir Herbert Maddock. This last was a member of the Governor-General of India's Council, and a leading coffee planter. He had a 'great reputation for wisdom and sagacity', and advocated stern measures of repression. Tennent had been less than three years in Ceylon, while the General's experience of the colony was even shorter than that of the Governor. They and with a few exceptions the whole of the civil servants greatly over-estimated the number of the rebels, and believed that a widespread revolt was about to break out. The real leaders were the Kandyan nobles and priests, whose object was to restore the independence of Kandy. In previous revolts they had failed because they had been unable to enlist the support of the raiyats; but in 1848 they had gained their adherence by arousing discontent against the new taxes and the Blue Book inquiries. The Government were not at first aware that the rebel leaders were robbers, and that their following was largely composed of marauders from the Maritime Provinces. The discovery of these facts did not shake the belief in the guilt of the priests and nobles. The ostensible leaders were merely figureheads who would be removed as soon as the rebellion had succeeded. The failure of the nobles to warn the Government proved their complicity since they undoubtedly knew of the impending outbreak. Careful investigation failed to discover any further incriminating evidence, and only a few priests and minor headmen were eventually convicted of participation in the rebellion. This was regarded by the Government merely as a tribute to the consummate duplicity of the principal nobles, and in no way as a presumption of innocence.[1]

As soon as the news of the outbreak reached Colombo the Governor and his advisers agreed that vigorous measures must at once be taken to 'crush the insurrection at its outset' and prevent it from spreading. The rebels were estimated to number 60,000, of whom 20,000 were armed with muskets; while there were only 680 British troops in Kandy. The large number of coffee plantations presented a serious problem since the troops were too few to protect them if the revolt became widespread. Apart from the danger to European lives, the destruction of the crop would be a serious blow to the struggling industry; while if the Tamil coolies were molested the news would be carried to India and might deprive the plantations of the labour on which they depended. Martial law was proclaimed on July 29 in the District of Kandy, and on July 31 in the Seven Korales. On General Smelt's advice Torrington sent to Madras for 300 troops who arrived at Trincomalee on August 5.[2] On August 6 they were sent to Matale, and at the same time reinforcements were dispatched from Colombo to Kandy. Meanwhile the

---

[1] C.O. 54. 250: Aug. 14 and 15, 1848; C.O. 54. 251: Sept. 13, 1848; C.O. 54. 264: July 11 and Aug. 5, 1848, and Nov. 13, 1849; *Parl. Pap. H.C.* 106 of 1850, vol. xii, 104; *Parl. Pap. H.C.* 36 of 1851, vol. VIII. i, 584–606. At his trial the Matale pretender stated that he was secretly aided by the majority of the nobles who were the real leaders of the revolt (C.O. 54. 264: Sept. 15, 1848). No weight can be attached to his statement, since it was so clearly to his advantage to minimize his guilt, and since the Government despite energetic efforts failed to obtain corroborative evidence.

[2] C.O. 54. 250: Aug. 9 and 14, 1848; C.O. 54. 264: Aug. 5 and 15, 1848, and Nov. 6. 1849.

planters and other Europeans in Kandy had volunteered, and were used to protect the coffee plantations. The Tamil coolies on the whole 'behaved remarkably well', and usually stayed on the plantations to guard them as long as the European planter remained with them. Colonel Drought, the officer commanding at Kandy, stationed small detachments in the disturbed areas to protect the plantations and to hunt down the rebels. Operations were greatly hindered by the lack of information and by the dense jungle which still covered a large part of the country. Since, however, the districts were fairly well provided with main roads, the task was much easier than in 1818.[1]

On August 16 Torrington visited Kandy and found that the country was 'perfectly peaceful' except in Matale, where Captain Watson reported the presence of large bands of armed rebels. A number of prisoners had been captured, and several had been tried by court martial and shot, including on August 4 the Kurunegala pretender. Among those arrested by Watson was the Dissawa of Matale, the principal Kandyan noble. Eighty years of age, he was the only surviving signatory of the Kandyan Convention of 1815, and had always been unswervingly loyal and thoroughly trusted. General Smelt believed that the Kandyans were preparing for a renewed revolt, and Torrington, while less pessimistic, agreed that 'the strong arm of power' was still required.[2] Many Kandyans had abandoned their homes, some to join the rebels and others from fear. The Government wished the return of innocent fugitives and of those who were only slightly implicated in the rebellion. On August 18 Torrington issued a proclamation that all save those who had actually fought against the British or had been guilty of plundering might return home without molestation. Unless they did so within twenty days their land would be sequestrated. Sequestration was 'extensively enforced, partly as a measure of terror and partly as one of protection', since unoccupied property was in grave danger of plunder from the bands of

[1] C.O. 54. 250: Aug. 14, 1848; C.O. 54. 264: Aug. 5 and 15, 1848, and Oct. 9, 1849.

[2] C.O. 54. 250: Aug. 14, 1848; C.O. 54. 264: Aug. 12, 1848, and *passim*; Henderson, *Ceylon*, 40–5 and 53–66.

marauders. After the revolt was suppressed the property was returned to the owners, save in the few cases where they had been convicted of high treason.[1] Torrington approved the retention of martial law because 'the rapidity and vigour of the measures adopted by Government combined with the terrors of martial law have . . . staggered the energies of the people', and prevented the spread of the rebellion. It was also 'a check upon the evil propensities' of the priests and nobles, who had undoubtedly planned the revolt. Furthermore the Matale pretender and large bands of armed rebels were still at large, and the summary powers of martial law were necessary to capture them and prevent plundering.[2] About the middle of September the troops were withdrawn except from Matale and Kurunegala, 'the most refractory places'. On September 21 the Matale pretender was captured by Captain Watson, and on October 10 martial law came to an end.[3]

A special session of the Supreme Court was held at Kandy on August 28 to try the prisoners who had been arrested before the proclamation of martial law. Seventeen were acquitted and 240 were released without trial, amongst the latter being the Dissawa of Matale. Seventeen, including the Matale pretender, were convicted of high treason and condemned to death; but in pronouncing sentence the Chief Justice, Sir Anthony Oliphant, recommended them all to mercy. Torrington censured his clemency and reluctantly commuted the sentences to imprisonment, the pretender being flogged and transported for life. The Chief Justice considered that since there had been so little fighting, and eighteen had been shot after trial by

[1] C.O. 54. 251: Sept. 14, 1848; C.O. 54. 259: Aug. 13, 1849. Sequestrated property was placed in charge of men appointed by the local commandants, and accounts of it were kept. Grain and cattle, &c., which could not safely be kept because of the disturbed state of the country were sold at once, and the proceeds returned to the owners if they were acquitted. No sequestrated lands were sold (C.O. 54. 252: Nov. 6, 1848). The value of the sequestrated property was about £20,000 (C.O. 54. 264: Oct. 9, 1849). Colonel Drought apparently originated the policy of sequestration on August 8 (*Parl. Pap. H.C.* 634 of 1851, vol. xxii, 195–9 and 232–3).
[2] C.O. 54. 251: Sept. 14, 1848.
[3] C.O. 54. 251: Oct. 14, 1848; C.O. 54. 264: Sept. 15 and Oct. 16, 1848. The customary Act of Indemnity was unanimously passed by the Legislative Council on Oct. 23 to safeguard those concerned in suppressing the revolt from prosecution for actions done in enforcing martial law (C.O. 54. 252: Nov. 6, 1848; C.O. 55. 91: Jan. 16, 1849).

N

court martial, 'the blood which has been already spilt is sufficient'.[1]

The severity with which the revolt was suppressed caused a sharp division of public opinion in Ceylon. On the side of the Governor were the majority of the civil servants and the coffee planters, an uncertain number of the European merchants at Colombo, and apparently a large number of Sinhalese. The planters were convinced that only the strict enforcement of martial law had saved their estates from pillage. Torrington's policy was condemned by the remainder of the Europeans and the burghers, under the leadership of Doctor Elliott and two prominent burghers, Morgan and Alwis. They contended that his taxes and above all his Road Ordinance had brought about a revolt which was little more than a series of riots. The proclamation of martial law and its retention for two-and-a-half months were entirely unnecessary, while the sequestration of property and the severe sentences imposed by the courts martial were nothing less than criminal. The object of the Governor's enemies was to bring about his dismissal from office, while the more ardent hoped for his impeachment. In August 1848 they petitioned the Secretary of State for the appointment of a Parliamentary Commission of Inquiry. Lord Grey refused since he entirely approved of Torrington's actions; and throughout the whole of the controversy which followed, the Governor was firmly supported by the Colonial Office.[2]

The Governor's opponents replied by further petitions, and appointed as their London agent Mr. T. J. McChristie, who had acted in the same capacity during the agitation against the Verandah Ordinance. He enlisted the support of Joseph Hume and several other members of the Radical wing of the Liberal party in Parliament. The London *Chronicle* and *Herald* together with the *Aborigines' Friend* and the powerful missionary influences ranged themselves on the side of the attack.[3] Morgan

---

[1] C.O. 54. 250: Sept. 14, 1848; C.O. 54. 251: Sept. 23 and 25, and Oct. 14, 1848; C.O. 54. 252: Nov. 6 and Dec. 5, 1848; C.O. 55. 91: Jan. 31, 1849. The pretender died of dropsy in prison at Malacca in 1849 (*Parl. Pap. H.C.* 36–II of 1851, vol VIII. ii. 405).

[2] C.O. 54. 261: *passim*; C.O. 55. 91: Oct. 24, 1848; Digby, *Morgan*, 141–62.

[3] In 1849 the *Aborigines' Friend* condemned Torrington's administration

and especially Elliott busied themselves in collecting information which they forwarded to Hume. Elliott made a tour of
Kandy and, according to Torrington, represented himself to
the Kandyans as authorized by the Queen to inquire into their
grievances. The Governor's supporters were equally active in
preparing addresses and petitions to the Secretary of State in
defence of his policy.[1]

Lord John Russell supported Torrington and at first refused
Hume's demand for a Committee of Inquiry. His majority in
Parliament however was far from secure, and on February 20,
1849, his Radical supporters allied with Sir Robert Peel forced
him to appoint a Committee of Inquiry of the House of
Commons. Speeches strongly condemnatory of Torrington were
delivered by Hume, Baillie, and Sir William Molesworth.
Having provoked the revolt by his taxes he suppressed it by
a brutal exercise of martial law. The real object of attack was
not so much Torrington himself as the Prime Minister and the
Colonial Office's methods of administration. Nepotism and
the Divine Right of Whiggism—a Whig peerage and relationship with the Prime Minister, were Lord Torrington's sole
qualifications for office. Inevitably he relied largely on the
advice of the Ceylon civil servants who, as Molesworth pointed
out, were lamentably ignorant of the native languages. Having
castigated Lord John Russell the attack turned upon the
Colonial Office. The Colonial Office was an honest but narrow-
minded and blundering tyrant whose ignorance and outworn
ideas drove the colonies to revolt. Lord Stanley's reforms had
increased the cost of the Ceylon Civil Service by about 50 per
cent. Ignorance completed the work which extravagance had
begun, and in 1847 the Colonial Office ordered the repeal of the
export duties in the mistaken belief that there was a surplus

and the whole Colonial Office system of government as 'a dark catalogue of
oppression, injustice, inhumanity, and impolicy' (vol. ii, 179–99).
[1] C.O. 54. 250: Aug. 15 and 16, 1848; C.O. 54. 251: Sept. 13, 1848; C.O. 54.
252: Dec. 12, 1848; C.O. 54. 257: *passim*; C.O. 54. 258: Apr. 12, 1849 and
passim; C.O. 54. 259: *passim*; C.O. 54. 260: Oct. 11 and 15, 1849; C.O. 54.
261: *passim*; C.O. 54. 264: Oct. 13, 1849; C.O. 54. 270: July 10, 1850; C.O. 55.
91: *passim*; *Parl. Pap. H.C.* 106 of 1850, vol. xii, 47–8 and 304–10; Digby,
Morgan, i. 141–62; Anon., *Ceylon and the Government of Lord Torrington*;
Colonist, *A Few Remarks upon Forbes' Pamphlet*; Colonist, *Is Ceylon to be
sacrificed at the Shrine of Party?*

in the Ceylon Treasury. To meet the resultant deficit the Colonial Office sanctioned the imposition of taxes which produced the revolt. Sir Robert Peel did not attack the Prime Minister or the Colonial Office, and he justified Torrington for proclaiming martial law and suppressing the revolt firmly. The harshness of some of his measures, however, and the discontent in Ceylon required investigation.[1]

The Committee of Inquiry was nominated on February 27, 1849, and included amongst its fifteen members Disraeli, Peel, Gladstone, Hume, Baillie, and Mr. (later Sir Benjamin) Hawes, Under-Secretary for the Colonies.[2] On July 27, 1849, the Committee resolved that since the evidence available in England was insufficient Parliament should appoint a Royal Commission to conduct an investigation in Ceylon as to the measures taken to suppress the revolt.[3] Baillie and Hume made a motion to this effect in the House of Commons on July 28; but Lord John Russell successfully opposed it since an inquiry in Ceylon would tend to weaken Torrington's authority and prestige as Governor. He promised that additional witnesses would be brought from Ceylon to give evidence on the administration of martial law, and the House rejected the motion. Hume characterized the charges against Torrington as 'amounting in fact to a capital offence'. He frequently hinted that grave crimes had been committed under cover of martial law, although the Committee had resolved that the incomplete evidence it had taken should not be disclosed to the House.[4] The reappointment of the Committee on February 11, 1850, in the following session of Parliament led to further debates in the House of Commons. On February 6, 1850, Baillie and Hume declared that 'acts of atrocity' had been committed under cover of martial law, Captain Watson at Matale being singled out for special attack. The courts martial were not 'legally and properly constituted', and sometimes inflicted disproportionate and unjust punish-

[1] Hansard's *Parliamentary Debates*, Series III, vol. cii, pp. 938–1027.
[2] *Parl. Pap.* H.C. 297 of 1849, vol. xi. The Committee was also appointed to investigate the condition of British Guiana.
[3] *Parl. Paps.* H.C. 573 and 591 of 1849, vol. xi.
[4] Hansard, III, cvii. 1079–1101. Although the Committee resolved that the evidence be treated as strictly confidential, Elliott 'printed verbatim' 'large extracts' in the *Colombo Observer* (C.O. 54. 264: Nov. 6, 1849).

ments. Lord Grey and Lord John Russell opposed summoning
the witnesses required from Ceylon; but the House voted that
they be brought to England.[1] On February 11 Hume and Disraeli accused the Government of trying to burke the inquiry
by withholding the witnesses and the official reports of the
courts martial.[2]

The majority of the witnesses examined by the Committee
were members of the Ceylon Civil Service, and with few but
important exceptions they defended the Governor's measures.[3]
The majority maintained that the pretenders at Matale and
Kurunegala were merely puppets, the real leaders being the
Kandyan nobles and priests. They provoked the raiyats to
revolt by working upon the discontent caused by Torrington's
financial measures, and by spreading the rumour of the proposed
thirty new taxes. The rebellion had been long in preparation
and would have spread to the whole of Kandy if the rebels had
met with initial success. The immediate proclamation of martial
law, together with the sequestration of property and the summary executions, were essential to prevent the revolt from
spreading and to save the coffee plantations from pillage. The
continuance of martial law was necessary because the civil
power alone could never have captured the pretender, since he
was screened by the nobles on whom it relied for information.
So long as he was at large it was impossible to restore quiet and
confidence amongst the raiyats.[4]

One of the principal witnesses against Torrington was
Mr. T. J. McChristie, who had been well supplied with information by his principals in Ceylon. He claimed to be the spokes-
man for the whole population of Ceylon, but under cross-
examination he finally admitted that he was the authorized
representative only of Elliott, the burghers, and a few others.
The Verandah Ordinance and the refusal to concede popular
control of the Legislative Council were amongst the com-

---

[1] Hansard, III, cviii. 417–58.   [2] Hansard, III, cviii. 643–61.
[3] The proceedings and the evidence taken by the Committee are printed in
Parl. Paps. H.C. 297, 573, and 591 of 1849, vol. xi; [1018] of 1849, vol. xxxvi;
H. C. 66, 106, and 605 of 1850, vol. xii; *H. C.* 36 of 1851, vol. viii, part i;
H. C. 36–II of 1851, vol. viii, part ii; *H. C.* 99 and 634 of 1851, vol. xxii;
[1301] and [1413] of 1851, vol. xxxv.
[4] C.O. 54. 264: Nov. 13, 1849.

plaints. Torrington had also forbidden Government clerks to write to the newspapers or give them information. His 'misrepresentation and disrespectful language' towards the burghers were dwelt upon, his gift for hasty and arrogant remarks affording ample material. Turning to the revolt McChristie ascribed it to the injustice of the Road Ordinance and the new taxes. The rebellion was little more than a riot, and was put down with excessive brutality and injustice. The skirmish at Matale was a 'slaughter', and at Kurunegala there were 'vast numbers killed'. Martial law was totally unnecessary, while the courts martial were travesties of justice conducted by young and inexperienced officers. Sequestration was used by many as a cloak to steal the property of the Kandyans. While McChristie's evidence contained much that was true, it was on the whole a judicious selection from the facts combined with a fair measure of misstatement.[1]

One of the most valuable witnesses was Major Skinner, a Ceylon civil servant of long experience and great ability. The real causes of the revolt—the inefficiency of the Civil Service, the growing demoralization of the raiyats, and the alienation of the native officials—had been in operation for many years prior to Torrington's arrival. His taxes were merely the immediate cause of the outbreak; while his inexperience placed him at the mercy of his advisers, who greatly overestimated the danger. Granted the exaggerated and false information which was all that Torrington had to guide him, his stern measures in July and early August were the only right ones. Furthermore they were 'decidedly the course of mercy, as in forty-eight hours the revolt would have spread rapidly'.[2]

Sir Anthony Oliphant, the Chief Justice, stated that the civil servants were inefficient and dependent upon the native officials for information. When the revolt broke out 'the general impression left upon my mind . . . was that nobody knew anything about it.' They were 'frightened out of their wits', and greatly exaggerated 'a futile and contemptible attempt at rebellion' engineered by the priests and minor headmen and by the criminal population. Lord Torrington was inexperienced and

[1] *Parl. Pap. H.C.* 106 of 1850, vol. xii, 307–43, and 473.
[2] Ibid. 278–98.

'of a timid and nervous temperament'. He was especially influenced by Sir Herbert Maddock, who was in favour of stern measures. The proclamation of martial law was unnecessary, since the civil power could have subdued the outbreak with the assistance of the troops.[1]

Important evidence was given by Mr. Anstruther, who had been a member of the Ceylon Civil Service for twenty-four years, and Colonial Secretary from 1833 until his retirement in 1846. He spoke Sinhalese fluently, and had very great knowledge of and influence over the Kandyans, by whom he was known as the 'One Armed Rajah'. He was in Kandy during the revolt, and believed that it broke out 'without any previous preparation on the part of the priests or of any great chiefs'. The raiyats were discontented because of the new taxes, and 'some few of the minor headmen' and others, 'robbers princi-pally', seized the opportunity to bring about a revolt, chiefly for the sake of plundering. Buller's estimate of 60,000 rebels was 'ridiculous'. 'There is a complete curtain drawn in Ceylon between the Government and the governed; no person con-nected with Government understands the language; very few of them have the remotest idea of the customs of the natives.' 'They are working in the dark, and that, in my opinion, is the reason why so many people were frightened.' The proclamation of martial law was perhaps 'excusable . . . under the ignorance of the members of the Government of the extent of the danger and real state of the people'; but its continuance for ten weeks was 'totally inexcusable'. The proclamation of August 18 sequestrating abandoned property he attributed to 'a panic proceeding from ignorance'.[2] Colonel Braybrooke of the Ceylon Rifles agreed with Mr. Anstruther's opinion concerning martial law.[3]

Mr. P. E. Wodehouse, Government Agent of the Western

[1] *Parl. Pap. H.C.* 36 of 1851, vol. VIII. i. 584–607.

[2] *Parl. Pap. H.C.* 106 of 1850, vol xii, 343–55. Subsequently Mr. Anstruther slightly modified his evidence, and stated that of the civil servants 'hardly any . . . can speak the language' (*Parl. Pap. H.C.* 36 of 1851, vol. VIII. i. 749).

[3] *Parl. Pap. H.C.* 36 of 1851, vol. VIII, i. 506–22. Colonel Braybrooke ap-proved the proclamation of martial law since owing to wrong information 'we were under the impression that we were on the eve of a great rebellion'. It should, however, have been repealed about the middle of August, when it became evident that the danger had been greatly exaggerated.

Province, was studiously guarded in his evidence, but conveyed the impression that Torrington and Sir Emerson Tennent had seriously mishandled the situation. The civil servants hesitated to proffer advice since they felt that they were discredited by Lord Stanley's strictures and that their opinions would be contemned. Lord Torrington frequently did not consult his Executive Council, relying on Sir Emerson Tennent who, like himself, had very recently come to Ceylon. The Governor and his chosen advisers considerably exaggerated the importance of the revolt: the civil power assisted by the troops could have suppressed it without the use of martial law. Many of the rebels were criminals from the Maritime Provinces, the priests and especially the Kandyan nobles having on the whole no share in the uprising.[1]

Serious charges were brought against Captain Watson for his conduct at Matale during the period of martial law. Elliott accused him of establishing a 'reign of Terror', burning the homes of all suspected rebels, sequestrating their property, and stealing part of it. The Matale court martial was composed of young and inexperienced subalterns who acted with undue haste and sometimes inflicted unjust punishments. The culminating charge was that on August 9, 1848, Captain Watson issued a signed proclamation at Matale ordering the Kandyans under pain of death to disclose the hiding-place of the property of certain rebels. The accusations were supported by native testimony collected at Matale by Elliott in 1849, and also by the evidence of Lieutenant Henderson, who was under Watson's command at Matale in 1848. Captain Watson appeared before the Committee of Inquiry on February 14, 1850, and for several days he was searchingly examined by Hume and Baillie.[2]

[1] *Parl. Pap. H. C.* 106 of 1850, vol. xii. 97–149, 188–207, and 247–69. Torrington, like his predecessors, frequently consulted his Executive Council only when an affair was so far advanced that he was already committed to a definite line of policy. Even if the Council disagreed it felt compelled to support him. Anstruther stated that Torrington consulted the Executive Council 'very little' (*Parl. Pap. H. C.* 106 of 1850, vol. xii. 354).

[2] Hansard, III, cviii. 424–7, Feb. 6, 1850; *Parl. Pap. H. C.* 66 of 1850, vol. xii, *passim*; *Parl. Pap. H. C.* 36 of 1851, vol. viii. i. 1–59, 145–61, 459–506, 534–41, 610–25, and 708–17; *Parl. Pap. H. C.* 634 of 1851, vol. xxii, *passim*; C.O. 54. 276: *passim*; Henderson, *Ceylon, passim*. Lieutenant Henderson included Watson, Drought, Torrington, and Tennent in his condemnation of the excessive and unnecessary severity displayed in suppressing the revolt. He

He appears to have been very careless in keeping accounts of the property sequestrated, but the charges of theft were not proved. The accusation was not substantiated that in several instances the Matale court martial acted so hastily that it condemned innocent men. It was clear, however, that Watson exaggerated the seriousness of the revolt, and that his measures of repression were needlessly severe.[1] He declared that the proclamation of August 9 was a forgery; but the Committee of Inquiry was not convinced. On February 19, 1850, it asked the House of Commons to appoint a Royal Commission to investigate the authenticity of the proclamation in Ceylon.[2] The Commissioners appointed were two members of the Madras Civil Service, Messrs. W. Morehead and J. Rhode, and they submitted their Report on June 20, 1850. After careful inquiry they concluded there was 'no reasonable doubt' that the proclamation was 'prepared in Captain Watson's office in Matelle, and issued under Captain Watson's orders after having been signed by him'.[3] Captain Watson was tried by court martial at Colombo on April 8, 1851, and acquitted, the court holding that the proclamation was a forgery.[4]

did not attend the courts martial and obtained his evidence from participants, since he was absent from Matale on duty. His testimony must be accepted with reserve, since it is far from impartial, and shows that he had a bitter grievance against the four whom he attacked. Henderson declared that he burnt the houses of rebels on Watson's written orders; but that when the inquiry began Watson denied that he had given such instructions. He insisted that Henderson had acted on his own initiative, and tried in vain to intimidate him into returning the written orders. Colonel Drought had a high opinion of Watson as had General Smelt, Tennent, and Torrington (C.O. 54. 260: Sept. 14, 1849); and they supported him against Henderson.

[1] C.O. 54. 260: Sept. 14, 1849: and C.O. Memo.; C.O. 55. 91: Dec. 18, 1849; *Parl. Pap. H. C.* 36 of 1851, vol. VIII. i. 594–5; Henderson, *Ceylon*, 40–5 and 53–66. As late as Sept. 22, 1848, Watson advised Drought that martial law was still necessary 'for the plot laid by the rebels is broad and strong' (C.O. 54. 264).

[2] *Parl. Pap. H. C.* 66 of 1850, vol. xii. 3; C.O. 54. 269: Apr. 16, 1850.

[3] C.O. 55. 91: Feb. 24 and July 5, 1850; C.O. 55. 92: Feb. 22, 1850; C.O. 54. 276: *passim*; *Parl. Pap. H. C.* 634 of 1851, vol. xxii, *passim*.

[4] C.O. 54. 276: *passim*. The report of the court martial was printed in [1413] of 1851, vol. xxxv. Watson rose to the rank of Lieutenant-Colonel and was appointed Inspector of Police at Galle in 1859. In 1862 and again in 1863 he tried to evade responsibility for irregularities by denying that he had issued orders, throwing the blame on his subordinates who had acted on his instructions. After the second offence the Secretary of State ordered that he be dismissed from his post for falsehood (C.O. 54. 377: Aug. 10 and Oct. 16, 1863). One is inclined to wonder whether Lieutenant Henderson's grievance were not justified.

The charges against Captain Watson were only one incident in the attack made by Hume and Baillie upon the use of martial law in Ceylon. They maintained that in so trivial a revolt to proclaim martial law was quite unnecessary, while to retain it for ten weeks—from July 29 to October 10—was infinitely worse. They also contended that the administration of martial law, notably the procedure of the courts martial and the sequestration of property, had been grossly irregular and illegal. The courts were not 'legally and properly constituted', since the members were young and inexperienced officers ignorant of the language and dependent upon interpreters, and in the majority of the trials a Judge Advocate was not present. The duty of this officer was to see that the trial was regularly conducted, and to advise the court upon doubtful points of law. The sentences were disproportionately severe and were immediately carried into effect without the confirmation of the Governor and Commander-in-Chief which the law required.[1]

As regards the proclamation of martial law the Governor was misled by false information, and greatly exaggerated the gravity of the situation. In view, however, of the state of lawlessness which existed amongst the raiyats in many parts of Kandy, weakness on the part of the Government might have encouraged them to join the rebels. The proclamation of martial law and the severity with which it was enforced obviated this possible danger. Whether this possibility was also a probability seems impossible to determine. In view of the circumstances the proclamation of martial law appears to have been natural and pardonable. Its retention for over two months after all resistance had ceased is another matter. Allowance must be made for an inexperienced Governor who would bear the responsibility for a wrong decision, and whose advisers continued to advocate its continuance. Even so the Governor was aware that the civil servants had no great repute for knowledge and efficiency, and that his most trusted advisers such as Tennent knew little more about Kandyan conditions than he did. Yet there is no evidence that Torrington sought the advice of Mr. Anstruther, for example, who was universally admitted to have an un-

[1] Hansard, III, cvii. 1079–1101; Hansard, III, cviii. 420–58; *Parl. Pap. H. C.* 36–II of 1850, vol. VIII. ii. 277–90.

rivalled knowledge of the Kandyans. The Governor preferred blindly to adopt the views of his chosen advisers, and he retained martial law long after the possible need for it had passed.

The drastic proceeding of sequestrating property does not seem to have been justified by the condition of the country. Furthermore, the circumstances under which Torrington issued the proclamation of August 18, 1848, ordering sequestration led to a dispute which injured his reputation. The measure was strongly advised by Colonel Drought and Sir Herbert Maddock; but before issuing the proclamation Torrington read it to Mr. H. C. Selby, the Queen's Advocate, although he did not formally ask his advice. Selby admitted that he voiced no objections, so that Torrington not unnaturally interpreted silence as assent and informed Lord Grey that the Queen's Advocate approved. In April 1849, when giving evidence before the Committee, Selby challenged the truth of the Governor's assertion, and denied that he had ever been formally consulted. Torrington's opponents did not overlook this reflection on his veracity. So far the dispute really reflected on Selby himself; but Torrington subsequently admitted that on August 22, 1848, he received a letter from Selby strongly advising against the proclamation. Torrington's excuse, which was scarcely convincing, was that he did not appreciate the strength of Selby's written protest until he gave evidence before the Committee in 1849.[1]

The procedure of the courts martial and the severity of their sentences was perhaps the strongest count in the indictment brought against Lord Torrington. Martial law was in force from July 29 to October 10, and courts martial were established at Kandy, Matale, Kurunegala, and Dambulla. They tried only those rebels and marauders who had been captured after the proclamation of martial law. Of those convicted, 18 were shot, 66 imprisoned, and 28 sentenced to transportation.[2] The ad-

---

[1] C.O. 54. 264: Aug. 7, Sept. 4 and Dec. 1, 1849; C.O. 55. 91: July 1, 1849; *Parl. Pap. H. C.* 36 of 1851, vol. VIII. i. 59–144 and 409–30.

[2] No prisoners were shot at Dambulla: two were shot at Kandy (Aug. 8 and 25): seven at Kurunegala (Aug. 5 and 10, and five on Sept. 2): and nine at Matale (Aug. 22, four on Sept. 6, and four on Sept. 14). (C.O. 54. 251: Drought's Memo.) The prisoners whose sentences had not expired were apparently released in 1850 (C.O. 54. 264: Feb. 22, 1850).

ministration of martial law was left to the unfettered discretion
of Colonel Drought, the Commandant of the Kandyan Provinces
with the Governor's 'entire concurrence and approbation . . .
by virtue of the powers which as Governor and Commander-in-
Chief I permitted him to use'. Torrington 'abstained on all
occasions from interfering in their proceedings in any manner
whatever', since he had the utmost confidence in Colonel
Drought and did not wish to embarrass him.[1] The membership
of the four courts varied, since Kandy had a fairly large garrison
while at the other stations there were only one or two companies.
At Kandy the court was composed of one major, three captains,
and one lieutenant, the sentences being confirmed by Colonel
Drought, who was not a member of the court. At Kurunegala
and Dambulla the court was composed of one captain and two
subalterns; while at Matale, the most active, it was made up of
three and occasionally five subalterns. In all three the sentences
were carried out after confirmation by the local officer commanding, who was not a member of the court. Very few of the
trials seem to have been held with the presence of a Judge
Advocate. Procedure was summary, and interpreters were used
since many of the officers were ignorant of Sinhalese.[2] The
courts differed markedly from those set up by General Brownrigg during the revolt of 1817 and 1818, which were composed
of five members of whom at least one was a field officer. A Judge
Advocate was 'invariably' appointed to each court, and was an
'experienced' civil servant or military officer; while all sentences
of death were confirmed by Brownrigg.[3]

One of the principal charges brought against Torrington was
the execution in August 1848 of a Buddhist priest in his robes
after conviction by the court martial at Kandy. Lord Torrington refused to commute the sentence when requested by
Mr. Selby, the Queen's Advocate, who was not present at the
trial. According to Selby's version the Governor refused in an
insulting manner, saying: 'By God if all the proctors in the

---

[1] C.O. 54. 251: Sept. 14 and Oct. 14, 1848; C.O. 54. 263: Nov. 14, 1849;
C.O. 54. 264: *passim.*

[2] C.O. 54. 263: *passim.* This volume gives the whole of the proceedings and
evidence taken before the courts martial. *Parl. Pap. H. C.* 36–II of 1851, vol.
VIII. ii. 270–5.

[3] *Parl. Pap. H. C.* 36 of 1851, vol. VIII. i. 506, 525–8, and 545.

place said the man was innocent he should die to-morrow morning.' Torrington's denial was not believed, and his remark did him great harm.[1] The Governor and the court were accused of executing an innocent man, and also of insulting the Buddhist religion by shooting a priest in his priestly robes of yellow. The charge broke down, since the accused man was convicted of complicity in the revolt after a fair trial, and confessed his guilt to Captain Fenwick, who commanded the firing party.[2] In 1849 the chief priests of the two principal Wiharas in Kandy voluntarily denied that Buddhists considered the execution of a priest in his robes to be an insult to their faith. Moreover the priest had no other garment.[3]

The courts martial at Kurunegala and especially at Matale were condemned because they executed 16 prisoners, 13 of them during September. This was over a month after resistance had ceased, and at a time when the Supreme Court at Kandy was simultaneously trying the prisoners captured prior to the proclamation of martial law.[4] Since Matale was only fourteen and Kurunegala about twenty-five miles from Kandy there seems no valid reason why the accused could not have been tried by the Supreme Court, or at any rate by a court martial of senior officers in Kandy. A decision of life and death was a serious matter to leave to the verdict of a court of subalterns who were usually not assisted by a Judge Advocate as at Matale, with Captain Watson as the final authority. The procedure adopted by General Brownrigg in 1818 was vastly preferable, and it is regrettable that Lord Torrington entrusted unfettered power to Colonel Drought, who in turn delegated it to his local commandants.[5]

[1] C.O. 54. 250: Sept. 14, 1848; C.O. 54. 269: May 30, 1850; C.O. 55. 91: Aug. 2, 1850; *Parl. Pap. H. C.* 36 of 1851, vol. VIII. i. 98 and 605.

[2] C.O. 54. 264: Oct. 14, 1849, and *passim.*

[3] C.O. 54. 258: Apr. 14, 1849; C.O. 55. 91: May 29, 1849.

[4] Hansard, III, cviii. 420–50; Hansard, III, cxvii. 6–33. The Chief Justice felt that the executions, especially those at Matale, were injurious to the British reputation. Finally he made such strong representations to Torrington that on Sept. 25 the Governor forbade further executions by martial law (*Parl. Pap. H. C.* 36 of 1851, vol. VIII, i. 594–5 and 601).

[5] Torrington was not unnaturally ignorant of the procedure of martial law, yet according to Colonel Braybrooke he never consulted either him or General Stewart, although both had served under General Brownrigg and were in Colombo in 1848 (*Parl. Pap. H. C.* 36 of 1851, vol. VIII. i. 542–3).

The Governor's opponents were mistaken when they declared that the courts were illegal because of their composition and because the sentences were not confirmed by Torrington himself. The error arose from confusing courts martial, which derived their authority from the Army Act and administered military law, with courts created in consequence of a proclamation of martial law. Military law is a 'peculiar and elaborate code of law, not applicable to civilians, but as much true law, being expressly authorized by Act of Parliament' for the maintenance of discipline in the army, 'as any other part of British law'. The composition, procedure, and powers of a statutory court martial are elaborately regulated, and a civil court will not interfere with its decisions unless it exceeds its jurisdiction.[1] Torrington's opponents confused military law with martial law, and were entirely mistaken in declaring the Ceylon courts martial illegal because they were not constituted and conducted in the same way as those authorized by the Army Act.[2] 'The proclamation of martial law is in fact no more than a declaration that in circumstances of public danger all law is for the time suspended.' A court martial established under martial law has little or nothing in common with the statutory court martial, and is strictly not a court at all. It is merely a committee formed for the purpose of carrying into execution the discretionary powers assumed by the Government. The purpose of the court is to prevent the punishment of innocent persons by instituting 'necessarily a very summary enquiry . . . the sentences of such courts add nothing to the legality of the punishment inflicted, and serve only to show that there was' due investigation before sentence was passed. So long as a state of war exists no civil court will interfere; but on the restoration of peace a member of such a court is liable both civilly and criminally for any breach of the law he may have committed. For this reason it is customary to pass an Act of Indemnity legalizing acts done in the administration of martial law.[3] The sentences are not founded on any precise law, but are merely

---

[1] Jenks, *Government of the British Empire*, 190 and 207; Hall, *Political Crime*, 63.

[2] E.g. Forbes, *Recent Disturbances in Ceylon*, 21 and 30.

[3] C.O. 54. 264: Feb. 22, 1850; Hall, *Political Crime*, 62–3; Jenks, *Brit. Empire*, 210–13.

acts done in the course of repressing disorder. The Duke of Wellington stated on April 1, 1851: 'Martial Law was neither more nor less than the will of the general who commands the army. In fact Martial Law meant no law at all. Therefore the general who declared Martial Law . . . was bound to lay down distinctly the rules and regulations and limits according to which his will was to be carried out.'[1] Sir David Dundas, the Judge Advocate General, made the same vital distinction. While military law was strictly defined and limited by statutes, martial law was vague, undefined, and not governed by regulations. Under martial law there were no rules determining the composition or procedure of the court: the right of the accused to a fair trial depended on the justice and wisdom of the officer presiding. Martial law was unwritten, without practices or precedents: 'I know of no rule except the rule of common sense and humanity.' The Government was entitled to proclaim it in a 'paramount necessity', and if it were executed 'honestly, rigorously, and vigorously, with as much humanity as the case will permit', Parliament could and should pass an Act of Indemnity.[2] Judged by these criteria Lord Torrington seems to be deserving of grave censure, nor can inexperience and apparently a blind confidence in a few trusted subordinates provide sufficient justification. He failed to lay down any rules for the guidance of the courts or to supervise their actions. The severe enforcement of martial law long after all justification for it had ceased was a breach of the principle that it must be exercised in accordance with common sense and humanity.

[1] Hansard, III, cxv. 880–1.
[2] *Parl. Pap. H. C.* 106 of 1850, vol. xii, 176–87. General Fitzroy Somerset, the Secretary to the Commander-in-Chief, stated: 'There are no written instructions that I can find out in any quarter for the administration of Martial Law' (*Parl. Pap. H. C.* 36 of 1851, vol. viii. i. 717–18). The Jamaican revolt of 1865 evoked a definition of martial law by Mr. Justice Ker which was endorsed by the Colonial Office. 'Martial law is the recurrence to physical force for the bringing about of a result beyond the scope and capabilities of the ordinary law.' Trial is summary, and acts otherwise illegal are justified by the emergency. While martial law sanctions every act that is genuinely necessary for the suppression of disorder, it does not authorize excess. Every act must be done in good faith, and must be 'adjudged to be necessary in the judgement, not of a violent or excited, but of a moderate and reasonable man. . . . Excess and wantonness, cruelty and unscrupulous contempt for human life, meet with no sanction from martial . . . law' (*Parl. Pap.* [3859] of 1867, vol. xlix. 12–13).

The conditions prevailing at Matale and Kurunegala perhaps made it impossible for the civil courts fully and freely to exercise their ordinary jurisdiction. Nevertheless, no adequate reason appears why the accused could not have been taken to Kandy for trial, at least after the middle of August.

The events which brought about Lord Torrington's recall were the disclosures made in 1850 before the Committee of Inquiry by Mr. P. E. Wodehouse and Sir Emerson Tennent. Wodehouse's evidence in 1849 while moderate in tone had been distinctly critical of the Governor's policy, and this was resented by Torrington and Tennent. They contended that Wodehouse while in Ceylon had acquiesced in their measures, and that his disapproval should have been voiced at the time instead of being reserved for the Committee of Inquiry. Tennent returned to England to conduct his own and the Governor's defence before the Committee in 1850. His attacks on Wodehouse's evidence were met by counter-attacks, and the hostility which had existed between them for several years became more and more embittered. Tennent declared that since his arrival in Ceylon he had had to struggle against the hostility of Wodehouse and a cabal of the principal civil servants, who resented his appointment to the Colonial Secretaryship. Torrington warmly supported Tennent and thereby incurred the hostility of the clique. Wodehouse, supported by Anstruther and other civil servants, denied the existence of a cabal or of resentment at Tennent's appointment. On his arrival the civil servants tried to support him, but soon became estranged by his lack of veracity and other personal faults. Finally, to substantiate his charges each of them produced private letters from Lord Torrington.[1]

The Committee of Inquiry drew up its Report in July 1850, after a sharp difference of opinion between Torrington's critics and supporters.[2] Hume moved that however necessary martial

---

[1] *Parl. Pap. H. C.* 36 of 1851, vol. VIII. i. 161–459, 662–70, 747–906; C.O. 54. 240: Nov. 10, 1847; C.O. 54. 261: Dec. 11, 1849; C.O. 54. 269: Apr. 12, 1850; C.O. 55. 92: *passim*; C.O. 54. 276: *passim*. Part of the correspondence is printed in [1301] of 1851, vol. xxxv, 4–24.

[2] *Parl. Pap. H. C.* 605 of 1850, vol. xii, *passim*. Although the Committee had again resolved in 1850 that the evidence be regarded as confidential, the Colombo newspapers continued to publish extracts.

law might have seemed on July 29 its continuance until October 10, together with the military executions and sequestration of property, 'were unnecessary and unjustifiable'. Lord Torrington had shown such 'want of judgement' that there was 'no prospect of his future usefulness' in Ceylon. Hawes moved that Lord Torrington was justified in proclaiming martial law in view of the information available and the 'universal alarm'. Its continuance until October 10 and the measures taken under it had the support of Smelt, Drought, 'and generally of all classes of the inhabitants'. The Committee felt 'general approbation' of the Governor's policy, although expressing 'their very strong disapprobation' of his private letters to Tennent and Wodehouse. These showed 'dissensions . . . highly detrimental to the public service' which demanded 'the prompt and decisive interference of Her Majesty's Government'. Neither of the proposed Reports proved acceptable, and finally as a compromise the suggestions of Lord Hotham were adopted. The Committee considered 'that the serious attention of Her Majesty's Government should be called to the evidence taken in the course of this Inquiry, and they recommend that a Royal Commission should be appointed to proceed to Ceylon to ascertain what changes may be necessary for the better government of that colony, unless some steps should forthwith be taken by the Government which may obviate the necessity of farther investigation'.

Torrington's critics were very far from content with the restrained wording of the Report. On July 26 and again on August 12, 1850, in the House of Commons Hume characterized Torrington's administration as an unparalleled tyranny and the executions under martial law as 'murders'. The most judicious speeches were made by Sir Joshua Walmsley and other members of the Committee. They approved of the initial proclamation of martial law since Torrington was misled by ignorant advisers, but condemned him for its continuance and for employing undue severity.[1] In 1851 Hume and Baillie again censured Torrington and the Government which had appointed him. The most effective speech was delivered by Gladstone, who considered that while the initial proclamation

[1] Hansard, III, cxiii. 339–43; 1043–56.

O

of martial law was justified the continuance long after all resistance had ceased was 'monstrous'.[1]

Nearly a year before this final debate Lord Torrington had been recalled. On this and later occasions Lord Grey made it clear that he entirely approved of the whole of the Governor's measures both before and after the outbreak of the rebellion. The sole reason for Torrington's recall was that 'it has appeared from the evidence and the documents submitted to the Committee that your Lordship has failed in maintaining amongst the' civil servants in Ceylon 'that harmonious co-operation with each other and that respect towards yourself, which are indispensable to the proper administration of its affairs'.[2] Selby was severely censured for his failure immediately to advise Torrington that he disapproved of the sequestration of property, and for disclosing the terms of the Governor's reply when he refused to pardon the Kandyan priest.[3] On December 3, 1850, Tennent and Wodehouse were dismissed from the Ceylon Civil Service, since their evidence before the Committee had disclosed such 'extreme animosity' that their future co-operation in Ceylon was 'impossible'. They were equally and 'greatly to blame', 'and each in his eagerness to discredit his adversary has thought himself justified in producing private letters of the most confidential character without the permission of the writers and to their manifest injury'.[4] In view of Wodehouse's excellent record of service Lord Grey appointed him Superintendent of British Honduras on December 17, 1850.[5]

---

[1] Hansard, III, cxvii. 6–98 and 130–2ʃ ι: May 27 and 29, 1851.

[2] C.O. 55. 91: Aug. 15, 1850; Hansard, III, cxv. 876–80: Apr. 1, 1851; Grey, *Colonial Policy*, ii. 188–91. Before the receipt of this dispatch Lord Torrington had already asked to be recalled owing to the publication of his private letters (C.O. 54. 270: July 20, 1850).

[3] C.O. 55. 92: Dec. 3, 1850.

[4] C.O. 55. 92: Dec. 3, 16, and 21, 1850; C.O. 54. 276: *passim*.

[5] C.O. 54. 276: Dec. 17, 1850. Sir Philip Wodehouse (1811–87) was Governor of British Guiana from 1854 to 1861, Governor of Cape Colony from 1861 to 1870, Governor of Bombay from 1872 to 1877, and was made a K.C.B. in 1862 (*Dictionary of National Biography, Supplement*, vol. iii. 516–17). Sir Emerson Tennent (1804–69) had accepted the Colonial Secretaryship of Ceylon as a step towards 'an early promotion to a Governorship' (C.O. 54. 276: Dec. 19, 1850). In December 1850 he was gazetted Governor of St. Helena, but never took up the appointment. In 1852 he became Secretary to the Board of Trade (*D.N.B.* lvi. 65).

XI

THE CINNAMON TRADE DURING THE NINETEENTH CENTURY

PRIOR to the nineteenth century the whole of the world's supply of cinnamon came from Ceylon; and the monopoly was one of the most lucrative branches of the Dutch East India Company's trade. Until 1769 the Dutch were entirely dependent upon the cinnamon which grew wild in the jungles, over three-fifths of the annual supply being obtained from Kandy. The situation was unsatisfactory, since the Kandyans frequently refused to permit the cinnamon peelers to enter their country. Governor Falck in 1769 established a cinnamon garden at Maradana near Colombo; and by 1795 four smaller plantations had been formed at Negombo, Kalutara, Galle, and Matara. In addition, the Dutch encouraged the Sinhalese to form 'an infinite number of small gardens'. The Dutch, however, never became more than partially independent of Kandyan supplies.[1] The cinnamon trade was a monopoly of the Company, and was preserved by a very stringent code of laws. The sale or export of a single stick of cinnamon except by the servants of Government, as well as the wilful injury of the tree, were punishable by death.[2] From 1691 to 1794, the date of the last Dutch shipment, the average annual export was limited to 400,000 lb., the estimated world consumption. The price was fixed at as high a figure as the market could be induced to pay, the profit on the sales averaging 200 per cent.[3] The collection and export of cinnamon were controlled by a Cinnamon Department under a European Superintendent; while the native cinnamon peelers formed a separate and privileged caste. Their own native headmen supervised the work of collection and also

---

[1] Tennent, *Ceylon*, ii. 51 and 163; Anthonisz, *Report on the Dutch Records*, 79–81; Cordiner, *Ceylon*, i. 414–16. Before 1769 all save 1,500 to 1,700 of the annual Dutch export of about 5,000 bales was obtained from Kandy (Bertolacci, *Ceylon*, 240–2 and 248–50).

[2] C.O. 54. 101: Dutch Proclamation of 1660; C.R. 52: Oct. 26, 1798; Bertolacci, *Ceylon*, 241.

[3] C.O. 54. 228: Oct. 22, 1846. The cinnamon was exported in 5,000 bales of 80 Dutch lb. each, or 436,000 lb. avoirdupois (C.O. 54. 9: Dec. 2, 1802).

administered their villages, subject to the control of the Superintendent of the Cinnamon Department.[1]

After the British conquest the East India Company carefully preserved the cinnamon monopoly. The export for 1797 reached the unprecedented volume of 1,173,427 lb., an amount which included not only the yield for 1796 but also the 732,885 lb. captured on the conquest of Ceylon. The average annual export from 1798 to 1800 inclusive was 438,017 lb., obtained by unwise exploitation of the sources of supply and particularly the Government plantations.[2] When Ceylon was transferred to the Crown in 1802 the Government took over control of the cultivation and collection of cinnamon.[3] An agreement was made in 1802 between the Crown and the Directors whereby the Company retained the monopoly, receiving annually 400,000 lb. of cinnamon and crediting the Ceylon Government with £60,000 at Madras.[4] For some years the British methods of controlling the monopoly followed closely those of the Dutch, although they modified the harsh penalties imposed for breaches of the cinnamon laws. The collection and preparation of the cinnamon remained in the hands of the caste of cinnamon peelers, who retained the Accommodessans or grants of land which they held in return for their services, as well as their other privileges. The Cinnamon Department was continued under a British Commercial Resident, the duties being the same as before the conquest.[5]

In 1800 Governor North attempted to restrict the cultivation to one principal and two subsidiary plantations, and to destroy all the small native gardens encouraged by the Dutch. He would thus facilitate the enforcement of the monopoly—since the high prices and the many scattered gardens encouraged smuggling—decrease the amount of labour required, and free native agriculture from the numerous restrictions imposed by

[1] C.R. 1: Pybus's Report of 1762; Bertolacci, *Ceylon*, 252–4.
[2] C.R. 52: Oct. 26, 1798; C.O. 54. 9: Dec. 2, 1802; Turner, *C.A. and L.R.* VI. ii. 76.
[3] C.O. 55. 61: Dec. 30, 1800.
[4] The Company was to receive annually 400,000 lb. in 4,324·5 bales of 92·5 lb. apiece, at a price of 3*s.* per lb. (C.O. 54. 5: Mar. 13, 1801). Turner, *C.A. and L.R.* VI. ii. 77–8; Cordiner, *Ceylon*, i. 416–17.
[5] C.R. 52: Feb. 26, 1799; C.R. 54: Major Robertson's MS.; Cordiner, *Ceylon*, i. 418.

the Dutch on all cultivation carried on near the cinnamon gardens.[1] North was confident that after two years the supply from the Government gardens would render the British entirely independent of the inferior Kandyan cinnamon.[2] These sanguine predictions were not realized: the yield of cinnamon sharply declined, and from 1802 to 1805 inclusively the amount sold to the Company fell short of the agreed quantity by about one-third. By the end of North's governorship in 1806 the deliveries were about 518,000 lb. in arrears. The gardens were almost 'entirely exhausted' by the large amounts collected in 1796 to 1800, and it proved necessary to depend upon Kandy for the bulk of the supply. Furthermore, labour was very difficult to obtain, since the cinnamon peelers were discontented by North's land reforms of 1801 which abolished their Accommodessans and substituted wages. A contributory cause was the Company's Agent at Colombo being the sole judge of the quality of the cinnamon submitted, and exercising freely his right of rejection.[3]

Sir Thomas Maitland soon discovered that the decline in production was largely due to North's mistakes. He restored the Accommodessans and abandoned the innovation of paying the cinnamon peelers.[4] Far from the Government gardens being able to supply all requirements they could produce only half. 'A considerable portion' of the balance was obtained from Kandy, but the greater part was made up from the small native gardens, which North had sold on the condition that the cinnamon trees were destroyed. Owing, however, to the 'inefficiency' of his administration the buyers had very rarely done so, and

---

[1] C.R. 52: Jan. 30, 1800; Bertolacci, *Ceylon*, 248–50.

[2] C.R. 52: Feb. 26, 1799; C.O. 54. 6: Sept. 10, 1802; Cordiner, *Ceylon*, i. 416–17.

[3] C.R. 52: *passim*; C.O. 54. 9: *passim*: C.O. 54. 20: Feb. 28, 1806; Cordiner, *Ceylon*, i. 405; Bertolacci, *Ceylon*, 247–53. The Company made no complaints, perhaps because in 1802 it had a surplus in London of 367,000 lb., or nearly a year's supply (Turner, *C.A. and L.R.* vi. ii. 78–9). Cinnamon rejected by the Company was sold in the Asiatic market, but was not allowed to be exported west of the Cape of Good Hope (Bertolacci, *Ceylon*, 246).

[4] C.O. 54. 20: Feb. 28, 1806. The cinnamon peelers presumed on their indispensability and proved inefficient. After ineffectual attempts at reform Governor Barnes in 1831 destroyed their monopoly of the work of cultivation by hiring part of his labourers from other castes (C.O. 54. 113: Sept. 5 and Oct. 11, 1831).

Maitland was thus 'able to deliver something near the amount of the contract'.[1] He also persuaded the Directors to abolish their Colombo Agency in 1808, Doctor High of the Ceylon Medical Staff being appointed to test the cinnamon for the Company.[2] While the deliveries increased during Maitland's governorship they still fell below the stipulated amount, the deficiency from 1807 to 1811 being apparently about 104,247 lb.[3]

In 1814 the Company's monopoly was renewed for seven years, the Ceylon Government undertaking to supply annually 450,000 lb. for £101,000.[4] During the period of the contract, from 1814 to 1821, there were sharp fluctuations in the quantity of cinnamon exported, the deliveries on the whole being less than the 450,000 lb. agreed upon. The independence of Kandy until 1815 and the revolt of 1818 were important causes, since the trade was partially dependent upon Kandyan supplies. The export in 1814 was only 274,262 lb., largely because the King refused to permit the cinnamon peelers to enter his territory. As a result of the Kandyan revolt the export for 1819 was only 323,102 lb.[5] The conquest of Kandy in 1815 was reflected in an increase of the annual export, the entire supply for 1817, 466,570 lb., being obtained from there.[6] Despite this advantage the average annual export from 1816 to 1821 inclusive was 429,949 lb., so that by 1821 the deliveries were 120,302 lb. in arrears.[7] Altogether apart from the Kandyan revolt, the cinnamon peelers were inefficient, and took advantage of their indispensability to resist the introduction of reforms. The principal cause, however, was that the Government plantations were too small to meet the demands made upon them.[8] In 1815 the four plantations had an area of about 11,126 acres,

[1] C.O. 54. 25: Feb. 28, 1807; C.O. 54. 27: Feb. 28, 1808; C.O. 54. 31: 1809: Maitland to Wood; Bertolacci, *Ceylon*, 245 and 251.

[2] C.O. 54. 33: *passim*.

[3] C.O. 54. 46: Mar. 4, 1813.

[4] C.O. 55. 62: Aug. 16, 1806; C.O. 54. 46: Mar. 4, 1813; C.O. 54. 80: Dec. 27, 1821; Bertolacci, *Ceylon*, 246–7.

[5] C.O. 54. 51: Feb. 28, 1814; C.O. 54. 70: Feb. 12, 1818; C.O. 54. 73: Jan. 9 and Feb. 8, 1819; C.O. 54. 80: Dec. 21, 1821. The 1819 export was only saved from a more serious decline by the inclusion of 74,000 lb. left in storage from 1818.

[6] C.O. 54. 66: Sept. 25, 1817; C.O. 54. 73: Feb. 8, 1819; C.O. 54. 80: Dec. 21, 1821.

[7] C.O. 54. 80: Dec. 21, 1821.   [8] C.O. 54. 46: Mar. 4, 1813.

and produced an annual average of 205,165 lb. An additional average of 196,007 lb. was collected from the gardens abandoned by North, and from trees growing wild in the jungle in British and Kandyan territories. The total amount of 401,172 lb. allowed no margin for rejections by the Agent appointed to test the cinnamon.[1]

The contract with the Company expired in 1821, and Sir Edward Barnes advised the Secretary of State not to renew it. The amount stipulated, 450,000 lb. of cinnamon of the first grade, was beyond the resources of the island, although the Government spent £5,000 or £6,000 annually out of its scanty revenue in increasing the amount of cultivation. Since 1811 the Company had made an average annual profit of £84,000, and Barnes urged that the Ceylon Government itself should be given the exclusive right to sell cinnamon. Assuming that the price in Europe remained at its existing average of 8s. per lb., he anticipated an annual increase in the revenue of at least £60,000. This would be still further increased by the sale in Europe of the coarser cinnamon which by the terms of the Company's contract could be sold only in Asia.[2] The Secretary of State refused to renew the Company's contract, and in 1822 the Ceylon Government took over the monopoly. The cinnamon would be classified into three grades, and packed in bales of 100 lb.; while public auctions would be held monthly at

---

[1] The four Government gardens were:

Kadirani	(near Negombo)	c. 4,106 acres—annual yield	c.	49,487 lb.
Ekele	(„ Colombo)	c. 1,598 „	„	c. 31,542 „
Maradana („	„)	c. 3,824 „	„	c. 103,970 „
Morotta („	„)	c. 218 „	„	c. 20,165 „

(C.O. 54. 56: June 8, 1815.)

The Government gardens had yielded about 240,500 lb. in 1807 (C.O. 54. 25: Feb. 28, 1807). The decline in production seems to have been due to poor methods of cultivation (C.O. 54. 46: Mar. 4, 1813; C.O. 54. 56: June 8, 1815). The discrepancy between the totals of 401,172 lb. for 1815 and 429,949 lb. for 1816–21 is probably due to an underestimate in the 1815 statement of the quantity of cinnamon obtainable from Kandy. The unspecified amount of Kandyan cinnamon in this total was an average based upon the fluctuating quantities previously obtained, since the Government only gradually secured accurate information after the conquest. The amount of cinnamon obtained from Kandy was greater after 1815 than before it.

[2] C.O. 54. 80: Dec. 27, 1821. There was reason to believe that much of the coarser cinnamon sold in Asia was re-exported to Europe under the alias of cassia (C.O. 54. 77: Aug. 18, 1820).

Colombo, and the purchaser might export it from there free from duty 'to any place whatsoever'.[1]

The attempt to make Colombo the centre of the cinnamon trade was abandoned in 1826, and thereafter all cinnamon was exported to London for sale. The auctions at Colombo were discontinued because the merchants made a tacit agreement to bid it in at much less than the reserve price. This they asserted was too high; while the Government maintained that it allowed for a reasonable profit.[2] The Government monopoly lasted from 1822 to 1833, the quantity exported being considerably in excess of what it had been under the East India Company. About one-third of the shipments, however, was made up of the coarse Grade III cinnamon which prior to 1821 had been sold only in Asia and had not been entered in the statement of exports.[3] The total exports from 1823 to 1825 are uncertain since the returns do not include the amounts sold in Colombo, but only the cinnamon sent by the Government to London for sale after it had been withdrawn from the auctions at Colombo. The Government exports reached their greatest volume during the quinquennium 1826–30, the average annual shipment being 517,760 lb. Owing to the decision to abandon the monopoly, the final shipments in 1831 and 1832 were only 162,600 lb.[4] Until 1828 the revenue realized from the sale of cinnamon was actually less than the £101,000 formerly received from the Company. When the contract expired in 1821 the Company had an unknown but very large surplus stock which largely supplied the London market until 1828. Moreover, though the quantity offered for sale was carefully restricted to maintain the monopoly price, nevertheless the value fell owing to the competition of the Ceylon Government and of the Colombo merchants who had bought cinnamon between 1822 and 1826.[5] By 1828 the Company's reserve stocks were exhausted, and from then until 1833 the Ceylon Government supplied the

[1] All attempts to evade the Government monopoly were punishable by a heavy fine and the confiscation of the cinnamon. The annual yield was estimated at 600,000 lb. including the inferior grade hitherto sold only in India (C.O. 54. 82: Mar. 12 and 13, 1822). C.O. 54. 104: Feb. 6, 1829.
[2] C.O. 54. 82: Dec. 6, 1822; C.O. 54. 84: *passim*; C.O. 54. 86: June 11, 1824; C.O. 54. 92: Mar. 15, 1826; C.O. 54. 110: July 31, Aug. 1 and 31, 1824.
[3] C.O. 54. 92: Mar. 15, 1826.   [4] C.O. 54. 140: Jan. 1, 1836.
[5] C.O. 54. 101: Dec. 19, 1828.

market. The average annual net revenue during the quinquennium 1828–32 was £115,817, as compared with the £184,000
which Governor Barnes had anticipated in 1821. By 1830 the
Government had accumulated in London a reserve stock of
1,442,247 lb. which was finally sold in 1833. The creation of
this reserve was due to the policy of restricting sales in order
to maintain a high price, combined with the Company's control
of the market until 1828.[1]

Another factor which contributed towards the small revenue
received from the sales was the increasing demand for cassia in
the London market. The East India Company and the Government had both adopted the Dutch doctrine that the average
annual world demand for cinnamon was about 400,000 or
500,000 lb., and that Ceylon had a natural monopoly which no
other country could challenge. Provided that the annual
quantity offered for sale were carefully restricted, the price
could be artificially maintained at a level which brought
enormous profit to the holder of the monopoly. The Colonial
Office and the Treasury fully accepted this doctrine despite the
far-sighted protests of Governor Barnes, and in 1829 ordered
that the annual export should not exceed 500,000 lb.[2] If Ceylon
had really possessed a natural monopoly, consumers would
presumably have been compelled to accept the situation. But
while the more delicate varieties of cinnamon could only be
grown on the island, there were inferior yet tolerable substitutes
which were beginning to invade the English market. Encouraged by the exorbitant price of Ceylon cinnamon the cultivation had been begun in India and Java, and although the
flavour was coarser, the much lower price made them dangerous
competitors. A still more formidable rival was the cassia which
was widely grown in Southern India, the Philippines, the East
Indian Archipelago, and above all in Southern China.[3]

As early as 1803 North had warned the Directors that Ceylon

[1] C.O. 54. 98: Sept. 5, 1827; C.O. 54. 101: Oct. 9, 1828; C.O. 54. 127: Mar. 9,
1833; C.O. 54. 136: Dec. 6, 1834; C.O. 54. 140: Jan. 1, 1836. The gross revenue
from 1823 to 1833 fluctuated between £50,000 and £170,000 (C.O. 54. 228:
Oct. 22, 1846).
[2] C.O. 54. 97: Oct. 29, 1823; C.O. 54. 101: Oct. 9 and Dec. 19, 1828: C.O.
Memos.; C.O. 54. 106: May 26, 1829; C.O. 54. 109: Apr. 20, 1830; C.O. 54. 113:
Aug. 5, 1831.
[3] C.O. 54. 228: Oct. 22, 1846.

cinnamon was losing the Indian and especially the Manila market, 'as the bastard cinnamon of China and the Malabar Coast has, notwithstanding its inferiority, gained a preference in the market by its cheapness'.[1] Twelve years later Doctor Marshall reported that the East Indian Islands were growing inferior cinnamon, and that the sale of Chinese cassia in the English market was small but rapidly increasing.[2] In 1817 Simon Sawers, the Commissioner of Kandy, wrote that 'it seems to be but little known that the Cinnamon of Ceylon does not constitute one-third of the quantity of that article which reaches the markets of Europe under the name of Cassia'.[3] From the beginning of his governorship Sir Edward Barnes foresaw the danger, and urged that by increasing the production of cinnamon and lowering the price the aggregate profit would be increased. In 1821 he pointed out that the average annual import of cassia into Great Britain was 382,673 lb., and that it sold for 1s. 6d. per lb., while the price of Grade I cinnamon was about 8s. a lb.[4] In 1828 he attributed the decline in the sales of cinnamon partly to the competition of Chinese cassia, and vainly advised the imposition in the United Kingdom of equal import duties on cinnamon and cassia.[5]

In the 'twenties and early 'thirties, however, cinnamon was by far the most valuable of Ceylon's exports, and few if any foresaw that within fifteen years the trade would be moribund. Commercial interests grew steadily more insistent that the Government should resign so lucrative an enterprise to private hands.[6] In 1832 Colonel Colebrooke, the Commissioner of Inquiry, advised the abolition of the Government monopoly because it was expensive to maintain, and was 'oppressive and injurious' to the Sinhalese. The charge of oppression

[1] C.O. 54. 11: Apr. 20, 1803.   [2] C.O. 54. 56: June 8, 1815.
[3] C.O. 54. 66: Sept. 25, 1817.   [4] C.O. 54. 80: Dec. 27, 1821.
[5] The import duty on cinnamon was 2s. 6d. per lb., and on cassia 1s. (C.O. 54. 101: Aug. 2, 1828). The average importation of cassia into Great Britain from 1827 to 1831 was 603,923 lb. (Ferguson, *All About Spices*, 236). During the quinquennium 1826–30 the average annual sale of Ceylon cinnamon in London was 479,398 lb. Between 1826 and 1833 the price of Grade I cinnamon varied between 7s. and 8s. per lb., that of Grade III was about 4s., and that of cassia 7½d. It was believed that cassia could not compete with Ceylon cinnamon because it was so much cheaper (C.O. 54. 109: Apr. 20, 1830; C.O. 54. 140: Jan. 1, 1836).
[6] Tennent, *Ceylon*, ii. 163.

referred to the cinnamon laws which declared all trees wherever situated to be Government property, and forbade their destruction or sale under heavy penalties.¹ Governor Horton scouted Colebrooke's charges as grossly exaggerated: since his arrival in 1831 he had received 2,842 petitions for the redress of grievances, but not one had asked for the abolition of the monopoly. In 1832 only twenty persons were convicted of breaches of the cinnamon laws, the fines amounting merely to £88. The Governor also urged that the monopoly should be gradually abandoned to obviate the danger of a serious loss of revenue.² The Colonial Office disregarded Horton's representations, and in 1832 ordered the Ceylon Government to abolish the monopoly on July 1, 1833. The Cinnamon Department and the cinnamon laws were to be abolished, the plantations were to be leased or sold, and cultivation and sale were to be free to all. The Government was 'to withdraw wholly from its participation in the trade', as soon as it had disposed of its plantations and of the reserve stocks of cinnamon which had accumulated in London and in Ceylon. The market for the public auction of cinnamon was to be transferred from London to Ceylon. An export duty of 3s. per lb. was to be imposed on each of the three grades of cinnamon. The Treasury computed that this duty would produce £50,000, the amount which Colebrooke had estimated as the annual net revenue from the sale of cinnamon.³

The liquidation of the Government's interests proved longer and more difficult than had been expected. The large reserve stocks which had accumulated in London were not entirely disposed of until the end of 1833.⁴ To obtain a fair price for the plantations proved impossible as the Governor had predicted;

¹ C.O. 54. 114: Nov. 9, 1831; C.O. 54. 121: May 22, 1832, and *passim*; C.O. 54. 122: Jan. 31, 1832.

² C.O. 54. 118: Oct. 2, 1832; C.O. 54. 127: Mar. 30 and 31, 1833; C.O. 54. 128: *passim*; C.O. 54. 129: *passim*; C.O. 54. 136: Dec. 6, 1834.

³ C.O. 55. 74: Oct. 12, 1832; C.O. 55. 75: Nov. 10, 1833; C.O. 55. 77: May 10, 1835; C.O. 54. 119: Sept. 18, 1832. The monopoly was abolished on July 10, 1833, exporters being required to ship cinnamon from Colombo or Galle (C.O. 54. 127: Mar. 9, 1833). The export of seeds and plants was forbidden on pain of a heavy fine or imprisonment. The prohibition was aimed at the Javan and other competitors who were trying to improve the quality of their cinnamon (C.O. 54. 129: July 9, 1833: Regulation No. 5 of 1833).

⁴ C.O. 54. 127: Mar. 9, 1833; C.O. 54. 140: Jan. 1, 1836.

and until 1846 the Government had no alternative but to collect and sell the cinnamon. The post of Superintendent of the Cinnamon Department was abolished, and four European Assistants with a reduced staff of native headmen and labourers carried on the cultivation. In 1835 the annual yield was estimated at 230,000 lb.; but it steadily decreased, since the lack of revenue forbade the employment of sufficient labourers to cultivate the plantations. Owing to the small shipments of 1831 and 1832 the Government stock of cinnamon in Ceylon amounted in 1833 to 1,179,900 lb., a quantity which steadily increased with yearly additions from the plantations. As early as January 1, 1835, the Government stock was 1,509,803 lb. Beginning with July 10, 1833, the Government cinnamon was sold by public auction at Colombo, subject to a reserve price.[1] The Governor's fears that the abandonment of the monopoly would injure the revenue were quickly justified. By August 1834 less than £31,000 had been realized from the sale of Government cinnamon and the export duty, as compared with an average net revenue of £115,817 from 1828 to 1832.[2] From August 1833 to December 1835 the total export of cinnamon was 720,369 lb., of which only 150,000 lb. had been bought from the Government.[3] Owing to the high reserve prices, the purchaser of Government cinnamon could not even cover his expenses when he sold it in London, except in the case of Grade III, on which a small profit could be made. If he bought from native growers, however, he could make a profit of from 57 per cent. to 62 per cent.[4] The cause of the low price of native cinnamon was 'the reckless and destructive manner in which the jungle cinnamon has been cut by the peelers' after the abolition of the monopoly in 1833. The Sinhalese were not

[1] C.O. 54. 127: Mar. 9, 1833; C.O. 54. 140: Jan. 1, 1836; C.O. 54. 154: Feb. 11, 1837; Tennent, *Ceylon*, ii. 162. The Senior Assistant managed the Colombo gardens, graded the Government cinnamon, and exercised general superintendence over the other three Assistants, each of whom was in charge of a plantation (C.O. 54. 117: Jan. 16, and July 16, 1832).

[2] C.O. 54. 129: Sept. 1, 1833; C.O. 54. 135: *passim*; C.O. 54. 136: Dec. 6, 1836; C.O. 54. 140: Feb. 9, 1835.

[3] C.O. 54. 140: Jan. 1, 1836; C.O. 54. 281: Nov. 28, 1851.

[4] C.O. 54. 136: Dec. 6, 1834. The Government reserve prices were: Grade I, 3s. 6d.; Grade II, 2s.; Grade III, 9d. Native growers sold Grades I and II at 1s. 6d. per lb., and Grade III at 4d. (C.O. 54. 141: Dec. 1835; C.O. Memo.).

forming new gardens because these required ten years before
they gave a profitable yield. They were making immediate
profits but were endangering the future of the industry, since
'a very considerable quantity of cinnamon' trees were being
destroyed. The Government considered that the reserve prices
could not be lowered because they were 'absolutely necessary
to remunerate the grower', and that the only solution was to
decrease the export duty. This would at least enable buyers
of Government cinnamon to make a moderate profit, although
it would not affect the vast disparity of profit between Government and private cinnamon.[1] The export duty on Grade III
cinnamon was reduced to 2s. per lb. on April 1, 1835; and on
January 1, 1837, that on Grades I and II was lowered to
2s. 6d.[2]

The new tariff did not have much effect on the sale of Government cinnamon, since, in addition to the disparity in profit, the
London price fell rapidly after 1835 owing to the competition
of cassia and Javanese cinnamon. The Ceylon trade became
steadily less profitable, and the Government found increasing
difficulty in disposing of its cinnamon and plantations. The
policy of fixing a high reserve price was continued until 1842, so
that Government was undersold by private cinnamon, and
reserve stocks steadily increased. The same causes explained
the failure to dispose of all but an insignificant part of the
plantations prior to 1840. With the London price of cinnamon
steadily falling no one was inclined to invest much capital in
so doubtful a speculation. The difficulty was accentuated since
the Government demanded a high reserve price 'fixed with
some reference to the . . . productiveness' of the plantations.
About 1840 the Ceylon Government reported that the 'extravagant' reserve price must be abandoned, and that there seemed
no hope of ever obtaining a fair value for the plantations.[3]
In 1842 the Colonial Office authorized the auction of cinnamon

[1] C.O. 54. 141: *passim.*
[2] C.O. 54. 135: Aug. 20, 1834; C.O. 55. 75: Apr. 14, 1836; C.O. 54. 157:
Ordinance No. 7 of 1837.
[3] C.O. 54. 140: Dec. 1835: C.O. Memo.; C.O. 54. 154: Feb. 11, 1837; C.O.
54. 171: June 29, 1839; C.O. 54. 177: Jan. 18, 1840; C.O. 54. 181: Aug. 10,
1840; C.O. 54. 190: Nov. 13, 1841; C.O. 54. 197: June 3, 1842; C.O. 54. 177–
201: *passim*; C.O. 55. 81: July 8, 1841; C.O. 55. 82: *passim*; Tennent, *Ceylon,*
ii. 163.

at current prices, and also approved the practice, begun about 1840, of selling the plantations for whatever they would bring.[1] In many instances the price obtained was less than one-quarter of the value of their annual produce. The last of the reserve stock of cinnamon was finally sold in 1845; and by 1847 the whole of the plantations had been disposed of, with the exception of two or three thousand acres of the Maradana Garden for which no offers were made. The Government abandoned the cultivation of the Garden and leased the right to collect cinnamon from it.[2]

The decline of the Ceylon cinnamon trade was due to the competition of cassia and other rivals combined with the crippling effect of the heavy export duty. The abandonment of the monopoly in 1833 by no means connoted the abandonment of the doctrine that the world demand was limited to about 450,000 lb., and that Ceylon had a natural monopoly which inferior competitors could never injure. The British Government felt absolutely secure in imposing an export duty which, added to the cost of cultivation and other charges, would just fall short of destroying the demand by fixing an impossibly exorbitant price. No measure could have been devised which was better calculated to foster the cultivation of cassia and of Javanese cinnamon. Their competition had begun to affect the London market in the 'twenties but did not become really serious until about 1835. The Ceylon Government and the Colonial Office gradually realized the effect of the duty; but the Treasury stubbornly resisted any effective change until the Ceylon trade was in danger of extinction.[3] The cultivation of cinnamon in Java was begun by the Dutch who were transported there after the British conquest of Ceylon. In 1825 a Dutch brig smuggled 3,000 plants from Ceylon to Java, and the plantations began rapidly to increase.[4] The cost of labour

[1] C.O. 55. 83: May 2, 1842.

[2] C.O. 54. 227: Oct. 30 and Nov. 6, 1846; C.O. 54. 228: Oct. 22, 1846, and Apr. 13, 1847; C.O. 54. 259: July 11, 1849.

[3] C.O. 54. 227: Oct. 30, 1846. The exorbitant Ceylon duties most successfully established the trade in Javanese cinnamon and Chinese cassia, for 'within the last few years we have been gradually pushed out of the market'. Ceylon cinnamon could only be sold in London at 'a figure which is actually below the sum for which it can by any possibility be delivered in London' (C.O. 54. 228: Oct. 22, 1846).

[4] C.O. 54. 98: May 1, 1827; C.O. 54. 107: Feb. 17, 1830.

was less, and above all the Javanese export duty was only
$\frac{1}{2}d$. per lb., so that the Ceylon export duty acted as a high
protective tariff for the Dutch benefit. The production increased
from 2,200 lb. in 1835 to 134,500 in 1845 and 250,500 lb. in
1848.[1] Southern India was a less serious competitor, but was
able to undersell Ceylon since the cost of labour was a quarter
of what it was in Ceylon. Moreover the Indian export duty
was only 3 per cent. of the value of the cinnamon, while that of
Ceylon was 'above 250 per cent.'[2] The most dangerous rival
was cassia, the importation of which into Great Britain increased very rapidly from about 1835. By 1844 the quantity
imported was 1,278,413 lb., more than double what it had been
in 1830. The flavour was much coarser, but 'its greatly inferior
price enabled it effectually to supplant the heavily taxed cinnamon of Ceylon in almost every market in the world'. Commercial dishonesty also played its part, for by 1846 'the greater
part of what is now sold in London as cinnamon is in reality
cassia'. The consumer gradually became satisfied with the
cheaper substitute, so that after about 1846 it no longer paid
to grow the finer qualities of cinnamon.[3]

The decline of Ceylon cinnamon is clearly marked by the
history of the sale price per lb. in London of Grade I cinnamon.
In 1835 it stood at 9s. 9d., by 1841 it had fallen to 5s. 1d., by
1846 to 3s. 9d., and by 1855 to 1s. 3d. During the same period
the price of cassia fluctuated between 6d. and 1s. per lb.[4] From
1835 to 1839 inclusive the average annual export of Ceylon
cinnamon was 521,492 lb., being an increase of 3,732 lb. per
annum over the shipments for 1826 to 1830. The average annual

[1] C.O. 54. 228: Oct. 22, 1846, and Apr. 13, 1847; C.O. 54. 281: Nov. 8,
1851; Pridham, *Ceylon*, i. 391–4. Prior to 1829 the United Kingdom import
duty was 2s. 6d. per lb. on British grown and 3s. 6d. on foreign cinnamon.
From 1829 to 1842 it was 6d. on British and 1s. on foreign cinnamon; and from
1842 to 1853 it was 3d. on British and 6d. on foreign cinnamon. The preference
was far too small to offset the effect of the Ceylon export duty (Danson,
Econ. and Stat. Studies, 208). The import duty was equalized at 2d. per lb. in
1853, and abolished in 1860 (Ferguson, *All About Spices*, 229).

[2] C.O. 54. 146: Dec. 24, 1835; C.O. 54. 177: Jan. 18, 1840.

[3] C.O. 54. 228: Oct. 22, 1846, and Apr. 13, 1847; Tennent, *Ceylon*, ii. 163–5;
Pridham, *Ceylon*, i. 391–3. The United Kingdom import duty on foreign-
grown cassia was 1s. per lb. from 1825 to 1842, when it was lowered to 3d.
(Danson, *Econ. and Stat. Studies*, 208–10).

[4] C.O. 54. 141: July 14, 1835; C.O. 54. 240: Dec. 13, 1847; Tennent, *Ceylon*,
ii. 165; Danson, *Econ. and Stat. Studies*, 209–10.

value, however, of the exports in 1835–9 was only £42,790, as compared with an average of £115,817, in the quinquennium 1828–32.[1] In 1837 the Ceylon merchants demanded a reduction of the export duties, but the Governor opposed it because the danger was imaginary.[2] In 1839 Governor MacKenzie reported that the duty was 'exorbitant', but that Ceylon could not afford the loss of revenue. Furthermore, it would be 'greatly preferable' to abolish the tax paid by the fishermen of a tenth of their catch. This was done in 1840, and as a result less fish were caught and the price doubled. Many of the fishermen were Roman Catholics, and transferred the payment of the tenth to their church.[3] In 1840 Governor MacKenzie finally became convinced of 'the very urgent necessity of an early alteration in the very exorbitant rate of duty'. The Colonial Office rejected his proposal that the duty be gradually reduced to 1s.; but as a compromise agreed that after June 1, 1841, the export duty on all grades of cinnamon should be 2s.[4] The reduction had no effect in improving conditions: the export declined from 389,373 lb. with a value of £29,583 in 1840 to 121,145 lb. valued at £15,207 in 1842.[5] The Ceylon Government and merchants continued their attempts to convince the Colonial Office that the duty must be drastically reduced. In 1841 the Collector of Customs advised a duty of 3d. per lb. 'When other places produce it [i.e. cinnamon] at the same, or nearly the same cost, the effect of the present high export duty will be to cause the market to be supplied from those places, even with Cinnamon of an inferior quality.' The argument that the Government could not afford to forego the revenue had lost its point since the export was steadily dwindling under foreign competition.[6] The Colonial Office lowered the duty to

[1] C.O. 54. 140: Jan. 1, 1836; C.O. 54. 157; C.O. 54. 188: June 30, 1841; C.O. 54. 281: Nov. 28, 1851; Ferguson, *Ceylon Commonplace Book*, 87–8.

[2] C.O. 54. 141: *passim*; C.O. 54. 154: Feb. 10, 1837.

[3] C.O. 54. 131: Dec. 9, 1833; C.O. 54. 154: Feb. 11, 1837; C.O. 54. 171: June 29, 1839; C.O. 54. 172: Sept. 2 and 18, 1839; C.O. 54. 228: Oct. 22, 1846; C.O. 55. 79: Oct. 2, 1837, and Jan. 10, 1840; C.O. 55. 81: May 22, 1840; Tennent, *Ceylon*, ii. 130–2.

[4] C.O. 54. 177: Jan. 18, 1840; C.O. 54. 182: Dec. 9, 1840; C.O. 55. 81: Apr. 27, 1840, and Mar. 7, 1841; C.O. 55. 82: *passim*.

[5] C.O. 54. 181: Aug. 10, 1840; C.O. 54. 189: Aug. 9, 1841; C.O. 54. 281: Nov. 28, 1851; Ferguson, *Ceylon Commonplace Book*, 87–8.

[6] C.O. 54. 190: Oct. 21 and Nov. 13, 1841; C.O. 54. 196: Apr. 27, 1842.

1s. per lb. in 1843, but refused to make further reductions since the £32,025 received from it was too important to be abandoned. Governor Campbell was censured for writing that 'the cinnamon revenue has dwindled down to a comparative trifle'. It seems clear that the opposition to Ceylon's requests came less from the Colonial Office than from the Treasury, which stubbornly resisted a change that might involve an additional charge upon Imperial revenues.[1]

The Ceylon merchants petitioned the Treasury that the new rate was 'wholly insufficient' to save the cinnamon trade. Even if it were greatly reduced the decline had gone so far that they despaired of retaining more than a fraction of their former trade.[2] The remonstrances proved of no avail, and the *débâcle* grew rapidly nearer. In 1846 the cinnamon export was 401,656 lb. with a value of £40,162, the amount of the duty being £13,800. The London price for Grade I cinnamon fell rapidly from 5s. per lb. in 1844 to 3s. 9d. in 1846, while for inferior varieties it was as low as 9d. The average price of Grade II cinnamon, which represented the average value of all kinds, was 2s. 6d. in 1846–8. The price of cassia during this period was 8d. a lb.[3] Barely to cover expenses the lowest price at which Ceylon cinnamon from the most economically managed plantations could be sold in London was 2s. 5d. per lb. This amount made no allowance for interest on the capital invested. 'A very large proportion of the shipments made' since 1844 'not only left nothing to the owner of the goods but in many recent cases' were actually sold in London at 'a heavy loss' As one instance out of many a shipment which cost the exporter £800 sold for £263 7s. 9d.[4] 'There is scarcely a house in the trade that could not multiply similar instances of loss and consequent ruin to native shippers . . . none of these native shippers are men of large capital. . . . the European owners of

---

[1] C.O. 55. 82: May 31, 1841, and *passim*; C.O. 55. 83: May 2 and Aug. 26, 1842; C.O. 54. 228: Apr. 13, 1847.

[2] C.O. 54. 197: June 3, 1842.

[3] C.O. 54. 227: Oct. 30, 1846; C.O. 54. 228: Oct. 22, 1846, and Apr. 13, 1847; C.O. 54. 240: Dec. 13, 1847; C.O. 54. 249: July 4, 1848; C.O. 54. 281: Nov. 28, 1851.

[4] C.O. 54. 225: July 10, 1846; C.O. 54. 227: Oct. 1 and 30, 1846. The items comprising the total of 2s. 5d. were: cost of cultivation 1s., duty 1s., freight and sales charges in London 5d. (C.O. 54. 228: Oct. 22, 1846).

P

gardens are also losing money.' 'A most unhappy unanimity prevails as to the rapidly declining condition of the trade, and the indispensable necessity for an immediate discontinuance of the Duty upon Export, to save the cultivation from utter abandonment under the pressure of successful competition from the cassia of China and the cinnamon of Java.'[1]

The Ceylon Government supported the merchants' demands, pointing out that a duty of 1s. was as effective in ruining the trade in 1846 as 3s. had been ten years previously. 'The simultaneous decline in the price of the article kept pace with this reduction in duty. . . . The relief therefore was only apparent and unsubstantial.'[2] The duty was equal to the whole cost of cultivation in Ceylon, while it was also between 50 per cent. and 100 per cent. of the sales price in London—sometimes indeed more than 100 per cent. when the price fell below 1s.[3] The export duty on Javanese cinnamon was only $\frac{1}{2}d$. per lb., and those on Indian cinnamon and cassia were also nominal. 'They have a protection at our expense of 1s. per lb., more than equal to the whole cost of production.' While the Ceylon export was stationary at best, and in some years declined, that of its rivals showed a steady and rapid increase. This was particularly true of cassia, the export of which 'has been doubled and even trebled since 1840'.[4] By 1846 it was clear that unless the duty were abolished the cinnamon trade was in danger of 'immediate and total extinction'. In 1847 Lord Grey's committee of Colonial Office and Treasury officials advised that the tariff must either be abolished or else reduced to 2½ per cent. of the cost of production, a tax of $\frac{3}{4}d$. per lb.[5] Owing to the heavy deficit in the Ceylon revenue, half-measures were again adopted, and in September 1848 the export duty was reduced to 4d. per lb.[6]

[1] C.O. 54. 227: Nov. 4, 1846.
[2] C.O. 54. 228: Oct. 22, 1846. The frequent changes in the duty 'have in some instances produced inordinate speculation, transient gleams of success have for short periods advanced prices only to make the reaction more severely felt'. Cinnamon 'has of late years presented more the appearance of a gambling transaction than the even tenor of a well-regulated trade' (C.O. 54. 227: Oct. 30, 1846).
[3] C.O. 54. 224: Apr. 14, 1846.
[4] C.O. 54. 226: Oct. 1846; C.O. 54. 227: Oct. 30 and Nov. 4, 1846; C.O. 54. 228: Oct. 22, 1846; C.O. 54. 240: Dec. 13, 1847.
[5] C.O. 54. 225: July 10, 1846; C.O. 54. 228: Apr. 13, 1847.
[6] C.O. 54. 240: Dec. 13, 1847.

The Ceylon planter could derive a profit from his sales providing the average London price continued at its existing level of 2s. 6d. per lb.—and the buyer was not allured by the superior cheapness of cassia.[1]

The immediate effect of the change was to increase the export of cinnamon from 448,369 lb. valued at £44,737 in 1847, to 733,782 lb. valued at £73,378 in 1849. In 1850 the export decreased by nearly 89,000 lb., and the decline steadily continued until 1852, when the shipment was 427,666 lb., with a value of £42,766.[2] Owing to the competition of cassia and of Javanese cinnamon the average London price per lb. fell from 2s. 6d. in 1848 to 1s. 8d. in 1852.[3] Once again the decline in price had kept pace with the reduction in duty, so that it was as impossible as before to sell Ceylon cinnamon at a profit, or even to cover the cost of placing it on the London market. In 1851 the Colombo Chamber of Commerce again demanded the total abolition of the export duty. The partial remissions had given 'no effectual relief . . . because they were never made until the trade had been paralysed by their continuance, and because a sufficient amount has always been retained to constitute an important advantage in favour of foreign growers'. So 'prostrate' was the condition of the trade and so thoroughly established were its rivals that even the abolition of the duty would not enable it to displace them. All that Ceylon could hope to do was to hold its own by a large increase in the export of coarse cinnamon.[4] The Colonial Office agreed that the immediate abolition of the duty was 'of paramount importance', since 'failing this repeal trade must be totally abandoned'. On the other hand, the loss of the £11,000 of revenue might 'curtail the expenditure for roads', so urgently required by the coffee plantations.[5] The budget estimates for 1852 fortunately showed a favourable balance, and the Secretary of State instructed the Governor to abolish the duty in 1853.[6]

[1] C.O. 54. 249: July 4, 1849.
[2] C.O. 54. 281: Nov. 28, 1851; Ferguson, *Ceylon Commonplace Book*, 87–8.
[3] C.O. 54. 281: Nov. 28, 1851; Tennent, *Ceylon*, ii. 165.
[4] C.O. 54. 278: Mar. 25, 1851; C.O. 54. 281: Nov. 8, 1851, and *passim*.
[5] C.O. 54. 281: Nov. 8 and 28, 1851, and Apr. 5, 1852; Steuart, *Notes on Cinnamon Revenue*, passim.
[6] The repeal of the duty was postponed to 1853 since the Governor in 1834

Subsequent events confirmed the prophecy made by the Colombo Chamber of Commerce in 1851. The repeal of the duty saved the trade from extinction; but until the 'sixties the growers were barely able to hold their own against their rivals. The majority of the European planters sold their estates, and the trade passed largely into native hands. The average annual export from 1853 to 1866 was 822,485 lb., valued at £42,440, as compared with 561,273 lb., valued at £56,130, from 1848 to 1852.[1] The explanation of the increased quantity exported was that under the pressure of competition the growers were compelled to sacrifice quality to quantity. The consumers had become satisfied with the cheaper substitute of cassia, and it no longer paid to grow the finer varieties of cinnamon. The change began about 1846, and thereafter the planters increasingly specialized in the coarser grades which could compete successfully in the market.[2]

The revival began about 1867 by still further debasing the quality through the inclusion of chips, the coarse and broken fragments which previously had been used in the manufacture of cinnamon oil. The discovery about 1867 that it was more profitable to export them caused 'a regular rush into the trade'. The export of chips and baled spice increased from 1,017,750 lb. valued at £50,887 in 1867 to the enormous quantity of 2,684,367 lb. valued at £134,269 in 1869.[3] 'This was the culminating point: the rubbish which was sent from the Island brought the chips into disfavour.'[4] In 1870 the export fell to 2,071,679 lb.

had promised that no reduction would be made without ten months' notice (C.O. 54. 136: Dec. 6, 1834; C.O. 55. 93: July 4, 1851 and May 22, 1852). In 1858 a small duty was reimposed on cinnamon and other exports to finance railway construction, the annual revenue being from £750 to £875 (C.O. 54. 378: Aug. 20, 1863).

[1] C.O. 54. 378: Aug. 20, 1863; C.O. 54. 404: Sept. 16, 1865; C.O. 54. 415: Oct. 15, 1866; C.O. 54. 437: Nov. 14, 1868. After 1852 the Ceylon records rarely referred to cinnamon, a testimony to the unimportant place it had come to occupy in the island's trade. Ferguson, *Ceylon Commonplace Book*, 179–81; Ferguson, *All About Cinnamon*, 4 and 8. From 1856 to 1870 the average annual importation of Chinese cassia into the United Kingdom was 736,855 lb., valued at £29,278. From 1870 to 1875 the average importation of all Chinese spices, the bulk of which was cassia, was 1,290,038 lb., the value being £44,005 (Ferguson, *All About Spices*, 225).

[2] Tennent, *Ceylon*, ii. 164.

[3] C.O. 54. 437: Nov. 14, 1868; C.O. 54. 457: Sept. 16, 1870.

[4] Ferguson, *All About Cinnamon*, 2–4.

valued at £103,584; and from 1871 to 1882 inclusive the average annual export was 1,460,756 lb. with a value of £69,570. From 1883 to 1887 inclusive the average annual export increased to 2,206,297 lb., with a value of £91,060, or about 1*d*. less per lb. than from 1871 to 1882.[1] 'The price has gone down until the cinnamon cultivators, nearly all Ceylonese, declare there is no margin of profit, and yet their exports still go on increasing, more particularly of chips.'[2] One reason for the low price was the poor quality of the chips, which seriously injured the sale in London of good cinnamon. 'A taste for coarse and inferior bark has been created, and we are paying the penalty for it in prices that leave but a narrow margin of profit.' An even more important cause was the competition of cassia, Javanese cinnamon being no longer so serious a rival as formerly.[3] By the close of the nineteenth century the cinnamon trade had come safely through its worst vicissitudes, and had established itself as 'one of the most important minor cultivations of the island, though not very remunerative'.[4] The value and quality of the bark had both suffered heavily in the struggle; but Ceylon had contrived to retain its position as a centre of the spice trade.

[1] *Parl. Pap.* [C. 2093] of 1878, vol. lxxviii. 37; *Parl. Pap.* [C. 4225] of 1884–5, vol. lxxxiii. 40; *Parl. Pap.* [C. 5507] of 1888, vol. cv. 43.

[2] Ferguson, *Cinnamon*, 2; Ferguson, *Ceylon in 1893*, 51.

[3] Ferguson, *Ceylon in 1893*, 236; Ferguson, *All About Spices*, 251 and 265; Ferguson, *All About Cinnamon*, 3–6.

[4] Willis, *Ceylon*, 62.

XII

COFFEE AND TRANSPORTATION DURING THE NINETEENTH CENTURY

UNDER the Dutch régime coffee was a monopoly of the Company; but little attempt was made to develop the cultivation, the average annual export varying from 40,000 to 100,000 lb. For a time the Dutch had plantations near Galle and Negombo, but abandoned them owing to the very indifferent results, contenting themselves with exporting the coffee bought from the Kandyans. The failure of the Dutch to develop the industry was due partly to their absorption in the cinnamon trade, and partly to the unsuitability of the districts near the coast for coffee growing.[1] In 1804 Governor North built a coffee mill, and again brought under cultivation the former Dutch plantations near Negombo. His expectation that coffee would 'soon become a principal Branch of our Produce' was not fulfilled, for in 1808 Governor Maitland reported that it was of small importance.[2] The cultivation increased to some extent, owing perhaps to the abandonment by the Government of the Dutch monopoly; but prior to 1812 the annual export never exceeded 3,000 cwt.[3] In 1810 General Maitland persuaded the Secretary of State to abolish Dundas's Regulation of 1801 which forbade Europeans to acquire land in Ceylon except within the District of Colombo. This prohibition, avowedly copied from the East India Company's practice in India, was 'striking at the only chance we have of making this either a very rich or a very valuable colony'. Ceylon was admirably adapted for coffee plantations, but the natives had neither the capital nor the industry to establish them.[4] One of the earliest European planters seems to have been a civil

[1] Tennent, *Ceylon*, ii. 226–7; Bertolacci, *Ceylon*, 156–7; Ferguson, *Ceylon in 1893*, 63–4. The Dutch received a profit of 200 per cent. from the sale in Europe (C.R. 54: Robertson MS.).

[2] C.O. 54. 9: Nov. 25, 1802; C.O. 54. 13: Jan. 1, 1804; C.O. 54. 16: Feb. 8, 1805; C.O. 54. 29: Aug. 19, 1808.

[3] Ferguson, *Ceylon in 1893*, 64; Bertolacci, *Ceylon*, 156–8.

[4] C.O. 54. 5: Mar. 13, 1801; C.R. 54: Douglass MS.; C.O. 54. 17: Mar. 6, 1805; C.O. 54. 22: May 21, 1806; C.O. 54. 38: June 5, 1810; C.O. 55. 62: June 5, 1810; Lord, *Maitland*, 126.

servant named Bletterman, who in 1812 had 'a coffee garden of some extent, and by which he appears hitherto to have been a considerable loser'.[1]

Neither the climate nor the temperature of the coastal plains were suitable for coffee growing, and little success was obtained until the conquest of Kandy made it possible to form plantations in the mountains. A further essential was the construction of a network of roads opening up the interior and linking it with the ports. While cinnamon was the staple industry roads were less essential, since the plantations were near the coast and the small yield could be carried by porters. The coffee crop was so much larger that the expense of conveying it from the interior to the ports by coolies would have been prohibitive even if the labour had been obtainable. Prior to the construction of the railway in the 'sixties the only means of transportation was the cumbrous bullock cart; but it could rarely be used except on made roads. Until 1820 there was not a mile of metalled road on the island outside a few of the principal towns, the only means of communication especially in Kandy being rough and narrow jungle paths. The numerous rivers could be crossed by fords or sometimes ferries in the dry season, but during the monsoons even small streams were often impassable. After holding the assizes in Kandy about 1830 the Chief Justice, Sir Hardinge Gifford, was moved to enshrine his tribulations in verse.

> Marshes and quagmires, puddles, pools and swamps,
> Dark matted jungles and long plushy plains,
> Exhaling foetid airs and mortal damps,
> By Kandyan perfidy miscalled a Road,
> Through which the luckless traveller must wade,
> Uncheered by sight of man or man's abode.[2]

---

[1] C.O. 54. 43: June 12, 1812; C.O. 54. 66: Nov. 19, 1817.

[2] Sir Hardinge's journey was made over Barnes's Colombo–Kandy road after it had been roughly graded but not metalled. Even this was a vast improvement over the former jungle paths; and his laments may be applied *a fortiori* to earlier conditions (*C.A. and L.R.* x. i. 58). *V.* also Haafner, *Ceylon*, passim. In 1831 the Governor reported that owing to the completion of Barnes's road 1,200 lb. were carried from Kandy to Colombo in a bullock cart for £1, whereas this amount formerly required 30 porters at a cost of £11 15s. 0d. A porter carried 40 lb. and received 7s. 6d. for the journey (C.O. 54. 114: Nov. 21, 1831).

The Kandyans indeed had a proverb that they would never be conquered until an invader drove a road from Kandy to the sea. Soon after the conquest in 1815 General Brownrigg determined to destroy their invulnerability by building roads through the country to the coast. The revolt of 1818 interrupted his plans, and after its suppression he began erecting forts to hold down the country. His successor, Sir Edward Barnes, arrived in 1819 and immediately made a tour of Kandy. He considered forts of less utility than roads, since without them 'we can never be said to have secure possession of the country, nor can it commercially improve'.[1] In 1820 Barnes ceased work on all forts and diverted the available labour and revenue to road building.[2] By comparison with the public works built by later Governors Barnes's 300 or 400 miles of roads may seem rather paltry. During the second half of the century, however, Governors were sustained by the comfortable certitude of a large and increasing surplus of revenue; while to Barnes fell the task of making a cartload of bricks with a fistful of straw. Eternally hampered by a small revenue and recurring deficits he contrived to build up the skeleton of what became a very fine system of communications. His roads made possible the formation of the coffee plantations, the ultimate basis of Ceylon's prosperity, and thereby enabled his successors to eclipse his modest achievements. The work of Sir Edward Barnes in the economic sphere was comparable with that of Sir Thomas Maitland in the administrative, and they stand together as the ablest of the early British Governors.

The greater part of Barnes's roads was built by exacting a fortnight's compulsory labour from the natives who held their lands by service tenure.[3] Had it not been for the existence of Rajakaria the work could not have been accomplished. The Governor also utilized the Ceylon Pioneer Lascars, a corps which had been formed early in the nineteenth century for the construction of public works. This 'most useful body of military labourers' was composed of Indians, many of them trained artisans, and was commanded by European officers. Despite various attempts to disband it in the name of economy it

[1] C.O. 54. 74: Nov. 13, 1819.   [2] C.O. 54. 77: May 19, 1820.
[3] C.O. 54. 77: May 19, 1820; Forbes, Ceylon, i. 56; Skinner, Ceylon, 29–36.

successfully withstood all assaults of the Treasury and the Colonial Office; and during the nineteenth century the corps was invaluable in providing trained men for constructing roads and other public works.[1] Most of the officers in charge of road building belonged to the Royal Engineers and were controlled by the Quartermaster-General, until in 1832 the construction of public works was transferred to the Department of the Civil Engineer and Surveyor-General.[2] The most important of Barnes's roads was the carriage road from Colombo to Kandy via the Kadugannawa Pass, which was begun in 1820 and completed in 1831. A triumph of military engineering, the road nullified the natural obstacles which had made possible the disaster of 1803; while from an economic viewpoint it was invaluable since it linked the coffee-growing districts with the port of shipment. A second road was built from Colombo to Kandy via Kurunegala, and was extended some distance towards Trincomalee. By 1831 many of the principal towns in Kandy were accessible from Colombo by road, and the coast road, which eventually encircled Ceylon, was completed from Puttalam to Hambantota.[3]

Amongst the officers in charge of road building the most distinguished was Lieutenant, later Major, Thomas Skinner, C.M.G., who entered the Ceylon Rifles in 1818 at the age of fourteen. In 1820 he was seconded for road work in Kandy, and from then until his retirement in 1867 he was concerned with the construction of nearly every road and bridge in Ceylon. Barnes soon saw his value, and in 1829 placed him in charge of the building of all roads in the interior. The Department of the Civil Engineer and Surveyor-General fell into 'inextricable confusion'; and in 1841 the Governor transferred road building,

---

[1] C.O. 54. 46: Jan. 25, 1813; C.O. 54. 77: May 19, 1820; Skinner, *Ceylon*, 261–2.

[2] C.O. 54. 77: May 19, 1820; C.O. 54. 80: June 1 and July 21, 1821; Skinner, *Ceylon*, 95. Captain Dawson of the Royal Engineers was in charge of the construction of all the Kandyan roads until his death from over-exertion in 1829. 'The Giriagam and Galgeddera, but more particularly the Kaduganawa Pass will stand the test of time as lasting monuments of his fame' (C.O. 54. 82: Apr. 2, 1822).

[3] C.O. 54. 77: May 19, 1820; C.O. 54. 82: May 29, 1822; C.O. 54. 92: Feb. 8 and June 1, 1826; C.O. 54. 97: Apr. 27, 1827; C.O. 54. 101: Aug. 11, 1828; C.O. 54. 104: Mar. 11, 1829; C.O. 55. 79: Oct. 2, 1837.

its most important work, to Major Skinner, who was appointed Commissioner of Roads. The Civil Engineer's Department again fell into confusion in 1850 and was incorporated with Skinner's Road Department. From that time until his retirement he controlled the entire public works of the colony. In 1867 he retired on a pension of £1,000, refused a knighthood since he was too poor to support the title, and died in 1877.[1] He gave to Ceylon 3,000 miles of good roads and a very efficient Road Department. The remarkable growth of the coffee plantations was made possible by his work; and Sir Emerson Tennent stated no more than the truth when he wrote that 'to him more than to any living man the colony is indebted for its present prosperity'.[2]

The establishment of plantations in the Kandyan mountains was probably due to the efforts of Sir Edward Barnes. He believed that the higher elevation was more suitable than the plains of Maritime Ceylon, and that Ceylon had a brilliant future as a coffee colony. In 1823 his friend George Bird, a former cavalry officer, formed the first European coffee plantation in Kandy.[3] In the same year the Governor established a Government plantation of 200 acres near the Botanic Garden at Peradeniya which he had founded in 1822. Several Government Agents also opened Government plantations, the labour being obtained by Rajakaria.[4] To foster cultivation Barnes in 1824 exempted coffee plantations from the land tax of one-tenth of the produce.[5] The plantation at Peradeniya was sold in 1832, in accordance with the orders of the Colonial Office that the Government should sever all connexion with trade.[6] The plantations proved unprofitable and some at least were abandoned, owing to the combined effect of faulty methods of cultivation and of the tariff discrimination in the United

---

[1] Skinner, *Ceylon*, passim. The making of land surveys was transferred in 1846 to the new and separate Department of the Surveyor-General (C.O. 55. 87: Aug. 20, 1846).

[2] Tennent, *Ceylon*, ii. 120–1.

[3] C.O. 54. 84: Dec. 31, 1823. Bertolacci (*Ceylon*, 156–7) seems to have been the first to believe that Kandy was more suitable for coffee growing than Maritime Ceylon. Bird died in 1857 after growing coffee for 33 years 'with singular want of success' (Ferguson, *Pioneers of the Planting Enterprise*, ii. 5–8).

[4] C.O. 54. 84: Dec. 31, 1823; C.O. 54. 98: June 11, 1827.

[5] C.O. 54. 118: Aug. 25, 1831.   [6] C.O. 54. 118: Dec. 31, 1832.

Kingdom against Ceylon coffee.[1] In 1830 there was 'only one European agriculturalist settled in the island',[2] and as late as 1836 there was a bare handful of European planters in Ceylon.[3] The bulk of the coffee was grown by the Kandyans on small plantations which seldom yielded more than a few pounds apiece. The yield slowly increased, the average export from 1828 to 1835 inclusive being 20,911 cwt., with a value of £24,862.[4]

Gradually the correct methods of cultivation were evolved by the process of trial and error, and by about 1840 the technique of coffee growing was fairly well understood. The improvement was largely due to the work of R. B. Tytler (1819–82), a trained tropical agriculturalist who studied the Jamaican methods from 1834 to 1837, and in 1837 introduced them on his Ceylon plantation.[5] The discriminatory import duties in the United Kingdom—6d. per lb. on West Indian and 9d. on all other coffee, including that of Ceylon—continued to handicap the planters until 1835. In that year the duty was reduced to 6d. per lb. on East and West Indian coffee.[6] A decisive factor in promoting coffee cultivation in Ceylon was the increasing demand in Europe combined with the simultaneous decline in West Indian production, which formerly had been the principal source of supply. The change was partly due to the diminishing consumption of wine in western Europe which increased the demand for coffee, especially in France and Belgium. The liberation of the slaves in the West Indies and Guiana paralysed Ceylon's most formidable rivals, since the freed slaves refused to work on the plantations. The West Indian export to the United Kingdom rapidly declined from 291,897 cwt. in 1827 to 148,554 cwt. in 1835, and 63, 559 cwt. in 1845.[7] The Ceylon

[1] C.O. 54. 104: Mar. 11, 1829; C.O. 54. 107: Rept. of Supt. Botanic Gardens; Ferguson, *Pioneers of the Planting Enterprise*, ii. 5–8.

[2] C.O. 54. 112: Sept. 10, 1830.

[3] C.O. 54. 146: Jan. 2, 1836; Lewis, *Ceylon in Early British Times*, 2.

[4] C.O. 54. 84: Mar. 5, 1823. C.O. 54. 157: Report of Colombo Collector of Customs. This Report apparently includes the exports from Galle given in a Report of June 8, 1836, by the Galle Collector of Customs. Very few statistics can be found for the period prior to 1828.

[5] Ferguson, *Ceylon in the Jubilee Year*, 61; Pridham, *Ceylon*, ii. 871.

[6] C.O. 54. 105: July 15, 1829; C.O. 54. 109: Feb. 8, 1830; C.O. 54. 112: Sept. 10, 1830; C.O. 54. 114: Dec. 10, 1831; C.O. 54. 121: Dec. 10, 1831.

[7] Tennent, *Ceylon*, ii. 228–30; Ferguson, *Pioneers of the Planting Enterprise*, i. 3; Danson, *Econ. and Stat. Studies*, 205.

growers were thus offered an expanding market combined with dwindling competition at the same time that the United Kingdom import duty was equalized and successful methods of cultivation were introduced. In a few years coffee from being a minor and speculative cultivation became the principal export of Ceylon.

The period of rapid development began about 1835, and continued with ever-increasing intensity for some ten years. Coffee was the certain road to affluence, and a veritable mania arose for plantations. By 1839 extravagant expectations combined too frequently with inexperience led to a period of rash speculation, which was more like a land boom in Western America than a sane business investment.[1] The sale of Crown lands in the Kandyan provinces, a reliable index of the growing interest in coffee, increased from 49 acres in 1834 to an average of 6,412 acres in 1835 to 1838.[2] From 1840 to 1845 the average annual sale was 42,880 acres, the largest amount being 78,685 acres in 1841.[3] A great part of the land was bought by speculators and left uncultivated; but in 1845, 37,596 acres were under coffee as compared with 4,000 in 1836. In 1848 there were 367 plantations, while approximately 60,000 acres were under cultivation out of the 400,000 which had been sold.[4] The average annual export of coffee in 1836 to 1840 inclusive was 49,322 cwt. with a value of £142,239.[5] This was more than double the quantity and four times the value of the coffee exported in 1831 to 1835 inclusive, when the production had been 24,069 cwt. with a value of £31,863.[6] During the quin-

[1] C.O. 54. 188: June 30, 1841.

[2] C.O. 54. 153: Jan. 18, 1837; C.O. 54. 157: Jan. 21, 1837; C.O. 54. 196: Apr. 5, 1842.

[3] Pridham, *Ceylon*, ii. 849; Tennent, *Ceylon*, ii. 230.

[4] C.O. 55. 85: Apr. 27, 1844; C.O. 54. 240: Dec. 3, 1847; C.O. 54. 249: July 4, 1848; Tennent, *Ceylon*, ii. 230; Ferguson, *Pioneers of the Planting Enterprise*, i. 3. The Sinhalese refused to do the hard and continuous work on the plantations; but the labour problem was solved by the emigration of Tamils from Southern India. The influx began in 1839, when about 2,432 came to Ceylon, and rapidly increased. Few of the coolies brought their families, the overwhelming majority returning to India with their savings after about a year (C.O. 54. 235: Apr. 21, 1847).

[5] C.O. 54. 188: June 30, 1841; Pridham, *Ceylon*, ii. 849; Ferguson, *Ceylon Commonplace Book*, 87.

[6] C.O. 54. 157: Report of Colombo Collector of Customs.

quennium 1841 to 1845 the average annual export of coffee was 121,559 cwt., the value being £257,925.[1]

'The mountain ranges on all sides of Kandy became rapidly covered with plantations'; and it was estimated that £3,000,000 were invested between 1837 and 1845.[2] 'The East India Company's officers crowded to Ceylon to invest their savings, and capitalists from England arrived by every packet. . . . So dazzling was the prospect that expenditure was unlimited; and its profusion was only equalled by the ignorance and inexperience of those to whom it was entrusted.' 'The previous Governor [Stuart MacKenzie] and the Council, the Military, the Judges, the Clergy, and half of the Civil Servants' were amongst the buyers.[3] While civil servants were debarred from trade the Colonial Office had decided in 1836 that the prohibition did not include agriculture.[4] During the 'thirties the Ceylon Government encouraged them to establish coffee plantations in order to supplement their inadequate salaries and also to foster the industry. Until the close of the decade Ceylon's economic development had always been strangled for want of capital, and the civil servants with their meagre savings were the nearest approach to financiers the island could provide. As pioneers they did useful work in calling attention to the potentialities of coffee, and most of them met the usual fate of pioneers. A few were very successful, but the majority lost heavily because of 'bad soil, lavish expenditure, and inexperience, combined with the disastrous crisis of 1847.'[5] The interests of Government also suffered since the civil servants paid more attention to their plantations than to their administrative duties. In 1845 Lord Stanley ended a thoroughly unsatisfactory situation by forbidding the acquisition of plantations by officials, and at the same time restoring adequate salaries.

The coffee industry during the early 'forties was resting on

[1] C.O. 54. 252: Dec. 11, 1848; Ferguson, *Ceylon Commonplace Book*, 87.

[2] Ferguson (*Ceylon Commonplace Book*, 144–5) and Tennent (*Ceylon*, ii. 231) rejected the general opinion that £5,000,000 were invested in five years.

[3] Tennent, *Ceylon*, ii. 231. Only 10 per cent. of the pioneer coffee planters benefited financially while 90 per cent. lost money, health, or life (Ferguson, *Ceylon in 1893*, 101–2).

[4] C.O. 54. 148: July 27 and Nov. 30, 1836.

[5] Sabonadière, *Coffee Planter*, 3–5; Skinner, *Ceylon*, 208.

very unsound foundations which went far to explain the partial collapse of 1847. As in all forms of tropical agriculture it was essential that a planter should have a capital of several thousand pounds to cover the heavy cost of developing a new estate. The plantations were situated in the Kandyan mountains at an elevation of from 1,500 to 4,500 feet and were covered with dense forest. In addition to buying and clearing the land, erecting buildings and machinery, and planting coffee, the owner had to maintain the plantation for three years until the first crop was ready for picking. Moreover, he was usually compelled to build a road at his own expense to the nearest Government road, perhaps fifteen miles away. The coffee boom ran true to type in underestimating expense and exaggerating returns, with the result that many planters found they had undertaken a task beyond their means. Since credit was easily—in many instances too easily—obtained, they borrowed money at 9 per cent. or 10 per cent. by 'mortgaging every available security', with the result that when the depression set in they were unable to meet their debts and lost everything.[1] Furthermore, the management of the estates was usually extravagant and unscientific, since the majority of the owners knew nothing of coffee-growing and paid little attention to the cultivation of their plantations. Many of them returned to England, entrusting the care of their interests to Colombo merchants. Subject to this supervision the actual direction of the estates was in the hands of superintendents who were often unsatisfactory. Trained agriculturists were few, and the superintendents 'were frequently of no or very poor education, people who as adventurers came to the country or were bought out of the regimental ranks'. The annual salary was usually £200 or less; but though inadequate it was apparently as much as most of them were worth.[2] Weeding was neglected until the bushes were seriously affected, 'an immense quantity of coffee' was lost by wasteful picking,

---

[1] C.O. 54. 249: July 4 and 5, 1848; Ferguson, *Pioneers of the Planting Enterprise*, i. 48; Speculum, *Ceylon*, 113–14; Officer of Ceylon Rifles, *Ceylon*, ii. 308; Baker, *Eight Years in Ceylon*, 92–4; Brown, *Coffee Planter's Manual*, 157 and *passim*; Knighton, *Life in Ceylon*, i. 115–26.

[2] Millie, *Ceylon*, chaps. ix, xxv, and xxvi. Millie came to Ceylon as a coffee planter in the early 'forties, and his reminiscences give a valuable account of planting conditions.

and the methods of manufacture and storage were 'better fitted for spoiling coffee than curing it'. Heavy losses were also caused by the uncertainty which prevailed as to the proper methods of cultivation.[1] In 1838 to 1840 the sale price of coffee in London was so high, 120s. per cwt., that 'coffee planting had become a mania . . . every intermediate outlay was looked upon as a bagatelle compared with the prodigious profits which were speedily to be realized by the sale of the produce on such terms. The result was a more than oriental extravagance in every item of expenditure, and a wild race of competition as to who would first have their estates in bearing, which raised the wages of labour and the cost of every article of consumption to a pitch actually absurd.' Ceylon officials sometimes paid salaries of £300 or £400 to superintendents 'who had never seen a tree planted, or a crop of coffee prepared for market'.[2]

The rapid growth of the plantations made heavy demands upon the Department of the Civil Engineer and Surveyor-General, which was understaffed and inefficient. Even before the period of expansion began, the work of land surveying was heavily in arrears; and in 1841 the Department became so seriously disorganized that the Governor transferred road building to Major Skinner.[3] The Department was still unable to cope with its duties, and the failure to survey land before it was sold indirectly entailed a considerable loss of revenue. According to the Regulations of 1833, Crown lands were sold by public auction at a reserve price of 5s. an acre, applicants being allowed to select unsurveyed land and mark off its boundaries, subject to the chance of being outbidden at the auctions.[4] Since this entailed great trouble and expense 'it has become a principle of honour in the community not to bid against parties who have thus selected land'. In consequence, Crown land which was frequently worth 20s. an acre sold for only 5s., often to speculators who resold it at a large profit. The reserve price of Crown land was therefore raised to 20s. per acre

[1] C.O. 54. 249: July 4 and 5, 1848; Millie, Ceylon, chaps. iii, iv, v, vi, vii, and xv.
[2] C.O. 54. 249: July 4, 1848.
[3] C.O. 54. 189: Aug. 9, 1841; C.O. 54. 190: Oct. 12, 1841; C.O. 55. 85: Apr. 27 and May 10, 1844; Skinner, Ceylon, 198–237; Millie, Ceylon, chap. xx.
[4] C.O. 54. 130: July 11, 1833; C.O. 54. 190: Oct. 12, 1841.

about 1845, and intending buyers were no longer allowed to demarcate their own boundaries. In 1846 the Department was divided, land surveying being assigned to the newly created Department of the Surveyor-General, while the Civil Engineer continued in charge of the construction of all public works except roads. The number of surveyors was increased; but apparently it was not until about 1860 that the staff was sufficient to survey all lands before they were sold.[1]

With the establishment of the plantations the amount of the annual appropriation for road construction became the most important issue between the Europeans and the Government. The demands for popular control of the Legislative Council were really due to the planters' resentment at the Government's failure to satisfy their demands. They were justified in their contention that the few hundred miles of trunk roads which had been built by the late 'thirties were quite inadequate to convey the coffee to the ports. The planters, however, were less than fair to the very great difficulties which hampered the Ceylon Government. Owing to the frequent deficits the Imperial Treasury insisted upon rigorous economy; while the abolition of Rajakaria in 1832 deprived the Government of Barnes's principal supply of labour. The raiyats were very unwilling to do paid road work; and there was rarely sufficient revenue to hire many of them. The Ceylon Government was compelled to do what it could with its scanty force of pioneers and hired labour, alternately censured by the Treasury for extravagance and badgered by the planters for parsimony. It did not always make the most of its available revenue; but no government in the circumstances could possibly have satisfied its critics. It might be added that whenever the Government proposed to increase its revenue by taxation the planters and merchants were unwilling to consent.

During the 'thirties the criticism of the planters was directed not only against the failure to build roads, but also against the bad condition of those which actually existed. Between 1832 and 1841 'the roads were left to decay', so that after 1841 no

[1] C.O. 55. 85: Apr. 27, 1844; C.O. 55. 87: Aug. 20, 1846; C.O. 54. 322: May 15 and June 9, 1856; C.O. 54. 335: July 5, 1858; C.O. 54. 353: June 25, 1860; Millie, *Ceylon*, chap. xx; Skinner, *Ceylon*, passim.

small part of the available revenue had to be used in restoring them.[1]   Colonel Colebrooke, the Commissioner of Inquiry, censured Barnes for extravagant expenditure upon roads.[2]   The Treasury and the Colonial Office entirely concurred, and during the 'thirties economy was the keynote of all dispatches.[3] Nevertheless, the Governor, Sir Wilmot Horton, contrived to accomplish a considerable amount of construction owing to the annual revenue surplus produced by a series of successful pearl fisheries from 1829 to 1836. He developed the insidious tactics of first beginning a road on the plea of urgent necessity and asking for Treasury sanction afterwards. By 1837 he had roughly completed the Kandy–Trincomalee road begun by Barnes, and continued it as far as Jaffna and Pt. Pedro. He also built main roads from Arippu to Anuradhapura, from Puttalam via Kurunegala to Kandy, and from Kandy to Bintenne and Badulla.[4] From 1837 to 1842 there was an average deficit of £16,000 owing chiefly to the failure of the pearl fisheries and the annual payment to the Imperial Treasury of £24,000 towards the cost of Ceylon's garrison. In addition to this charge, which was imposed in 1837, Ceylon contributed annually about £55,000 towards its military expenses. The expenditure on roads was curtailed at the very time when the rapid growth of the plantations made it 'of the most vital importance'; but the Treasury was 'inexorable' in its refusal to cancel the £24,000. 'The difficulties of access to many of the districts of the interior which have been occupied by settlers are almost incredible'; and 'numbers of planters who have invested very large sums . . . must be ruined if the roads are not rapidly extended'. 'There appears no prospect of more being done than keeping up the roads already opened, and indeed that is hardly done.'[5]

Owing principally to the large sale of Crown lands there was

[1] C.O. 54. 228: Apr. 13, 1847.   [2] C.O. 54. 114: Nov. 21, 1831.

[3] e.g. C.O. 55. 72: Mar. 29, 1832, and C.O. 54. 130: Oct. 25, 1833.

[4] C.O. 54. 117–56: *passim*, e.g. C.O. 54. 127: Jan. 4 and Feb. 23, 1833, and C.O. 54. 155: Aug. 14, 1837; C.O. 54. 228: Oct. 22, 1846; C.O. 55. 79: Oct. 2, 1837.

[5] C.O. 54. 181: Sept. 15, 1840; C.O. 54. 188: Jan. 16, 1841; C.O. 54. 189: Aug. 9, 1841; C.O. 54. 190: *passim*; C.O. 54. 196: Apr. 11, 1842; C.O. 54. 228: Oct. 22, 1846; C.O. 54. 243: Feb. 16, 1843; C.O. 55. 81: May 31, 1841; C.O. 55. 83: May 2 and Sept. 21, 1842.

Q

an average annual revenue surplus of £44,430 from 1843 to 1845; and between 1843 and 1847 1,247 miles of road were built or restored.[1] The perennial deficit soon reasserted itself as a result of the reduction of the Ceylon tariff in 1847 combined with the partial collapse of coffee. From 1847 to 1855 expenditure was stringently curtailed by order of the Treasury and the Colonial Office, many roads falling into 'a miserable state' and few new ones being built. Lord Torrington conferred one great benefit upon Ceylon by the Road Ordinance of 1848, which required every male inhabitant except Buddhist priests to give six days' compulsory labour annually to road construction or repair, or else to pay a commutation tax of 3s. Many districts and even provinces, e.g. Ratnapura and Batticaloa, were almost destitute of all means of communication except jungle paths 'intersected by deep and rapid streams infested by alligators'. The prosperity of every part of Ceylon was retarded, native interests suffering as much as those of the coffee planters. Since the revenue was 'wholly inadequate' 'it will be barely possible to keep existing roads in efficient repair; and . . . to open others still urgently required will be quite out of the question'.[2] The Ordinance made possible the construction of a very fine system of communications, and benefited the natives as well as the planters, since it led to the development of remote districts which had stagnated from lack of roads. Sir George Anderson seems to have been more criticized than Lord Torrington, the planters asserting that many roads were 'in a state of positive ruin' and could not be used for transporting coffee. The Governor insisted that they were 'in tolerable good order'; but the planters seem to have had substantial grounds for their complaints.[3] It would appear that he adhered with undue rigidity to his instructions, and accumulated a fairly large revenue surplus by allowing the roads to fall into 'a most unsatisfactory state'. Sir George's memory survived as the Governor during whose régime 'men with long

[1] C.O. 55. 83: May 28, 1843; C.O. 54. 203: Feb. 16 and May 11, 1843; C.O. 54. 228: Oct. 22, 1846, and Apr. 13, 1847.
[2] C.O. 54. 249: July 4, 1848.
[3] C.O. 54. 309: Aug. 24 and Sept. 26, 1854; C.O. 54. 310: Nov. 23 and Dec. 22, 1854; C.O. 54. 311: Dec. 29, 1854, and C.O. Memos.; C.O. 54. 314: Jan. 13, 1855.

poles were sent in advance of carts and carriages to sound the holes, anything more than three feet deep being deemed dangerous' [1] Sir Henry Ward, who became Governor in 1855, defended the policy of his two predecessors since 'the most rigid economy was required to balance the expenditure with the receipts'. 'It is to the firmness with which this hard and painful duty was fulfilled . . . that I am indebted for the very different state of things which I have had the good fortune to find here.'[2]

The necessity for economy was largely the result of the depression which began in 1847. In this as in other respects the period of speculation ran true to type: the panic was in proportion to the extravagant hopes of the early 'forties, and ruin was widespread amongst the planters. Estates which a few years before had been worth a small fortune were almost unsaleable: a plantation which had been bought in 1843 for £15,000 was sold by auction in 1847 for £440. Many owners who had mortgaged their estates were unable to meet their payments, and the creditors foreclosed to find the property almost valueless. About one-tenth of the plantations were abandoned, and more than one-third were sold 'at almost nominal rates'.[3] The causes of the crisis were 'wild speculation followed by depression and stagnation, intensified by the low price to which coffee had fallen after the abolition of the differential duty which protected British-grown from the competition of Java and Brazil coffee'.[4] 'It is no exaggeration to say that there is not a single well-established principle which now guides the management of estates and the conduct of their proprietors, that was not preceded by a directly opposite policy prior to 1845.'[5] The average planter gave scant attention to such a detail as careful cultivation; and paid 'unreasonable' prices for labour and every other cost of production in his eagerness to place his coffee on the market before his competitors. Economy was out of fashion: credit was easy to obtain

[1] Millie, *Ceylon*, chap. iv.   [2] C.O. 54. 322: June 9, 1856.
[3] Two estates in Badulla which had cost £10,000 sold for £350, and another worth £10,000 for £500 (Tennent, *Ceylon*, ii. 232).
[4] Ferguson, *Pioneers of the Planting Enterprise*, i. 48; C.O. 54. 249: July 4 and 5, 1848; C.O. 54. 251: Oct. 3, 1848; Knighton, *Life in Ceylon*, ii. 159–60.
[5] Tennent, *Ceylon*, ii. 232–3.

and estates were opened or maintained by mortgages bearing interest at 9 per cent. or 10 per cent. Permanent prosperity was impossible on a basis of unsound finance and unscientific estate management.[1] The financial crisis of 1845 and 1846 in Great Britain hastened the inevitable reaction in Ceylon in 1847 and 1848, since credit could no longer be obtained and mortgagees began to press for repayment. The planters tried to reduce their expenses; but 'the vast majority of them had become chargeable with liabilities and mortgages' too heavy for their resources.[2] About the same time the sale price of coffee in London began to fall rapidly, owing to the reduction in 1844 of the preference granted to Ceylon coffee imported into the United Kingdom from 4d. to 2d. per lb. The costs of production in Java and Brazil were much lower than in Ceylon; and owing to the tariff reduction their coffees were able to undersell Ceylon's in the London market. The full effects were not felt for some years after 1844, but by 1848 the London price had declined from 100s. per cwt. to 45s., an amount which barely equalled the cost of production in Ceylon. Some shipments sold for as little as 28s., and in 1849 the price reached its lowest level at 27s.[3] Two further misfortunes occurred in 1847, a plague of rats which gnawed the young shoots, and a coffee blight which ruined large areas by killing the trees.[4]

The crisis paralysed the coffee industry for three years, and when the recovery began it was retarded by the inadequacy of the roads. By 1853, however, coffee had completely recovered and entered upon a period of increasing prosperity. The crisis had really been a blessing in disguise, effectually though it had concealed its gifts in 1847. So many estates had changed hands at very low prices that a large number of proprietors were able to start without the crippling burden of their predecessors' debts, in addition to the benefit of their dearly-bought ex-

---

[1] A 'very few' prudent and economical planters had weathered the storm; and 'on the whole . . . the instances of failure are but the natural results of indiscretion or inexperience' (C.O. 54. 249: July 4 and 5, 1848). Speculum, *Ceylon*, 113–14.

[2] C.O. 54. 249: July 4, 1848.

[3] C.O. 54. 249: July 4, 1848; C.O. 54. 251: Oct. 3, 1848; Tennent, *Ceylon*, ii. 231; Ferguson, *Pioneers of the Planting Enterprise*, i. 48; Knighton, *Life in Ceylon*, ii. 159; Skinner, *Ceylon*, 208; Pridham, *Ceylon*, ii. 849.

[4] C.O. 54. 249: July 4 and 5, 1848.

perience. The extravagance and unscientific cultivation of the early 'forties were replaced by sound finance and an increasingly careful attention to every detail of estate management. A reckless adventure towards El Dorado had become a sober business enterprise, and the new prosperity was based on much firmer foundations than the old.[1] The cost of production had also greatly decreased owing to the fall in the price of labour and of all other items of expenditure.[2] Simultaneously the price of coffee in London rapidly increased to about 41s. per cwt. in 1850. Apart from minor fluctuations it remained at this figure till 1856 when it rose to 44s., values which together with the diminished costs of production allowed a handsome profit to the planters.[3] The export of coffee increased from 278,473 cwt. with a value of £609,263 in 1850, to 506,540 cwt. with a value of £1,025,282 in 1855.[4] Despite occasional fluctuations the export steadily increased until in 1870 it attained its maximum volume with an export of 1,054,030 cwt. valued at £2,753,005.[5] By 1857 the number of European plantations was 404 with an acreage under cultivation of 80,950, as well as about 48,000 acres owned by natives, giving a total of about 128,950 acres.[6] In 1867 the acreage of the European plantations was 168,000, and in 1878 it reached the maximum of 275,000.[7] While the rapid development of the plantations and the introduction of

[1] Tennent, *Ceylon*, ii. 232–3.
[2] Knighton, *Life in Ceylon*, ii. 160; Speculum, *Ceylon*, 113–15 and 128.
[3] Speculum, *Ceylon*, 115; Ferguson, *Ceylon Commonplace Book*, 118.
[4] Ferguson, *Ceylon Commonplace Book*, 88; C.O. 54. 378: Aug. 20, 1863.
[5] The average annual export of coffee was:
1851–5: 393,092 cwt., valued at £782,556 (Ferguson, *Ceylon Commonplace Book*, 88; C.O. 54. 378: Aug. 20, 1863).
1856–60: 559,501 cwt., valued at £1,371,404 (C.O. 54. 378: Aug. 20, 1863).
1861–5: 736,079 cwt., valued at £1,863,313 (C.O. 54. 378: Aug. 20, 1863; C.O. 54. 404: Sept. 16, 1865; C.O. 54. 415: Oct. 15, 1866).
1866–70: 964,330 cwt., valued at £2,485,280 (C.O. 54. 437: Nov. 14, 1868: C.O. 54. 457: Sept. 16, 1870; *Parl. Pap.* [C. 2093] of 1878, vol. lxxviii. 37).
[6] Ferguson, *Ceylon Summary of Useful Information*, passim. This most useful and detailed account was based on the information collected by the Planters' Association, and was extensively used by Tennent (*Ceylon*, ii. 234 ff.). Of the area of 80,950 acres 63,771 were in bearing, while 17,179 were planted but not yet yielding a crop. The average number of acres cultivated on each estate was 200, and the average production per acre was 5½ cwt. In addition to the above total, the area of the abandoned estates was 10,000 acres. 'A good many once abandoned have been resuscitated.' The number of coolies required on the estates was 128,200.
[7] Ferguson, *Ceylon in the Jubilee Year*, 67.

scientific methods of cultivation were due to the Europeans, the natives profited to an increasing degree from their example. They largely increased the area of their plantations, and also improved the quality of their crop, which appears at first to have been inferior. It was estimated that from 1849 to 1869 the export of native-grown coffee was between a half and a quarter of the total quantity.[1]

During the years which immediately followed the crisis of 1847 the recovery of coffee was hampered by commercial dishonesty in the United Kingdom. The adulteration of coffee with chicory was prohibited by law, but a Treasury Regulation of 1840 forbade its enforcement, with the result that by 1852 the 'consumption of real coffee has actually declined' in England despite the 'vast increase' of coffee drinking. This was due to 'the enormous adulteration of coffee with chicory . . . half the (so called) coffee consumed by the poorer classes consists of spurious matter'; while even 'chicory itself is largely adulterated'. Chicory was sold at less than 3*d*. per lb., the amount of the United Kingdom import duty imposed in 1851 on colonial and foreign coffee alike. The Ceylon planters petitioned either that the duty be abolished, since it acted as a protective tariff on chicory, or else that the sale of chicory be prohibited. As an alternative they asked for 'protection against fraud': adulterated coffee should be sold as such, and not as pure coffee. The Treasury refused to abolish the duty or prohibit the sale of chicory; but an Act was passed forbidding adulterated to masquerade as pure coffee. After a large number of fines had been inflicted for breaches of it the planters ceased to complain of fraudulent adulteration.[2]

The renewed prosperity of coffee roughly coincided with the arrival in 1855 of Sir Henry Ward, the ablest and most popular Governor since Sir Edward Barnes.[3] He soon decided that what

[1] Ferguson, *Ceylon in 1883*, 56–7.
[2] C.O. 54. 288: Mar. 9, 1852; C.O. 54. 300: *passim*; C.O. 55. 95: Nov. 23, 1853, and Feb. 2, 1854.
[3] In 1858, 4,000 Europeans, burghers, and natives successfully petitioned that Ward's salary be increased from £7,000 to £10,000, although their normal attitude was that official salaries were undeserved and excessive (C.O. 54. 337: Oct. 20 and 29, 1858; C.O. 55. 100: July 11, 1859). In 1860 Ward was appointed Governor of Madras (C.O. 55. 103: June 21, 1860), and died soon after his arrival in India.

the island most required was a liberal expenditure on irrigation works and the construction or repair of roads. Apart from the Galle–Colombo–Kandy road they 'were in the rudest and most primitive state'; while many like the Kandy–Trincomalee road had 'been for many years impassable for wheel carriages'.[1] Circumstances were entirely favourable: the Treasury had a balance of £120,000 accumulated by 'the watchful economy of my predecessors',[2] while the rapid development of coffee was reflected in a steadily growing annual surplus of revenue. The revenue increased by nearly £70,000 in 1855, and between 1854 and 1860 rose from £408,000 to £747,000. During this period the Governor spent £1,080,295 on public works, so that by 1860 Ceylon had about 3,000 miles of road in good repair, of which nearly 213 were open at all seasons. The remainder were impassable during the monsoon rains since the necessary bridges had not yet been built.[3] 'Every town of importance in the island is now connected with the two principal cities by roads either wholly or partially macadamized'. A continuous road 769 miles in length encircled the whole island; and 'no portion of British India can bear comparison with Ceylon, either in the extent or the excellence of its means of communication'.[4] While most of the expenditure was in the coffee districts the Governor also devoted large sums to the repair of roads and irrigation works in the Southern, Eastern, and North-Western Provinces.[5] From 1861 to 1864 the Colonial Office and the Treasury considerably reduced the expenditure upon roads to accumulate a large reserve towards the cost of constructing the Colombo–Kandy railway. The Governor, Sir Charles MacCarthy, became very unpopular since the building of necessary new roads was refused or long postponed, while existing roads fell into disrepair.[6] The

[1] C.O. 54. 316: July 11, 1855; C.O. 54. 317: Oct. 26, 1855; C.O. 54. 318: Nov. 15, 1855; C.O. 54. 322: *passim*; C.O. 54. 329: July 22 and 24, 1857; C.O. 54. 353: June 15, 1860; C.O. 55. 98: Aug. 27, 1855, and May 26, 1857.

[2] C.O. 54. 318: Nov. 15, 1855.

[3] C.O. 55. 98: May 26, 1857; C.O. 54. 335: July 5, 1858; C.O. 54. 353: June 15 and 25, 1860; C.O. 54. 360: June 7, 1860.

[4] Tennent, *Ceylon*, ii. 120–1, and 571.

[5] C.O. 54. 329: July 22, 1857; C.O. 54. 334: Mar. 20, 1858; C.O. 54. 343: Jan. 8, 1859.

[6] C.O. 54. 377: July 31, 1863; C.O. 55. 106: Nov. 22, 1863; *v.* p. 115, note, chap. vii. The need for roads into newly-opened coffee districts was 'excessively urgent'; but to obtain them Skinner had constantly to fight hard

next Governor, Sir Hercules Robinson, spent lavishly on road construction; and 'the result has been the advance of the colony with almost unexampled rapidity.'[1] Sir William Gregory, Governor from 1872 to 1877, gave special attention to the roads in the North Central Province which he established in 1873, and also restored the trunk road from Kandy to Jaffna which had fallen into ruin.[2] The failure of the coffee plantations in the late 'seventies necessitated a curtailment of expenditure; but with the gradual return of prosperity in the 'eighties the extension of roads and railways was resumed.[3]

The most ambitious project undertaken during this period was the construction in the 'sixties of the Colombo–Kandy railway. The planters were dependent on native-owned bullock carts to take the crop to Colombo and to bring up supplies. This caused 'serious and frequent fluctuations in the price of rice . . . which . . . sometimes rises in Kandy to upwards of 200 per cent. on the Colombo price, and the mere carriage of 72 miles under the most favourable circumstances adds about 60 per cent. to the prime cost in Colombo on the staple food of the community'. The cost of transport by road was much heavier than by rail, and the difficulty was accentuated by the necessity of conveying the whole crop to the coast in the few weeks which elapsed between the time it was ready and the beginning of the South-West monsoon. After this date many of the roads were impassable because of swollen streams and the absence of bridges. As the plantations increased, the threat of a complete breakdown of road transport became more imminent. By about 1855 it was clear that unless a railway were built the further development of coffee would be prevented.[4] The con-

against 'the niggardly cheeseparing policy . . . pressed upon the governor' (Skinner, *Ceylon*, 244–7).

[1] C.O. 54. 457: Sept. 16, 1870; Skinner, *Ceylon*, 249–50. 'Sir H. R. has been an excellent governor and Ceylon has made great advances.' 'Yes! a complimentary despatch. He deserves it. K[imberley]. Nov. 25/71' (C.O. 54. 467: Sept. 14 and Oct. 14, 1871 and C.O. Memos.).

[2] C.O. 54. 498: Sept. 8, 1875; C.O. 54. 504: Oct. 27, 1876; Ievers, *North Central Province*, 52–76 and 203–7. Gregory built roads from Anuradhapura to Kandy, Trincomalee, Jaffna, and Puttalam (Gregory, *Autobiography*, 297–325 and 386–7).

[3] C.O. 54. 554: Nov. 11, 1884; Ferguson, *Ceylon in 1883*, 17–18.

[4] C.O. 54. 298: Mar. 23, 1853; C.O. 54. 315: June 8, 1855; C.O. 54. 322: June 9, 1856; C.O. 54. 360: June 7, 1860.

struction of the railway was first proposed in 1845, a company
being formed under the chairmanship of Philip Anstruther, the
former Colonial Secretary. A survey was made and the cost of
the line estimated at £800,000; but the plan was abandoned
owing to the financial crisis in England and the Ceylon depression of 1847.[1] In 1853 the Ceylon merchants and planters
petitioned the Secretary of State to arrange a contract with the
company formed in 1845; and from 1853 to 1856 negotiations
were carried on in London by the Colonial Office.[2] In 1855
Sir Henry Ward reported that the railway was an 'absolute
and imperative necessity' or Ceylon would 'cease to exist as
a coffee producing colony' in the face of Brazilian and Javanese
competition.[3] In July 1855 the Legislative Council unanimously
agreed to his proposal that the Ceylon Government should
guarantee the interest at 6 per cent. on a loan of £800,000.
No private company would undertake the construction without
this security; and the Colonial Office refused to permit the
Government itself to build the line.[4] Meanwhile the company
had offered to build the first 55 miles (the total length being
about 75) if Ceylon would guarantee the interest at 6 per cent.
on a loan of £500,000.[5]

In 1856 a provisional contract was made by the Colonial
Office and the company, which was ratified by the Legislative
Council after much opposition. The railway from Colombo to
Kandy was to be completed within five years after the company
had received the land required; and for that purpose 'the Company shall raise a capital of £800,000 to be augmented if
necessary'. If, however, 'the line . . . shall exceed 90 statute
miles in length . . . the Company shall not for the purpose of
completing the Railway, be bound to raise and provide a capital
exceeding in amount £1,200,000' unless it preferred to do so.
For 99 years the Ceylon Government was to pay the company

[1] C.O. 54. 316: July 11, 1855; C.O. 55. 98: June 9, 1856; *Parl. Pap. H. C.* 716
of 1847, vol. lxiii; Ferguson, *Pioneers of the Planting Enterprise*, iii. 68–70.

[2] C.O. 54. 298: Mar. 23, 1853; C.O. 54. 308: Aug. 8 and 17, 1854; C.O. 54.
311: Dec. 29, 1854; C.O. 54. 314: Jan. 12, 1855; C.O. 54. 315: Mar. 17, 1855;
C.O. 55. 95: Nov. 14, 1854; C.O. 55. 98: June 9, 1856.

[3] C.O. 54. 315: June 8, 1855.

[4] C.O. 54. 316: July 11, 1855; C.O. 54. 318: Nov. 15, 1855; C.O. 55. 95:
June 25, 1855; C.O. 55. 98: Aug. 27, 1855.

[5] C.O. 55. 95: June 25, 1855.

interest 'on the Capital of the Company for the time being paid up' at the rate of 6 per cent. on a maximum of £800,000, and 5 per cent. on all additional capital. The payment should cease if the line were not completed within the specified time, unless the company had already spent £1,200,000 and were not bound to raise additional capital owing to the length of the line exceeding 90 miles. If thereafter the company finished the construction the payment should be resumed. The net traffic receipts were to be applied towards the payment of the interest; while after 99 years the railway was to become the property of the Government, which had also the right to buy it at the end of 25 or 50 years. As with Indian railways, the Board of Directors in London would include a Colonial Office nominee with the power of veto.[1] The Europeans were afraid that the company might indulge in 'an almost unlimited expenditure'—even beyond the £1,200,000 in the contract—'to have the benefit of a larger investment of capital at 5 per cent. interest'. The Governor and the Colonial Office considered it most improbable that the cost of the railway would exceed £1,200,000, and regarded the contract as exceedingly favourable to Ceylon. The company would not be able needlessly to increase expenditure since the contract gave 'the government and the Secretary of State the entire and absolute control over all the operations of the Company'. Finally the Legislative Council resolved, at Ward's suggestion, that the contract should not become operative until another survey had made certain that the utmost cost of the line would not exceed £1,200,000. At the same time an Ordinance was passed authorizing the imposition on January 1, 1858, of export duties of 2½ per cent. to cover the expense of the Government guarantee of the interest.[2] The Secretary of State appointed Captain Moorsom, an engineer unconnected with the company, to make a survey. In 1857 he estimated the total cost as £856,557, and the contract went into effect.[3]

Construction began in 1858 and advanced very slowly under

[1] C.O. 55. 98: May 9 and June 9, 1856; C.O. 54. 323: Ordinance No. 1 of 1856: Supplemental Agreement [undated]: and Second Supplemental Agreement of Dec. 5, 1856.
[2] C.O. 54. 323: *passim*; C.O. 54. 328: Jan. 23, 1857; C.O. 55. 98: Dec. 12, 1857; C.O. 55. 100: July 9, 1859.
[3] C.O. 55. 98: *passim*; C.O. 55. 100: *passim*; C.O. 54. 329: May 23, 1857.

the superintendence of Doyne, the company's engineer.[1] He surveyed the route and discovered that Moorsom's survey had been made 'with culpable haste and inaccuracy'. Doyne's estimate of the cost of the railway was nothing short of a high explosive in Ceylon: In place of Moorsom's £856,557 his figure was £2,214,000.[2] 'There can be no doubt now that whatever the cost may be the Colony is legally bound to provide interest at 6 and 5 per cent. upon the capital required to complete the line between Colombo and Kandy, subject to the sole condition that that line shall not exceed ninety miles in length. . . . Nothing can be more improbable than the occurrence of this case . . . we must either go on with the work at a cost which I cannot regard without some apprehension; or negociate with the company at a disadvantage for leave to cancel or modify the Agreement.'[3] The publication of Doyne's estimate caused widespread despondency in Ceylon and bitter attacks on the Governor, the Colonial Office, and the company. There was 'universal opposition' to the contract and a general desire to cancel it.[4] Negotiations began between the Colonial Office and the company; and in 1860 the shareholders asked the Ceylon Government to suggest a settlement.[5] The Legislative Council resolved in 1860 that the contract should be cancelled and debentures issued to repay the company the whole of its paid-up capital with the interest due, the Ceylon Government assuming all the company's 'property rights and liabilities'.[6] The company accepted, and on August 21, 1861, the contract was annulled, the payment made for paid-up capital and interest being £299,947 13s. 0d.[7] The total cost to the colony was

[1] C.O. 54. 343: Apr. 14, 1859.

[2] C.O. 54. 343: Apr. 26, 1859; C.O. 54. 344: June 7, 1859; C.O. 54. 345: July 25, 1859; C.O. 55. 100: Sept. 13, 1858; Doyne, *Construction of Railways in India*, passim.

[3] C.O. 54. 345: July 22, 1859; C.O. 55. 100: *passim*; *Parl. Pap. H. C.* 457 of 1860, vol. xlv.

[4] C.O. 54. 345: Aug. 16 and 30, 1859; C.O. 54. 346: Sept. 15, 16, and 17, 1859; C.O. 55. 100: Nov. 10, 1859.

[5] C.O. 55. 103: Sept. 26, 1860; C.O. 54. 349: *passim*.

[6] C.O. 54. 355: Dec. 15 and 29, 1860.

[7] C.O. 55. 103: Aug. 26, 1861, and *passim*; C.O. 54. 359: Feb. 28 and Mar. 27, 1861; C.O. 54. 364: Aug. 19, 1861: Printed Report of Directors to the Proprietors of the company; C.O. 54. 366: undated Memo. of Agreement of Aug. 19, 1861, cancelling the contract. The payment was met partly from general

£368,275 10s. 4d., while the value of the assets salvaged from the wreck was £59,134 5s. 11d.[1]

In July 1861 the Legislative Council resolved that the Government should employ a contractor to build the railway.[2] The contract was awarded in 1863 to Favielle, a London contractor, whose tender of £873,039 was the lowest of the eight received. The Government estimated that the total cost of construction inclusive of past expenditure would be £1,382,039.[3] The Colonial Office aroused keen resentment amongst the Europeans because it ordered the curtailment of expenditure upon public works 'to reduce the railway debt by contributing from current revenue as largely as possible'.[4] Construction began in March, 1863, and the whole line from Colombo to Kandy, 75 miles in

revenue and the export duties, and partly by floating a loan of £100,000 in London (Perera, *Ceylon Railway*, 66).

[1] C.O. 54. 438: Aug. 17, 1868: printed enclosure with Governor's dispatch of Dec. 11, 1868. An incomplete estimate gave the company's assets as £126,454 2s. 2d. and liabilities as £31,612 10s. 0d. (C.O. 54. 366: June 30, 1861). Perera (*Ceylon Railway*, 66) gave the assets as £125,000.

[2] C.O. 54. 361: July 1 and 30, 1861; C.O. 54. 370: Sept. 4, 1862.

[3] C.O. 55. 106: Feb. 3, 1863, and *passim*. 'The works executed, materials, stores, &c., will be taken over by the Contractor after arbitration.' The items in the estimate were:

Favielle's tender	£873,039
Value of survey, works executed, land, materials, stores, &c., and interest paid to company's shareholders	£283,000
Future expenditure on rolling stock, land, machinery, &c. . .	£226,000
Total	£1,382,039

The Government accepted Favielle's additional tender of £155,400 for maintenance of the line after completion for seven years (C.O. 54. 371: Nov. 29, 1862).

[4] C.O. 55. 103: July 18, 1860; C.O. 55. 106: Apr. 7 and June 6, 1863; C.O. 55. 112: Oct. 13 and Nov. 26, 1866; C.O. 55. 115: *passim*; C.O. 54. 377: July 31, 1863; C.O. 54. 378: Aug. 20, 1863; C.O. 54. 400: Jan. 12, 1865; C.O. 54. 414: Aug. 30, 1866; C.O. 54. 417: Dec. 12, 1866. In addition to the export duties Ceylon paid £250,000 from the Treasury surplus, and from 1863 to the completion of the railway made an annual contribution of £35,000 from current revenue (C.O. 55. 106: Oct. 31, 1864; C.O. 55. 110: Sept. 26, 1864, and Mar. 27, 1865). £800,000 of 6 per cent. debentures were also issued in London (C.O. 54. 454: Mar. 7, 1870). Owing to the unexpectedly large amount of the traffic receipts the export duties were abolished in 1870 as unnecessary to repay the loan (C.O. 54. 457: Sept. 16, 1870). The Europeans strongly opposed the Government policy of extinguishing the railway debt by 1883. They vainly demanded that repayment should be spread over a long period, 'so that it might be shared by those who are to succeed them' (C.O. 54. 392: Aug. 30, 1864).

length, was opened for traffic on October 1, 1867.[1] The total cost under the company and under Favielle's contract was £1,738,483 3s. 2d.[2] The railway was owned and operated by the Ceylon Government; and from the beginning it proved an important and increasing source of revenue.[3] In 1871 the railway was extended from Peradeniya to the important coffee district at Nawalapitiya.[4] Lines were built from Colombo to Kalutara in 1877–83, and from Kandy to the plantations at Matale in 1878–83. In 1880–5 the railway was extended as far as Nanu Oya.[5] The plantations brought an increasing amount of shipping to Galle and Colombo; and to make the harbour safe the Colombo breakwater was built between 1874 and 1886.[6] Before it was completed the coffee plantations which had called it into being had almost ceased to exist.

The catastrophe was caused by a fungus which attacked the leaves of the tree and ultimately destroyed it. Officially known as *Hemileia vastatrix* it was popularly referred to as the Coffee Bug. Every attempt to discover a remedy failed, and comprehensive disaster inevitably resulted from 'the limitation of cultivation to one plant, and one only, over hundreds of square miles of country'. The blight appeared in 1868 when coffee was at the height of its prosperity, and rapidly spread throughout the planting area. For the first few years the crops were only slightly affected; and the disease was regarded as unimportant by all save Doctor Thwaites, from 1849 to 1880 the Superin-

---

[1] C.O. 54. 399: *passim*; C.O. 54. 400: Feb. 27, 1865; C.O. 54. 437: Nov. 14, 1868; C.O. 55. 115: Feb. 6, 1868.

[2] When the accounts were closed a surplus of £127,143 remained from the funds devoted to the cost of construction, which was transferred to form the nucleus of a sinking fund. Deducting this from the railway loan of £800,000 the real debt of the colony was £672,857 (C.O. 54. 454: Mar. 7, 1870).

[3] C.O. 54. 425: Apr. 23, 1867; C.O. 54. 457: Sept. 5 and 16, 1870; C.O. 55. 115: Sept. 7, 1867; C.O. 55. 117: *passim*.

[4] C.O. 54. 463: Feb. 5, 1871; C.O. 54. 497: May 25, 1875.

[5] C.O. 54. 493: Aug. 1, 1874; C.O. 54. 502: Aug. 12, 1876; C.O. 54. 503 and 504: *passim*; C.O. 54. 507: May 4, 1877; C.O. 54. 508: July 27, 1877; C.O. 54. 513: *passim*; C.O. 54. 514: July 6 and 22, 1878; Ferguson, *Ceylon in 1883*, 20.

[6] In 1856 Governor Ward proposed the building of a breakwater at Galle (C.O. 54. 323: Oct. 10, 1856), and from 1866 to about 1871 the Colonial Office strongly pressed its construction (C.O. 55. 112: Nov. 28, 1866; C.O. 55. 115, 117, and 120: *passim*). Sir Hercules Robinson and Sir William Gregory persuaded the Colonial Office to build the breakwater at Colombo (C.O. 54. 425: May 28, 1867; C.O. 54. 473–8, 487, and 489: *passim*).

tendent of the Royal Botanic Gardens at Peradeniya.[1] The planters attributed the falling off to seasonal fluctuations; and they were also blinded by the 'sudden and unprecedented rise in the value of coffee in Europe and America, a rise equivalent in a few years to more than 50 per cent'.[2] While the quantity of the export declined the value was actually greater than it had been before the blight appeared. The decreased production of the older plantations was still further disguised by 'a vast extension of cultivation into the only large reserve known as the Wilderness of the Peak, extending from Newara Eliya to the Adam's Peak Range, covering some 400 square miles'. A cycle of favourable seasons produced good crops in the new district; and coffee was profitably cultivated at an altitude of 5,500 feet, whereas previously the limit of growth had been believed to be about 4,500 feet.[3] So far were the planters from realizing the danger that the 'seventies were a period of land speculation, forest land which had been worth about £1 an acre rising in 1874 to £5 7s.[4] During the quinquennium of 1871 to 1875 the average annual export was only 856,570 cwt., but it reached the unprecedented value of £3,155,922.[5] In 1876 to 1880 inclusive the average annual export fell to 743,098 cwt., with a value of £3,599,486.[6] In 1881 to 1885 inclusive the full effects of the blight showed themselves, and the average annual export rapidly declined to 364,488 cwt., with a value of £1,378,454. In 1886 the export was 179,254 cwt., the value being £630,643.[7]

Even in 1878 most of the planters and civil servants believed that coffee would eventually recover, although many were

[1] Gregory, *Autobiography*, 285.
[2] In 1873 the average Ceylon sale price rose from £2 14s. od. to £4 10s. od. per cwt. (C.O. 54. 493: Aug. 11, 1874).
[3] C.O. 54. 467: Sept. 14, 1871; C.O. 54. 493: June 10, 1874; C.O. 54. 494: Oct. 6 and 12, 1874; C.O. 54. 534: Nov. 22, 1881; Ferguson, *Ceylon in 1883*, 58–60 and 63; Lewis, *Sixty-Four Years in Ceylon*, 68.
[4] C.O. 54. 493: Aug. 11, 1874; Anon., *Ceylon and her Planting Enterprise*, 44; Ferguson, *Ceylon in 1883*, 60–1. 'All the time the leaf disease got worse and worse, and men got madder and madder, and prices got higher and higher, and crops got small and smaller' (R. W. J., *Ceylon in the Fifties and Eighties*, 55–6).   [5] *Parl. Pap.* [C. 2093] of 1878, vol. lxxviii. 37.
[6] *Parl. Pap.* [C. 2093] of 1878, vol. lxxviii. 37; *Parl. Pap.* [C. 4225] of 1884–5, vol. lxxxiii. 41.
[7] *Parl. Pap.* [C. 4225] of 1884–5, vol. lxxxiii. 41; *Parl. Pap.* [C. 5507] of 1888, vol. cv. 43.

becoming alarmed. Sulphur, 'liberal cultivation with manure'—
every expedient that was suggested had been tried in vain: and
the Botanic Gardens at Peradeniya had completely failed to
discover a remedy.[1] In 1879 the Governor reported that
Hemileia vastatrix had 'disastrously affected the productiveness of the coffee trees'; and by 1882 it had 'spread over the
whole island'.[2] From every part of Ceylon came the same tale
of declining production and abandoned plantations; and in
1883 the export fell to 305,702 cwt., the lowest figure since
1848. While the blight also wrought havoc in Java it did not
affect Brazil, the most important coffee-growing country; and
under the pressure of Brazilian competition the European price
fell heavily, 'reacting disastrously on the Ceylon enterprise'.
The universal commercial depression of 1876 to 1880 in Europe
intensified the difficulty of obtaining credit; and as a final blow,
the good seasons of the early 'seventies were replaced by a
series of wet seasons.[3] By about 1880 'anxiety was becoming
greater and greater. People were trying to sell out'; but
estates found no buyers. 'All around me there seemed to be
an air of expectation of disaster . . . the crisis was acute: the
colony was practically in a state of paralysis',[4] and about 400
of the 1,700 European planters left Ceylon. To an increasing
extent coffee was abandoned for cinchona and tea, until by
1887 the area of the coffee plantations had fallen from 275,000
acres in 1878 to a little more than 100,000, while the export
was only 178,562 cwt. with a value of £905,169. By 1895 the
acreage had fallen to 22,475, the export being 56,618 cwt. and
the value £323,330; while in 1905 the acreage was 3,591, the
export 5,310 cwt., and the value £19,845.[5] The destruction of

[1] C.O. 54. 494: Oct. 6 and 12, 1874; C.O. 54. 508: Aug. 20, 1877; C.O. 54.
509: Nov. 22, 1877; *Parl. Pap.* [C. 2598] of 1880, vol. xlviii. 224; *Governors'
Addresses to Legislative Council,* iii. 28, 57, and 106; Lewis, *Sixty-Four Years
in Ceylon,* 29, 56, 68, and 78–83; Brown, *Coffee Planter's Manual,* 181–4;
Hughes, *Ceylon Coffee Soils,* passim.

[2] *Parl. Pap.* [C. 2829] of 1881, vol. lxiv, 233; *Governors' Addresses to Leg.
Council,* iii. 131 and *passim*; Ward, *Morphology of Hemileia Vastatrix,* passim.

[3] *Parl. Pap.* [C. 2829] of 1881, vol. lxiv. 228; *Parl. Pap.* [C. 3794] of 1883,
vol. xlv. 7; *Parl. Pap.* [C. 4583] of 1885, vol. lii. 181–2; *Governors' Addresses
to Leg. Council,* iii. 67 and 148; Anon., *Private Life of Coffee Planter,* pt. ii.
1–5; Ferguson, *Ceylon in 1883,* 62.

[4] Lewis, *Sixty-Four Years in Ceylon,* 56–128.

[5] *Parl. Pap.* [C. 5507] of 1888, vol. cv, 43; *Parl. Pap.* [Cd. 2679] of 1905, 72

coffee threatened the existence not only of the plantations but also of the prosperity of Ceylon. The system of communications, the restoration of irrigation works, the employment given to thousands of natives in the coffee mills, these and numerous other benefits were due to the coffee plantations.

Salvation was found in the substitution of tea and cinchona for coffee. If any one man deserved especially to be remembered for his share in this work it was Doctor Thwaites: he saw the danger of confining cultivation to a single staple, and for many years before the collapse tried without much success to interest the planters in tea and cinchona. In 1845 a small tea plantation was established at Peradeniya, and from 1860 Doctor Thwaites experimented to determine the variety best suited to Ceylon and the proper methods of cultivation. Cinchona 'was almost wholly the creation of the efforts of Doctor Thwaites', who in 1861 established a plantation at Hakgala.[1] Sir William Gregory in the 'seventies induced a small but increasing minority of the planters to grow cinchona. They were rewarded by 'extraordinary success' since the Ceylon bark proved superior to the Indian and in 1872 brought 'a very high price' in London.[2] The majority refused to interest themselves in cinchona until about 1878, when their conversion was brought about by the continued failure of coffee coupled with the excellent price paid in London for Ceylon bark. From about 1878 to 1883 the reaction was as great as the previous indifference and the cultivation increased very rapidly. Doctor Thwaites rendered invaluable services by supplying the planters with young trees and instructing them in the best methods of cultivation.[3] The area under cinchona, which had been 500

and 257; *Parl. Pap.* [Cd. 9051] of 1918, 88 and 344; Ferguson, *Ceylon in the Jubilee Year*, 67 and 330. 'There are no cultivations of Arabian coffee now remaining in the Colony, although there are still considerable numbers of trees to be found scattered in all the planting districts. These trees thrive and produce good crops. . . . In recent years . . . there has been some planting of the robusta types of coffee, and good crops are now being reaped' (Turner, *Handbook of Commercial and General Information for Ceylon*, 1927, p. 133).

[1] C.O. 54. 531: Jan. 18, 1881; Ferguson, *Ceylon in 1893*, 73; Ferguson, *Pioneers of the Planting Enterprise*, i. 52–5 and 65–71.

[2] C.O. 54. 477: July 1, 1872; C.O. 54. 487: July 30, 1873; C.O. 54. 488: Oct. 13, 1873; C.O. 54. 493: June 10, 1874; Ferguson, *Pioneers of the Planting Enterprise*, i. 65–6.

[3] C.O. 54. 531: Jan. 18, 1881; Lewis, *Sixty-Four Years in Ceylon*, 78.

acres in 1872 and 6,000 in 1876, increased by 1881 to 33,000 and by 1883 to 65,000.[1] The export increased from 14,932 lb. in 1876 valued at £1,288 to 7,489,005 lb. valued at £365,088 in 1883. The profits did 'a good deal to bridge over the gap between the ruin of coffee and the introduction of tea'; but the feverish expansion defeated its own object. The cause of the high price of cinchona during the 'seventies was that the world demand exceeded the annual supply of about 2,000,000 lb. The enormous increase of production in Ceylon, together with the heavy exports from Java and elsewhere, exceeded the demand and caused a rapid fall in price from 1880 onwards. While the export for 1884 was 11,865,280 lb. the value was only £337,315. The sale price which was 12s. 2d. per ounce in 1878 and 10s. in 1880, fell to 2s. 4d. by 1886 and to about 1s. by 1892.[2] The planters were unwilling to sacrifice their investments and for a few years the exports continued to grow, attaining in 1886 the maximum of 14,675,663 lb. with a value of only £345,977. From about 1884, however, tea increasingly supplanted cinchona, 'and over a wide expanse young plants of the latter were pulled out as weeds'. The number of trees fell from 60,000,000 in 1883 to 7,000,000 or 8,000,000 in 1893; and by 1902, cinchona had become a minor industry with an export of 307,063 lb. valued at £1,842. In 1915 the export was 20,393 lb and the value £88.[3]

The planters were even slower to recognize the possibilities of tea than of cinchona despite the exhortations of Gregory and Thwaites, who predicted that it would become 'one of the most important staple products of the island'. The number of acres planted was only 350 in 1874 and 9,274 in 1880; and the export for the same years rose from 3,217 lb. valued at £817 to 228,680 lb. valued at £17,878.[4] The preference for cinchona

[1] C.O. 54. 532: Apr. 29, 1881; Ferguson, *Ceylon in 1883*, 66; Ferguson, *Ceylon in 1884*, 66.

[2] *Parl. Pap.* [C. 5507] of 1888, vol. cv. 43; C.O. 54. 531: Dec. 14, 1880; *Governors' Addresses to Leg. Council*, iii. 18, 157, and 220–1; Lewis, *Sixty-Four Years in Ceylon*, 105, 117, and 184; Ferguson, *Ceylon in 1893*, 238.

[3] C.O. 54. 552: Feb. 18, 1884; *Parl. Pap.* [C. 5249] of 1888, vol. lxxii. 7; *Parl. Pap.* [C. 5507] of 1888, vol. cv. 43; *Parl. Pap.* [Cd. 9051] of 1918, 88 and 89; Ferguson, *Ceylon in 1893*, 238; Ferguson, *Ceylon in 1903*, 69.

[4] C.O. 54. 478: Sept. 25, 1872; C.O. 54. 487: July 30, 1873; C.O. 54. 493: June 10, 1874; C.O. 54. 532: Apr. 29, 1881; *Parl. Pap.* [C. 5507] of 1888, vol. cv. 42–3.

R

was above all due to the high degree of skill and care required to prepare tea for the market. Other causes were the much greater cost of tea seed, the immense profits to be made from cinchona and the preference in the United Kingdom for Chinese tea. Owing to the fall in the value of cinchona, the cultivation of tea began rapidly to increase about 1884. By 1887 tea had become the staple product of Ceylon, the export in that year being 13,824,701 lb. with a value of £587,967, or more than five times as much as in 1884. The acreage increased from 35,000 in 1883 to 70,000 in 1884 and about 150,000 in 1887.[1] The planters had realized that tea was more suited than coffee to Ceylon since it was hardier, was not ruined by untimely rain, and grew better in the comparatively poor soil. The price of seed had decreased, and the planters had gained skill in preparing tea for the market. The former preference in the United Kingdom for Chinese tea was also being replaced by a demand for Ceylon and Indian tea which exceeded the supply; and in 1888 the importation of the two last was for the first time greater than that of Chinese tea. Since that date the demand for Chinese tea has steadily declined, and in 1924 it was less than 4 per cent. of the total quantity imported into the United Kingdom.[2] While the disastrous results of the collapse of coffee had not yet been eliminated, the plantations were rapidly recovering, and Ceylon was entering upon a period of greater prosperity than it had ever known.

[1] *Parl. Pap.* [C. 7526] of 1895, 47; Lewis, *Sixty-Four Years in Ceylon*, 126–7, 184, and 195; Ferguson, *Ceylon in the Jubilee Year*, 74–6.

[2] Ferguson, *Ceylon in the Jubilee Year*, 72–7; Anon., *Ceylon and her Planting Enterprise*, passim; Lewin, *Resources of the Empire*, 198.

XIII

THE EVOLUTION OF CEYLON
1889–1932

1. *Agriculture*

ONE of the most striking developments of the past fifty years in Ceylon has been the changes which have occurred in its agricultural industries. The former overwhelming dependence upon coffee has been replaced by three staple exports, tea, rubber, and coco-nuts, so that a repetition of the disastrous 'eighties is improbable. Moreover, the Ceylonese themselves have a far larger direct share in the export trade than formerly, since almost the whole of the coco-nut and about half the rubber cultivation is in their hands. The minor products are also more numerous and more important than in the coffee era, including cacao, cardamoms, and cinnamon. A very important change in European and to a lesser extent Ceylonese agriculture has been the increasing use of scientific methods of cultivation, due to the emergence of the science of tropical agriculture.

The tea industry developed very rapidly until 1896 owing to the expanding market in the United Kingdom. In that year the acreage under cultivation was 330,000 as compared with 220,000 in 1890;[1] but thereafter 'the rush began to fall off rapidly'. In consequence of the rapid increase in production in India and Ceylon the London market became overstocked, and the average London price fell from 8*d*. per lb. in 1896 to about 7*d*. in 1900. This left 'little or no margin of profit' to planters in the less suitable districts, the more so since the decrease in costs of production did not keep pace with the decline in price.[2] In 1900 the export was 149,265,053 lb., and the value £3,582,361.[3] The planting of new areas almost entirely ceased, and plantations in some of the poorer districts were abandoned, so that the total acreage declined from 406,000 in 1903 to

---

[1] *Parl. Pap.* [Cd. 2679] of 1905: 256.
[2] Ridgeway, *Administration of Ceylon*, 71; Willis, *Agriculture in the Tropics*, 59 and 64.
[3] *Parl. Pap.* [Cd. 2679] of 1905: 73.

388, 753 in 1904.[1] The methods of cultivation and manufacture were improved until by 1903 tea-planting had become more scientific, efficient, and economical than any other Ceylon culture. The planters received great assistance from the staff of the Royal Botanic Gardens. New markets also were energetically developed in the British Dominions, Russia, China, and the United States, green tea being prepared for American and other customers who refused to accept black tea. Owing to the rapid expansion of these markets the percentage of tea exports taken by the United Kingdom decreased from $\frac{7}{8}$ in about 1895 to $\frac{2}{3}$ in 1903.[2] With the passing of the depression additional areas were brought under cultivation; but the danger of renewed over-production was prevented by the continued expansion of the new markets and by the counter-attraction of rubber-planting. A further cheapening of the costs of management and manufacture was obtained by grouping together estates and establishing large factories to deal with their crops. The majority of the plantations were owned by London companies which exercised control through the medium of a firm of agents in Colombo. The agency in turn supervised the work of the estate managers by means of a visiting agent who was himself an experienced planter. The success of the industry was 'a conspicuous instance of the success of good methods and modern machinery'. In 1910 the amount exported was 182,070,094 lb., and the value £5,280,033.[3]

During the War many estates were compelled to curtail their operations owing to the shortage of shipping, exchange difficulties, the rising cost of fertilizers, and the 'extraordinary' fluctuations in sale prices in 1917. In 1918 the export was 34,814,983 lb. less than the record shipment of 215,632,727 lb. in 1915.[4] The establishment of Government control of the trade had the effect of making it more profitable to produce coarse than fine grades of tea. The over-production of the coarse

[1] *Parl. Pap.* [Cd. 2679] of 1905: 256.
[2] Ridgeway, *Administration of Ceylon*, 71–3; *Parl. Pap.* [Cd. 2238/2] of 1904, Ceylon Report 1903, No. 425: 28–9.
[3] Willis, *Agriculture in the Tropics*, 60–5; Ceylon Reports 1900–10: *passim*; *Parl. Pap.* [Cd. 9051] of 1918: 351.
[4] *Parl. Pap.* [Cd. 8172/30] of 1916, C. Rep. 1915, No. 904: 5; *Parl. Pap.* [Cd. 8973/20] of 1918, C. Rep. 1917, No. 971: 7 and 18; *Parl. Pap.* [Cmd. 1/30] of 1919, C. Rep. 1918, No. 1007: 1, 6, and 21.

varieties coupled with the post-war sale of Government stocks led to a serious fall in prices in 1920, and the majority of estates worked at a loss. The quantity of tea exported in 1920 was 184,770,231 lb., and the value £8,078,154. Once again the planters adapted themselves to the emergency, and in the end profited from a most unpromising situation. The demand was largely confined to fine quality teas, and from this date the industry gave increasing care to their preparation. The methods of cultivation and manufacture became steadily more economical and scientific.[1] A very important factor in obtaining this result was the co-operation between the planters and the Department of Agriculture; and in 1925 they established the Tea Research Institute to supplement its investigations. In 1921 the market began to improve, and the industry entered upon a new period of prosperity owing to the great improvement in the quality and the methods of production.[2]

In 1929 the area under tea was over 457,000 acres, divided into about 1,200 estates of which some 80 per cent. were owned by British companies—few proprietary planters remained—and the remainder (chiefly small gardens) by Ceylonese. Nearly 80 per cent. of the plantations were in the Districts of Kandy, Nuwara Eliya, and Badulla, the finer teas being all grown at altitudes of between 4,000 and 6,000 feet. Good medium qualities were grown between 2,500 and 4,000 feet, and a little inferior tea at lower levels. The average yield per acre on a well-managed estate was between 650 and 800 lb.; while on the best cultivated estates it was as high as 1,000 lb. Ceylon is after India the most important tea-producing country, and the trade is one of the most progressive, most scientific, and best organized industries in the world. The export in 1929 was 251,588,012 lb., the value being £15,389,556.[3] The existing depression has seriously affected the trade both in Ceylon and India. In 1931 Empire tea sold 'at the Mincing Lane auctions at prices which do not nearly cover the bare cost of production', particularly of the low and medium grade teas. Plantation

[1] C. Rep. 1920, No. 1086: 6, 7, and 13; *Parl. Pap.* [Cmd. 2738] of 1926: 102.
[2] C. Reps. 1921–9: *passim*, e.g. C. Rep. 1927, No. 1404: 14; Lewin, *Resources of the Empire*, 198–9.
[3] *Parl. Pap.* [Cmd. 3131] of 1928: 97 and 173; *Parl. Pap.* [Cmd. 3235] of 1928: 78 and 88; C. Rep. 1929, No. 1507: 9–11 and 48.

staffs have been reduced and wages curtailed, dividends have declined, and there has been serious danger that large areas might go out of cultivation. An important contributory cause has been the rapid increase in the sale of the cheap and inferior Javanese and Sumatran teas in the United Kingdom market. The imposition in 1932 of the United Kingdom import duty of 4*d*. per lb. on foreign and 2*d*. on Empire teas has given the trade a very necessary measure of protection.[1]

Rubber was introduced into Ceylon from Kew in 1876, the seedlings being planted at Heneratgoda and Peradeniya. The Ceara flowered before the Hevea trees, and by 1883 977 acres had been planted with Ceara rubber. The cultivation did not pay owing to the low price, incorrect methods of tapping, and small yield of latex. Many of the trees were replaced by tea, and few planters interested themselves in rubber until 1899. When the Hevea trees began to flower in 1881 almost all the seeds were sent to Botanic Gardens in the British possessions and Java; but after 1889 increasingly large quantities became available for Ceylon planters. By 1898 only 1,071 acres had been planted, almost all with Hevea. The general lack of interest was due to the assured success of tea as contrasted with the doubtful prospects of rubber. In 1897–9 the future of the industry was revolutionized by the experiments of the staff of the Ceylon Botanic Gardens. These were the rediscovery of wound response which greatly increased the yield of latex, the discovery that trees could be tapped when 6 or 7 instead of 10 years old, and various improvements in the manufacture. At the same time the London price of tea fell, while that of rubber rapidly rose from about 2s. to 4s. per lb. in 1901 and 6s. in 1904–6.[2]

Profits were very large until about 1907, and the acreage under rubber increased from 2,500 in 1901 to 150,000 in 1907 and 200,000 in 1910. The export was 8,223 lb. valued at £859 in 1900 and 3,802,624 lb. valued at £1,308,934 in 1910. The extension of cultivation was temporarily checked by the fall in

[1] Woolacott, *United Empire*, xxii. 541; McLeod, *United Empire*, xxii. 670–3; *Times Weekly Edition*, Mar. 31, 1932: 377.

[2] Petch, *Annals of the Royal Botanic Gardens Peradeniya*, v. vii. 434–512; Willis, *Agriculture in the Tropics*, 123–9.

the London price to about 4s. per lb. in 1907; but in 1910 Brazilian growers temporarily forced it up to over 12s., and a large number of new companies were formed. Between 1910 and 1920 prices were considerably less than in 1910, but never fell below 2s., and were sufficient to yield a profit. In 1920 the acreage was 266,962 in bearing and 130,932 planted but not yet in bearing, the export being 88,552,500 lb., and the value £8,996,110. While the majority of the plantations were owned by British companies the Ceylonese had a much larger share in the rubber than in the tea industry. For the most part their holdings were small, but the number steadily increased, cinnamon and paddy being sometimes replaced by rubber.[1]

The rapid expansion of rubber-planting was due to the development of the motor industry particularly in the United States, which normally required 72 per cent. of the annual world output. By 1920 world production had outstripped consumption, and surplus stocks were still further increased by the sharp curtailment of American purchases owing to the depression of 1920–2. The average London price per lb. for standard crêpe fell rapidly to 10d. in 1920, 7d. in 1921, and 6d. in 1922, while inferior grades were 'practically unsaleable'. Many of the plantations both in Ceylon and Malaya were faced with bankruptcy.[2] In 1920–1 the planters voluntarily reduced their output by 25 per cent. for one year; but the plan was only temporarily successful in raising the price and was not continued.[3]

The British Government in 1922 adopted the report of the Stevenson Committee advising the restriction of rubber exports from British colonies, although the Netherlands Government had refused to co-operate. The Dutch East Indies produced 25·5 per cent. of the world's rubber, partly on large plantations owned by Dutch and British, and partly on small native holdings. The Government felt that the Dutch planters, or at any

---

[1] *Parl. Pap.* [Cd. 2679] of 1905: 281; *Parl. Pap.* [Cd. 9051] of 1918: 377; *Parl. Pap.* [Cmd. 2738] of 1926: 102; C. Reps. 1901–20: *passim*; Petch, *Annals*, v. vii. 470; Lawrence, *The World's Struggle with Rubber*, 9–17.

[2] *Parl. Pap.* [Cmd. 1678] of 1922: 3–4; Figart, *Plantation Rubber Industry in the Middle East*, 7–9, 95–6, and 127–45; Liversedge, *The Nineteenth Century and After*, ciii. 767 and 770; Bois, *United Empire*, xvii (New Series), 157.

[3] C. Rep. 1920, No. 1086: 7; C. Rep. 1921, No. 1137: 6 and 7; C. Rep. 1922, No. 1172: 7.

rate the most efficient of them, would survive the depression without assistance. Moreover, the Dutch policy was to foster native prosperity and loyalty by encouraging their cultivation of rubber. The Stevenson Committee at first regarded Dutch co-operation as essential; but in its final report of October 1922 it advocated single-handed British restriction. Ceylon and Malaya together produced 70 per cent. of the world supply; and in addition the majority of British planters in the Dutch colonies agreed voluntarily to restrict their output, thus giving the British control of about 75 per cent. of the annual production. The object of the Stevenson plan was to stabilize prices at 1s. 3d. per lb. (raised to 1s. 9d. on May 1, 1926) by a system of variable export quotas. The production of each estate was ascertained for the year November 1, 1919, to October 31, 1920, and was the Standard Production, or 100 per cent. The Exportable Percentage, initially fixed at 60 per cent., was raised or lowered according to whether the average London price of standard quality smoked sheet during the preceding quarter had been above or below 1s. 3d. An Advisory Committee in London was appointed to assist the Secretary of State for the Colonies in operating the scheme. A nominal export duty was levied on the Exportable Percentage; but exports in excess of this were subject to a graduated and heavy duty.[1]

Restriction was enforced from November 1, 1922, to November 1, 1928. While the attempt to stabilize prices failed, the plan was successful in raising them and enabling planters to sell at a profit. During the first two years prices were kept fairly stable in the neighbourhood of 1s. 3d. per lb.; but in 1925 they rose rapidly to over 4s. due to the recovery of the American market. In 1926 the price fell to about 1s. 8d. owing to the growth of Dutch exports, and in 1928 to 8d.–9d. This last 'left only a small margin over cost of production'. While the European planters supported restriction the Ceylonese and their members in the Legislative Council became increasingly hostile. The plan was defeated partly by the development of the American reclaimed rubber industry, but principally by the

[1] *Parl. Paps.* [Cmd. 1678] and [Cmd. 1756] of 1922: *passim*; C. Reps. 1922–8: *passim*; Bois, *United Empire*, xvii (New Series), 157–8; Liversedge, *Nineteenth Century and After*, ciii. 767–72.

immense stimulus which it gave to European and especially to
native production in the Dutch East Indies. The Dutch growers
reaped the benefit of the higher prices, and being unfettered by
a quota had every incentive to enlarge their exports. By 1927
the British share of world production had fallen to 52 per cent.
and the Dutch had increased to over 40 per cent. The greater
part of this increase, which rendered restriction progressively
more ineffective in regulating world prices, was native rubber
planted in 1919 and 1920. Moreover, under the stimulus of
high prices the area under native rubber in the Dutch East
Indies had grown from 444,600 acres in 1923 to about three
times that amount in 1927. It was clear that as this rubber
came into bearing the waning efficacy of the Stevenson plan
would be nullified.[1]

The abolition of restriction found the British plantations
seriously handicapped in the competition with their rivals. The
expenses of the native cultivator were less than those of the
European plantation company, whose principal hope of salvation lay in the increase of output by more scientific cultivation.
In 1928 the Dutch methods were more advanced than the
British, particularly in improving the yield of latex by bud-
grafting and selection. The British research workers and many
of the planters realized the situation, and set to work to make
up for lost time. The present depression has made radically
worse what must have been a serious position under the most
favourable conditions. Since 1929 consumption of rubber has
fallen to an alarming extent, while production has very largely
increased as the new areas planted during the restriction period
have come into bearing. By August 1931 the price per lb. had
fallen to under 3*d*. Lack of capital has prevented many planters
from incurring the expense of research and improvement of
methods. Proposals for restriction of output were revived; but
as formerly the Netherlands Government declined to co-operate.
The scheme was dropped, and the British plantations are
faced with the task of recovery under peculiarly adverse
circumstances.[2]

[1] *Parl. Pap.* [Cmd. 3235] of 1928: 135–41; House of Commons Debates:
216: 5: 1161–1220.

[2] *Parl. Pap.* [Cmd. 3235] of 1928: 119–21 and 140–56; C. Rep. 1923,

The products of the coco-nut palm form the third of Ceylon's staple exports. While the cultivation is of great antiquity its rapid extension has taken place during the last half-century. In 1870 the value of the coco-nut exports was about 4 per cent. of the total export trade, in 1880 9 per cent., in 1890 15 per cent., and in 1900 17 per cent. By 1910 it was 24·5 per cent., and by 1920 about 27 per cent. The volume continued to increase, but owing to the fall in prices the export percentage in 1929 was only 16 per cent. The acreage has grown from about 650,000 in 1902 to approximately 1,100,000 in 1929, chiefly in the North-Western, Western, and Southern Provinces, in the Jaffna Peninsula, and along the coast of the Eastern Province. The greater part of the cultivation is in Ceylonese hands. Much could be done to increase the output by better methods of cultivation; and the Department of Agriculture has been trying to achieve this result by research and by propaganda amongst the cultivators.[1]

2. *The Nation-Building Services*

The organization of the Ceylon Civil Service experienced no essential change until the radical alterations introduced by the Constitution of 1931. The nation-building services, however, were transformed both in personnel and in their fields of operations. Between 1900 and 1911, for example, the expenditure upon them increased by 85 per cent. This was made possible by the growth of the revenue from £1,217,158 in 1890 to £8,086,370 in 1929.[2] The importance to an agricultural colony of adequate roads and railways can scarcely be over-estimated; and the Government has made their extension one of its principal duties. In 1929 there were about 16,400 miles of roads and cart-tracks, of which 5,260 miles were metalled, in addition to 8,200 miles of bridle-paths. In Ceylon as elsewhere the post-war period has seen a remarkable development of

No. 1243: 42; C. Rep. 1928, No. 1455: 10–12; C. Rep. 1929, No. 1507: 11–14; Lawrence, *The World's Struggle with Rubber*, 91–3.

[1] C. Reps. 1890–1929: *passim*; *Parl. Pap.* [C/3502] of 1883: 40; *Parl. Pap.* [C/7526] of 1895: 46; *Parl. Pap.* [Cd. 2679] of 1905: 72–3; *Parl. Pap.* [Cd. 9051] of 1918: 89; *Parl. Pap.* [Cmd. 2738] of 1926: 102; Willis, *Agriculture in the Tropics*, 76–9.

[2] *Parl. Pap.* [Cd. 2679] of 1905: 14; C. Rep. 1929, No. 1507: 3; Denham, *Ceylon at the Census of 1911*, 7.

motor traffic; and motor-lorries, of which there were about 2,800 in 1929, are gradually replacing bullock-carts in the movement of estate goods. The length of railway lines open in 1928 was 951 miles, of which 834 miles were broad and 117 narrow gauge. The lines are owned and operated by the Ceylon Government Railway Department. The system consists of five main lines radiating from Colombo and linking up the principal ports and inland towns. Combined with the branch lines and the road system the plantations and the Ceylonese agricultural districts are well supplied with means of communication. The northern railway is connected with the Indian railways by a ferry service from Talaimannar to Dhanushkodi, and is the principal means of transport for Tamil estate labour. The extensive additions to the Colombo harbour works have also increased the prosperity of the colony.[1]

The restoration of irrigation works was continued on an extensive scale until 1905. In 1900 Governor Sir West Ridgeway established a separate Irrigation Department, the Provincial and Central Irrigation Boards established in 1887 having proved unsatisfactory. In 1905 the Government made an important change in its policy, deciding 'to push forward the completion and full development of existing works, and to refrain from the initiation of new schemes of any magnitude until greater advantage is taken of the facilities for paddy cultivation that have already been supplied'. 'Irrigable lands have been provided in excess of all probable requirements', often at a heavy and unremunerative cost to Government. Many of the restored works lacked a sufficient supply of water at all seasons owing to the provision of 'too limited a catchment area', while the system of distribution channels was often incomplete.[2] The effect of the new policy was 'generally speaking to stop the construction of new works . . . and to stop improvements or completion of existing works, because such improvements could not be shown to be business proposals'.[3]

[1] C. Reps. 1889–1929: *passim*, e.g. C. Rep. 1929, No. 1507: 55–60; Ridgeway, *Administration of Ceylon*, 19–45.

[2] Keane, *Report on Irrigation*, passim; Ridgeway, *Administration of Ceylon*, 46–8; C. Reps. 1890–1905: *passim*.

[3] Ceylon Sessional Papers, xxii, 1920: *Papers relating to the Resumption of an Extensive Irrigation Programme*, 3.

After the Great War the Government altered its policy, and large sums were spent upon the completion of existing and the construction of new systems. In 1929 153,680 acres were irrigated by 'Crown' irrigation works constructed and maintained by the Irrigation Department; while an additional 210,268 acres were irrigated by small village works largely repaired by the raiyats themselves under Government supervision. The prevalence of malaria, however, in many instances discouraged settlers and thus prevented the full utilization of the irrigable area.[1]

Less striking but at least as important as irrigation has been the work of the Royal Botanic Gardens (reorganized and enlarged in 1912 as the Department of Agriculture). Prior to 1896 the small staff were largely concerned with the study of the Ceylon flora and similar subjects of scientific inquiry. Save in exceptional emergencies like the attacks of *Hemileia vastatrix* little research was done on practical problems such as plant diseases or improved methods of cultivation. The principal contribution to Ceylon's prosperity, and a very important one, was the acclimatization of rubber and other new cultures. After 1900 the acclimatization of new cultures became of decreasing importance since 'most of the new products that can possibly be brought in are now introduced'. In 1896 the present policy was adopted of systematic research in the problems of tropical agriculture, combined with the dissemination of advice to the planters and the Ceylonese cultivators. The science of tropical agriculture was in its infancy, and the investigation of its manifold problems has been the principal cause of the prosperity of the planting industry in the twentieth century. In 1897 the *Agricultural Journal* was founded, and in 1899 a botanical laboratory was built. The number of subsidiary gardens was increased to five, and in 1901 the Gangaruwa Estate of 500 acres near Peradeniya was bought for an experiment station. By 1903 the staff had been increased from three to eight, a Mycologist and an Entomologist being appointed, and subsequent additions included an Economic Botanist and an Agricultural Chemist. One of the first results of the new policy was the

---

[1] C. Reps. 1906–29: *passim*, e.g. C. Rep. 1929, No. 1507: 79; *Parl. Pap.* [Cmd. 3235] of 1928: 79.

discovery of wound response which radically altered the position of the rubber industry. The tea-planters especially availed themselves of the advice of the Department, and became 'every year more and more scientific in their methods'.

The Ceylonese cultivators were slow to make use of the Department's services, and an elaborate system of propaganda was devised which included vernacular leaflets, agricultural instructors, and demonstration gardens. The establishment of school gardens was begun in 1901, and by 1929 the number was 908. The children were taught the value of new products and improved methods of cultivation. In 1904 the Agricultural Society was established to supplement the efforts of the Department. It was financed partly by membership dues, and partly by a Government subsidy. In 1916 the School of Tropical Agriculture was established at Peradeniya to train Ceylonese members of the Department's staff and private students. Selected school-teachers were also instructed in the management of the school gardens.[1] The Veterinary Department established by Governor Sir West Ridgeway has done valuable work in research and the diminution of cattle diseases.[2] Ceylon was the first Crown Colony to combat the problem of rural debt by the creation in 1911 of Co-operative Credit Societies. In 1927 there were 303 societies with a membership of 35,112, operating under Government supervision. The societies were primarily concerned with the provision of credit for their members at reasonable rates of interest; although they were also used as one medium for the introduction of improved methods of cultivation and co-operative marketing. Recently reforms were introduced to remedy various defects such as too great a dependence on Government loans.[3]

During the past twelve years important developments have occurred in the Department of Agriculture, the staff being increased, larger laboratories built, and a Tea Research Institute

[1] C. Reps. 1899–1929: *passim*, e.g. *Parl. Pap.* [Cd. 8434/21] of 1917; C. Rep. 1916, No. 934: 4–5; Ridgeway, *Administration of Ceylon*, 66–8; Willis, *Agriculture in the Tropics*, 32, 162–4, and *passim*.
[2] *Parl. Pap.* [Cmd. 3235] of 1928: 90; Ridgeway, *Administration of Ceylon*, 122–3.
[3] C. Reps. 1909–29: *passim*; *Parl. Pap.* [Cmd. 3235] of 1928: 159–63; *Parl. Pap.* [Cmd. 3629] of 1930: 103–11.

formed in 1925 under the control of the Government and planters. The Rubber Research Scheme was established on its present footing in 1921 by combining the two separate research organizations founded prior to the Great War. Financial support was provided partly by the planters and partly by a Government grant. Since 1927 the Scheme has been especially concerned with research in bud-grafting. The proposals of the Colonial Office Conferences of 1927 and 1930 for a unified Agricultural Service for the Crown Colonies, with the Imperial College of Tropical Agriculture at Trinidad as the training centre, should still further increase the efficiency of the Ceylon Service. The results of its work during the past half-century are an excellent commentary on the truth of Lord Lovat's dictum that: 'The prosperity of the people, the trade, and, not least, the revenue of each Colony is mainly dependent upon the efficiency of agriculture.'[1]

The Medical Department shared the development of the other nation-building services. In 1926 the medical branch of the Department of Medical and Sanitary Services had a staff of 294 Medical Officers, the sanitary branch had 24 Medical Officers and 234 sanitary inspectors, and the research branch had 8 specialists in various fields of research. The number of Medical Officers in 1903 was 134. In 1929 there were 102 Government hospitals and asylums with 10,761 beds, and 601 dispensaries. In addition there were 85 hospitals and 706 dispensaries on the plantations, supervised by 6 Medical Officers. The Colombo Medical College, which was founded in 1870, supplied part of the medical staff together with the apothecaries in charge of dispensaries. The hospitals were models of efficiency, and 'Ceylon possesses probably the most extensive hospital system of any British possession'. Research, public health services, and preventive medicine, however, were 'not up to modern standards. . . . Ceylon has concentrated all her energies on attempts to cure and alleviate disease, but is behind many other parts of the Empire in preventing the need for such efforts.'[2]

[1] *Parl. Pap.* [Cmd. 730] of 1920: 6 and 12; *Parl. Pap.* [Cmd. 2883] of 1927: 18–40; *Parl. Pap.* [Cmd. 3049] of 1928: 44 and *passim*; *Parl. Pap.* [Cmd. 3235] of 1928: 80–9 and 154–6; *Parl. Pap.* [Cmd. 3628] and [Cmd. 3629] of 1930: *passim.*
[2] *Parl. Pap.* [Cmd. 3235] of 1928: 91.

The medical problems of Ceylon were the same as those of other tropical colonies—the widespread prevalence of such diseases as malaria and hookworm, and insanitary living conditions. The De Soysa Bacteriological and Pasteur Institute was established in 1899, and a clinic for tropical diseases in 1905; but in 1927 the Institute was reported to be 'hopelessly inadequate in staff and accommodation'. In 1915 a campaign against hookworm was begun by the Medical Department in collaboration with the International Health Commission of America, and a distinct improvement was made in the health of the population. Since 1921 systematic attacks have been made on malaria, and 'very marked results are shown by the decrease in the number of patients admitted to hospitals'. To effect improvements was both costly and difficult 'owing to the excessive rainfall, and the presence of large masses of water in the form of lagoons, canals, and paddy fields'. Sanitary reforms were urgently required in the towns and villages at the beginning of the twentieth century. The two obstacles were the heavy expense and the insanitary habits of the people. One of the first steps was to provide Colombo, the population of which was rapidly increasing, with an adequate supply of pure water. A complete system of drainage and sewage disposal was also begun in 1903 and completed about 1924. The sanitation of other towns was gradually improved; but their condition and especially that of the villages remained unsatisfactory.[1]

During the greater part of the nineteenth century the limited revenue of the colony allowed only a small expenditure upon education. In addition to Government schools, largely situated in the towns, grants in aid were made to mission schools. In 1869 the Department of Public Instruction was established; and grants in aid were made available for non-Christian as well as mission schools which conformed to the Government standards of instruction. In addition to the aided there were a number of unaided schools of dubious value. In 1885 the Government decided to devote the greater part of its available

---

[1] C. Reps. 1888–1929: *passim*; *Parl. Pap.* [Cmd. 3235] of 1928: 91–6; Ridgeway, *Administration of Ceylon*, 90–107; Bridger, *Administration Report of the Director of Medical and Sanitary Services for 1926*, passim; Balfour and Scott, *Health Problems of the Empire*, 141–7.

funds to education in the vernacular, leaving education in English almost entirely to the aided schools. To avoid duplication the provision of rural schools, particularly in the interior, was undertaken mainly by the Government, since the majority of the aided schools were in the Maritime Provinces and in the towns. The rapid increase of the revenue which began in the 'nineties with the prosperity of tea and later rubber was accompanied by a steady growth of the expenditure upon education. Concurrently the popular demand for education, and particularly English education, increased to a remarkable degree with the growing prosperity of the Ceylonese. 'The small landowner and cultivator who has prospered believes that education will make a clerk of his son or fit him for a learned profession. . . . The younger generation seek escape from rural life.' In 1906 and 1907 permissive Ordinances were passed empowering the local authorities to introduce compulsory vernacular education in the towns and rural districts. The areas affected were gradually extended as funds for the provision of sufficient schools became available. Where compulsory education was enforced in a district provided for by mission schools pupils of other creeds were exempted from the religious instruction unless the consent of their parents was given. To an increasing extent vernacular schools were established on the plantations.

The progress of education prior to the War is shown by the following table:

	Government.		Aided.		Unaided.		Total.	
	Schools.	Pupils.	Schools.	Pupils.	Schools.	Pupils.	Schools.	Pupils.
1890	436	40,290	984	73,698	2,617	32,464	4,037	146,452
1900	500	48,642	1,328	120,751	2,089	38,881	3,917	208,274
1910	759	96,600	1,910	203,020	1,546	36,754	4,215	336,374

The percentage of literacy per 100 of the population increased from 24·6 per cent. in 1881 to 40·4 per cent. in 1911 for males, and from 2·5 per cent. in 1881 to 10·6 per cent. in 1911 for females. In 1911 3·3 per cent. of the males and 1·2 per cent. of the females were literate in English. Technical education was provided in the Government Technical College founded in 1893, in aided industrial schools, in manual training courses attached to the ordinary schools, and in the school gardens.[1]

[1] C. Reps. 1884–1916, e.g. Parl. Pap. [Cd. 8434/21] of 1917, C. Rep. 1916,

The main distinction was not between secondary and elementary education, but between the schools in which the medium of instruction was English or one of the vernaculars. The real elementary education of the country was provided in vernacular schools attended in 1929 by 89·76 per cent. of the school-going population. 'In the English schools a large majority of the pupils are learning a language which is not their own, and none of these can be regarded as receiving a purely elementary education. A small number of schools called Anglo-vernacular schools combine education in the vernacular with a small amount of elementary instruction in English.' All three types were divided into lower and higher grades, and the subjects taught in the lower grades did not differ materially with the medium of instruction employed. In the higher grades of the English schools the standard of instruction reached was the entrance examination to a university. All vernacular education was free, but fees were charged in English schools.[1]

The post-war period was marked by a continued expansion and an increasing demand for English education. In 1920 there were 919 Government vernacular schools with 131,320 pupils, and 1,868 aided vernacular schools with 197,640 pupils. There were 278 English and Anglo-vernacular schools (the majority aided) with 48,125 pupils.[2] In 1921 Colombo University College was founded, the courses of study leading to the intermediate and final Arts, Science, and Economics examinations of London University. In 1928 the Legislative Council decided to establish a University at Kandy. In 1929 the number of schools and pupils was as follows:

	English.		Anglo-vernacular.		Vernacular.		Total.	
	Schools.	Pupils.	Schools.	Pupils.	Schools.	Pupils.	Schools.	Pupils.
Government	16	2,402	123	33,370	1,199	176,695	1,338	212,467
Aided . .	251	55,086	56	11,445	2,055	251,096	2,362	317,627
Unaided .	55	2,407	13	862	522	14,025	590	17,294
							4,290	547,388

No. 934: 18; *Parl. Pap.* [Cd. 2873] of 1906: *passim*; Denham, *Ceylon at the Census of 1911*, 157–71, 399, and 400–44; *Imperial Education Conference Papers, III, Ceylon*, 1914, *passim*; Ridgeway, *Administration of Ceylon*, 59–65 and 141–6.

[1] C. Rep. 1929, No. 1507: 87–90; *Imperial Education Conference Papers, III, Ceylon*, 9–10.   [2] C. Rep. 1920, No. 1086: 25–6.

S

There were also 81 Government and aided technical and industrial schools, and 3 Government and 10 aided training schools for teachers. In 1928 approximately 50 per cent. of the children of school age in Ceylon were receiving education. As in India large sections of the population were unfavourable to female education: in 1929 348,632 boys and only 198,756 girls were attending school.[1]

The criticisms passed by Mr. Ormsby Gore in 1928 were very reminiscent of those brought against Indian education. 'The chief fault . . . has been the over-emphasis of the purely clerical and literary traditions . . . popular opinion had demanded that the elementary school must lead to the secondary school and the secondary school to the University, and thereby the whole course and aim of education became controlled by . . . the Cambridge Junior and the Cambridge Senior local examinations. . . . The social consequences are seen in the vast army of competitors for every minor clerical appointment . . . and a large body of unemployed, disappointed, discontented youths with an English education of a kind and a Cambridge certificate of no commercial or intrinsic value.' The Education Department was aware of the weakness and was attempting to deal with it.[2]

3. *The Constitution of Ceylon*

In Ceylon as in India the demand for self-government was to a large extent the result of Western education. It was significant that while the earlier protests against Crown Colony government had been almost entirely confined to the Europeans and the burghers the movement which began in the 'nineties was conducted by the educated Ceylonese. In 1909 Low Country Sinhalese and Tamil societies petitioned the Secretary of State for the election of Ceylonese members to the Legislative Council and representation on the Executive Council. The petitioners, 'mostly belonging to the professional and commercial middle classes' in the towns, were a 'very small minority . . . of the natives of Ceylon who have assimilated

---

[1] C. Reps. 1921–9, *passim*, e.g. C. Rep. 1929, No. 1507: 87–93 and 105–6.
[2] *Parl. Pap.* [Cmd. 3235] of 1928: 96–105.

an education of a purely Western type'. The Secretary of State remodelled the Legislative Council on the principle 'that the possession of Western education must be attended in future by the exercise of popular franchise'. The membership was increased to 11 official and 10 unofficial members of whom 4 were elected, viz. the European Rural and Urban, the Burgher and the Educated Ceylonese representatives. The Governor continued to nominate 6 members, viz., 1 Kandyan and 2 Low Country Sinhalese, 2 Tamil, and 1 Moorman.[1]

In 1919 the Low Country Sinhalese and Tamil societies united to form the Ceylon National Congress, and demanded that the majority of the Legislative and at least half the Executive Council should be Ceylonese. In 1920 the composition of the Legislative Council was altered to 14 official and 23 unofficial members. They were allocated amongst the various races so that 'no single community can impose its will on the other communities if the latter are supported by the Official Members'. In 1921 the Tamils withdrew from the National Congress, which thus became practically a Low Country Sinhalese organization, and formed a separate society. The cause of the rupture was that the Tamils as well as the other minorities insisted on the retention of communal representation since they feared Sinhalese predominance. The Congress advocated territorial constituencies with as its consequence a Sinhalese majority, and were opposed to the retention of communal electorates except as a temporary concession.[2]

In 1924 the constitution was again amended, the Legislative Council being composed of 12 official and 37 unofficial members. Of the unofficials 23 were territorially and 11 communally elected, while 3 were nominated by the Governor. An educational and property qualification for the franchise limited the electorate to 204,997, or 4 per cent. of the total population. Four unofficial members were added to the Executive Council. The Legislative Council's control of legislation and finance was practically unrestricted save for the Governor's powers of veto

[1] *Parl. Pap.* [Cd. 5098] of 1910: *passim*; *Parl. Pap.* [Cd. 5427] of 1910: *passim*.
[2] *Parl. Pap.* [Cmd. 1809] and [Cmd. 1906] of 1923: *passim*; *Parl. Pap.* [Cmd. 2062] of 1924: *passim*; *Parl. Pap.* [Cmd. 3131] of 1928: 13–15.

and certification. Any Bill which he considered to be of paramount importance to the public interest became law when passed by the 12 official members.[1]

The Donoughmore Commission which investigated the working of the constitution in 1927–8 emphatically condemned it. Cordial co-operation between Executive and Legislature was essential for success; but 'if it has been a partnership at all, at times it has been rather like holy matrimony at its worst'. The Ceylonese members were critical and suspicious, and convinced 'that they could administer the country more efficiently themselves'. Their attitude was intensified by the divorce of power from responsibility which was the most striking characteristic of the constitution. 'Denied all prospects of office, the unofficial members were in no danger of being called upon to translate their criticisms into action.' They 'came gradually to regard themselves as a permanent Opposition', and 'the launching of continuous and irresponsible attacks on the members of the Government collectively and individually became the distinctive feature of their policy'. While theoretically independent the Executive in practice was largely controlled by the 'overwhelming' Ceylonese majority in the Legislative Council, owing to their 'complete control over expenditure'. This power was used to hold endless and searching inquiries into the detailed working of the executive departments 'which were outside its legitimate sphere'. At these investigations Government officials found themselves treated as hostile witnesses, 'subjected to grave discourtesy if not on occasion to personal insult'. Moreover, the attitude of the Council made them uncertain of the safety of their positions and pensions. 'The effect on the *moral* of the public services [was] disastrous': unsupported by the Government they were left 'bewildered and disheartened'. The Governor was placed in a very difficult position: his power of certification was no substitute for an official majority in the Legislative Council. Furthermore, he adopted the policy of gaining the co-operation of the Ceylonese members by conciliation and concession. In addition to achieving a measure of success he thereby encouraged them in their policy of interference and hostile criticism. The Donoughmore

[1] *Parl. Pap.* [Cmd. 3131] of 1928: 16.

Commission considered that the constitution was 'reducing the Government to impotence without providing any means of training the unofficial members in the assumption of executive responsibility'.[1]

The Secretary of State promulgated a new constitution based upon the recommendations of the Donoughmore Commission which finally came into force in 1931. It excited strong opposition amongst the Ceylonese unofficials in the Legislative Council, but was finally accepted. The Legislative Council was replaced by the State Council composed of 50 members elected for territorial constituencies, a maximum of 8 nominated by the Governor, and 3 *ex-officio* Officers of State. These last were the Chief Secretary, the Legal Secretary, and the Financial Secretary (the former Colonial Secretary, Attorney-General, and Treasurer). Their role was advisory: they could take part in debates but could not vote. Two outstanding characteristics of the State Council were the disappearance of the official minority and the abolition of communal representation, apart from the Governor's power to nominate a limited number of members. The franchise provisions practically instituted universal suffrage for all male and female Ceylonese of 21 years of age. Additional qualifications gave the vote to Tamil immigrants from India who intended permanently to reside in Ceylon, and to European British subjects in Ceylon. The Donoughmore Commission estimated that the electorate would be increased from 204,997 to 2,175,000. The qualifications for candidates were the same as for members, with the exceptions that they must be literate in English and must not hold any public office under the Crown in Ceylon. The abolition of communal representation and the wide extension of the franchise were strongly opposed by Ceylonese members of the Legislative Council.

All Ordinances were enacted by the State Council with the assent of the Governor, who had power to veto, to refer back

---

[1] *Parl. Pap.* [Cmd. 3131] of 1928: 18–30 and 125–7; Woods, *United Empire*, xxi. 322–9; Bandaranaike, *Remembered Yesterdays*, 290–1. The Governor of Ceylon contended that the constitution had worked as successfully as could be expected. Distrust and suspicion had become 'much less acute'; and the description given of the policy of Government and the general attitude of the Ceylonese members was 'too sweeping' (*Parl. Pap.* [Cmd. 3419] of 1929: 4–13).

for further consideration, or to reserve them for the decision of the Crown. The Crown retained full power to legislate and to disallow or amend Ceylon legislation. For the control of internal affairs the Council by secret ballot divided its members (except the three Officers of State) into seven Executive Committees. Each of these exercised general control over one of the ten groups into which the Government departments were divided; while an Officer of State supervised each of the remaining three. Each Executive Committee elected a chairman, the Minister, who together with the three Officers of State formed the Board of Ministers, the Executive Council being abolished. The centralized control of the Colonial Secretary over all departments was thus replaced by ten separate Ministries. In important questions a Committee's decision required the approval of the State Council sitting in executive session and of the Governor, each being empowered to accept, reject, or refer back any proposal. The Board settled the order of business for the Council and prepared the annual budget and other financial measures. Decisions of a Committee or of the Board were made by a majority vote. The Officers of State had no vote, but were to advise their inexperienced colleagues. The Ministers were individually responsible to the Council, although an adverse vote there or in a Committee would not necessarily require resignation. They were, however, collectively responsible for the budget, the total rejection of which entailed a new election. So far as the Executive Committees were concerned the principle of the reforms was that of the London County Council.

The Governor's authority became 'supervisory rather than executive', and normally he acted according to the advice of his Ministers. He was, however, authorized to carry out any executive or legislative measure upon certifying that it was 'of paramount importance to the public interest', as for example the prevention of injustice to minorities. He might also assume control of any department if he considered that a state of emergency had arisen. To safeguard the position of Government officials all measures affecting them were placed under the control of the Governor and the Secretary of State. The Governor 'will no longer be responsible himself for the administration of the Island; his duty will be, first and foremost, to see that those on whom the responsibility will now fall do not infringe the principles enunciated in the constitution for their guidance'.[1]

[1] *Parl. Pap.* [Cmd. 3131] of 1928: *passim*; *Parl. Pap.* [Cmd. 3419] of 1929: 15–56; *Parl. Pap.* [Cmd. 3862] of 1931: Constitution of Ceylon: *passim*; *Parl. Pap.* [Cmd. 2884] of 1927: 69–72; Bertram, *The Colonial Service*, x–xii and 188–92.

APPENDIX

Draft of a Commission passed under the Great Seal of the United Kingdom appointing William Henry Gregory, Esquire, to be Governor and Commander-in-Chief of the Island of Ceylon and its Dependencies.[1]

VICTORIA, by the Grace of God, of the United Kingdom of Great Britain and Ireland, Queen, Defender of the Faith, to Our trusty and well-beloved William Henry Gregory, Esquire, Greeting:

I. Whereas by certain letters-patent, under the Great Seal of Our United Kingdom of Great Britain and Ireland, bearing date at Westminster, the fourth day of March, one thousand eight hundred and sixty-five, in the twenty-eighth year of Our Reign, We did constitute and appoint Our trusty and well-beloved Sir Hercules George Robert Robinson, Knight, now Knight Commander of Our Most Distinguished Order of Saint Michael and Saint George, to be Our Governor and Commander-in-Chief, in and over Our Island of Ceylon, with the territories and dependencies thereof, during Our Will and Pleasure: Now know you that We have revoked and determined, and by these presents do revoke and determine, the said recited letters-patent, and every clause, article, and thing therein contained. And further know you that We, reposing especial trust and confidence in the prudence, courage, and loyalty of you the said William Henry Gregory, Esquire, of Our special grace, certain knowledge, and mere motion, have thought fit to constitute and appoint, and by these presents do constitute and appoint you to be, for and during Our will and pleasure, Our Governor and Commander-in-Chief in and over Our said Island of Ceylon, with the territories and dependencies thereof, and of all forts and garrisons erected and established, or which may be erected and established within the same. And we do declare that, in the interpretation of this Our Commission, and of any such instructions as hereinafter are mentioned, the term 'Our said Island' shall be understood to include the said Island of Ceylon, and all such territories, dependencies, forts, and garrisons as aforesaid. And We do hereby authorize and command you to do and execute all things in due manner that shall belong to your said command, and the trust We have reposed in you, according to the several powers and directions granted or appointed you by this Our present Commission, and the instructions given to you, or by such further instructions as may hereafter be

[1] C.O. 381. 28: Printed Letters-Patent dated Jan. 8, 1872.

given by Us under Our sign-manual and signet, or by Our Order in Our Privy Council, or through one of Our Principal Secretaries of State, and according to such laws as are now, or shall hereafter be, in force in Our said island.

II. And whereas His late Majesty King William IV did, by certain letters-patent, under the great seal of Our said United Kingdom of Great Britain and Ireland, bearing date at Westminster, the nineteenth day of March, one thousand eight hundred and thirty-three, in the third year of His reign, grant, ordain, and appoint that there should be within the said Island of Ceylon two separate Councils, that is to say, one Council to be called the Legislative Council, and one other Council to be called the Executive Council: Now We do hereby declare Our pleasure to be that the said Councils shall be respectively constituted in such manner and of such persons as may be directed by the instructions accompanying this Our Commission, or by any other instructions which may from time to time be addressed to you by Us under Our sign-manual and signet, or by Our Order in Our Privy Council.

III. And We do hereby authorize and empower you with the advice and consent of the said Legislative Council, to enact laws for the peace, order, and good government of Our said island, subject nevertheless to all such rules and regulations as We, by Our instructions under Our sign-manual and signet, may from time to time make for your and their guidance therein: Provided, nevertheless, that nothing herein contained shall affect the undoubted right of Ourselves, Our heirs and successors, with the advice and consent of Parliament, or with the advice of Our or their Privy Council, to repeal or amend any law so made as aforesaid, or to make from time to time all such laws as may to us or them appear necessary for the peace, order, and good government of Our said island, as fully and effectually as if these presents had not been made.

IV. And We do hereby authorize and empower you to keep and use the public seal of Our said island for sealing all things whatsoever that shall pass the said seal.

V. And We do hereby authorize and empower you to make and execute in Our name and on Our behalf, under the said public seal, grants and dispositions of any lands which may lawfully be granted or disposed of by Us within Our said island, either in conformity with instructions under Our sign-manual and signet, or in conformity with such regulations as are now in force, or may be made by you in that behalf, with the advice of Our said Executive Council, and duly published in Our said island.

VI. And We do hereby authorize and empower you to constitute and appoint all such Judges, Commissioners of Oyer and Terminer, Justices of the Peace, and other necessary officers and ministers as may lawfully be appointed by Us, all of whom are to hold their offices during Our pleasure.

VII. And We do hereby authorize and empower you, upon sufficient cause to you appearing, to suspend from the exercise of his office within Our said island any person exercising any such office under or by virtue of any Commission or Warrant granted or to be granted by Us in Our name or under Our authority, which suspension shall continue and have effect only until Our pleasure therein shall be made known and signified to you. And we do strictly require and enjoin you, in proceeding to any such suspension, to observe the directions in that behalf given to you by Our instructions accompanying this Our Commission.

VIII. And We do hereby authorize and empower you, as you shall see occasion, in Our name and on Our behalf, when any crime has been committed within Our said Island, to grant a pardon to any accomplice, not being the actual perpetrator of such crime, who shall give such information and evidence as shall lead to the apprehension and conviction of the principal offender; and further, to grant to any offender convicted of any Crime in any Court, or before any Judge, Justice, or Magistrate within Our said island, a pardon, either free or subject to lawful conditions, or any respite of the execution of the sentence of any such offender for such period as to you may seem fit, and to remit any fines, penalties, or forfeitures which may become due and payable to Us.

IX. And We do hereby declare Our pleasure to be that in the event of your death, incapacity, or absence from Our said island, all and every the powers and authorities herein granted to you shall be, and the same are hereby vested in such person as may be appointed by Us under Our sign-manual and signet to be Our Lieutenant-Governor of Our said island, or if there shall be no such Lieutenant-Governor, then in such person or persons as may be appointed by Us under Our sign-manual and signet to administer the Government of Our said Island, and in case there shall be no person or persons within Our said Island so appointed by Us, then in the Senior Officer for the time being in command of Our regular troops in Our said island.

X. And We do hereby require and command all officers and ministers, civil and military, and all other the inhabitants of Our said island to be obedient, aiding, and assisting unto you the said William Henry Gregory, or, in the event of your death, incapacity, or absence, to such other person or persons as may, under the provisions of this Our Commission, administer the Government of Our said island.

In witness whereof We have caused these Our letters to be made patent. Witness Ourself at Westminster, the eighth day of January, in the thirty-fifth year of Our reign.

By warrant under the Queen's sign-manual.

C. ROMILLY.

Draft of Instructions passed under the Royal Sign Manual and Signet to William Henry Gregory, Esquire, as Governor and Commander-in-Chief of the Island of Ceylon and its Dependencies.[1]

VICTORIA R.

Instructions to Our trusty and well-beloved William Henry Gregory, Esquire, Our Governor and Commander-in-Chief in and over Our Island of Ceylon and its Dependencies, or in his absence to our Lieutenant-Governor or the Officer administering the Government of Our said Island and its Dependencies for the time being.

Given at Our Court at Windsor this eighth day of January 1872, in the Thirty-fifth Year of Our reign.

I. Whereas by a Commission, under the Great Seal of Our United Kingdom of Great Britain and Ireland, bearing even date herewith, We have constituted and appointed you to be for and during Our will and pleasure Our Governor and Commander-in-Chief in and over Our Island of Ceylon, with its Territories and Dependencies, and have further authorized and commanded you to do and execute all things in due manner that shall belong to your said Command and the trust We have reposed in you, according to the several powers and directions therein mentioned, and particularly according to such instructions as should therewith be given you: Now, therefore, We do, by these Our Instructions, under Our sign-manual and signet, being the instructions so referred to as aforesaid, declare Our pleasure to be that you shall, with all due solemnity, cause Our said commission to be read and published in the presence of the Chief Justice, or in his absence, of any other Judge of the Supreme Court of Our said island, and that you shall then and there take the oath of allegiance in the form provided by an Act passed in the Session holden in the thirty-first and thirty-second years of Our reign, intituled, 'An Act to Amend the Law relating to Promissory Oaths'; and likewise that you take the usual oath for the due execution of

[1] C.O. 381. 28: Printed Instructions dated Jan. 8, 1872.

the office of Our Governor and Commander-in-Chief in and over Our said island and for the due and impartial administration of justice, which said oaths the Chief Justice or other Judge as aforesaid is hereby required to tender and administer unto you.

II. And We do hereby authorize and require you, from time to time, and at any time hereafter, by yourself or by any other person to be authorized by you in that behalf, to administer to all and every person or persons as you shall think fit, who shall hold any office, or place of trust or profit, the said oath of allegiance, together with such other oaths as may from time to time be prescribed by any Laws or statutes in that behalf made and provided.

III. And whereas We have, by Our said commission, declared Our pleasure to be that the Executive Council of Our said island shall be constituted in such manner and of such persons as shall in that behalf be directed by Our instructions given you, with Our said commission, or according to such further powers, instructions, and authorities as therein are mentioned: now We do, by these Our instructions, direct and appoint the undermentioned officers to be Members of Our said Executive Council, that is to say, the senior military officer for the time being in command of Our regular troops within Our said island, and the persons for the time being lawfully discharging the functions of Colonial Secretary, of Queen's Advocate, of Colonial Treasurer, and of Auditor General for our said island: Provided always, that when the senior officer for the time being in command of Our regular troops within Our said island shall be in the administration of the Government thereof, his place in the said Council shall be filled by the next senior officer in command of our regular troops therein.

IV. And We do direct and appoint that you do forthwith communicate to Our said Executive Council these Our instructions, and likewise all others, from time to time, in the execution of which their consent and concurrence are requisite, or which you shall find convenient for Our service to be imparted to them.

V. And We do further direct and appoint that Our said Executive Council shall not proceed with the dispatch of business unless duly summoned by your authority, nor unless two Members at least, exclusive of yourself, or in your absence of the Presiding Member, be present and assisting throughout the whole of the Meetings at which any such business shall be dispatched.

VI. And We do further direct and appoint that you do attend and preside at the Meetings of Our said Executive Council, unless when prevented by some necessary and reasonable cause, and that in your absence the Senior Member of the said Council actually present shall preside at all such Meetings.

VII. And We do further direct and appoint that a full and exact journal or minute be kept of all the deliberations, acts, proceedings, votes, and resolutions of Our said Executive Council, and that at each Meeting of the said Council, the minutes of the last preceding Meeting shall be read over, and confirmed, or amended, as the case may require, before proceeding to the dispatch of any other business, and that twice in each year a full transcript of all the said minutes for the preceding half-year be transmitted to us through one of Our principal Secretaries of State.

VIII. And We do further direct and appoint that, in execution of the powers and authorities committed to you by Our said Commission, you do in all cases consult with our Executive Council, excepting only in cases which may be of such a nature that in your judgement Our service would sustain material prejudice by consulting the said Council thereon, or when the matters to be decided shall be too unimportant to require their advice, or too urgent to admit of their advice being given by the time within which it may be necessary for you to act in respect of any such matters: provided that in all such urgent cases you do subsequently, and at the earliest practicable period, communicate to Our said Executive Council the measures which you have so adopted, with the reasons thereof.

IX. And We do further direct and appoint that no question shall be brought before Our said Executive Council for their advice or decision excepting only such questions as may be proposed by you for that purpose: provided, nevertheless, that if any Member shall, by application in writing, request you so to propose any question, it shall be competent to any such Member to record upon the said minutes such his written application, together with the answer which may be returned by you to the same.

X. And We do authorize you in your discretion, and if it shall in any case appear right so to do, to act in the exercise of the power committed to you by Our said Commission in opposition to the advice which may in any such case be given to you by the Members of the said Executive Council: provided, nevertheless, that every such proceeding shall be fully reported to Us by the first convenient opportunity, together with the grounds and reasons thereof: and we do further direct that in every case it shall be competent to any Member of the said Council to record at length on the said Minutes the grounds of any advice or opinion he may give upon any question brought under the consideration of such Council.

XI. And Whereas we have by our said Commission declared Our will and pleasure to be that the Legislative Council of Our said Island shall be constituted in such manner and of such persons as shall in that behalf be directed by Our instructions given you with our said Commission, or according to such further powers, instructions and authorities as therein are mentioned; now We do by these Our instructions direct and appoint that our said Council shall consist of Official and Unofficial Members, and that the undermentioned persons shall be the Official Members of Our said Council, that is to say, the Senior Officer for the time being in command of Our Regular Troops within Our said Island not being in the administration of the Government thereof, and the persons for the time being lawfully discharging the functions of Colonial Secretary, of Queen's Advocate, of Auditor General, of Colonial Treasurer, of Government Agent for the Western Province, of Government Agent for the Central Province, of Surveyor General, and of Collector of Customs at Our port at Colombo: provided always, that when the Senior Officer for the time being in command of Our Regular Troops within Our said Island shall be in the Administration of the Government thereof, his place in the said Council shall be filled by the next Senior Officer in command of Our Regular Troops therein.

XII. And We do hereby revoke all appointments heretofore made of unofficial Members of Our said Council, and We do authorize and empower you from time to time to nominate and appoint, by any instrument under the Public Seal of Our said Island, any fit and proper person or persons to be such unofficial Members. Provided that the total number of the unofficial Members resident in Our said Island, and capable of acting in the exercise of their offices, shall at no time exceed the number of six. Provided also, that in case any unofficial Member of Our said Council shall at any time be absent from Our said Island, or incapable of acting in the exercise of his office, it shall be lawful for you to appoint, provisionally, any fit person to be a Legislative Councillor in place of such Member, and so soon as such Member shall return to Our said Island, or shall be declared by you to be capable of exercising his office of Legislative Councillor, the person so provisionally appointed shall forthwith cease to be Member of Our said Council: Provided also that the appointment by you of any unofficial Member of the Legislative Council shall be forthwith signified to Us, and may be disallowed by Us through one of Our Principal Secretaries of State, and that every Member of the said Council shall hold his office during Our pleasure.

XIII. And We do further direct that in the said Council the official Members shall take precedence of the unofficial Members, and that the official Members shall between themselves take precedence according to the order in which their respective offices are herein enumerated, and the unofficial Members according to the priority of their respective appointments.

XIV. And We further hereby authorize and require you to frame and propose to the said Council, for their adoption, and with the advice of the said Council, from time to time to make, alter, revoke, and renew, such standing rules and orders as may be necessary to ensure punctuality of attendance of the Members of the said Council, and to prevent Meetings of the said Council being holden without convenient notice to the several Members thereof, and to maintain order and method in the dispatch of business and in the conduct of all debates in the said Council, and to secure the due deliberation in the passing of laws, and to provide that before the passing of any law intended to affect the interest of private persons, due notice of the same is given to all persons concerned therein; all which rules and orders, not being repugnant to your said Commission, or to these Our instructions, or to any other instructions which you may receive from Us, shall at all times be followed and observed, and shall be binding upon the said Council, unless the same or any of them be disallowed by Us.

XV. And whereas We have by Our said Commission given and granted to you full power and authority, with the advice and consent of the said Council, to enact laws for the peace, order, and good government of Our said Island, subject, nevertheless, to all such rules and regulations as We, by Our instructions under Our sign-manual and signet, may from time to time make for your and their guidance therein: Now We do hereby direct and appoint that in the execution of the powers vested in you and the said Council you do observe the following rules and regulations (that is to say):

XVI. The said Council shall not be competent to act in any case unless six Members at the least of such Council, in addition to yourself, or to the Member who may preside therein in your absence, shall be present at and throughout the Meetings of such Council.

XVII. You shall attend and preside in the said Council, except when you may be prevented by some insuperable impediment; and at any Meeting of the said Council which may be holden during your absence, the Member shall preside who shall be first in precedence of those present.

XVIII. All questions proposed for debate in the said Council shall be decided by the majority of votes, it being Our pleasure that you, or the Member presiding in your absence, shall have an original vote, in common with the other Members of the said Council, and also a casting vote, if upon any question the votes shall be equally divided.

XIX. It shall be competent for any Member of Our said Council to propose any questions for debate therein, and if such proposal shall be seconded by any other Member, such question shall be debated and disposed of accordingly, excepting only that no ordinance shall be enacted, nor any vote or resolution passed, nor any question admitted to debate at the said Council, where the object of such ordinance, vote, resolution, or question may be to dispose of or charge any part of Our revenue arising within Our said Island, unless such ordinance, vote, resolution, or question shall have been first proposed by yourself, or the proposal of the same shall have been expressly allowed or directed by you.

XX. Every Ordinance to be enacted by you with the advice and consent of the said Council shall henceforth be styled 'Ordinance enacted by the Governor of Ceylon, with the advice and consent of the Legislative Council thereon'.

XXI. All Ordinances made by you with the advice of the said Council shall be distinguished by Titles, and the Ordinances of each year shall be also distinguished by Consecutive Numbers, commencing in each successive year with the Number One, and every such Ordinance shall be divided into successive Clauses or Paragraphs consecutively numbered, and to every such Clause there shall be annexed in the margin a short Summary of its contents.

XXII. In the passing of all Ordinances each different matter is to be provided for by a different Ordinance without intermixing into one and the same Ordinance such things as have no proper relation to each other; and no clause is to be inserted in or annexed to any Ordinance which shall be foreign to what the title of such Ordinance imports; and no perpetual clause is to be part of any temporary Ordinance.

XXIII. You are not to propose or assent to any Ordinance whatever respecting the Constitution or Proceedings of the said Council in relation to any of the matters mentioned or referred to in your said Commission, or in Our Letters-Patent of the 19th day of March, 1833, or in these Our Instructions, which shall be in anywise repugnant to or inconsistent with such Commission, Letters-Patent, or Instructions, or repugnant to any Act of Parliament, or to any Order made or to be made by Us in Our Privy Council, extending to or in force within Our said Island, and any such Ordinance, or pretended

Ordinance, shall, to the extent of such repugnancy or inconsistency, be absolutely null and void to all intents and purposes.

XXIV. You are not to Assent in Our Name to any Ordinance of any of the Classes herein specified, that is to say:

1. Any Ordinance for the Divorce of Persons joined together in Holy Matrimony.

2. Any Ordinance whereby any Grant of Land or Money, or other Donation or Gratuity, may be made to yourself.

3. Any Ordinance whereby any increase or diminution may be made in the Number, Salary, or Allowances of the Public Officers.

4. Any Ordinance whereby any Paper or other Currency may be made a Legal Tender, except the Coin of the Realm, or other Gold or Silver Coin.

5. Any Ordinance imposing differential duties.

6. Any Ordinance, the provisions of which shall appear inconsistent with obligations imposed upon Us by Treaty.

7. Any Ordinance interfering with the discipline or control of Our forces in Our said Island by land and sea.

8. Any Ordinance of an extraordinary nature and importance, whereby Our prerogative or the rights and property of Our subjects not residing in Our said Island, or the trade and shipping of Our United Kingdom and its dependencies, may be prejudiced.

9. Any Ordinance whereby persons not of European birth or descent may be subjected or made liable to any disabilities or restrictions to which persons of European birth or descent are not also subjected or made liable.

10. Any Ordinance containing provisions to which Our assent has been once refused, or which have been disallowed by Us:

Unless such Ordinance shall contain a clause suspending the operation of such Ordinance until the signification in Our said Island of Our pleasure thereupon, or unless you shall have satisfied yourself that an urgent necessity exists requiring that such Ordinance be brought into immediate operation, in which case you are authorized to assent in Our name to such Ordinance, unless the same shall be repugnant to the Law of England or inconsistent with any obligations imposed on Us by Treaty. But you are to transmit to Us, by the earliest opportunity, the Ordinance so assented to, together with your reasons for assenting thereto.

XXV. No private Ordinance is to be passed whereby the property of any private person may be affected in which there is not a saving of the rights of Us, Our heirs and successors, and of all Bodies politic and corporate, and of all other persons, except such as are

T

mentioned in the said Ordinance and those claiming by, from, through, and under them; and you are not to give your assent to any private Bill until proof be made before you in the said Legislative Council, and entered in the Council Book, that adequate and timely notification was made by public advertisement, or otherwise, of the Parties' intention to apply for such Bill before any such Bill was brought into the said Council; and a certificate under your hand shall be transmitted with and annexed to every such private Ordinance, signifying that such notification has been given, and declaring the manner of giving the same.

XXVI. And We do further direct and appoint that when any Ordinance shall have been passed by you with the advice of the said Council, the same shall forthwith be laid before Us for Our final assent, disallowance, or other direction thereupon to be signified through you; for which purpose We do hereby require you, by the earliest occasion next after the enactment of the said Ordinance, to transmit to Us, through one of Our Principal Secretaries of State, a transcript in duplicate of the same, together with a marginal abstract thereof, duly authenticated under the Public Seal of Our said Island, and by your own signature.

XXVII. And We do further direct you to transmit to the Chief Judge of the Supreme Court of Our said Island, to be enrolled in the said Court, a transcript duly authenticated in the manner before mentioned of every Ordinance passed by you with the advice and consent of the said Legislative Council. You are also, from time to time, to transmit to the Chief Judge of the said Supreme Court, to be enrolled in the said Court, a certificate under your hand and seal of the effect of every order which you may have received from Us, confirming or disallowing or amending the provisions of any such Ordinance, which certificate shall, in like manner, be enrolled in the said Supreme Court and there remain on record, to the intent that the Judges of the said Court may, without further or other proof, take cognizance of all Ordinances to be made and promulgated for the peace, order, and good Government of Our said Island: Provided always, and We do hereby declare, that the Judges of the said Court have not, and shall not have, any right or authority to prevent or delay the enrolment of any such Ordinance, and that the validity thereof doth not and shall not depend upon any such enrolment.

XXVIII. And We do further direct and appoint that in the month of January, or at the earliest practicable period at the commencement of each year, you do cause a complete collection to be published, for general information, of all Ordinances enacted during the preceding year.

XXIX. And We do further direct that Minutes be regularly kept of the proceedings of the said Legislative Council by the Clerk thereof, and that the said Council shall not proceed to the dispatch of business until the Minutes of the last preceding meeting have been first read over, and confirmed or corrected, as may be necessary; and that twice in each year you do transmit to Us, through one of Our Principal Secretaries of State, a full and exact copy of the Minutes of the said Council.

XXX. And whereas We have by our said Commission authorized and empowered you to make and execute in Our name and on Our behalf, under the public seal of Our said Island, grants and dispositions of any lands which may be lawfully granted or disposed of by Us within Our said Island: Now We do direct and enjoin you, before disposing of any vacant or waste lands to Us belonging in our said Island, to cause the same to be surveyed, and such reservations made thereout as you may think necessary or desirable to be reserved and set apart for public roads or other internal communication by land or water, or for purposes of military defence, or for any other purposes of public safety, convenience, utility, health, or enjoyment. And we do further direct and enjoin that you shall not directly or indirectly purchase for yourself any of such lands without Our special permission given to you in that behalf through one of Our Principal Secretaries of State.

XXXI. And We do further direct and appoint that all Commissions to be granted by you to any person or persons for exercising any office or employment be granted during pleasure only; and that whenever you shall appoint to any vacant office or employment any person not by Us specially directed to be appointed thereto, you shall at the same time expressly apprize such person that such appointment is to be considered only as temporary and provisional until Our allowance or disallowance thereof be signified.

XXXII. And whereas We have by Our said Commission authorized you, upon sufficient cause to you appearing, to suspend from the exercise of his Office within Our said Island any person exercising the same under and by virtue of any Commission or Warrant granted or to be granted by Us in Our name or under Our authority: Now We do charge and require you that before proceeding to any such suspension you do signify by a statement in writing to the person so to be suspended the grounds of such your intended proceedings against him; and that you do call upon such person to communicate to you in writing a statement of the grounds upon which, and the evidence by which, he may be desirous to exculpate himself, which statement and exculpation you will lay before the Executive Council of Our said Island; and having consulted the said Council thereupon, you will cause to be recorded in the Minutes of the said Council whether they or the majority of them do or do not assent to the said suspension; and if you thereupon proceed to such suspension you are to transmit both of the said statements, together with the Minutes of Council, to Us, through one of Our Principal Secretaries of State, by the earliest conveyance; but if in any case the interests of Our service shall appear to you to demand that the person shall cease to exercise the powers and functions of his office instantly, or before there shall be time to take the proceedings hereinbefore directed, you shall then interdict such person from the exercise of his powers and functions, preserving to him, however, until such proceedings shall have been taken, the emoluments and advantages of his office.

XXXIII. And whereas We have by Our said Commission given and granted unto you power and authority, as you shall see occasion, in Our name and on Our behalf, to grant to any offender convicted of any crime in any Court or before any Judge, Justice, or Magistrate within Our said Island, a pardon, either free or subject to lawful conditions: Now We do require and enjoin you to call upon the Judge who presided at the trial of any offender who shall have been condemned to suffer death by the sentence of any Court within Our said Island, to make to you a written Report of the case of such offender; and such Report of the said Judge shall by you be taken into consideration at the first meeting thereafter which may be conveniently held of Our said Executive Council, where the said Judge may be specially summoned to attend: and you shall not pardon or reprieve any such offender as aforesaid, unless, upon receiving the advice of Our Executive Council thereon, it shall appear to you expedient so to do; but in all such cases you are to decide either to extend or withhold a pardon or a reprieve, according to your own deliberate judgement, whether the members of Our said Executive Council concur therein or otherwise, entering nevertheless on the Minutes of the said Council a Minute of your reasons at length, in case you should decide any such question in opposition to the judgement of the majority of the members thereof.

XXXIV. And Whereas you will receive through one of Our Principal Secretaries of State a Book of Tables in blank, commonly called the Blue Book, to be annually filled up with certain returns relative to the Revenue and Expenditure, Militia, Public Works, Legislation, Pensions, Population, Schools, Course of Exchange, Imports and Exports, Agricultural Produce, Manufactures, and other matters in the said Blue Book more particularly specified with reference to the state and condition of Our said Island of Ceylon: Now We do hereby signify Our Pleasure that all such Returns be accurately prepared and punctually transmitted to Us from year to year through one of Our Principal Secretaries of State.

XXXV. And Whereas great prejudice may happen to Our Service and to the Security of Our said Island by your Absence from thence, you are not upon any pretence whatever to quit Our said Island without having first obtained leave from Us for so doing under Our Sign-Manual and Signet, or through one of our Principal Secretaries of State. V.R.

BIBLIOGRAPHY

PRIMARY AUTHORITIES

MANUSCRIPT

The most important source of information for the period from 1798 to 1885 is the Colonial Office archives in the Public Record Office. Series C.O. 54 contains the Governors' dispatches with the majority of their enclosures, the Colonial Office Memoranda, and drafts of dispatches from the Secretaries of State. The volumes in C.O. 54 catalogued as *Public Offices and Miscellaneous* contain the Colonial Office correspondence with the Treasury and other Government departments, the Crown Agents, and miscellaneous correspondents. Series C.O. 55 contains the dispatches of the Secretaries of State to the Governors of Ceylon, together with the Commissions and Instructions to the Governors prior to 1831. C.O. 381. 26, 27, and 28 contain the Commissions and Instructions to the Governors and Lieutenant-Governors from 1837 to 1872.

The Ceylon Records in the India Office Library cover the period from Pybus's embassy to about 1802. After 1798 many of the dispatches are duplicates of those in the early volumes of series C.O. 54. Volume 54 contains contemporary copies of manuscripts written in 1799 by Major Robertson and about 1801 by Sylvester Douglass, later Lord Glenbervie, with marginal notes signed 'H.D.' (Henry Dundas). North's letters to the Marquess Wellesley, Governor-General of India, are in British Museum Additional Manuscripts Nos. 13865, 13866, and 13867.

PRINTED

Aitchison, C. U. *A Collection of Treaties, Engagements, and Sanads Relating to India and Neighbouring Countries.* Vol. x. Calcutta 1909. Published by authority of the Foreign Department of the Government of India.

Anthonisz, R. G., Government Archivist. *Report on the Dutch Records in the Government Archives at Colombo.* Colombo, 1907.

Boyd, Hugh. *The Miscellaneous Works of Hugh Boyd, the Author of the Letters of Junius. With an Account of his Life and Writings, by L. D. Campbell.* 4 vols. London, 1800.

Ceylon Government. *Addresses Delivered in the Legislative Council of Ceylon by Governors of the Colony. Together With the Replies of Council.* 4 vols. Colombo, 1876, 1877, 1900, and 1905.

Ceylon Government. *The Ceylon Civil List.* Colombo, 1863 ff.

Ceylon Government. *Papers Relating to Buddhist Temporalities.* N.D. This contains the Reports of the Temple Lands Commissioners, 1857–65, and the Report of the Buddhist Temporalities Commissioners, Oct. 17, 1876.

Codrington, H. W., ed. *Diary of Mr. John D'Oyly.* Published by the Ceylon Branch of the Royal Asiatic Society. Vol. xxv, No. 69. Colombo, 1917.

Colonial Office. *The Colonial Office List.* London, 1862 ff. Since 1927 the title has been *The Dominions Office and Colonial Office List.*

Colonial Office. *Regulations for His Majesty's Colonial Service.* London, 1919.

Dickman, C. *The Ceylon Civil Service Manual, Being a Compilation of Government Minutes, Circulars, &c. With an Appendix Containing a Summary of Colonial Regulations, a List of the Legislative Enactments in Force, and a Glossary of Ceylon Terms. Published with the Permission of Government.* Colombo, 1865.

Dickman, C. *The Ceylon Civil Service Manual, Being a Compilation of Government Minutes, Colonial Regulations, Circulars, &c. With an Appendix containing a Glossary of Ceylon Terms. Published with the Permission of Government.* Ed. 3. Colombo, 1883. The third edition was revised and considerably lengthened.

Hansard's Parliamentary Debates. The most important references relate to Lord Torrington's administration and are cited in the footnotes.

Ievers, R. W. *Manual of the North Central Province, Ceylon.* Colombo, 1899. An official publication by the Government Agent of the Province.

Keane, Captain Sir John, Bt., R.A. *Report on Irrigation in Ceylon.* Colombo, 1905. Also published in Sessional Papers Ceylon, xlv 1905.

Malmesbury, Earl of, ed. *Diaries and Correspondence of James Harris, First Earl of Malmesbury; Containing an Account of his Missions to the Courts of Madrid, Frederick the Great, Catherine the Second, and The Hague; and his Special Missions to Berlin, Brunswick, and the French Republic.* 4 vols. London, 1844.

Mesurier, C. J. R. Le. *Manual of the Nuwara Eliya District of the Central Province, Ceylon.* Colombo, 1893. An official account by the Assistant Government Agent.

Neil, Rev. Wm. *The Cleghorn Papers, A Footnote to History, Being the Diary, 1795–1796, of Hugh Cleghorn of Strathvithie.* London, 1927.

Parliamentary Papers are cited in the footnotes.

Pybus, John. *Account of Mr. Pybus' mission to the King of Kandy in 1762.* Printed from the records of the Madras Government. Colombo, 1862.

War Office. *Manual of Military Law.* London, 1916.

Ward, Sir H. G. *Speeches and Minutes of the late Sir Henry George Ward, K.G.C.M.G., Governor and Commander-in-Chief in and over the Island of Ceylon with the Dependencies thereof. With other papers connected with his administration of the Government of Ceylon, 1855–1860.* Colombo, 1864.

Ward, Sir H. G. *Ceylon Papers.* N.D. An unofficial and incomplete collection of his addresses and minutes, but containing Moorsom's Report on the cost of the railway which is lacking from the publication cited previously.

SECONDARY AUTHORITIES

Alexander Alexander. *The Life of Alexander Alexander, written by himself.* John Howell, ed. 2 vols. Edinburgh, 1830.

An Officer, Late of the Ceylon Rifles. *Ceylon, A General Description of the Island, Historical, Physical, Statistical, Containing the Most Recent Information.* 2 vols. London, 1876. The author is believed to have been Captain H. Suckling (*Ceylon Literary Monthly Register*, i. 288).

Anon. *A Narrative of Events Which Have Recently Occurred in the Island of Ceylon, Written by a Gentleman on the Spot.* London, 1815. The author was Captain William Tolfrey (J. H. Lewis, *C.A. and L.R.* vi. iii. 145).

Anon. *Ceylon and her Planting Enterprise: in Tea, Cacao, Cardamoms, Cinchona, Coconut, and Areca Palms. A Field for the Investment of British Capital and Energy.* Colombo, 1885.

Anon. *Ceylon and the Government of Lord Torrington, Containing A Correction of the Errors in an Article in the Quarterly Review for December 1850, Entitled 'The Mysteries of Ceylon'.* London, 1851.

Anon. *Days of Old: Or the Commencement of the Coffee Enterprise in Ceylon.* Colombo, 1878.

Anon. *History of the Connection of the British Government with Buddhism and Hindu-Buddhism, from its Origin in 1815 to the Present Date showing the Existing State of Serfdom in the Island of Ceylon.* Colombo, 1889. The author attacked the Ceylon Government because it respected the rights of the Buddhist church.

Anon. *The Private Life of a Ceylon Coffee Planter.* Colombo, N.D.

B., F. *Memorials of the late Honourable Sir Samuel Grenier, Attorney-General of Ceylon.* Colombo, 1892.

Baker, Sir Samuel W. *Eight Years' Wanderings in Ceylon.* London, 1855.

Barrow, Sir George. *Ceylon Past and Present.* London, 1857.

Bertolacci, Anthony. *A View of the Agricultural, Commercial, and Financial Interests of Ceylon, with an Appendix; Containing Some of the Principal Laws and Usages of the Candians: Port and Custom-House Regulations: Tables of Exports and Imports, Public Revenue and Expenditure, &c., &c.* London, 1817. Bertolacci and his father, a Corsican judge, were Royalists who assisted the British when they occupied Corsica and were forced to accompany them on their departure in 1796. Bertolacci had been North's Assistant in Corsica and went with him to Ceylon in 1798, retiring in 1814 on an annual pension of £500 as Controller-General of Customs and Acting Civil Auditor-General (C.O. 54. 3: Jan. 1, 1804; C.O. 54. 38: Apr. 13, 1810; *C.A. and L.R.* ix. i. 17–19). His book on the economic history of Ceylon is detailed and valuable.

Bingham, P. M. *History of the Public Works Department, Ceylon.* 3 vols. Colombo, 1921, 1922, and 1923.

Brown, Alexander. *The Coffee Planter's Manual. To Which is Added A Variety of Information useful to Planters, Including a Summary of Practical Opinions on the Manuring of Coffee Estates, &c. Thoroughly Revised with Notes by Practical Planters in 1880.* Colombo, 1880.

Bruce, Sir Charles, G. C. M. G. *The Broad Stone of Empire: Problems of Crown Colony Administration.* 2 vols. London, 1910.

Bussche, Captain L. de. *Letters on Ceylon, particularly relative to the Kingdom of Kandy.* London, 1826.

Butts, Lieutenant de. *Rambles in Ceylon.* London, 1841.

Campbell, Lieutenant-Colonel James. *Excursions, Adventures, and Field-Sports in Ceylon; Its Commercial and Military Importance, and Numerous Advantages to the British Emigrant.* 2 vols. London, 1843.

Ceylon Almanac and Compendium of Useful Information for the Year 1835. Colombo, 1835.

Ceylon Almanac and Compendium of Useful Information for the Year 1836. Colombo, 1836.

Ceylon Almanac and Annual Register For the Year of our Lord 1859. Colombo, 1859.

Ceylon Antiquary and Literary Register, The. Colombo, 1915 ff. Contains many valuable articles on the early British period.

Ceylon Calendar for the Year of Our Lord 1815, Containing Lists of His Majesty's Civil, Judicial, Naval, Military, and Medical Establishments in the Island with other matters of useful information. Ceylon (?), 1815. The Bodleian Library copy has contemporary notes of changes in the civil and military services.

Chitty, Simon Casie. *The Ceylon Gazetteer, containing an Accurate Account of the Districts, Provinces, Cities, Towns, Principal Villages, Harbours, Rivers, Lakes, &c., of the Island of Ceylon.* Ceylon, 1834.

Codrington, H. W. *A Short History of Ceylon.* London, 1926.

Colonial Intelligencer, or Aborigines' Friend, The. London. Vol. II, Nos. xii and xiii, new series, Apr. and May 1849.

Colonist. *A Few Remarks upon Colonel Forbes' Pamphlet on Recent Disturbances in Ceylon.* Colombo, 1850.

Colonist. *Is Ceylon to be Sacrificed at the Shrine of Party?* Colombo, 1850.

Cordiner, Rev. James. *A Description of Ceylon, containing an Account of the Country, Inhabitants, and Natural Productions, with Narratives of a Tour Round the Island in 1800, the Campaign in Candy in 1803, and a Journey to Ramisseram in 1804.* 2 vols. London, 1807. Cordiner was chaplain to the Colombo garrison 1799–1804. The book is valuable but strongly biased by friendship for North, especially in the account of Kandyan policy and the Davie massacre.

Danson, John Towne. *Economic and Statistical Studies, 1840–1890.* London, 1906.

Davy, John, M.D., F.R.S. *An Account of the Interior of Ceylon and of its Inhabitants, With Travels in that Island.* London, 1821. Davy served in Ceylon on the Army Medical Staff, 1816–20.

Dictionary of National Biography, Sir Sidney Lee, ed., London. Vol. lvi, 1898: and Supplement Vol. iii, 1901.

Digby, W. *Forty Years of Official and Unofficial Life in an Oriental Crown Colony; being the Life of Sir Richard F. Morgan, Kt., Queen's Advocate and Acting Chief Justice of Ceylon.* 2 vols. Madras, 1879.

D'Oyly, Sir John. *A Sketch of the Constitution of the Kandyan Kingdom.* London, 1832.

Doyne, W. T. *The Causes Which have Retarded the Construction of Railways in India, Referring especially to the Ceylon Railway; with Remedies suggested.* London, 1860.

Ferguson, A. M. *Ceylon Summary of Useful Information and Plantation Gazetteer for 1859.* Colombo, 1859.

Ferguson, A. M. *The Ceylon Commonplace Book; Directory; Road Book; and Compendium of Useful Information for 1861.* Colombo, 1861. A. M. Ferguson (1816–92) came to Ceylon in 1837, was a pioneer coffee planter, and later was one of the first to substitute cinchona and tea. He took a prominent part in the agitations for road and railway construction, and from 1859 was owner and editor of the *Colombo Observer.* His books and those of John Ferguson are valuable for the economic history of Ceylon.

Ferguson, A. M., and J., eds. *The Tropical Agriculturist: A Monthly Record of Information for Planters of Coffee, Tea, Cocoa, Cinchona, &c.* Colombo, 1881 ff.

Ferguson, A. M. and J., eds. *All About Spices.* Colombo, 1889.

Ferguson, A. M. and J., eds. *All About Cinnamon: Including Practical Instructions for Planting, Cultivation, and Preparation for Market, with Information from a Variety of Sources.* Colombo, 1900 (?).

Ferguson, John. *Ceylon in 1883: The Leading Crown Colony of the British Empire; with an Account of the Progress made since 1803.* London, 1883.

Ferguson, John. *Ceylon in 1884: The Leading Crown Colony of the British Empire; with an Account of the Progress made since 1803.* London, 1884.

Ferguson, John. *Ceylon in the Jubilee Year, with an Account of the Progress made since 1803.* London and Colombo, 1887.

Ferguson, John. *Ceylon in 1893, describing the progress of the island since 1803.* London and Colombo, 1893.

Ferguson, John. *Ceylon in 1903, describing the progress of the island since 1803.* Colombo, 1903.

Ferguson, John, ed. *Pioneers of the Planting Enterprise in Ceylon; From 1830 Onwards.* 3 vols. Colombo, 1894, 1898, and 1900.

Forbes, Major (later Lieut.-Col.). *Eleven Years in Ceylon, Comprising Sketches of the Field Sports and Natural History of That Colony, and an Account of Its History and Antiquities.* 2 vols. London, 1840.

Forbes, Lieutenant-Colonel J. *Recent Disturbances and Military Executions in Ceylon.* Edinburgh, 1850. Colonel Forbes served in Ceylon from about 1826 to 1837, and was Commandant, Assistant Government Agent and District Judge of Matale. He was an able man with wide knowledge of the Sinhalese language and customs (C.O. 54. 154: May 10, 1837).

Gregory, Lady, ed. *Sir William Gregory, K.C.M.G., Formerly Member of Parliament and Sometime Governor of Ceylon. An*

Autobiography. ed. 2. London, 1894. A valuable account of Ceylon in the 'seventies.

Grey, Earl. *The Colonial Policy of Lord John Russell's Administration.* 2 vols. London, 1853.

Haafner, J. *Travels on Foot Through the Island of Ceylon.* London, 1821.

Haeckel, Ernst, trans. Clara Bell. *A Visit to Ceylon.* London, 1883.

Hall, Wilfred G. C. *Political Crime: A Critical Essay on the Law and Its Administration in Cases of a Certain Type.* London, 1923.

Henderson, Capt. J. M. *The History of the Rebellion in Ceylon, during Lord Torrington's Government. Affording a Comparison with Jamaica and Governor Eyre.* London, 1868.

Hughes, John, F.C.S. *Ceylon Coffee Soils and Manures. A Report to the Ceylon Coffee Planters' Association.* London, 1879.

Ireland, Alleyne. *Tropical Colonization.* New York, 1899.

Ireland, Alleyne. *The Far Eastern Tropics, Studies in the Administration of Tropical Dependencies.* Boston, 1905.

J., R.W. *Ceylon in the 'Fifties and 'Eighties, A Retrospect and Contrast of the Vicissitudes of the Planting Enterprise During a Period of Thirty Years, and of Life and Work in Ceylon.* Colombo, 1886.

Jenks, Edward. *The Government of the British Empire as at the End of the Year 1917.* London, 1918.

Johnston, Major A. *Narrative of the Operations of a Detachment in an Expedition to Candy in the Island of Ceylon, in the Year 1804.* London, 1810.

Journal of the Ceylon Branch of the Royal Asiatic Society. Colombo, 1845 ff.

Keith, A. B. *The Constitution, Administration, and Laws of the Empire.* London, 1924.

Knighton, W. *Forest Life in Ceylon.* 2 vols. London, 1854.

Lewin, Evans. *The Resources of the Empire and Their Development.* London, 1924.

Lewis, Frederick. *Sixty-Four Years in Ceylon: Reminiscences of Life and Adventure.* Ceylon, 1926.

Lord, Walter Frewen. *Sir Thomas Maitland, the Mastery of the Mediterranean.* London, 1897.

Lowell, A. L., and Stephens, H. Morse. *Colonial Civil Service; The Selection and Training of Colonial Officials in England, Holland, and France. With an Account of the East India College at Haileybury (1806–57).* New York, 1900.

Lucas, Sir C. P., K.C.B. *A Historical Geography of the British Colonies.* Vol. i, ed. 2, revised by R. E. Stubbs. Oxford, 1906.

Lucas, Sir C. P., K.C.B. *British Colonial Administration and its Agencies*, in *The Oxford Survey of the British Empire*. Ed. A. J. Herbertson and O. J. R. Howarth. Vol. vi. Oxford, 1914.

Marshall, Henry. *Notes on the Medical Topography of the Interior of Ceylon; and on the Health of the Troops Employed in the Kandyan Provinces, During the Years 1815–1820; with brief remarks on the prevailing diseases.* London, 1821.

Marshall, Henry. *Ceylon: A General Description of the Island and its Inhabitants; with an Historical Sketch of the Conquest of the Colony by the English.* London, 1846. Marshall was an army surgeon in Ceylon 1808–21, accompanied the troops to Kandy in 1815, and was senior medical officer in Kandy 1816–21. He was the most impartial and accurate of the early British writers on Ceylon.

Mellor, James R. *The Case of Ceylon.* London, 1868.

Methley, Miss V. *Transactions of the Royal Historical Society*, IV. i. 96–125. London, 1918.

Millie, P. D. *Thirty Years Ago: or Reminiscences of the Early Days of Coffee Planting in Ceylon.* Colombo, 1878.

Mills, Arthur. *Colonial Constitutions: An Outline of the Constitutional History and Existing Government of the British Dependencies: with Schedules of the Orders in Council, Statutes, and Parliamentary Documents Relating to Each Dependency.* London, 1856.

Mills, L. A. *British Malaya, 1824–1867.* Singapore, 1925.

Payne, C. W. *Ceylon, Its Products, Capabilities, and Climate.* London, 1854.

Percival, Captain Robert. *An Account of the Island of Ceylon, Containing its History, Geography, Natural History, with the Manners and Customs of its Various Inhabitants; to which is added the Journal of an Embassy to the Court of Candy. With an Appendix Containing some Particulars of the recent Hostilities with the King of Candy.* ed. 2. London, 1805. Interesting but inaccurate.

Perera, G. F. *The Ceylon Railway, the Story of Its Inception and Progress.* Colombo, 1925.

Philalethes. *The History of Ceylon from the Earliest Period to the Year 1815; with Characteristic Details of the Religion, Laws, and Manners of the People and a Collection of Their Moral Maxims and Ancient Proverbs.* London, 1817. Philalethes was the Rev. Robt. Fellowes, who obtained his information partly from previous writers and partly from his relative, Lieutenant Fellowes of the Second Ceylon Regiment (Lewis, *C.A. and L.R.* VIII. iii. 214–15).

Pieris, P. E. *Ceylon and the Hollanders, 1658–1796.* Tellippalai, Ceylon, 1918.

Pohath-Kehelpannala, T. B. *The Life of Ehelapola, Prime Minister to the Last King of Kandy; with Notes Relating to the King and the Court.* Colombo, 1896.

Pohath-Kehelpannala, T. B. *How the Last King of Kandy was captured by the British.* Colombo, 1896.

Pridham, Charles. *An Historical, Political, and Statistical Account of Ceylon and Its Dependencies.* 2 vols. London, 1849.

Sabonadière, Wm. *The Coffee Planter of Ceylon.* ed. 2. London, 1870.

Sirr, Henry Charles. *Ceylon and the Cingalese; Their History, Government, and Religion, The Antiquities, Institutions, Produce, Revenue, and Capabilities of the Island; with Anecdotes Illustrating the Manners and Customs of the People.* 2 vols. London, 1850.

Skinner, Major Thomas, C.M.G. *Fifty Years in Ceylon, An Autobiography.* Miss Skinner, ed. London, 1891. Very valuable and reliable.

Speculum. *Ceylon, Her Present Condition, Revenues, Taxes, and Expenditure, Described in a Series of Letters Addressed to 'The Ceylon Observer'.* Colombo, 1868. The author was George Wall, one of the unofficial members of the Legislative Council who resigned in 1864 (Ferguson, *Pioneers of the Planting Enterprise*, i. 82; Digby, *Morgan*, i. 268–73, and ii. 44).

Steuart, James. *Observations on Colonel Forbes' Pamphlet on the Recent Rebellion in Ceylon.* Colombo, 1850.

Steuart, James. *Notes on the Monetary System and Cinnamon Revenue of Ceylon.* Colombo, 1850.

Steuart, James. *Notes on Ceylon and its Affairs, During a Period of Thirty-Eight Years Ending in 1855. To Which are Appended some observations on the Antiquity of Point de Galle, and on the Pearl Fishery.* London, 1862.

Tennent, Sir James Emerson. *Ceylon, An Account of the Island Physical, Historical, and Topographical, with Notices of its Natural History, Antiquities, and Productions.* 2 vols. ed. 5. London, 1860. Reliable for the economic history of Ceylon.

Turner, L. J. B. *Handbook of Commercial and General Information for Ceylon.* Colombo, 1927.

Valentia, George, Viscount. *Voyages and Travels to India, Ceylon, the Red Sea, Abyssinia and Egypt, in the years 1802, 1803, 1804, 1805, and 1806.* 4 vols. London, 1811.

Ward, H. Marshall. *On the Morphology of Hemileia Vastatrix, The*

Fungus of the Coffee-Disease of Ceylon. London, 1881. Ward was brought to Ceylon by the Government to find a remedy, but failed.

Willis, J. C. *Ceylon, A Handbook for the Resident and the Traveller.* Colombo, 1907.

Wright, Arnold, ed. *Twentieth Century Impressions of Ceylon; Its History, People, Commerce, Industries, and Resources.* London, 1907.

SELECT BIBLIOGRAPHY, CHAPTER XIII

PRIMARY AUTHORITIES

The principal sources of information for the period from 1886 to 1931 are the Annual Ceylon Reports, the British Parliamentary Papers, and the Ceylon Sessional Papers. The Annual Ceylon Reports were published as Command Papers until 1919 inclusive. Occasional references are found in the House of Commons Debates. Citations from these authorities are given in the footnotes.

Valuable information is also found in:

Board of Education. *Imperial Education Conference Papers. III. Educational Systems of the Chief Colonies not possessing Responsible Government. Ceylon.* London, 1914.

Bridger, J. F. E. *Administration Report of the Director of Medical and Sanitary Services for 1926.* Colombo, 1927.

Denham, E. B., Superintendent of Census Operations. *Ceylon at the Census of 1911, being the Review of the Results of the Census of 1911.* Colombo, 1912.

Figart, David M. *The Plantation Rubber Industry in the Middle East.* Washington, D.C. 1925. Published by the Department of Commerce, Bureau of Foreign and Domestic Commerce. Trade Promotion Series, No. 2. Crude Rubber survey.

Keane, Captain Sir John, Bt., R.A. *Report on Irrigation in Ceylon.* Colombo, 1905. Also published in Sessional Papers, Ceylon, xlv. 1905.

Ridgeway, H.E. the Right Honourable Sir West. *Administration of the Affairs of Ceylon, 1896 to 1903.* Colombo, 1903.

SECONDARY AUTHORITIES

Balfour, A., and Scott, H. H. *Health Problems of the Empire, Past, Present, and Future.* New York, 1924.

Bandaranaike, Maha Mudaliyar Sir Solomon Dias, K.C.M.G. *Remembered Yesterdays.* London, 1929.

Bertram, Sir A. *The Colonial Service.* Cambridge, 1930.

Lawrence, J. C. *The World's Struggle with Rubber 1905–1931.* New York, 1931.

Lewin, Evans. *The Resources of the Empire and their Development.* New York, 1924.

Liversedge, A. J. 'Rubber, the Stevenson Scheme and International Goodwill': *The Nineteenth Century and After*, ciii. 765–74. London, 1928.

Petch, T. 'Notes on the History of the Plantation Rubber Industry of the East': *Annals of the Royal Botanic Gardens, Peradeniya*, v. vii. 433–520. Colombo, 1914.

United Empire, the Journal of the Royal Empire Society. London. Citations are given in the footnotes.

Willis, J. C., Director of the Royal Botanic Gardens, Ceylon. *Agriculture in the Tropics.* Cambridge, 1909.

INDEX

U

NOTE ON MAP

The discrepancies between the provincial boundaries of 1885 and 1925 (apart from the creation of the two new provinces of Uva and Sabaragamuwa) are due to the inaccuracy of all maps of Ceylon up to the end of the nineteenth century. The Survey L ·artment was understaffed, and owing to ιe heavy demands for land it was compelled largely to confine its work to surveying lands offered for sale. In 1897 Governor Sir West Ridgeway began a Topographical Survey of the island. 'The existing map of the Island, compiled chiefly from General Fraser's map made early in the century, contained errors so numerous and so gross as to make it useless for administrative purposes and for the purposes of the general public. For example, 400 miles of province boundaries and about 2,800 miles of district boundaries were still unsurveyed: only three of the larger rivers had been completely surveyed, while in the case of the largest in the Island, the Mahaweli Ganga, there was a gap of over twenty miles' (Ridgeway, *Administration of Ceylon*, 52–3).

70
71
72
74
75
76
77
79
83
88